MOSAIC VOICES

An Anthology of
Winning Stories and Poetry
From the 2024 Writing Contest

Sponsored by
SouthWest Writers

ISBN: 9798336390285
Formatted by: RMK Publications, LLC.
Published by SouthWest Writers
Printed in the U.S.A.

Table of Contents

Artwork by Allen Herring

Acknowledgements

A mosaic of talents have come together to produce the anthology you hold in your hands. Thanks to the members of the 2024 SouthWest Writers Contest Team:

- Judy Castleberry, Chair
- Chris Allen
- Brenda Cole
- Rose Kern
- Kathy Wagoner
- Dollie Williams
- ReVaH Loring, Administrative Support

Special thanks to our sister organizations for providing workshops for writers as well as judging the contest:

New Mexico State Poetry Society

Society of Children's Book Writers and Illustrators, New Mexico Chapter

More information about our sister organizations and SouthWest Writers can be found at the end of this book.

Artwork by Allen Herring

Foreward

The mission of SouthWest Writers is given in our tagline "writers help writers." The purpose of our annual contest is to fulfill this mission by encouraging writers to use their voice in the world. This year we had over 400 entries in twenty-five categories from talented writers and artists eager to share their work.

First, a huge congratulations to everyone who entered the contest! Entering a contest is a big step for a beginning writer or even a more experienced one. No matter where you are on your writing journey, this is a way to test your work in public. You are a winner because you took a chance on yourself and your writing.

The second phase of the contest is to judge the entries. We called on a panel of expert judges to evaluate the entries, including our sister organizations New Mexico State Poetry Society and the Society of Children's Book Writers and Illustrators New Mexico Chapter. This anthology highlights the winning entries in all categories. We are delighted by the quality of these entries and hope our readers will be too.

Our winning entries came from all over the country and beyond. The writers are from a wide variety of backgrounds, experiences, and education. Like the pieces of a mosaic, these voices come together in beautiful patterns that enrich each other while also maintaining their own identity.

Enjoy this mosaic of voices!

Section One:

Haiku

Crow Sees All by Carol Rawie

HAIKU – 1st Place Michelle Smith

All hallow eves night

over a red horizon

a blue moon rises

Michelle Smith is an award-winning writer and poet. A top-10 finalist in the 2019 She Writes Press and SparkPress Toward Equality in Publishing competition, and a First Place winner in the 2021 SouthWest Writers annual writing competition, she placed 19th in the *Writer's Digest* 2023 international poetry competition.

HAIKU – 2nd Place   Wanda Whittlesey-Jerome

pale water lilies
delicate beauties sip mud
turn darkness to light

Wanda Whittlesey-Jerome (aka Wanda W. Jerome and Ella Volé) received two awards from the 2023 New Mexico Press Women's writing contest. In 2024 she collaborated with Jasmine Tritten on *Magical Morning Moments: Awakening to Love and Light* and *Crow Wisdom: A Seasonal Journey.* Currently crafting a poetic trilogy, Wanda is happily living with her artist husband in beautiful New Mexico.

HAIKU – 3rd Place William Stotts

Deep within the Earth
Hidden kingdoms lit by quartz
My secret retreat

[Carlsbad Caverns]

Will Stotts, Jr. is a retired teacher of Creative Writing, Theatre, and English. He studied Criticism at UT-Austin. His play, *Tales of Lavender Youth*, was performed in Milwaukee by Different Drummer. His poetry is published in *Espresso Poetry*. He is currently completing a YA fantasy series in Albuquerque, NM.

Section Two

Short Story

We, The Dream by Raymund Tembreull

Short Story – General 1st Place Robert Temple

The Wolf-Gray War Bonnet

At the shadow edge of a stand of post oaks and stubby cedars, Man Too whistled the mating call of a bobwhite hen three times, each two-note repetition softer than the one before. The buffalo grass of the rolling plains west of the Clear Fork Brazos was still brown, but the side oats were new green, and the sand sage all a bright smoky hue. Man Too had hoped for a deer browsing shoots of skunk bush and hackberry crowding the fringes of the post oak—green venison to sting his mouth with sharp bitter juices! His Mayeyes band of The People Who Gather Together had eaten the last of their fall pemmican two moons ago. The meat and grease of four thin buffalo had only gone so far, but white hide hunters had long since scattered the once great herds of the Texas plains. His band had struggled through the last half of winter begging at newly re-opened Fort Griffin for rations the returning blue-coat soldiers had promised for scouting against Comanche, Kiowa and gray-coat Texans. Chunky bobwhite cocks would be a welcome change from stringy, dry, salt beef.

A dazzling flash at the western horizon caught his eye—an immense horse the color of a woman's milk. It bore a warrior who led two smaller mustangs. Comanche. Man Too slid behind the bole of a post oak whose stunted and knotted branches aped those huge dolls the whites set in their corn fields as signs of power. From his quiver, he drew a long, iron-tipped arrow, his line of sight darting here and there among the mesquite brush and shin oaks dotting the horizon. No Comanche mounted on so fine a horse ever rode alone. Yes, there they were, five—no, six—mounted warriors trailing half a bowshot behind their leader. Each man led a single remount—not enough horses for a war party. What did the leader carry in the crook of his left arm? Too short for a lance. Most likely a rifle, adorned with scalp locks bouncing with each beat of that horse's mincing trot.

Oh, such a horse! It must be seventeen, maybe eighteen hands tall, but the barrel of its chest was that of a runner, not the huge girth of a draft horse, such as the whites used to rip holy cottonwoods out of rich bottomland. For his seven feet in height, the elders of his tribe had given him the name Man Too Tall for a Horse. Yet with that horse, Man Too could win a new name. But was something wrong with its head? At more than even Man Too's bowshot away, the horse's ears and skull looked cropped. What foul medicine had the dwarf Comanches worked on this god of a war horse?

But no, as the horse trotted nearer, wolf-gray ears and mane at the crown of its head emerged from the greasy background of the Comanche's flowing black hair.

A sacred war bonnet stallion! And its bonnet the color of the wolf—spirit kindred and protectors of The People Who Gather Together. Surely, this was a sign.

The Comanche leader drew within easy bowshot of Man Too's hiding place. One arrow—and Man Too never missed—the horse would be his. On that stallion, Man Too, who had never won a horse race in his life, knew he could outrun his enemies to the safety of the Mayeyes camp. Then let the Comanches attack if they dared. He would eat their flesh. But could he leap from behind the tree, catch and mount the horse before the other six Comanche were upon him?

An eastern breeze fluttered the post oak leaves, and the war bonnet, nostrils flaring, sidled to the left and snorted. The Comanche leader reined to a halt and scanned the copse of trees where Man Too hid. Then he hoisted a four foot branch of holy cottonwood, green leaves shining in the morning light. He came in peace. On that horse.

Bow and arrow both gripped in his left hand, Man Too stepped away from the post oak and held up his right hand, palm to the Comanche leader, fingers spread. The Comanche extended the cottonwood branch toward Man Too and nodded, but the other six Comanche, bows or lances at the ready, spread in a semi-circle behind their leader. Man Too glanced at them and then stared eye to eye with their leader.

The Comanche chieftain called to his warriors in the harsh grating language of the most hated enemy of The People Who Gather Together. The other six Comanche rested their weapons across the backs of their spotted ponies, so when the leader again locked stares with him, Man Too grunted and sat cross-legged on the ground, laying his bow and quiver behind him. In one smooth motion, the leader dropped the war bonnet's reins, swept his right leg over its arched, gleaming neck and slid off its back. But once on the ground, with the cottonwood in the crook of his arm, he waddled toward Man Too with the bow-legged roll of a child who had just learned to walk and settled himself like an old woman whose bones troubled her on the ground five steps from Man Too. Then he looked at Man Too with the dark, burning eyes of a hawk, and he was once again a leader of the fierce Comanche who had driven Apache, Wichita, Osage and Man Too's people from the Llano Estacado.

In sign language, the leader asked if Man Too spoke the language of the Snake, the Comanche. Man Too replied in sign no, but he spoke the language of the whites, did the Comanche also? Yes, signed the Comanche.

"I am called Buffalo Horn of the Nawyehkuh band of the Nerm," he said. "The Wanderers band of the People in the foul language of the whites. It is of the whites that I wish to speak to my enemies, the Tonkawa—who should be my friends."

"I am called Man Too Tall for a Horse, of the Mayeyes band of the People Who Gather Together." Man Too looked down at Buffalo Horn. Even sitting on the ground, the Comanche looked like a dwarf across from Man Too. "The whites are the only friends my people have."

Buffalo Horn shook his head. "Friends? Do they even know your people's rightful name? Are you not, to the whites, just 'Tonks'?"

Despite himself, Man Too felt his eyes narrow. Yes, that was what the Rangers, the gray-coat Texans, and their white enemies, the blue-coats, called his people. Oh, this Buffalo Horn was clever. He knew how to use words as weapons. Yes, he must be a great leader among his people. A man of power. A man the spirits favored—even if he was a Comanche. Did he not ride that wolf-gray war bonnet?

"Tonk." Buffalo Horn repeated. "Just another 'dirty Injun'?"

Curse that filthy word! The meanest of Texas farmers, scratchers in the dirt like their pigs and chickens, tossed that in Man Too's face without a thought.

"Yes, dirty Injuns, Tonkawa, Caddo, Wichita, Kiowa and Comanche." Buffalo Horn smacked a fist into his palm. "They mean to crush us beneath their heels. You call the whites friends, but how did the gray-coat Texans repay you for leading their Rangers against Kiowa and Comanche? Did they not cry that all 'dirty Injuns' must leave Texas and drive you north of the Canadian River? On the whites' reservation beside the Arkansas, did the blue-coats stand beside you when Cherokee, Caddo and Wichita came to burn your villages, rape your women, and kill your children? Or did they stand aside and say just a bunch of 'dirty Injuns' killing one another?"

Taking a deep breath, Man Too squared his shoulders. Even though Buffalo Horn spoke truth, this man was still his enemy. "There were Comanche among Cherokee and Wichita that night. They, too, scalped our warriors, killed our children and carried off our women."

Buffalo Horn turned his head and spat. "Reservation Comanches—reservation Injuns! The whites have enslaved them with their whiskey. They lick the boots of their blue-coat masters for drops of whiskey. They are your enemies, and they are mine, as well."

"The whites do not steal our land, our children, our horses. They bring us gifts." But Man Too felt shame in his own voice. Yes, the blue-coats had stood aside that night and placed bets on the outcome while Man Too's people were slaughtered and driven south of the Arkansas River. Harried by Wichita and Caddo to the north, driven away by Texas Rangers to the south, The People Who Gather Together had drifted west away from the white settlements of central Texas into the scrub wastelands bordering the Llano Estacado, their old homeland before the Comanche had driven them from those prime grasslands generations ago. Then in the middle of this wasteland where game was scarce and the soil fit only for mesquite and stunted post oaks, the blue-coats had dared to re-open Fort Griffin, an outpost for raiding the gray-coat Texans. The same blue-coats who had laughed at their slaughter now offered gifts to the People Who Gather Together to scout against their old enemies.

"Yes, their gifts." Buffalo Horn smiled. "Did your people feed well this winter on the blue coats' leavings? Did it make your warriors strong? Do your women and children sing and play in your village? Or are their bellies swelled tight with the whites' tainted, wormy swill? Does your campsite not reek with the stench of the running sickness?"

Man Too scowled. Air gusted in and out of his nostrils. Buffalo Horn turned his upper body and swept his right arm toward the two spotted mustangs beside the war bonnet.

"I bring gifts to my enemy whom I would call friend—gifts befitting a warrior."

At fourteen hands each, the two mustangs were sturdy horses with straight legs and powerful haunches. Any other man would have counted them splendid gifts, but Man Too scratched at a tick dug into the flesh above his knee. In a squirt of blood, Man Too popped the tick between the nails of his thumb and index finger. This Buffalo Horn spoke as if he had brought these mustangs just for Man Too, as if he had sought Man Too alone of all The People Who Gather Together as worthy of meeting with him to discuss the fates of their peoples. But the horses were far too small to carry Man Too. Yes, this Buffalo Horn was clever, taking whatever came and turning it to his advantage, as if he had planned it. Here was a warrior to make the whites tremble in their log fortresses. Man Too said, "They are fine gifts. Perhaps, they might interest others of my people." Despite himself, his eye sight flickered a moment to the gray war bonnet before returning to Buffalo Horn. "But I have nothing to give in return for such gifts."

"You have the bow that no man but you can bend," Buffalo Horn said and smiled at the flare of Man Too's eyes. "We Nerm know well the bow of Man Too Tall for a Horse. Your arrows fly as far as the migrating geese and strike as hard and sure as the eagle."

"What use would you have for a bow you cannot bend?" The skin of Man Too's face stretched tight as he fought off a smile. Again, this Comanche acted as if Man Too were the sole object of his journey.

"For the bow, none." Buffalo Horn made a chopping motion with his right hand. Then he swept the same hand palm up toward Man Too. "But for the man who bends it, much."

Man Too regarded Buffalo Horn for several moments. Yes, this was a man of power among his people, the Comanche. The dark eyes bespoke a man of foresight—and of daring. What visions of the days to come had the spirits shown Buffalo Horn that he sought his most ancient enemies of the plains? Offered their strongest warrior gifts? Yes, the strongest warrior, but horseless, one who could never lead a raiding party. The man destined to be the scout who stalked days ahead of the raiding party, who dared to sneak into his enemy's camp and count their warriors and horses, horses that the raiding party would steal, but Man Too would never ride. He deliberately let his eyes stray again to the gray war bonnet. Now,

Buffalo Horn's eyes narrowed, but just for a moment, and then a tight smile creased his face.

"It is said on the plains that you share the blood of the race of giants—the Karankawa."

Man Too felt the muscles of his neck stiffen. What did Buffalo Horn mean by this—tribute or insult? The Karankawa had been a people apart, many over seven feet tall, fearsome giants who had stalked the islands and marshes of the gulf coast. But their enemies had feared the Karankawa far more for what they did than for their awesome height. They were eaters of human flesh. A tattooed tribe of monster shaman who bewitched the souls of their living enemies by consuming the flesh of their kindred. A combined army of Tonkawa, Lipan Apache and early white settlers had wiped out the last band of Karankawa on their island hideout more than forty years ago. But for years afterward, the Lipan Apaches whispered that Tonkawa warriors had carried off a beautiful Karankawa woman. From her black spells, they said the Tonkawa had learned to gain the strength of their enemies by eating their hands and hearts. From her corrupt bloodline, the Lipan said the Tonkawa had grown taller than their enemies. Man Too's grand-father, a small but hardy warrior, had led his people's war against the Karankawa. Then Man Too's father had grown over six feet tall. And yes, Man Too was far taller than his father or any other Tonkawa. Next to this Buffalo Horn, Man Too was a giant.

But a giant condemned to hunt alone through post oak stands and dry creek bottoms for bobwhite hens, like a bear sniffing out bird eggs and grubs, while other men—men who rode horses—chased down buffalo. When Man Too brought his kill to the Mayeyes women, they said at least it was good to gnaw a hen or jackrabbit to still the pangs of hunger. But when other hunters rode from the far plains to bring word of buffalo they had slaughtered, the Mayeyes women rushed from camp, singing all the long miles to the kill site. Yes, the young, unmarried, Mayeyes women sang for the mounted warriors to climb down and eat their fill of sweet buffalo tongue the women had cooked in their honor, and when the young single men strode among them, the unmarried women thrust hips in the men's paths. Man Too had seen twenty-five springs but never once heard a woman's song.

Man Too stared at the wolf-gray war bonnet, the magnificent stallion that could carry him as if he were no more than a tick lodged on its back. Dimly, he heard this Buffalo Horn try to distract him from the horse with more words of Man Too's enormous strength, his mighty bow that would strike the blue-coat and gray-coat sentries who guarded the white men's war camps, opening the way for mounted Comanche and Tonkawa warriors to slaughter the rest while they slept. If only, Buffalo Horn said, Man Too would take him to the Tonkawa camps so Buffalo Horn could propose this alliance to his tribe's elders. The whites warred among themselves. Now was the time. The other men of Man Too's tribe would surely see Buffalo Horn's wisdom. Kiowa, Caddo, Wichita, Lipan Apache, all other tribes would see his wisdom. Together, they would drive the divided whites from all of

Texas. The old ways would return. The buffalo would thrive again. The old trails into Mexico for plunder would once again be open for all the mounted warriors of the plains.

Man Too turned his eyes to Buffalo Horn. "Give me the war bonnet."

"I have given you two spotted horses." Setting the cottonwood aside, Buffalo Horn uncrossed his legs and pressed his left hand against the ground. His right hand slid to the pommel of his knife on his hip. Man Too set the fingertips of both hands against the ground.

"I have no use for a child's ponies. Give me the war bonnet."

For a fleeting moment, Buffalo Horn regarded Man Too, who saw in those dark eyes the Comanche at war with himself. Which would the Comanche choose—his dream or the horse? Then behind him, the great stallion nickered.

"AIIIYYEEE!" Buffalo Horn sprang to his feet, knife in hand, but Man Too hurled himself backwards in a somersault, seized bow and arrow, and shot Buffalo Horn through the heart. The war bonnet snorted and fled galloping to the northwest. Three of Buffalo Horn's warriors raced to catch him while the other three charged Man Too. He dropped two of their horses with bolts through their lungs, but lance thrusting for Man Too's throat, the third was on top of him. With his right hand, Man Too batted the lance aside, and with a smash of his heavy bow, broke the Comanche's skull. Roaring like the great gray bear, Man Too charged the other two Comanche who turned and fled on their squat bowed legs. With his giant's strides, he caught each one in turn, and with his enormous hands, snapped each one's neck. Tossing aside the corpse of his last victim, Man Too crouched with hands on knees, gasping.

Air in his lungs at last, he straightened and scanned the distant horizon for the other three Comanche and the wolf-gray war bonnet.

But the great horse was gone.

* * *

Born in Alaska, **Robert Temple** grew up a military brat across the United States. He taught creative writing, composition, and literature at several Florida colleges. Throughout his career, Robert kept writing, publishing the novel *The Strange Courtship of Kathleen O'Dwyer* and numerous short stories, winning several awards for fiction.

Short Story – General 2nd Place Maria Meier

Holy Child

In wizard-like fashion, Angel stretched out his arms, scrunched his eyes closed, and willed his desire to manifest. Daring to peek, he saw just enough through the front window of his small home to know that the silent, wet snowflakes continued to fall. Resigned to the fact that his attempt at magic didn't work, he sighed deeply and sank back onto the mattress in the living room corner that served as his bed. As he did with everything in his young life, Angel took it all in stride.

In the gray light of the cloudy morning, he burrowed deep under his flea market blanket dotted with images of winged cherubs. From his vantage point, he watched the sky stubbornly refuse to transform, ending his plans for a morning exploration.

Deemed "shy" and "withdrawn" by well-meaning teachers, Angel preferred to amble alone along the endless rocky trails behind the trailer park where he lived rather than to hang out with kids his age. He wished he could find the words to explain to those who worried about him that he didn't wander because he wanted to; it was something he felt he had to do.

If he possessed the words, he would have explained how he felt most at home in the expanse of the great open spaces and boundless sky. He would tell them about the pull of the silent force deep within him.

Sometimes, he would return from one of his adventures, bursting with a story to share - like about the old woman he found who now lived alone in her decrepit house that once held so many. She explained to Angel that her family was days late with their grocery delivery, and he suddenly understood why he had felt compelled to fill his pockets with snacks before leaving for his walk. She gratefully accepted his gift. Often, though, his mother's headaches kept her from being able to listen to what she assumed were his made-up tales.

The sound of the bathroom door slamming brought him back to the cold and dreary day. It also told him his mother was up and likely not in a good mood.

Silently, he watched her make her way into the kitchen where she opened and then quickly shut the refrigerator door.

"Hey, you two, get up!" Eppie bellowed.

"We forgot to go to the grocery store yesterday. You're supposed to remind me of this stuff!"

His mother often found it challenging to manage the practical aspects of life, like food, and that realization only added to her long list of stresses.

At the thought of breakfast, Angel's stomach grumbled. Dutifully, he rolled off the mattress and began to pull on his clothes.

"Then can we go to McDonald's?" his young sister, Jazmin, asked sleepily as she padded into the living room. "You said we would go last night."

"Maybe," her mother replied dryly.

Dressed and bundled as best they could against the cold air, they headed out the door. Angel felt the wet wind find the rip in one of his shoes. The icy coldness of the ground pushed through the worn-out sole of the other.

As he slid across the stained back seat of his mother's multi-colored sedan, he heard a crunch and pulled out from under him the remnants of a plastic fireman's hat, his Halloween costume from the night before. His mother, who worked part-time at the local discount store, brought the hat and a sparkly tiara home for the siblings, ecstatically explaining that she had learned of a Halloween party they could attend.

The gathering was held at a community center, and by the time they got there, most of the candy was gone, but Eppie and his sister both reveled in the social aspect of it all. For his part, Angel was content to keep company with a slightly older boy who didn't say a word all evening.

The snow was slowing as Eppie navigated their way down the two-lane road. She constantly shifted her ample bottom to avoid a spring pushing through the worn upholstery of the driver's seat but kept her gaze focused.

Sitting silently, Angel studied his mother's pearly white face offset by her long dark curls still pinned to the top of her head. Jazmin was her mirror image. He, however, matched the shades of desert dirt after a summer downpour. The deep dimples bookending his mouth were a constant reminder, he was told regularly, of his absent father.

Lost in their thoughts, they passed familiar landmarks spread vast distances from each other. The Catholic church's parking lot, the anchor of their little community for so long, was beginning to fill up, a signal that services would start soon.

A little farther along, the car began to sputter despite his mother's efforts to put her whole weight on the gas pedal. Coasting would only get them so far, so she instinctively steered onto the wet shoulder, where they rolled to a stop.

"Damn it! You didn't remind me to get gas," she cried, slamming her hand against the steering wheel.

Any response was pointless, so with practiced measures, they reluctantly climbed out of the car and zipped jackets to prepare for the walk.

"Let's go," she said in a flat tone. "Someone at church will give us a ride."

Grabbing her daughter's hand, Eppie left Angel to follow behind. The snow had stopped, but muddy puddles dotted their path, and it didn't take long for the dampness to soak his shoes and socks.

After about ten minutes of walking, they spotted the small adobe building. Next to the church sat a modern prefab that served as a community gathering site; its open door revealed a crowd of people.

"This way. I want to see what's going on," Eppie said, steering them inside. A dozen costumed children were milling about while family members primped and prodded final details into place.

"Oh look, it's a Halloween party!" she cried in glee, thrilled at having chosen the more social of the two options available.

"Epefina," a voice sounded.

"No, it's not a Halloween party. The first communion class is dressing up as their patron saints for a procession at mass today in honor of All Saints Day."

Eppie dropped her eyes before the stern expression of the petite woman who had approached them. Hearing her full name made her feel like a misbehaving child.

She could never remember Mrs. Padilla's first name, though they were somehow related; the older woman intimidated her. On rare occasions when they ran into each other, it was at some event for which Mrs. Padilla was in charge.

With her graying hair in a neat bun, plaid skirt, and wool blazer, she was dressed like she was headed to an important meeting. Her matter-of-fact manner kept almost everyone in check, including the parish priest.

"Shouldn't Angel be coming to classes on Sunday? He's in the second grade, isn't he?" Mrs. Padilla queried.

If she believed in superpowers, the older woman would say hers was the ability to retain even the smallest detail about everyone who entered her orbit.

"Oh, he always forgets to tell me about these things," Eppie replied with an awkward laugh. She thumped the back of her son's head playfully to avoid the older woman's gaze.

The smack landed harder than she had intended, causing Angel to lurch forward. As he righted himself, he characteristically dropped his chin and lifted his eyes just enough to filter his view through the veil of his long, dark bangs.

In her practiced method of taking charge, Mrs. Padilla declared that Angel was now part of the class and would be a participant in the procession.

"Come on, let's get you something to wear," she said as she directed him toward the open door of a nearby supply closet.

In the shadows of the far side of the room, pots and pans clanged as a group of women in bright aprons prepared food to be served after mass. One of them arranged pastries on decorative plates. Unwilling to wait, Eppie ignored the woman's scowl and helped herself to a chocolate donut, which she split between herself and her children.

Angel chewed his piece while he watched Mrs. Padilla rummage through an assortment of odds and ends. To him, the closet looked like a place of special powers, and he was not wrong. On more than one occasion, Mrs. Padilla had seen the contents of her closet work miracles.

Growing restless, the young group surrounded Angel and began petitioning for treats. A single "sush" from the older woman was enough to quiet them.

"His shoes are all dirty," a young voice's pronouncement broke through the silence.

Immediately, all heads turned to stare at Angel, scanning him from tussled hair to mud-caked shoes.

"What?" Mrs. Padilla asked, not registering what she had heard.

"His shoes are all dirty," Tonie repeated, rocking back on her heels as if to contrast the pristine condition of her shiny ones.

Prepared to reprimand her, Mrs. Padilla paused, then silently gave thanks for the divine inspiration.

"Well, class," she said, turning and straightening her spine to better use her teacher's voice. "Who do we know whose shoes are also dirty because he wanders at night performing miracles for those in need?"

"El Santo Niño de Atocha!" they knowingly cried in unison.

No matter their age, all parish members had been raised on stories about the unnamed child who delivered the answers to prayerful requests. As a sign of their devotion, the faithful dressed statues of Santo Niño in baby clothes and shoes. Everyone seemed to know someone who had a tale about seeing that the little shoes on the statue had become dirty or worn. What more proof did one need of the saint's holy journeys?

It did not matter to them that this belief was nearly eight centuries old and from a distant land. The holy child was theirs - as much part of their community and lives as the red earth mountains that had nestled them and their families for so many generations.

Something about Tonie's voice made Angel feel brave enough to lift his head to see who had singled him out. He recognized her; they were classmates, and their teacher often paired them, hoping Tonie's loquaciousness might draw him out.

Today, she stood before him, an otherworldly apparition resembling the princesses in his sister's storybook. A flouncy skirt of purple tulle puffed out from beneath a shiny material that encased her upper body.

"I'm wearing my sister's Easter dress," she explained in response to his stare. And I'm being Joan of Arc. She's my patron saint 'cause I was born on her feast day. That's why they named me Maria Antoinetta *Joan*."

Unconcerned with being the lone participant in the conversation, she continued, "And she was a soldier. That's why I have a sword and this. She pointed to the foil-covered cardboard serving as battle armor that covered her torso.

"And she's French. That's a country far away. My sister Clara says she's going to move there when she's all grown up. See, she let wear her French hat." Tonie paused for a breath.

Angel studied the red-felt beret, which was too big for Tonie's head, and sat low on her forehead.

Mrs. Padilla emerged from her closet holding a child-sized cowboy hat that had been abandoned in a church pew months earlier. It fit Angel perfectly, eliciting a smile from him that made his dimples appear. She prodded him to take a long branch that would be his walking stick and placed in his other hand a repurposed Easter basket that represented the one Santo Niño used to carry food to those in need.

"There you go," she exclaimed with the highest level of pride she would allow herself in church. Just like Santo Niño, you're all set."

"With dirty shoes," Tonie added.

"Yes, with dirty shoes," Mrs. Padilla replied with exasperation.

Eppie came up behind Angel, beaming with maternal pride. It was as if she had planned everything that led up to this moment when her son would become the embodiment of a revered community icon.

Angel struggled to sort out what was happening, but he liked the hat and could see that wearing it made his mother and Mrs. Padilla happy. That was enough for him.

The saintly procession wound its way to the back of the church as Miss van Dyke, a visiting faith instructor, took her position at the pulpit. The organist had declared that she would not learn a new song, so the young woman was left to fend for herself.

She invited the congregation to sing along to the words on the papers she had distributed and, holding her portable CD player aloft, pushed play. The pulsing sounds of New Orleans jazz bounced off the adobe walls, and the saints went marching in.

An enraptured Joan of Arc, gazing heavenward, could not see where she was going and cut a crooked path down the center aisle. The motley assembly of self-conscious holy beings followed. Some held statues or traditional wooden paintings bearing images of their patron saints; others tried not to trip over their saintly robes.

With embarrassed grins and arm punches, they passed beaming family members who snapped photos.

At the end of the line, Angel trudged with downcast eyes, his wet shoes squishing and leaving a trail of muddy footprints to mark his route. Eppie followed, waving at acquaintances and relatives who ignored her. Halfway down the aisle, she squeezed herself and her daughter into the end of one of the rows, seemingly unaware of the dirty looks from the occupants she displaced.

Despite her efforts to encourage the congregation to join her singing, Miss van Dyke was met with stoic looks and closed mouths. The more exuberant her efforts, the quieter they became. Suddenly, from somewhere in the back, a deep chuckle burst out. No longer able to contain themselves, the snickers spread.

They didn't intend to be mean, nor could anyone point to any one target of their laughs. Maybe it was Eppie, the foil-covered Joan of Arc, the scraggly kid leaving a mud trail, or the white woman from back East who was trying to get them to sing along to Fats Domino. Maybe it was just a little bit of everything.

Eppie began to feel the return of a too-familiar gripping sensation that squeezed her head in a vice-like grip. She didn't like the idea that these people might be laughing at her son, or at anyone's kid for that matter. They simply needed to understand.

Cupping her hands around her mouth as if at a ball game, she shouted to be heard. "He's Santo Niño! *Mi'jo,* Angel, at the end there. See! His shoes are dirty because he's being El Santo Niño!"

Heads bobbed as the congregation released a collective "ah" of faithful understanding.

"*Santo Niño de Atocha ruega por nosotros*!"

"Pray for us, Holy Child," an aged voice cried out.

Gasps of awareness erupted. The saints, as ragtag and imperfect as they were, walked among them. Light claps became full applause, replacing the chuckles. Angel swayed his bowed head to capture glimpses of those who watched him intently. Still tentative about the whole situation, he locked this moment deep inside himself and created a place in his heart to which he would return in later years.

The overheated social hall buzzed with the mingled voices of the parishioners who had gathered for food and socializing following mass. Conversations from the huddled groups created an indistinguishable hum.

Alone at the end of one of the long folding tables, Angel slurped the bowl of posole that sat in front of him. He liked the prickly sensation that hit the back of his throat as the warm, spicy liquid passed through. As he ate, he studied the scene around him. His little sister was involved in a rowdy game of tag; his mother was making the rounds to plead her case for a ride to the gas station. Near the door, Tonie posed for pictures with her family.

Sated and warm, Angel jumped slightly when Mrs. Padilla's voice boomed above the chatter, asking for everything she had lent from her closet to be returned. A wave of sadness washed over him as he realized his special day was ending. Dutifully, he approached the older woman, handing her his walking stick and basket. As he reached to remove the hat, Mrs. Padilla grabbed his wrist to stop him.

"That thing's been around here for a while, and no one's claimed it, so I don't see why you can't keep it," she told him. He glanced up at her to ensure he heard correctly and thought he saw a wink.

Buoyed by the unexpected gift, Angel skipped back to the table to finish his breakfast; his dimples deepened from his wide grin. As he approached the plastic chair he had been sitting on, he saw an orange rectangular box on his seat. Reverently, he lifted the lid. The smell of new leather and rubber hit him square on. Slipping down to sit on the floor, he began to put on his new pair of shoes..

* * *

Maria Robles Meier won her first national writing competition at age ten for her short story about dog food. In the ensuing years, she has focused on non-fiction writing and mass communication, including at the national political level. She is on a personal mission to find magic in everyday life.

Short Story – General 3rd Place Ramona Gault

The Sun and the Moon

There was no moon that warm August night, except the one Marisa outlined over the table, her work-roughened hands circling a make-believe sphere in the air. A not-so-young woman with silvery hair flowing over her shoulders watched the young man with a hip haircut and wireless earbuds sitting across from her on the café's patio.

"So describe for me where you want to install my piece in your new house," Marisa said to Sean. Zack, the teenage waiter, was disappearing into the kitchen, having taken their orders: two chiles rellenos plates.

Impatience twitched on Sean's face. Marisa cringed inwardly and forced a smile.

"It's the outdoor living space that faces San Francisco Bay," he said. "Don't be concerned about scale." He paused. "But if you really want it, I'll have a schematic sent."

She was junk DNA to Sean Jorgensen's calibrated process of acquiring art. Greta, manager of her gallery in Santa Fe, had warned Marisa that afternoon. "Sean says he's really busy," she'd said. Marisa had persisted. "Greta, you know I like to see where my work is going. I want to meet him."

If he bought it. Somehow she'd have to get through dinner despite Sean's chilly distancing. She leaned back and glanced around the familiar patio, cobbled together out of odds and ends. Like her sculptures. Salvaged window frames and weathered doors. Part of a stained glass window. Slabs of local sandstone slate mosaicking the floor.

"Have you ever been in a restaurant like this?" She arced one hand in front of him, sweeping in the room.

Eyelids lowered, Sean gave the tiniest shake of his head. "Not really."

"I thought not." Heedless, she plunged on, her deep blue eyes glowing. "People in this village have always had to make do with what's in the environment. They were isolated and poor. But wouldn't you say the whole of this space is greater than the sum of the parts?" She leaned toward him, willing him to see what she was seeing.

"It's charming. Rustic."

She sucked in a breath. "That's what 'The Sun and the Moon' is for me. Not just a collection of found objects that I assembled artfully. When I look at it, I see much more, I feel like it has its own life." Hot tears sprang into her eyes. With effort she batted them back. "What other kinds of art do you collect?"

He hesitated half a second, eyes unfocused. She suspected he was listening to another information stream coming through those earbuds. With his right hand, he pulled an iPhone from somewhere. The fingers of his left hand caressed the glowing surface one, two, three times in precise sweeps.

"Great room." He angled the phone so she could see the screen. Marisa beheld a multicolored diagram—a room plan—and then his fingers elicited a panorama of paintings and sculptures rolling across the screen. She recognized many as the work of Native American artists of high repute.

"Foyer." Now the slideshow was tribal art from around the world: Australian Aboriginal, African, Pacific Islander, South American.

"Media room." This room held breathtaking Chinese and Japanese calligraphy and brush paintings, probably all antique.

She shook her head in disbelief. "It's a stunning collection! Where does my style fit in?"

He actually smiled. "I'm diversifying into contemporary works. The outdoor living room needs something naturalistic."

"Naturalistic. I see." She sat back, suddenly conscious of her faded denim work shirt, no makeup or jewelry. She couldn't imagine this San Francisco software billionaire dandling a child on his knee or petting a dog. How could she let this man take the best thing she had ever created? How could she even keep this conversation going?

"Weathering is a consideration with bronze pieces outdoors, you know," she said. To her surprise, his eyes narrowed—he hadn't thought of that.

"Weathering partly depends on the types of patinas used," she went on. "The rich golden-yellow for the sun disk is a completely different chemical process from the misty blue of the moon disk. I can tell you more about how to care for the piece later, though. It's manageable."

To her relief, Zack appeared with a large oval plate of food balanced on each arm. He batted his long eyelashes at Marisa and she grinned back—she had known Zack since he was a toddler. He was plump and good-natured and worked hard in his parents' café.

"Here you are, lady and gentleman!" Zack slid a plate in front of Marisa with a flourish and sidled around to Sean's side to ease that plate down.

"Watch out—plates are very hot," he murmured.

Then he backed up a step, looked at each of them in turn, and opened his mouth in alarm. "Oh, wait! Excuse me! Oh dear! I mixed these up!" Bowing, chagrined, he deftly slipped Sean's plate out from under the man's upraised fork.

"*You* have the chiles rellenos," he declared to Marisa, setting Sean's plate in front of her with one hand while pulling her plate away with the other. He set that plate in front of Sean with another little bow.

"I'm so sorry, sir. Here are *your* chiles rellenos."

By this time Marisa was laughing and shaking her head at the teenager's prank. Sean looked genuinely puzzled and then annoyed, but Zack was unfazed.

"Now is there anything else I can do for you?"

"We're fine, thanks, Zack," Marisa said. Zack gave her a parting flirty glance and sauntered off to the kitchen.

"I've watched these village children grow up. They're so much fun! I even have an apprentice. She's a talented high school junior," Marisa said, turning back to Sean. But he had a fork in one hand and his iPhone in the other, head bent over the small screen.

So she ate in silence for several minutes while Sean nibbled at his meal, his eyes darting back and forth across the screen.

"That's a great way to show your collection—that slideshow on your phone. I should do that with my work."

Sean looked up. "Yeah, I wrote the app for that. When you drill down, you can get the artists' bios and reviews."

When Zack laid the bill on the table, Sean paid with a credit card and then stood up. "I'll ping your gallery in the morning," he said. Then he dashed out to his rental car. No goodbye, it-was-nice-to-meet-you.

"I guess he hasn't really decided," she said to Zack, who had strolled over to clear the table.

Zack cocked an eyebrow at her.

"That man is considering buying one of my sculptures, Zack dear. I thought he was ready to sign but now he sounds ambiguous."

"Don't worry, Marisa. He will buy it. And now I'm bringing you a slice of my mama's raspberry pie so you can celebrate."

Marisa ate her dessert—it was the best raspberry pie in the county—but it didn't bring that happy rush she was expecting.

Under stars and wispy night clouds, she walked up the hill to her house, dragging her feet. The yard between house and studio was dark but she knew the way. Unlocking the studio door, she flicked on the overhead lights.

There was the maquette she had made of papier-mâché. The sun and moon disks, suspended from wires, wavered in the air stirred up by her arrival. The maquette was kind of a joke, because she'd made it after the sculpture was nearly done. It was for the gallery, to show Greta what she had been working on for weeks.

Her abstract assemblages of cast bronze disks had sold well for several years. In spare moments, she scouted the arroyo behind the village, where people had dumped their trash for generations. Window sills throughout her house and studio were lined with her findings: half-melted blue medicine bottles, vintage barbed wire, the rusted-out hulks of cast-off clocks and cameras, broken tools.

The heavy, curved iron piece that would eventually enfold the sun and moon disks had come from the county dump. She had dug it up after spotting one end of it emerging from the baked red soil. The idea had hit her in a flash as she stood over the iron scrap, panting from the exertion of wresting it out of the dirt. It would unite the parts of the sculpture. Greta had been ecstatic over it, predicting it would sell quickly, and Sean Jorgensen had expressed his interest after seeing it on the gallery's website.

Standing in her studio now, Marisa shuddered remembering the chilly young tech millionaire. *It's just a trophy for him,* a voice in her head said. She turned off the lights and locked the door and got into her car, heading for Santa Fe. *It would pay the mortgage for the next year,* a countering voice said. With a growl, she kept driving. Half an hour later she parked behind the gallery under a security light. As she got out, the night watchman walked into view around the corner of the building. Most galleries had expensive alarm systems, but Greta was waiting a few more years for Jerry to retire before installing one.

She talked her way past Jerry's skepticism and inside. With Jerry's help, she lifted "The Sun and the Moon" from its anchors on the wall and onto a trolley.

Jerry held the door open for her, his voice following her into the parking lot: "Maybe I should call Greta? She didn't mention anything about you picking it up tonight . . ."

Marisa looked back over her shoulder. "Sure, you can call her but I doubt she wants to be disturbed. She said she was dining out tonight with a client."

She eased the sculpture into the trunk of her car and went up to Jerry, who was still standing at the door.

"It's okay, Jerry. Really. I'll let her know first thing in the morning that I took it." She waved goodbye and eased the car out of the parking lot. *He won't call Greta, but I'll have to come clean. Apologize to him for the white lie, explain it all to Greta, whatever "it all" is.*

Back at her studio, she climbed on a ladder and used her pulley to hoist the sculpture up to a heavy hook planted in a ceiling beam. It trembled slightly as she reached out to steady it, the disks glowing in the dim light. To her it spoke of sun and moon imagery in the indigenous Aztec and Pueblo Indian art that was all around her, but also of her own roots in nearly forgotten European myths and legends.

"The whole is greater than the sum of its scrappy parts," she said aloud. She couldn't have made that sculpture when she was thirty. What would anyone who visited Sean Jorgensen's mansion know of that? They'd put their own spins on it, or else glide past like it was part of the décor, which it would be.

Her body sagged as a wave of helplessness washed over her.

"You don't really want to part with this piece, do you?" Greta had asked her this afternoon. "Don't you want the recognition selling it to Sean Jorgensen would bring?"

Don't you want . . don't you want? Marisa closed her eyes as a memory swept over her. "You're too much!" her exasperated mother had declared to the teenage Marisa. "What do you want, girl? The sun and the moon?"

"Yes!" Marisa had shouted back. "And I'm going to get them!"

She opened her eyes, rebalancing herself on the ladder, reached out and stroked the yellow sun disk, the blue moon disk, and climbed down. Exhausted, she went to bed.

At dawn, she surfaced slowly from a sweet dream of being young again and courted by a gentle lover. The open window revealed a soft, shadowy gray, not the clear desert morning. Puzzled, she tiptoed over and leaned out.

It was raining just enough for her to hear the drops pattering on the ground. A dark, wet, fecund scent was arising from the earth, mixing with the rain, richer than anything she could remember. A breeze poured over her, lifting tendrils of loose hair from her shoulders. Raising her head, she sniffed the air like an animal.

* * *

Most of **Ramona Gault**'s fiction is set in New Mexico, her heart place. Her first novel is *The Dry Line*, about the aftermath of the Vietnam War in a New Mexico village. She has three more novels in progress and several short stories. She loves mesas and autumn and green chile.

Short Story – Honorable Mention Amber Train

Summer Snow

I found the ballet shoes with their dirty pointes and stretched elastic inside a crate in my dead parents' attic. They are the size of my 12-year-old feet in 1945. Worn to that summer dance camp in the mountains of New Mexico while my father was off somewhere unknown, drafted into war, and my mother was back home in Texas in a constant state of fatigue and sadness.

I am surprised to feel my face flush when I find them, the same hot flush perhaps on my 63-year-old face as that which rose to my cheeks that long ago summer, although now it rises on skin that is saggy and dull. Yet the flush pulls me back and I am gangly and loosed limbed with developing breasts. Inside the dance studio at camp, the vanilla smell of ponderosa pines in the high desert mountains competes with the tangy hormonal sweat of girls on the brink of becoming women. I am on that cusp myself, with a body full of the aches of menstrual cramps and longing. I finger the faded soft leather of the shoes and think of Betty's fingers in my mouth and other places that summer – thus the flushing back then.

Of all my pairs of dance shoes, I wonder that these are the ones that were saved. My parents surely could not have known the significance of this particular pair of shoes and the summer they represented to me. I sniff the insides, searching I guess for some olfactory gate through time that can reunite me with that other me. Disappointingly, they smell of moth balls and nothingness. I stow them in my tote as I continue the momentous task of sorting through a lifetime of my parents' accumulated stuff amidst dust motes and mouse droppings.

As I sort and clear, my mind continues to wander back to that summer. I had longed to go to summer dance camp for the past two years. It was run by my dance instructor, Ms. Penny, in an old carriage house off main street of downtown San Antonio, Texas. Once the girls at Ms. Penny's studio turned ten, we were invited to join the summer camp "to get away from the goddamn Texas heat" as Ms. Penny put it.

The way Ms. Penny put it had been a big part of the problem. We were a family of staunch Pentecostals. My faith leaned toward the fantastical, with frequent imaginings of a fire scorched earth full of sinners left behind to suffer, while me and my absolved loved ones floated gently up to heaven. My father's faith, on the other hand, tended to manifest more literally in the here and now. Women cursing, such as Ms. Penny was prone to do, was almost as sacrilegious as fornication or adultery in my father's eyes. And my father's faith was generally as unyielding as the hardpacked caliche that made up our back yard. In that spirit, he had deep suspicions about women in the arts, particularly those that were unsaved, unmarried and went gallivanting across state lines with a string of impressionable young girls in their wake. So, I had not been allowed to flee "the goddamn Texas heat" for the cooler mountain clime of the mountains in southern New Mexico.

But the summer I turned thirteen, fate intervened on my behalf in a way that was both terrible and liberating. The previous year, the war effort was in need of fresh bodies, so the government opened the draft to include married men; by fall, my father's draft number had been called and by spring of the following year he was shipped off as a United States Marine. My mother had begged him to seek some sort of deferment but my father, if nothing else, considered himself a man bound by duty. By the time Ms. Penny posted the flyer in her studio announcing the summer camp in Ruidoso, New Mexico, my father was conveniently beyond reach for questions of permission. And my mother, who had become increasingly tired and withdrawn since my father had left, needed no convincing to allow her teenage daughter to go away so she could rest in solitude for a few weeks that summer. I was thrilled of course, even as some dark energy nibbled at the edges of my happiness. I suppose that was the guilt I felt running off to camp, contrary to my father's wishes while he was off fighting a war.

As I went through the attic, I found a single pair of dress blues from my father's time in the Corps. I remember him wearing it during the annual parades to celebrate San Antonio's veterans. I was always so proud to see him dressed up in his uniform, my dad a hero returned from a victorious war. The funny thing was, the war took the fight out of him about many things. For instance, once he returned, he never forbade summer dance camp again, perhaps believing that battle had been lost in his absence.

After clearing my parents' house to ready it for sale, I fly home to California. I drink the cheap white wine served on the flight, which perhaps leads me to being a tad maudlin. I imagine the pillowy white line my plane might be drawing as we cross the same cerulean blue New Mexican sky I had danced under those summers long ago. And I remember that first time with Betty. We were cabinmates in one of the dozen or so two-cot, wood-shingled cabins at camp. She has been rubbing my back because I have been complaining about being achy from having my period. I got my period for the first time while at camp. Betty had to lend me Kotex because I hadn't even thought to pack such a thing and my mother certainly hadn't brought it up.

We are both on my bed. My face close to the wall as she rubs my shoulders. Even with the stormy mountain air drifting in from the window that we left slightly ajar, the air feels close and warm. The light is shifty from the anemic glow of the porchlight getting occasionally washed out by lightning flashes. Betty's hands are firm and confident as they rub my shoulders. At first, I tense at the unfamiliar intimacy of her touch but begin to relax as my muscles loosen under her fingers. She distracts me from my discomfort with stories about her family.

Betty's oldest sister got pregnant at the age of fifteen. She says "we all thought our daddy was gonna kill our pregnant sister when he found out. Then he stormed out and we thought he was gonna kill the boy." I laugh softly when Betty explains that in the end nobody ended up getting killed, but they did end up with a very speedy, very white wedding. By this point I forget all about my cramps. Betty's hands move into my hair and her fingers scrape my scalp. The sensation is calming and something else I can't name. Betty says that is probably why she gets shipped out of Dallas every summer to some camp in the middle of nowhere – less chance of getting knocked up.

I listen silently, not wanting to interrupt the quiet confidences she shares. And now I can feel Betty's breath on my bare neck. The room feels even warmer than before. The cot feels smaller. The room closer. The wall is inches from my face and the white plaster looks petaled and delicate in the dim light of the porch. Betty's hands move down my neck again and forward to my clavicle. I can no longer tell if it is the weighty humidity of Betty's breath on my neck or Betty's actual lips. My own breath catches in my throat and my body is suddenly taut again, but not in the painful contracted way of cramps. And then Betty's hands move down along my rib cage and are cupping my breasts and then Betty presses her body into mine and I exhale a moan and press back. One of Betty's hands moves to my mouth and I surprise myself by opening it to take in Betty's fingers. And that is when suddenly the sun explodes. High noon with no sunrise or other preface. But not sun. No, some cosmic rupture. The white walls flash blinding and brilliant, so much so that I bring my hands instinctively to cover my eyes as I feel Betty's hands abandon my body and mouth. Betty stumbles out of bed and just as suddenly we are plunged back into the dark, a dark that seems darker than before in the aftermath of so much light.

I'm definitely more than a little drunk now on this flight. And I feel overly hot between the wine and the memories. I reach up to twist on the air vent and point it at my face. A stewardess asks if I would like some water. I accept and then fall asleep dreaming of cottonwood trees and musty camp cabins for the rest of the flight home.

Once home, I am slow to unpack. It is almost a full week later that I run across the ballet slippers again when I finally unpack the bag holding my tote. I am unpacking in my bedroom where my husband is already in bed reading. He must have felt a shift in me when I pull the shoes from my bag, because he sits his book aside and asks "what are they?"

I place the faded pink shoes in the fifth position on the floor beside me, arranging them unnecessarily precisely as I consider how to answer the question. All at once, Betty is dancing pirouettes beside me. Betty is rubbing my back when I am crying after getting my first period. Betty is in my mouth. The apocalyptical light flashes in the cabin. A short time later Betty and I feel a hard tumbling like noiseless thunder. I am suddenly filled with dread; the Rapture had been a foundation of my upbringing and I fear I have sinned monumentally at the worst possible time. Then minutes later we hear a tremendous boom and most of the camp is awakened. Girls are wandering around in their pajamas, unnerved and shivering in the thin high-altitude air. A camp counselor runs to the facilities building to check to see if a boiler has exploded. But then everything is silent again, aside from some hooting owls and tree boughs trembling in the wind.

We never found out what the cause of the night time disturbance was, at least not for many days after. None of us girls get back to sleep that dawn and we proceed to have breakfast and activities as normal. I convince myself that the Rapture is not upon us but walk around flushed from guilt and shame over what Betty and I had been up to. I start to feel better as Ms. Penny leads us through our morning calisthenics. Then one of the girls yells that it was snowing outside! In July!

Indeed, when I look outside, I see soft flakes swirling through the branches of the cottonwoods and ponderosas. Us girls, overcome by the mysterious delight of July snow, race outside, ignoring Ms. Penny's commands to stay put.

Once outside, I glance toward Betty, noticing tiny flakes had begun to catch on her long dark lashes. I know that is not the Rapture, but it is something else strange and mystical and beautiful, and I feel giddily alive. Some of the girls begin to twirl like fairies in the snow. I stick out my tongue to catch the flakes - they are soft and warm. It is all so wrong and, yet, so ecstatically wondrous.

I am back in my old body in my bedroom with my husband. I answer "just an old pair of ballet shoes, silly of me to bring them home I know. I think they are from that year that they tested the atomic bomb in New Mexico." I am twirling the slippery lace of one shoe around my index finger. "Remember how I told you I was in a nearby dance camp when it happened and the fallout was like summer snow?"

My husband peers at me over his readers. "Of course I remember. What a frightful thing for you to have experienced."

I want to correct him and explain that at the time it had been glorious and magical and only terrible in hindsight. I see his kind eyes waiting for me to answer. Our love is so steady and good. I don't know how to describe to him that other kind of earth-shattering love without hurting his feelings. Or how to explain that when we married, I knew I was trading that other kind of love for the peaceful love we had built our marriage upon. And that the vast majority of days, I am content with that decision.

I suddenly feel very tired. "Yes," I say. "It was something." He nods and returns to his book. I push the ballet shoes under my bed to be forgotten - or to be found perhaps by my own daughter, cleaning up someday after her dead parents, left to wonder why they were saved.

* * *

Amber Train lives in Santa Fe, New Mexico. She's most interested in reading and writing about the weird and beautiful. She was recently honored to win the Grand Prize for the 2023 Santa Fe Pasatiempo Writing contest. Her work is also in *Dust Up*: An Anthology by New Mexican Writers.

Short Story – Honorable Mention Roberta Summers

Manhattan Rodent Control Operations

Monsieur Le Chat, a one-eyed cat with a black eye patch prowled the New York City waterfront. He waited for the luxury ocean liner, Kaiser Wilhelm II to dock. Cat Tales, the grapevine for news and gossip in the feline community said the infamous ratter, General von Katz would soon be arriving.

As the unanointed and unofficial head of Manhattan Rodent Control Operations (MRCO) the handsome orange tomcat Le Chat wanted to meet the famous rodent control general. Word was he had gained three-star general status in 1909 for rodent control in Germany at fancy hotels and as the Chief Rodent Control Officer on cruise ships. Le Chat thought it would be good to have his expertise in eradicating rats.

Le Chat's nemesis, El Raton ruled the burgeoning rat population in Midtown Manhattan. To date, the rat had evaded capture, handily escaping all efforts to exterminate him. He and his gang grew fat from raiding pantries in the best hotels.

Le Chat's daughter Mimi, was a champion mouser who patrolled at the Port Authority, a news center for Cat Tales. She'd heard about von Katz arrival and organized a welcoming committee comprised of half a dozen of her feline friends. When von Katz disembarked, they surrounded him purring, nuzzling and rubbing against him. The large handsome black and gray cat had a haughty arrogant air about him, nonetheless he welcomed the ladies attentions. Mimi introduced him to her father who escorted him to rodent control headquarters in the newly built Knickerbocker Hotel on Times Square.

Le Chat called together the members of MRCO to introduce General von Katz, extolling his virtues in rat control.

The new arrival spoke. "I hear there is a rat that needs expulsion," he said. "I have some expertise in these matters. I call upon you to locate El Raton and tell him I'm issuing a challenge. He is to meet me at midnight tomorrow at a location of his choosing." Von Katz had heard about Manhattan's chief rat while aboard ship, the rat's reputation having preceded him.

The MRCO audience cheered with loud meows and growls affirming their eagerness to locate El Raton and arrange for a showdown. They scattered to attend to the task of finding the rat.

El Raton weighed over two pounds, more than double the size of the average rat. He was a cross between an apricot rat and a black rat—all black with a pale orange spot on his head, dark ruby eyes, large Dumbo ears—an ugly mix and meaner than any other rat in town. He ruled the sewer and subway rats with an iron paw and was responsible for infestations, sneak attacks and raids on the city's finest hotels, not to mention searches through alley trash cans for tasty delicacies. None would mess with him—that is until von Katz arrived in New York.

MRCO troops located El Raton, delivered the challenge and asked where he would like to meet for the showdown.

When El Raton arrived at the designated time in the alley behind the Astor hotel and saw von Katz, he squeaked, "Whoa, this Hessian chap is huge." El Raton had never taken on a cat so big. *I can always skedaddle if the outcome looks grim.* He circled the cat and slipped between his legs nipping at von Katz' inner thighs.

It was the fight of the century. Cats cheered for von Katz with hisses and snarls. Rats on the other side squeaking and jumping up and down, all of them expecting their side to win or at least for El Raton to escape if the fight went against him. The daring rat harried the cat with repeated nips at his legs landing an occasional bite on the face. Von Katz yowled when the rat's teeth sank into his tail. The big cat managed to spin around. In a swift lunge, he grabbed El Raton in his mouth, shut it with a crushing bite. He tossed him high into the air. The rat plummeted—smashed onto the concrete platform where the big cat landed a final deadly blow. Defeated, the notorious El Raton lay dead at von Katz' large paws. The conqueror poked him a couple of times to ensure the rat's demise, before raising a victorious paw.

El Raton's cheering section fled, scampering through the subway tunnel. A squadron of MRCO cats dashed after the rats until they disappeared into the opening to the sewer. Cats patrolled around the opening until it was evident their foes had eluded capture. No way were they going to pursue them into the stinky sewer. After a time, they gave up their prowling.

That victory cemented von Katz position as commandant of the Manhattan Rodent Control Operation. He headed up the operation from his office in the tunnel at the subway station that connected underground to the Knickerbocker Hotel. This was a good location for Command Central since there was sewer access in the subway tunnel, a well-known route for rat traffic. Von Katz could monitor rodent activity from his post there. Although the new commandant was respected by the cats, his stiff and authoritarian manner didn't endear him to them.

In a brilliant strategic move, General von Katz promoted Le Chat as his second in command.

Le Chat had the most knowledge of all the mouse and rat hidey holes in Midtown Manhattan and was fully familiar with the cats most experienced at rodent control. Further, Le Chat had fathered a loyal family of fighters. He had taught his children all the ins and outs of protecting New York's hotels against rodent infestations. They took orders well and fought valiantly at the side of their father. Moreover, they willingly patrolled the alleys for trash rats sending them scampering into the sewers.

Monsieur Le Chat looked down upon the assemblage of cats meeting in the basement of the Astoria Hotel. He scanned his troops before asking, "Who is in charge of policing the Plaza Hotel tonight?" His golden eye searched the feline crowd. Owners and managers of luxury hotels welcomed the cats especially kitchen staff who often offered dishes of cream to reward rodent control cats for their efforts.

Ebony, a green-eyed black cat, small in stature but tough, swished his tail and came forward. "I'm in charge. I'm taking Georgie and Henriette with me. I received your message that Pierre the head chef, is beside himself with mice nibbling at his prized cheeses." Henriette, a diminutive calico and Georgie a chubby black and white cat lined up next to Ebony. Le Chat knew the black cat and his team were skilled mousers who were willing to take on the most difficult jobs, so the three of them could easily clean up any mouse problems.

A beautiful blue-eyed Persian, Koko slipped forward, "Where do you want me?" She purred at Le Chat.

"Stay right here with me, Koko. There's been a report that we have rats in the attic. How they got past our front lines mystifies me." Le Chat kept patrols at all entrances to the hotel.

She sidled next to the handsome orange cat and rubbed her lush creamy long hair against him.

He moved away, and muttered under his breath, "Non, Ma Cheri. Not here. Not now."

Koko tossed her head and smacked Le Chat in the face with her fluffy tail. "Humph, you're no fun." She hissed at him before prancing back to her place elbowing cats out of her way.

After adjusting his black eye patch, Le Chat said, "Paco El Gato, please get over to the Hotel Victoria and see how our patrol is doing. A rat was spotted in the dumb waiter by a maid. Her shriek could be heard clear down to the Bowery."

Paco raised a gray paw in salute, "Si Senor," and scampered up the stairs.

"Report back to me ASAP," he called after him." I need to update Commandant von Katz."

Le Chat was immensely popular, but because of the loss of an eye, he lacked the confidence to cement his position as head of MRCO, so when von Katz gained popularity, and proved his mettle by ridding New York of El Raton, he was promoted over him by acclamation.

When Le Chat was just a playful kitten, he and his sister Simone came across a mouse caught in a trap. The bar that was supposed to provide instant death by smashing him across the neck had instead just caught his tail at the base. The little gray mouse protested by squeaking, jumping and dragging the wooden trap around the basement laundry room of the Astoria Hotel where Le Chat's mother had given birth to him and his siblings. Torturing and playing with the mouse seemed like great sport, so the kittens batted at the entrapped mouse and the device he dragged behind him. When the mouse leaped flipping the trap Simone jumped, mistakenly striking Le Chat. One of her claws caught in his eye gouging a deep scratch. Le Chat screeched in pain.

The game was over and the injured kitten headed for his mother who snuggled in a corner with his siblings. Le Chat whimpered and cried rubbing at his painful eye with his paw. His mama licked the eye in an attempt to heal and comfort her baby. Simone purred and rubbed against him in apology. Le Chat's eye never recovered from the injury and he became blind in his right eye – a lifetime infirmity. But he'd adapted well and wore a black eye patch. He'd learned to cope with his disability and limited vision.

As the unspoken and unanointed head of rodent control, the cats had looked to Le Chat for instructions. MRCO had been loosely organized until von Katz arrived and took control, leaving Le Chat on the outside looking in.

Le Chat had once hoped to pull MRCO together and be Commandant, but when the new cat from Germany arrived, he was admired and instantly popular. It seems the old adage, *nobody is a prophet in his own land,* was true among cats too.

Although handsome and attractive to the lady cats, von Katz ran a tight ship with his strict authoritarian style. Le Chat was the opposite. He was easy going, charming and popular. The lady felines loved him and found his black eye patch sexy. He never lacked for female companionship.

In the attic, Koko and Le Chat searched in every corner for the reported rats without success. The lover in Le Chat rose and he sought out Koko. They'd become separated while they conducted their investigation. Now, she was gone, but where? He recalled her early advances and his rebuke. Now that he was in the mood for love, he began to worry. *Could she have gone seeking companionship?*

He caught her scent going down the stairs to the hallway and onto the elevator. "Where *has mon amour gone?" Not waiting for the elevator to arrive, he scampered down the remaining* fifteen floors to the lobby where he caught her scent and followed it to the front doors and out onto the street.

"Oops dogs." The orange hair on his back stood at attention as he executed a U-turn back into the lobby until two standard black poodles on leads proceeded up the street. They had their noses so high in the air, they didn't see him. Scolding himself for being incautious, he proceeded with care.

Peeking down a nearby alley, LaChat saw two of his offspring monitoring trash for scavenging rats, but no Koko. Hurrying down the street, he checked every alley purring hello to his eldest daughter who was lurking in the shadows contentedly munching on a brown rat.

Mouser Henriette caught up with him. "I have a report from the Plaza," she said.

Le Chat paused in his quest to hear what she had to say. "Yes, go ahead, but I'm in a hurry."

Henriette fell into step with him. "I'll make it brief. Chef Pierre has invited Ebony, Georgie and me to stay until the mouse problem in under control—at least a week. I'll report in as needed.," With that she raised a paw in salute, turned and headed back to The Plaza.

Ebony discovered the Plaza had lost their resident rodent control cat. He, Georgie and Henriette observed the damage done to Chef Pierre's treasured, Camembert, Brie and Gouda cheeses. The cats laid out their strategy to eradicate all mice from the chef's kitchen. It would require some time and they'd need to find a new resident cat. The Plaza was a desired assignment so it shouldn't be difficult.

Le Chat continued running toward the Knickerbocker until he saw an elegant lady step out of her carriage. At the end of a leash, stood a seal point Siamese. Le Chat stopped in his tracks. She was gorgeous, sleek and slender, her blue eyes rivaled Koko's. His heart raced as she looked him up and down. *Wow, is she a looker, but so gorgeous she's probably already spoken for.*

Koko--he shook his head remembering his mission. *Well, a fella can look, can't he?* And hurried on his way.

Von Katz barked orders from a concrete shelf in the subway tunnel. Fluent in three languages including English, albeit with a harsh accent, he gave orders. "Achtung. You there check out the Knickerbocker kitchen to make sure rodents haven't infiltrated." He snapped at a pair of calicos before turning to the rest of his troops. "The rest of you locate find Monsieur Le Chat. I need his report."

Arriving at the Knickerbocker Hotel, Le Chat followed a human couple entering the doors. He scurried through the lobby toward the entrance to the subway station following a faint trace of Koko's scent. He tracked it onto the platform. *What is ma cheri doing here?* Le Chat scurried down the walkway adjoining the tracks. He was soon to know. His worst fears were about to be realized. Rounding a curve next to the subway tracks, there was his love in the embrace of von Katz. He arched his back and emitted a loud hiss. Koko was locked in the paws of his commanding officer. Jealousy seized him blinding him to reason. He attacked the larger cat. Fur flew as growling, snarling and biting ensued. Despite being much smaller than von Katz, Le Chat, fueled by rage got in several blows, scratches and bites before his commandant realized his opponent was beating the crap out of him.

A crowd of cats and rats gathered to watch the two leaders in a fight to win Koko who stood watching—amused by the battle for her affections. She secretly hoped Le Chat would win, but would settle for von Katz. She wanted a family and dearly needed a mate now.

His position and dignity at stake, von Katz viciously struck back turning the fight in his favor. Le Chat tried to keep the larger cat on his blind side in an effort to protect his good eye. Unable to see the blows coming from that side, he was at a disadvantage. His right ear was bleeding and a chunk of orange hair had been yanked off his back. He was losing—badly.

Koko couldn't watch any longer and covered her eyes with her paws. She realized how much she cared for her one-eyed lover. *He can't die.* She joined with Le Chat's supporters cheering him on although it was apparent he was out matched.

Le Chat lay panting trying to regain strength. Pride and his love for Koko kept him from slinking off in defeat. This was a battle to the death. Von Katz knew he had weakened his opponent and leapt to strike a fatal blow. Le Chat rolled onto his back and with all his strength he kicked his powerful back legs up into von Katz's belly catapulting his foe off the walkway. He somersaulted in mid-air and plummeted onto the third rail of the subway train tracks electrifying him into eternity.

Le Chat managed to stand just as Koko crept up and rubbed against him. She purred and licked the gashes on his face. Despite his wounds, he was a happy cat. He'd won his love in battle.

Together they strolled back to the Astoria—home. But not before being cheered by the rodent control cats, and Le Chat being voted in as the new Commandant of Manhattan Rodent Control Operations.

* * *

An award-winning author with a creative writing degree from San Juan College, **Roberta Summers** lives in Farmington, NM. Summers lived in Hawaii for 25 years. Formerly owner of Silverjack Publishing, Roberta served as a contest judge for Pikes Peak Writers and editor of *Perspectives*, a San Juan College literary journal.

Short Story – Humor - 1st Place   Bonnie Hayes

Enlighten Up

I have meditated, medicated, sublimated, introspected, and prayed to find the inner bliss that mystics and life coaches rhapsodize about. And, I must say, it has been a decades-long monumental waste of time. Debating, demanding, disciplining, and all my "Yang-ish" will-powered attempts have also failed miserably.

What is the problem? Are my charkas clogged? Is my Inner Child intransigent?

I don't know and I don't care, because...***I give up.***

Optimists might call my new state of mind "Enlightened Acceptance." They would be dead wrong. Euphemistic "Enlightened Acceptance" does not move me. Hardcore "Grudging Resignation" does. Only Grudging Resignation could force me to invent better ways to manage myself, inspiring new strategies that simplified my life and dramatically improved my relationships. Let me share some of them with you now:

Begin with my new motto: "Put your faults to work." We all have faults. A fault is simply a misused or abused virtue. For example: Humility is commendable. But, when it is phony or if it degenerates into Timidity, it mutates into a fault. Humility then becomes deplorable. Any virtue pushed to its extremis will turn into a vice. Miserable misers were once simple frugal folks. (Sadly, when we are truly insufferable, everyone knows it but us.)

Powerful forces within each of us generate and maintain our faults and vices. In fact, the more obdurate and intractable they (and we) are...the more latent power they pack. Acknowledge that power and half the battle is won. Stop calling it a battle and the possibilities are amazing.

As Alexis de Tocqueville observed:

"We succeed in enterprises which demand the positive qualities we possess, but we excel in those which can also make use of our defects."

My new, improved strategies coordinate my faults, deploy my bad habits productively, and focus my character flaws on worthy targets. I find the following approaches particularly useful. I think you will, too.

First Strategy – Scheduling (Control the Agenda)

How many times have you discovered your brain whirling and chattering, sapping your energy with a barrage of drivel, criticism, and fear? Limit the number of minutes a day you indulge such nonsense. Let your competent compulsions master it.

Here is a transformational schedule for a date-book-addicted, time-obsessed individual. (It is a working person's schedule – adjust it to fit your week.) Notice how well faults (compulsivity/punctuality-panic) function as management tools.

Monday Morning – Prioritizing, Planning and Scheduling

7:04 to 7:14 "Prioritize Procrastination" Review Milestones. Set weekly goals.

7:15 to 7:24 "Schedule Faults and Bad Habits" Delegate and Schedule responsibilities.

7:25 to 7:36 "Fussing and Fuming" Limbering-up session – focus on minor irritations.

7:37 Move on.

Tuesday Morning – Worrying

7:04 to 7:14 "Obsessing – Improvisational"

7:15 to 7:26 "Imagining the Worst" Daily news, podcasts, and talk radio can inspire you.

7:27 to 7:36 "Silent Screaming" Unleash the volume only if the car windows close tightly and carpool riders are joiners.

7:37 Time's up! All additional worrying must be postponed to next session (Thursday.)

Wednesday Morning – B*tching and Blaming (B&B)

7:04 to 7:09 "Warm-up – Ranting and Indignation" Venting of dissatisfaction with the world and its rulers, society and its institutions, friends, family, and self.

7:10 to 7:16 "Blaming – Impersonal and Generalized" Institutions and public figures.

7:17 to 7:26 "Blaming – Personal and Specific" Family, friends, business contacts, and call center representatives.

7:27 to 7:36 "Blaming – Self-recrimination"

7:37 Shut Up! Abstain from all B&B until next scheduled session (Friday morning.)

Thursday Morning – Repeat Tuesday Worrying Schedule

"Free-floating Anxiety" may be substituted for the first two agenda items.

Friday Morning – Repeat Wednesday B&B

Use your option to reapportion blame as desired.

Saturday Morning – Wallowing, Whining and Whipping *(Limit to 54 minutes.)*

8:04 to 8:12 "Maudlin Sentimentality, Tears, and Regrets" Perform it all self-indulgently:

"Should have"..."Could have"... "Might have"..."If only"... etc., etc., ad nauseam.

8:13 to 8:28 "Reform Family Members"

Note: It is imperative, if you have live-in family or a significant other, to enforce a rigid weekly schedule for their improvement. A fixed, predicable day and time empowers them to "forget" unerringly and to prearrange escapes to traditional sanctuaries (such as the golf course or the mall). This maintains harmony in the home all week (except for 8:13 to 8:28 am Saturday morning).

8:29 to 8:58 "Reform Friends" This time commitment will rapidly shrink. The number of friends who will tolerate browbeating, at this early hour, on their day off, is small.

Caveat: The Reformer (you) may not intentionally awaken the Reformees (them) by subterfuge. This restriction protects most family members and saves many friendships.

Sunday Morning – Inspiration and Elucidation *(Maximum time limit – two hours)*

(If necessary, trade Sunday for another day to accommodate a specific faith's holy day.)

Go to an extremist religious service, watch a proselytizing religious channel, or tune into the Sunday morning TV News. Study the advanced techniques of professional rabble-rousers and pontificators. Learn how to motivate yourself with humiliation and intimidate yourself with righteous rage. Keep a running list of the words and phrases that hit home with you, triggering your nerves or tripping your inner alarms – reclaim them from the preachers, pendants and politicians.

Comments: If you choose robust personal faults, this scheduling technique will amplify its power over time. Schedules will compress. A week's worth of worrying will be done in half an hour. Imagine what a bonanza of time and energy that will liberate!

Second Strategy – Efficiency, Efficacy, and Multitasking

- Speed up your procrastination. Begin immediately and do it more efficiently.

- Develop productive avoidance ploys. Instead of binge eating or watching gameshow reruns, polish the doorknobs, or brush the dog.
- Be prepared. Stockpile frequently needed excuses. Reinventing them wastes time.
- Use broad generic excuses which will defend several failings simultaneously.
- Multitask your memory lapses. Utilize your ADD distractions and Senior Moments. For example: before you are transfixed or distracted by the sight of clothes spinning in the front-loading washer (again), post-hypnotically suggest to yourself to transcend your body and, while you are out there, to look for the long lost car keys. (Who knows, it might work.)
- Use the "Three Things Strategy." If you find yourself standing in a room for no apparent reason, choose three random things. Dust them, toss them, or put them away. Usually, before you finish, you will remember why you are there. (If you don't remember, you can pretend it was for one of the Three Things.)
- Spontaneously Exercise. While trying to recall why you walked to the other end of the hallway, stand in a doorway and push energetically on the frame, performing an upper body workout until your purpose resurfaces.
- Use a pedometer. Record all your valuable wasted steps. The more you wander around forgetful and indecisive – the more physically fit you become.
- Elevate your memory lapses – dedicate them to a higher purpose. Forget to be hurt or angry at least four times every day (so much easier than forgiveness.)

Refocus *all* your old routines and habits to empower *Your* unique new chronic "virtues."

Third Strategy – Rename, Reframe*, Redefine

The power of language and your creativity can work miracles.

Rename shortcomings, and obstacles. Leaders in all fields do this routinely:

Stubbornness becomes "Determination."

Insoluble Problems are "Challenges."

Dead Children are "Collateral Damage."

The possibilities for this technique are limited only by your imagination, vocabulary, and brazenness. To see masters in action, watch the presidential debates.

Reframe the situation. (*We are doing this right now!)

Some professional Reframers are so skilled that, given the incentive ($$$), they can shift the blame for all the Earth's ills onto the dolphins, while convincing you that tobacco cures old age (which it does, actually.)

Redefine your world. Take control of the most profound of all these techniques. It is in your power, at any time, to redefine your world and anything in it... including yourself.

Try it!

For example: What if you choose to redefine what constitutes a "CRISIS"?

Simply decide that, no matter what,

If there is no 911 number for it – it is NOT a CRISIS!

(Therefore, panic is NOT needed.)

You will deal more effectively with serious matters sans your self-inflicted dramas.

And, to reinforce that last point, let me suggest that, in these times, and at any age...

ANY DAY THAT HAS NOT REQUIRED A 911 CALL IS A GREAT DAY!

GO ENJOY IT!

* * *

Inventor of her own world and interloper in several others, **Bonnie Hayes** has a unique perspective, cherished by her friends and tolerated by her family (usually). Fame and fortune have not yet tested Bonnie's humility – but she is ready and willing to take up that challenge (ASAP).

Short Story Mystery/Crime/Thriller - 1st Place Suzanne Stauffer

Effie's Tale

The doctors say I don't have much longer, but I knew that. I might make it another year or two — I've got the money for the best long-term medical care — but I've already had well beyond my biblically-allotted three score and ten. In fact, I've had a full four score, so I can't complain. Life's been pretty good to me these past forty years or so. I've had pretty much everything that money can buy. Certainly everything that money could buy that I wanted.

Before I go, I'm setting down the story of where and when and how I got all that money, which is also the story of what really happened to the black figure of a bird that they called the Maltese Falcon. As far as I can tell, no one ever did work it out, but in those days, no one paid attention to the secretary except to take a letter or get coffee. Especially one who was — and still is — that old I, the secretary who's hopelessly in love with her boss. In my case, he knew, and I knew that he knew, and he knew that I knew that he knew … but he took advantage of it, anyway. Yeah, he called me "Angel" and "Sweetheart" and "Doll," but that's what he called all the girls, when he wasn't calling them something worse. There were days I looked at myself in the mirror and thought, "Effie Perrine, you're a fool. You're forty years old and you've been nursing a hopeless passion for Sam Spade for the past twenty years. Twenty years from now, it'll still be hopeless and you'll be a dried-up old maid still living in the old family home with your mother." That's why, when fate or destiny or kismet or whatever you want to call it threw the opportunity in my lap, I decided to grab it and never looked back.

It all started when that Miss Wonderly — later I found out her name was really Brigid O'Shaughnessy –walked into the office to hire Sam and his partner Miles Archer supposedly to look for her missing sister. Not that I knew anything about the black bird at the point. None of us did. No, what started it for me were her furs and her jewels and her hat that cost a week's wages and the way that Sam looked at her when I ushered her into his office. He looked her up and down and grinned like the wolf he was. I'd said, "She's a knockout," just to show that I wasn't jealous, but I was. She had everything I didn't have and it was obvious that she'd have Sam next, although Miles tried to beat him to it. Which was a good thing, as it turned out, as Miles was murdered that same night. It could have been Sam. In fact, it would have been Sam.

Naturally, I was delegated to break the news to Miles' wife, Iva. It was my job to make Sam's life easier and, sap that I was, I never complained. I even went out of my way to look for ways to do it without being asked. He'd been avoiding her ever since breaking off their affair when she started talking marriage. It was always that way with him. That's why I kept a little hope alive, knowing that his affairs never lasted very long and one day he just might see me as someone besides a secretary sitting behind a desk. He also told me to keep her away from him, but he didn't tell me how. I still got the blame for her turning up at the office, all fake tears and widow's weeds. After she left, I couldn't help asking whether he was going to marry her. I knew it was a mistake to show him that I cared one way or the other, but you know how it is when the green-eyed monster gets his claws into your gut.

The first we heard of the black bird was when Joel Cairo showed up. I was curious what someone like him would have to say to my boss, and it wasn't too hard to hear what was said in Sam's office if I listened, even with the door closed. The walls of those cheap offices were thin and the doors didn't fit too tight and the transom might have been open an inch or two. When I heard the phrase "black figure of a bird," in Cairo's mincing words, I knew that fate had something in store for me. I'd seen a "black figure of a bird" in the window of a pawn shop that was on my way to the office. It was clear from what Cairo said that he'd either never seen the bird he was looking for, just heard it described, or had only had a brief glimpse of it. I couldn't see what he meant when he said it was "so high," but it couldn't be all that big if he thought it was hidden in Sam's office and was planning on carrying it away with him. I didn't know what made that black bird valuable and I didn't have any kind of plan right then, but I knew that I had to have that substitute bird ready when fate tipped me the wink. Cairo was offering five thousand dollars for it. Why shouldn't little Effie be the one to profit from it, if she could? I might even stand Sam to a cup of coffee and a sandwich after.

I stopped at the pawn shop on my way home. No matter how late I left work, it was always open. I bought the bird — it was about a foot tall, with a hooked beak. The owner of the shop thought it was a hawk or a falcon. He said it was too small to be an eagle. Someone who saw it later said it looked like a kestrel. I wouldn't know. I've lived in the city all my life. The only birds I can identify are pigeons and the odd seagull, although I hear there are some hawks in Golden Gate Park. Anyway, it was heavy and black and cheap enough. Mother said it gave her the willies and to keep it in my room.

The next thing I know, Sam's asking me what I think of Miss O'Shaughnessy — did he tell me that was her name then? I don't remember, but it doesn't matter, he told me then or later — and I say that "She's all right." What did he expect me to say? He hates it when I'm jealous and he was making no secret of his feelings for her. And then he has the nerve to ask me to put her up at home with Mother and me for a few days! What can I say but "Yes?" Besides, she really might be in danger and I have nothing against her. It's not her fault he's going for her and it's not like I have his ring on my finger. Mind you, I still didn't know that she had anything to do with the black bird. If I had … but I didn't.

She never did make it to our place, even though I put her in the cab myself and gave the driver our address. When I got home and she wasn't there, I figured that she had gone back to the office, but then I got a call from Sam later that night asking to speak with her. When he heard she wasn't there, he told me to go to the office and wait for him. And I went, because, well, because. When Sam finally showed up, he had a nasty bruise on his forehead where, he later told me, someone had kicked him when he was down. I made him let me clean it up. While I was doing that, he told me all about the black bird. I don't remember whether he called it the Maltese Falcon then or later, but that's what it was. He told me that it wasn't really black, just painted with a thick coat of black enamel; it was really solid gold and encrusted with jewels! I almost couldn't breathe. To think I had planned to sell it to Cairo for a measly five thousand! Or the fake, rather, but Cairo wouldn't have known that until later.

Just as I was thinking about maybe letting Sam in on my scheme of telling Cairo that the bird from the pawn shop was the one he was looking for, a dying man with several bullet holes in him stumbled into the office carrying a newspaper-wrapped bundle. He managed to gasp out "You know. Falcon," before he dropped dead in front of us. Sam cut open one end of the bundle and, yes, it was the genuine black bird! The solid gold jewel-encrusted bird! Finally, my ship had come in! Sorry, Captain Jacoby.

Before we could decide what to do with it, the phone rang. Like the good secretary, I answered it. It was Miss O'Shaughnessy. She told me that she was in danger and asked me to send Sam to her. She gave me an address, then screamed. I insisted that Sam go rescue her, mostly so that he wouldn't suspect how glad I was that it looked like she was out of the way, but also because I really didn't wish her ill. While I helped him on with his jacket and his coat, he told me to call the cops after he left and tell them about Jacoby, but to leave out the bundle and to say that he got the phone call and I didn't know where he was. I might have told him about my plan then if he hadn't said, "You're a good man, sister!" I'd heard him call Miss O'Shaughnessy "My own true love" earlier, so that really rankled. Then he took the bundle and scarpered, leaving me to clean up the mess, as usual. And I did. I did what he said and told the cops about everything except the bundle. Finally, I headed for home and bed. But not for long. Maybe two hours later he called to tell me that the address I had given him was no good, which was funny because I gave him the address that she gave me only because it hadn't occurred to me to send him on a wild goose chase. I went back to bed hoping that that was the last we'd heard of Miss Brigid O'Shaughnessy.

No such luck. Sam called me at home the next morning. It didn't matter that it was a Sunday and it was only a few hours since he'd called me the last time and that it was still dark outside. He told me to go to our post office box, get an envelope with a claim check in it, get the bundle from the baggage check at the bus depot, and bring it to his apartment. He called me "Precious." That was enough to silence any doubts I might have had about cutting him out of the deal.

Well, I got the bundle, but first I took it and the substitute bird to the office, where I made the switch. Fate really was looking out for me. The birds were not identical, but they were close enough in size and shape to fool anyone who hadn't had a good look at the original. Besides, what did it matter? I could have substituted just about anything that was the right size and weight. They'd know a switch had been pulled one way or the other, eventually. What mattered was that they didn't know who had pulled it or when or where. I stashed the real bird in the bottom drawer of my desk, headed over to Sam's, handed him the bundle, and told him I'd see him at the office the next day. A fat man smoking a cigar was standing behind him, but he didn't introduce us. I could see Cairo and Miss O'Shaughnessy in his apartment. So, she hadn't been taken care of and she was one of the gang. Even more reason for me to keep the black bird. I scooted before I gave the game away by smirking.

Next day, Sam told me that the black bird in the bundle had turned out to be a fake and the fat man and Cairo thought the switch had been made in Istanbul before they stole it, so they'd gone there to try to find it. I was glad that I'd been able to substitute a black bird, since it cast suspicion so far way. I had to work at not looking at the bottom drawer of my desk. To tell you the truth, I had to work at not opening that drawer and giving him the real bird, just to see the look on his face when he realized that I had pulled one over on him. He also told me that Miss O'Shaughnessy was going down for Miles' murder and would get at least twenty years, if not the death penalty. I pretended to be shocked and dismayed. I was, a little, but mostly at how this love affair of his had ended so differently from all the others. I could tell that Sam was going to enjoy playing the tragic hero for a while. I also knew that it would pass. It always did. But, until it did, he would mope around the office, sighing and drinking too much. Not that he needed an excuse to do that last one.

I took my time making my plans — I didn't want Sam to suspect that I had the bird. Not that he would have, but, if he had thought about it, I was the last one to have it … but I was just the secretary and I was in love with him, so … he didn't give me a second thought, as usual. I almost laughed out loud when he gave me the black bird, the one I had bought in the pawn shop, as a "souvenir" of our adventure with Captain Jacoby. It's a little scratched here and there, but it sits on my mantel piece today.

I'd worked for him long enough to know how to dispose of jewels without a bill of sale, although I only got a fraction of what they were worth. Still, they were worth millions, so as soon as I'd sold enough of them, slowly so as not to draw attention to myself, Mother and I moved to a mansion on Nob Hill. That's not what I told Sam when I turned in my resignation, of course. I told him I'd quit because I could never forgive him for turning Miss O'Shaughnessy over and he was never to contact me again. He didn't. Didn't even try. It all fit with his view of himself as a tough guy and a loner. I attended his funeral when the time came and I was the anonymous donor who paid for the marble tombstone. The heart has reasons of its own, they say. Besides, I could afford it, thanks to him.

I'll be putting this letter in my safe deposit box that holds what remains of the Maltese Falcon. I've converted nearly all of the jewels to cash, stocks, and bonds, so it's mostly the solid gold body that's left. No one wanted to touch that much gold back when it was illegal for private citizens to own gold. And my investments have done so well that even after the law changed, there was no need to bother. I'll leave it to my attorney, the executor of my will, to figure out what's best to do with it. I'd have left it to Miss O'Shaughnessy, but they did hang her by that pretty little neck until she was dead.

* * *

Suzanne Stauffer is a retired librarian, professor emerita of Library Science, and author living in Baton Rouge, but soon moving to Albuquerque. Her historical mystery, *Fried Chicken Castañeda*, set in Las Vegas, New Mexico in 1929, will be published in Spring 2024 by Artemesia Publishing.

Short Story Romance - 1st Place   Rhenna St. Clair

The Dance

Graciela puffs up the pleated sleeves of her *blusa*, the white one no longer pure white but graying and showing signs of wear. The once-red daisies embroidered around the blouse's neckline are now faded and fraying since the garment is almost as old as her relationship with *him*. They were but babies when they married each other at the age of sixteen but, still, it is a garment he had once much admired. It is a garment he will remember.

Resigned to her *blusa's* imperfections, Graciela secures her gold hoop earrings and plops down in the chair outside the door of her casita, the door facing onto the village plaza just like the doors of the houses of the neighbors she has known all her life. Late afternoon is fading away and the heat rising from the plaza's flagstone-paved surface shimmers and sways, its seductive waves resembling the ghosts that often wander into her dreams these nights. Such unwanted visitors, these parents, grandparents and other relations and friends who are gone. All gone. Do such visions mean her days left on God's good earth are few in number? It could be true for each day seems to pass away more quickly than the last one.

The square plaza rimmed by the village houses is not large, but to Graciela the distance across the plaza to the other side is far and away too long. *His* casa stands on the other side of the plaza exactly facing her own home here. The two hundred cobblestones, *precisamente*, between his home and hers seem always a no-man's-land. A barrier redoubtable. Perilous. If she could cover that distance by her heartstrings alone and not have to cross by foot over two hundred stones, and if only he understood her feelings then he would know the depth of both her love and her regret.

Graciela sighs. Stretching out her hand, she takes a tortilla from the blue plate on the wooden table next to her chair and spoons some shredded pork onto that corn surface and spreads pico de gallo onto that. *Sin duda*, she muses, she eats far too many tortillas. Sighing again, she rolls the morsel up and takes a bite and gazes again across the plaza toward the house he lives in. Later, in the cool of the evening he will step outside his home, sit in the chair beside his door and watch *la gente* dancing on the plaza. The dancing, tonight, on this first night of Fiestas, will begin when the cottonwood trees shade the stones and a cooling breeze sweeps onto the plaza and the church bell tolls eight times, and the band, los músicos, arrives to play its music.

He, Matteo, is the father of four of her five children. The name of the father of the fifth child, known to her, is still unknown to him and this is a good thing. Matteo stayed with Graciela and endured the label of cuckold until the fifth child, a male, was born and then, one day soon after the birth of the fifth, not his, he bundled up his best shirt and pants with his hair comb and toothbrush and left her house and moved into the casita on the opposite side of the plaza. He had had enough. He could no longer suffer such humiliation. No man could.

Graciela understands Matteo's feelings all too well and she weeps for her loss of this good man. Every Friday evening, on returning from the fields, he would tramp across the plaza to her house on the other side and give her money, money for the children, even to feed the fifth one, all the while never speaking one word to her. Who would have guessed the deep love Matteo felt and still feels for the fifth child, the boy who bears no resemblance to him but is, *en verdad*, the spitting image of the handsome drifter who was his father. *Ah*, Graciela recalls how she gave Matteo a stack of still warm tortillas every Friday evening when he placed those coins in her hand. *Ah*, yes, the years passed so quickly with those five children traveling back and forth across the plaza, eating and sleeping at one house or the other, his or hers, until they all grew up and went their separate ways. But not too far away from her, or him.

Every evening now Graciela sits in the chair beside her door and watches Matteo sitting on his chair next to his door and, wistful, she tries to summon up courage enough to cross over the flagstone paving of the plaza and wish him a good evening.

"Buenos tardes, Matteo," she wants to say but has yet to say although, perhaps, tonight, when the band starts playing she might do just that. *God willing*, he might return her greeting, but, chances are he will not. He is a good man. But like all men, he has much pride. And he is a man who was once deeply hurt. By her.

Sitting there in her chair, Graciela feels a slight breeze tickle her nose then pass by her and enter through the open door into her house to cool it. She hears the sagging rumble of the mariachi band's ancient truck struggling up the hill to the village, arriving in the same truck they arrive in each and every year. Soon they will arrange their chairs at the far end of the plaza near the church and begin tuning up their instruments. *Ahora es el momento*, she mutters to herself.

With determination Graciela rises from her chair and steps over the threshold into her house and peers into the mirror beside the door. Her hair is still black, although who knows for how long it will be so, and her skin is quite youthful. Moist. Dewy. Unwrinkled. And, well, so what if her waist is gone and her hips are wider? After all, she had borne five children. Alas, that fifth one. Alas, such sweet temptation! *Oye, that handsome man.*

Oye. How soon he had left her. *Gone.*

She shimmies out of her everyday skirt and into her best skirt, the red cotton one with many pleats that swish loosely with the swing of her hips. Just as the band strikes its warm-up notes, with her lipstick applied she again steps outside and stands beside her door. Hesitating. Her heart is willing but her feet won't move. She breathes ever faster and faster as she watches her neighbors in their bright feast day clothing swarm onto the flagstone plaza, now their dance floor, bow gracefully to their partners, and begin moving to the sound of guitar and horn and drum and gourd and flute.

Yes, now it is time. Yes, she might never have a better chance. Another chance. She might never again summon up enough courage. Forbidding her sandaled feet to turn around and stray back toward the front door, Graciela walks slowly across the still warm stones of the plaza with a firm tread, directing her steps toward the man seated in the chair by his front door directly across the plaza from her home. *Matteo*. One step, then two steps, then three, and she counts three hundred steps until she stands right in front of him and tries to smile, but is not at all sure of her success.

"Buenas Noches, Señor," she addresses him in a whisper, thinking perhaps it would be better if she had not come. *Señor.* Hah. Although they have by now been married for twenty-five years, she feels their peculiar circumstance requires this formality since they have lived apart for fifteen of those years. "Por favor, Señor, quiere usted bailar conmigo?" Another formality, *usted*, but at least the words are out of her mouth. A very dry mouth, but she has said it. "Good evening, sir. Would you like to dance with me?"

Matteo stares at her, grim-faced, scowling, his tightly curled upper lip revealing anger, injury, frustration, smitten pride and the sting of betrayal. The glint in his eye would pierce the hide of an armadillo or the skin of a rattlesnake. His sneer enlarges, he quivers, shoulders stiff with rage and, then, quite surprising himself more than Graciela, he emits a deep sigh as if by no choice of his own. The scowl vanishes. He opens his mouth but no sound emerges. He nods his head, but very slightly, and one could say this was no nod at all. He stands up, straightens his posture, kicks his chair to one side and steps toward his doorway.

"Matteo?" Fearing he means to slam the door in her face, Graciela croaks out his name because she has been holding her breath for far too long, her temples pounding, pounding, pounding like the strike of the *metate* on the *mano* when she grinds corn for tortillas. She watches Matteo pause. She sees his shoulders bend and soften. And when he turns to face her with a light in his eye no longer cold but yielding, she feels faint.

"El gusto es mio," Matteo states hoarsely, but still unsmiling. He clears his throat as he steps over his threshold and gazes into the mirror just inside the doorway of his casa, slicks back his hair with his comb, adjusts his best necktie worn only for Fiestas, and polishes the turquoise stone on his belt buckle. He steps outside again and picks up the sombrero lying beside his chair, dusts it off and places it on his head. Then removing the sombrero he bows to Graciela and replaces his hat on his head. He reaches for her hand, grasps it, and leads her onto the flagstone plaza, now a dance floor.

As if acknowledging the fine and precious nature of this long-awaited and never-expected-to-ever-occur moment of reconciliation, this clasping of hands, this mutual intention to dance with each other once again, his and hers, the villagers, as one, emit a sigh. This is a beginning and everyone knows it. The band members cock their heads and share a knowing look and commence their next tune as Matteo again bows to Graciela and she curtsies deeply to him and he takes her in his arms with a firm hand upon her back.

The two move slowly, amid but not with the throng of other dancers, at arm's length at first as, together, they begin to remember the rhythm of their dancing those many years ago, a pace which was always ever theirs alone. Never to be fully forgotten. With foot next foot, they now step closer to each other, as the music demands of them. The distance between their bodies lessens even further as the band's tempo increases. Matteo pulls Graciela toward him, his grip on her back now steely as they, by heart, reprise the steps they danced so well, together, as they did all those many years ago before the fifth child was conceived.

Again, the music's tempo alters, stealthily at first, drawing them in before it quickens as if she, Graciela, wills the strings on those guitars now hot to the fingers of the musicians, to be plucked ever more swiftly. Faster and faster.

Gripping her hand fiercely, releasing his clutch on the back of her *blusa*, Matteo thrusts her away from him in a swirl of skirt, those red pleats, and Graciela turns and turns and whirls while he never lets go her hand, not once. Reeling her in toward him yet again he stares into her eyes as the minutes melt away and the band plays on, tendrils of smoke rising from the weary strings of their instruments. Again, he thrusts her away as the frenzied pace of the music hastens ever more swiftly. To Graciela and Matteo the other dancers are now but a blur of movement and rainbow color as they try to sustain the pace these two and the marimba band have set for them, but fail. It is too much. The others, all, panting, abandon the flagstone plaza dance floor and drift into the shadows beyond the cottonwood trees. There they catch their breath and await the slow beginning of the second round of dancing when they will rejoin Graciela and Matteo, who continue to dance even when the band ceases to play.

It is the *descanso*, the intermission, and the band members remove their sombreros, wipe the sweat from their brows and their instruments, stagger off their chairs, retrieve their bottles cooling beneath the cottonwood trees, drink deeply from these, and then collapse onto the grass.

Graciela and Matteo dance on, perhaps unaware that the band no longer plays its tunes. It does not matter. They do not care but cling to each other, as close as two beings can cling, moving slowly with a rhythm all their own yet speaking not one word for there is no need for words. Although Matteo's head is presses tightly against her own, Graciela cannot see the sorrow in his eyes nor the tears escaping and traveling their course along the lines etched deeply into his countenance. Matteo hears Graciela sniff loudly but he cannot see the tears that blind her, the tears she tries so hard to hold back. Yet fails.

One hour passes, maybe more, and los músicos don their hats, settle into their chairs once more, pick up their instruments, tune briefly, and again begin to play as the chattering villagers reenter the dance floor and rejoin the man and woman lost in their own reverie.

At last, as the moon drifts beyond the plaza and behind the cottonwood trees, the band sleepily plays the last note of their final tune. The villagers, no longer gay and smiling but exhausted, feel the ache in their bones of one too many salsa tunes, with tired voices bid their neighbors "Buenas noches", and retreat into their casas. Those traveling from farther away saddle up their horses or hitch their horses to wagons and disappear into the darkness of night leaving the echo of hoofbeats and rusty wheels to linger behind them.

On hearing that last fading note and cherishing it to the very last vibration of audible sound, Graciela and Matteo stare into each other's eyes. With her hand in his, Matteo slowly turns and begins to walk the length of the plaza toward its end where, on opposite sides, his casa and Graciela's stand with open doors facing each other. Exactly between the two houses they stop and stand, and face each other, eye holding eye with a long look that tells how they, as one, in this instant, relive together all the years they have shared. Matteo presses Graciela's fingers and she returns that pressure, then their hands slowly part. Graciela's eyes speak more than her tongue ever could and Matteo's lips are held grimly tight even as his own eyes lavish her with love. She curtsies deeply and he, doffing his sombrero, bows low to her. They then turn away from each other and slowly begin, each, to pace across once hundred flagstones of the two hundred separating their two houses, Graciela to her casa, and Matteo to his.

* * *

Rhenna St. Clair loves writing, oil painting, and her cat. "I am always writing something. My novel, *Getting New Mexico*, was traditionally published by Pace Press in 2019. I am a licensed acupuncturist and Doctor of Chinese medicine. I currently work at Holy Cross Hospital in Taos, New Mexico."

Short Story Romance - 2nd Place Linda Triegel

Mary and the Gypsy

"Had we never loved sae kindly,
Had we never loved sae blindly,
Never met—or never parted,
We had ne'er been broken-hearted."

Mary listened to the lines with only half an ear inclined to the poetry lesson. The other ear-and-a-half and both eyes were fixed on the world outside the classroom window, a world of sunshine and clover and jack-in-the-pulpit pushing his way out of the damp, dark earth near the brook.

It was May of Mary's last year of school. She was going on sixteen, and even Mr. MacKenzie, the schoolmaster, had been unable to convince her mother that another year of learning would do Mary any good.

"And what do ye think o' that, Mary Morison?" Mr. MacKenzie asked again. His Scottish burr was always more pronounced when he taught poetry class. The schoolmaster was partial to poetry because it developed the imagination. Even more than common sense, in his view, imagination was a good thing to have. Common sense had its limits, but there was no stopping the imagination.

"Have ye no thought for pur Mr. Burns, Mary Morison?" he asked again.

Mary's last name was Rivers, but it might as well have been Hills or Meadows. Mary didn't know why Mr. MacKenzie chose to give her the name of every Robert Burns lass he introduced her to, but she accepted the Morison unquestioningly.

She said, still looking out at her window-world, "I think—I think being in love might be worth the broken heart!"

Giggles broke out around her, and Mary remembered her audience. Her red head spun around; her wide blue eyes widened even more. Then she lowered her face over her desk in shame. Mr. MacKenzie beamed.

"Well done, Mary Morison! You have passed this class with colors flying!"

#

When school was over, boys and girls burst from the small, wood-shingled building with shouts of joyful release. Twenty of them ran in twenty different directions. Only Mary, the twenty-first, walked on her way slowly, knowing her path without looking.

She walked to the bridge that spanned the creek near the Potter farm and thence led to her own home. She crossed the creek and entered a copse of birches, where the new leaves were still a sweet yellow-green. At the edge of the sun-dappled water, she sat down on a rock, closed her eyes, and waited.

What Mary waited for was a dream. She knew he was a dream, the product of her imaginings, but he was the best she could do until the genuine article came along. She never doubted that he would come; to that extent, Mr. MacKenzie's poetry had triumphed over the innate common sense that told her she was daydreaming.

What Mary's imagination conjured up was a gypsy, a romantic figure with curly black hair and green eyes, wearing a gold earring and a guitar slung over his shoulder. Mary had never seen a gypsy, but she had a fairly sound common-sense knowledge of such things as earrings and guitars, and her imagination fitted those images together into a picture of what the word 'gypsy' meant to her.

Her gypsy watched her from the far side of the creek, and then, with a flash of a smile, jerked his head toward the trees and dared her to follow him. She always did, picking up her skirts and crossing the creek in one quick leap. But no sooner did she enter the copse than he disappeared, dissolved like dew in sunlight. Then Mary went on her way alone. But one day, she knew, she would talk to him.

Mrs. Truman Potter saw Mary crossing the field as she stood in her yard taking laundry down from the line. She wagged her head sadly, not for anything Mary had done—Mrs. Potter knew nothing of gypsies—but for what she imagined, because Mary was "serious" and not prone to giggling like other girls, that Mary was missing in the way of a normal childhood. Where Mrs. Potter erred, however, was in thinking that the small, but already nicely rounded body crossing her field was still eight years old.

Mary's mother, on the other hand, kept a sharp eye on her daughter's rate of growth, anticipating the time when Mary, like her older siblings, would marry and leave home, leaving her and Eben to enjoy their old age and their rockers.

"You just missed Billy Potter," she said as Mary came into the kitchen. She was putting cornbread into the big brick oven and did not turn around.

Mary sat down at the long table and picked up the glass of milk her mother put out for her every afternoon.

"He knew I'd be in school."

"He hadn't reckoned on you walking home over Worcester, I guess," Frances said, banging shut the oven door.

If there was a note of sarcasm in her mother's voice, Mary did not hear it. Sarcasm was not a tune she danced to. Billy was the boy the childless Potters had hired out from the Orphanage ten years before to do chores on the farm and later adopted. Frances Rivers, who frequently lectured Mary on her expectations, listed Billy as the best of them.

Billy was eighteen and a good-hearted cub of a boy. Everybody between Cook's Corners and Ambleside knew from the way he shuffled around after Mary Rivers that he had set his cap for her. But Mary discouraged Billy on the grounds that he had no imagination. No imagination was worse than the dirty fingernails that Billy, a hard worker, could not avoid. Billy was kind and dependable and, given half a chance, probably had a sense of humor. But he was no gypsy.

"Mama...?"

Frances pushed back the straggling gray hairs that fell over her forehead, then settled herself wearily into a chair opposite her daughter.

"Yes, Mary?"

"Where's Papa?"

Mary had already changed her mind about what she was going to say, and Frances, who had trouble getting through to Mary at the best of times, sensed that she had just missed another opening in the fence. She sighed.

"He went back with Billy. Tru Potter has a leaky roof. People seem to think your father is the only man around who can hold a hammer, or he's just too soft-headed to say no to every fool who asks a favor."

She stood up again and began opening cupboard doors, a sure sign that she was starting supper and Mary had better make herself useful or scarce. Mary elected to do both.

"I'll go to the well," she said. She rose and handed her mother the empty milk glass and picked up a bucket, all in one swift movement.

She stood outside the kitchen door for a moment, waiting. He didn't come. But he wouldn't come here, to the farm, anyway, so she was not troubled. Mary walked down to the well, swinging the bucket as she went.

#

It was August when Mary, now fully fledged sixteen and wearing a new bonnet to prove it, accompanied her father on a buying expedition to Cook's Corners. Eben Rivers knew as well as Mary did that the only buying to be done there was at Will Jamison's general store. But both Eben and Mary were capable of making a safari out of a trip to the springhouse for milk.

Eben finished his purchases and was now standing next to the loaded wagon, getting down to the important business of the morning, which was Being Neighborly. At the moment, he was so being with Seth Bishop, who generally had plenty to say about his neighbors.

Mary sat very still on the wagon seat. The air around her was very still and she wanted to blend in, to become as the air. But August was hot and heavy, and Mary was by nature cool and light, and she floated above the heat. She closed her eyes and felt the ripening of wild grapes on the wall running alongside the road.

When she opened her eyes again, it was to the sight of a pair of large brown eyes staring at her, like a spaniel's. Their owner raised a hand to his forehead and bade her good day. Mary sighed.

"Good morning, Billy."

"Nice day, Miss Mary."

"Yes, Billy."

"I . . . admire your bonnet, Miss Mary. Right smart color, I mean."

"Thank you, Billy."

Mary lowered her eyes modestly, and in the hope that he might go away. When she raised them again, Billy was still there, but he was no longer looking at her.

The Pittsfield stagecoach was coming up the pike, trailing a cloud of dust. Eben and Seth stopped talking to observe this phenomenon, and movement in general ceased around the store as the coach pulled to a halt.

Then Mary saw him.

He got out of the coach and turned to help a lady passenger—a round-faced, all-round round lady who was perspiring delicately —down from it. Then he turned and Mary had a better look. Billy, her father, Seth, the road, the wall—everything vanished from Mary's sight but the stranger.

There was no earring, no guitar; his hair wasn't black but chestnut—her mother would have called it plain brown—but it was just the right degree of thick and curly. He *was* handsome and his eyes *were* green. It was him all right.

He had been talking to the driver, who now motioned in Mary's direction. Her gypsy turned too and looked directly at Mary. She turned her head quickly and fixed her gaze on a spot between their old mare's ragged mane and the scrape on her swayed back

. . . and held her breath.

Seconds later, she heard, "Mr. Rivers?"

Mary moved her eyes as far to the left as she could without turning her head, which was just far enough to see the leather glove on his hand and the carpetbag hanging from it. Eben acknowledged his name.

"This is my daughter Mary, my friend Seth Bishop, and—afternoon, Billy, didn't see you there—my neighbor, William Potter."

The stranger said something to Mary, but the words were lost in a strange buzzing sound inside her head. She nodded, but he had already turned to shake hands with the men.

"Mr. Rivers, my name is Jared Kincaid. They tell me you're the best carpenter hereabouts."

"I'm the only carpenter hereabouts," said Eben, being an honest man.

Now Mary threw all show of indifference over the side of the wagon and was staring at Mr. Kincaid with all the foreign intensity of the August sun, but he did not seem to notice. He laughed, showing strong white teeth and a twinkle in his green eyes.

"Be that as it may, Mr. Rivers, I'd like to talk business with you. You see, I've inherited some land nearby, and I understand the buildings on it are about falling over. I want to build a home there."

A home! On his own land! That seemed very solid and respectable; not very gypsy-like. Of course, "inherited" made it sound a little chancier; one had no control over eccentric uncles and such dying and leaving their holdings to one. . . .

"Well, sir," Eben said, considering. "I'd be pleased to help you. If you're planning anything stately, though, August's starting pretty late. You got someplace to put up in the meantime?"

"I was aiming to pitch a tent for the time being."

A tent! Mary brightened. Eben was less enthusiastic, but allowed as how Mr. Kincaid was young and could probably sleep in anything, especially in August.

Bidding Eben good day, Mr. Kincaid looked up at Mary. Just for a moment, the heat outside her and the glow inside Mary made him think, *Why, she's really very pretty!* He took off his hat and smiled.

"Please to have met you, Mary."

Mary glowed.

#

All through the rest of August and September, Mary broke away from her chores whenever she could to go and watch the new house abuilding. If Eben wondered at the sudden desire to be of help to him in a daughter who had never before shown herself to be devious, he did not question it. He had as much faith in Mary's common sense as he had in her imagination, and it never occurred to him to set her right about gypsies.

Mary brought pitchers of lemonade for her father, and watched Jared drink them. She ran to Mr. Jamison for a pound of nails, and watched Jared up on a ladder pounding them into the roof. He worked with a good will, even a certain flair, but he wielded a hammer like any other man and sweated under the summer sun like any other man.

And when Jared spoke to her father, she could not help noticing that there was little poetry about it. Apart from the house, Jared had set his mind on an orchard, and he needed advice from Eben on soils, fertilizers, and storage temperatures.

It was a clear case of imagination against common sense, earrings against apples. Mary knew the virtues of both, and if she couldn't have the one, she could make do with the other. But at sixteen, "making do" held little attraction. She feared that Jared, for all his looks, might be just as steady as her father seemed to think, but she had seen that he was not above laughing and even dancing a jig now and then, so she thought she would hold out a little longer, for imagination's sake.

#

When his home was finished enough to live in, Jared washed off the sweat and put away his tools and dressed himself again in the linen shirt and leather jacket he had arrived in. And one morning, Mary came out of the kitchen to see him outlined against the early sky, walking straight toward her. She held her breath. But then he turned and took the path to Cook's Corners.

Mary dropped the bucket she was carrying and, staying out of sight and some distance behind, followed him. She'd follow him this time, she thought, wherever he might lead, because something told her that this time he would not disappear into the morning mist. This time was too real.

He walked quickly and with a springing step, as if he were eager to get to wherever he was going. Mary picked up her skirts and ran to keep up.

Jared crossed the bridge over the creek, and by the time Mary, breath coming quicker, heart pounding, caught up with him at the Corners, he was standing at the edge of the pike, looking up it in the direction of Pittsfield.

Mary was suddenly seized with a sense of foreboding. She sat down on the bench in front of the store, half hidden by the shade of the big oak tree.

Jared began to pace, with an intensity that would have worn a rut in the dirt road if at that moment—precisely on time—the stagecoach had not come clattering up the pike.

He stood still now, in a tense, waiting attitude. The coach stopped, its rattlings and bumpings subsiding into a faint jingle of harness as the passengers alighted.

The first was an elderly gentleman in a beaver hat, who stepped down and held up his hand to help the lady behind him.

The lady had soft blond hair and a bone-china complexion; her eyes were the blue of forget-me-nots. She put up her hand to shade them just as Jared bounded to the door of the coach, nearly knocking down the elderly gentleman, and picked the lady up in his arms. He gave her a hearty kiss and swung her to the ground. Squeals of "Papa! Papa!" came from the coach, and Jared helped two children, a boy and a girl both dressed in pale blue, out of it and embraced them too. The elderly gentleman smiled at the charming family scene.

#

Mary sat on the bench for a long time, her hands clasped in her lap, staring straight ahead in a kind of trance. Jared and his family left, and the coach went on its way, and the Corners returned to its usual morning stillness, broken only by the song of an unfeeling thrush.

Mary continued to sit. But soon, uninvited, ordinary sensations began to return to her. She heard the thrush, and Mr. Jamison's door being opened, and the distant neighing of a horse. And a voice in her ear.

"Morning, Miss Mary."

Billy took off his hat and stood in front of Mary, holding it over his heart. He looked down at her, but her head was lowered and she did not answer for a moment. But then she looked up, smiled and tossed her red head.

"Good morning, Billy!"

Billy, startled by this reception, nevertheless recovered bravely. He clutched a bedraggled bunch of marigolds in his hand, obviously plucked in haste when he saw they might suit the occasion. He thrust them at Mary, who took them with a delicate air and pressed her nose to them as if they were hothouse roses.

"Are ye—waitin' for somebody, Miss Mary?"

Mary stood up. "Why, no, Billy. No one at all. I was just going home." She looked expectantly at Billy, who took the hint.

"I'd be pleased to walk with ye, Mary!"

"Thank you, Billy."

She slipped her arm through his and, holding her head high and the marigolds in front of her, allowed him to lead her. Billy's arm was strong and the day was fine and Mary's common sense told her, not unkindly, that she wasn't really broken-hearted after all.

Billy, of the sorely underrated imagination, might have thought:

"How blythely wad I bide the stour
A weary slave frae sun to sun,
Could I the rich reward secure,
The lovely Mary Morison!"

* * *

Linda Triegel states: "I'm a Connecticut Yankee by upbringing and moved to the Southwest in 2006. I'm a member, and newsletter editor, of Croak & Dagger, the New Mexico chapter of Sisters in Crime. I've published several historical romances as Elisabeth Kidd and am working on my second cozy mystery."

Short Story SciFi/Fantasy/Horror - 1st Place Charles Botsford

The Leader

I write this with a pen.

It's midnight and I sit against a grimy office wall on the fifth floor of an abandoned building. A big rat scurries by with a french-fry in its mouth. A sign across the street shines just enough light for me to write.

I'm old and know how to use this pen, which is one of those cheap plastic jobs with Hilton running down the side. Only the H and two other letters remain, the rest rubbed away through use. It's my last. A computer would have been my writing preference but those are hard to come by for the common folk. They are anathema, which is partly why we're in this mess.

Decision time approaches. I either do something, or wither away as I've done for far too many years. Death greets me either way, and withering carries little risk, except to my soul.

This was a dentist's office by the look of the wrecked chair with its parts missing. The office stinks of decay, as do many places. I close my eyes and imagine a better time when doctors and dentists tended to patients here. It was a cleaner time.

The morning's event gives me hope, though, and also terrifies me.

Today I saw beauty.

Pursuit of beauty is why I stay alive.

Today's was so unexpected.

Real beauty is deep. It stays with you, overflowing your soul with joy. It's so rare you despair you'll never see it again. The child who lovingly hugs her stuffed penguin experiences real beauty and remembers it forever, or so she told me.

Today's beauty caught me by surprise, stripped my defenses, and made me vulnerable to those who would have me dead and gone.

It was a boy—actually a young man.

His actions, and the events that followed, affected me so, and allowed me to understand the nature of the beauty.

It was seven am, the morning wind above was chill, the patrols circumspect, and anyone who didn't have business above, was not. I was not. It was breakfast time if food had been available. I had none, so I found a secluded alcove off a secondary sewer channel and made myself at home. The sewer channel stench was positively mild compared with most mornings. I'd come down the back way through a manhole with the cover marked, "Chicago Sewer." With no food, I partook of an ancient bottle of whiskey.

A couple of months ago, during one of my late-night scavenging forays, I'd discovered a cache of whiskey bottles in an accountant's abandoned office behind a mop and boxes stuffed with dusty file folders . . . a veritable gold mine, or death sentence, depending how you look on such things. Whiskey doesn't dull my guilt, but does warm my soul.

My penance is to observe those around me. This does little to assuage my guilt, but I've taken it up as my job for now. At times I do my job with less diligence than at others, as I did in the alcove this morning, my life sipping away.

I heard rustling, but not the rustling of rats. Someone tried to run quietly from something bad, and hoped they wouldn't be noticed. It's a common noise below, but my little alcove was well hidden. A few nasty rags covered me, so that anyone looking my way would merely see a lump of disgusting filth. Besides, I was well into the bottle and not of a mind to move anytime soon.

The quiet rustling turned into the rumble of thumping feet and heavy breathing. I peeked between a rag and a threadbare beach towel, still not worried, and still not wanting to move. A woman stumbled, fell, and turned on her back staring backward with wide eyes as she skidded. A flyer or something fluttered from her jacket and landed several feet away in a puddle of water. It was actual paper. A second later a man slid to a stop and bent down to tend to her. Was the woman his wife?

The couple, Asian, appeared to be in their fifties, though they could have been younger. The underground does that to you. The woman, who had black hair shot through with white streaks, wore black beat-up poly-blend pants, a tattered green blouse, a thin black jacket, and worn-out boots. The man had a similar look, except he was mostly bald. He alternated tending to his wife and glancing toward the horror that followed them.

I've seen this play out countless times. Like a wolf cutting the weak sheep from the flock, the agent would show up to harass, arrest, or sometimes just kill the prey. Agents are bastards through and through. They pick 'em that way. They pick them for many vile traits and capabilities. Mostly they pick them for their ability to instill fear.

Then the agent sauntered up, a boy.

They must train them in sauntering. He had it down. He also had the ferocious glare down. The weapon helped. He had it trained on the couple, which meant that was it for them . . . no harassment, no arrest, just kill them there like dogs.

The agents get younger and younger. He was probably twenty-five, tall, skinny, mocha-colored skin, and obviously had a few years of experience refining that glare and pointing his weapon so cavalierly. His uniform was immaculate, but by no means new, which also said he'd been on the job a while.

I had no idea what the couple had done. It needn't have been much: selling contraband like coffee and methamphetamines, pushing counterfeit scrip, or even stealing from one of the State stores. They probably hadn't done anything big like trade in slavery, offer protection, or make book. They wouldn't have done the unthinkable: plot revolution, the R word. None but fools did that, and I hadn't seen any fools around for years.

However, it was odd that an agent had come to the depths of the underground that early in the morning. Not unheard of, just unusual.

Should I interfere? What would I do? Tell the agent to leave the couple alone and be on his way? Right. Not a chance. This was the norm. It was the new world to which I'd resigned myself. My hands shook so bad I feared he would hear me. I was close to bolting.

Instead of killing them immediately, he knelt down as if to torment them before doing the deed. Then he whispered to them. I almost didn't hear him. I was sure I misheard.

"Play dead."

My eyes widened, and I nearly dropped my bottle. This was new.

He took their threadbare jackets and shot holes in the chests and sleeves. His weapon was a relatively new energy gun that burned hot holes in things. The agent handed the jackets, smoking holes and all, back to the couple. Agents used to have lasers, but they were crap, always breaking. The energy guns are nastier and deliver more terror.

The agent shot the man in the leg, just enough to singe the pants and skin, which made the air reek of burning flesh. The man whimpered until the woman elbowed him.

The couple played dead.

The agent's partner finally showed up half a minute later munching on a protein bar. She, too, was tall and skinny, but white and early thirties, with an expression ten times meaner than the boy. The gnarly scar of mottled skin on her cheek gave the expression extra depth. The boy must have had a good reason for setting up such an elaborate hoax to deceive a brute like her. She surveyed the bodies and smiled. It was an ugly smile.

"Good work, Jack," the female agent said. "Just leave them there. That'll give the other liquor runners something to think about."

"Yeah sure. No worries."

"Central reported your comm unit is out," the female agent said. "You'd better get it fixed."

"Sure. Let's take a break at Antoine's. I'm starving."

The female agent nodded, and immediately started back through the side channel.

"Jack" stared at the "dead" couple, smiled, and then stared directly at me, as if he knew I were there all the time. Then he turned and followed his partner.

I waited a full five minutes, sitting still like a rock, my hands shaking uncontrollably. The couple returned to life, looked around, and the wife helped the man limp down the channel. I got up, tossed the grimy rags and beach towel aside, and bent down to pick up the soaked flyer. The woman agent had been wrong. They weren't liquor runners, or at least that wasn't their worst offense. The couple flirted with the R word. They truly were fools to consider revolution an option, brave fools.

I wadded up the flyer and tossed it in a pile of rotting trash. Then I strolled away, leaving the bottle. You don't want to get caught red-handed with contraband. I wandered the underground all day trying to process what I'd just witnessed, my heart thumping. They'd discovered me. By evening, I left the underground and wound up in this abandoned medical building, depleting the ink from my last pen, resigned.

That was it, an act of beauty. It may not sound like beauty to you, whoever reads this. If it's me reading this a year from now—if I survive that long—I want to remember what happened, and try to understand the importance of the events.

In the frigid darkness, I shiver. A soft recliner would be much kinder to my back than the cold office wall. Never going to the same place twice, it's the first time I've been here. By the state of debris, no one has been here for years.

I used to be someone. Now, I'm one of the common folk.

Being old gives me perspective on the good and the bad times. We live in grim times. When I still had hair, Chicago was an ugly place, but filled with pockets of beauty. Granted you had to look, and sometimes you had to look hard. Now, it's just an ugly place.

At least here I'm alone and out of sight. I don't hang out in homeless encampments on the street . . . too dangerous, too exposed, too monitored. Why make it easy for them? Even here I run the risk of discovery. During the day, I usually roam the underground rail lines and sewers. They monitor those as well, but it's easier to slip through their net.

I come above to scrounge for supplies and to escape the bleak feel of below. I need the escape. The underground oppresses everyone with its prison-like atmosphere, the weight of the city above, the competition for food, the competition among gangs, the competition for life. That's why they don't mess much with people below. They let the underground do their work for them.

Why do I bother to write this at all? Let's call it a journal of destiny. Only that which affects me to the core makes it into this journal. Today's beauty is worthy.

I pick up my pen and consider the grimy sheaf of paper on my lap. Paper is harder to scrounge. I snagged this and a few other pieces from a butcher who'd tossed odd-sized wrapping scraps in a bin behind her shop. I keep my "journal" between two slabs of cardboard and a string wrapped around the bunch to keep everything in place.

I used up the last of six magnificent leather-bound notebooks a month ago and hid them in the small library of an abandoned house. The notebooks were a luxurious treasure I'll never find again. I've stashed my journal collection in many such hideaways throughout the city. I'm like a squirrel with nuts, waiting for winter to settle in. Only, this type of winter isn't like the squirrel's winter. It's darker, harsher. My collection awaits a spring that will never come.

I fear running out of ink and paper. My pen is almost out.

I do my best writing at midnight. The early morning buzz of the whiskey has worn off, especially since I didn't drink another drop after the agent left. The hard part is interpreting what happened. That's what's taken me all day to understand.

I could easily pass off the agent's action as one of kind-hearted sympathy. Agents are people after all. It's possible one bad apple, at least from the State's perspective, got through screening and did something human. It has to happen. Their recruits can't all be sociopathic bastards.

But that's not what happened.

He'd stared directly at me.

His gaze said, "This was all for your consumption, something for you to think about."

He'd known I was there.

Trying to imagine who they are isn't difficult. They have embedded agents in the system, which is impressive. They aren't the State. Otherwise, I'd be dead. I know who they are, but I also know they shouldn't exist. I know what they're up to. It's one of the deadly sins, the worst of the deadly sins. Revolution.

My pen stops writing. Damn.

It may be nothing. Sometimes it's not the pen. Sometimes the paper gets grease from a finger, and the pen doesn't have enough friction for the ink to flow. The cure is to find a non-greasy part of the paper and get the ink to flow again. It takes a few squiggles, which wastes paper, and ink.

Yep, that was it. Close call. I didn't want my pen to crap out on me at this point.

This morning's beauty lies not in the act of kindness. It lies in the act of brilliant strategy, and of course the thought behind the strategy. This morning's act was a setup. They did it to get my attention. They want me.

Damn.

Well sure, I'll just jump right back in. Why wouldn't I? Together, we could turn this whole thing around. We'll overthrow the bastard oppressors, save the people, and save the planet.

Right.

Or die. Or worse. We'll get folks hopes up just to watch their hopes crash on the rocks after being beckoned by the sirens of freedom, and get a lot of people killed, and not accomplish anything, because that's the most likely outcome. Did I mention revolution is for fools?

The question is, are these organized fools or just idiot wannabe fools? It makes a difference. I know about fools. I'm a recovering fool. Idiot wannabe fools are typically harmless because they only get themselves killed, not having the brains or charisma to bring the innocent into their schemes, and thus limiting the damage they do.

Organized fools, however, are dangerous. These ones are definitely organized because their schemes have brains behind them. They understand strategy, which is very dangerous.

They think they need me.

Sure, I'm a writer, currently, but that's not why they need me. Previously, I was the voice of reason. I was eloquent, could fire up imaginations, get hopes up, even walk on water.

Fortunately, they don't have enough money to bring me into their fold. My price is astronomical because the cost to me is my soul. If I should fail and crush the hope of millions of other souls, or cause them to lose their lives, I could not bear the cost.

A noise alerts me.

Someone comes for me. They know I'm here. Question is, is it the State or the fools? I'm ready for either, long ready. I've been ready ever since the rise. The plateau followed the rise, and then the fall, all in the space of ten years. I've had many dismal years to cement my readiness. The cement hardened long ago when beauty left my life, the beauty of my wife and daughter. I was an oblivious fool.

It's easy if it's a fool who approaches. I decline their offer and slip into whiskey until the bottles run out. One way or the other I end up retired from life. I find comfort in my high price since it has nothing to do with money.

The scuffling comes closer. The person does it on purpose to alert me, possibly giving me a chance to flee if I wish.

And then the time arrives. It's Jack, the agent from this morning, who stands over me. In the near darkness he stares at me much the way he did this morning. The light from the street sign gives his face a boyish cast. It must be hell for someone who must appear fearsome to have such a boyish face. It must be hell for someone with his skin tone—neither light enough, nor dark enough—to fit in anywhere.

I stop writing and stay seated, my back against the wall. The scraps of papers on my lap suddenly seem worthless, trivial even, the musings of a drunken old man, a dead man. What is it I'm trying to accomplish? I've lost hope ages ago.

Jack says nothing. Instead, he extends his left hand, which holds the half-empty bottle from this morning. I'm surprised, but not overly. This is obviously the low offer. I take the bottle, set it aside, and go back to my journal, pretending to ignore him.

Then he reaches into his tunic pocket and brings out a pen, a newer twin for the one in my hand and offers it to me.

I gaze in wonder.

Damn.

As if by magic he's met my price.

I take it and nod.

The agent turns to leave and nods back, as if he respects me.

Wither or not. Not.

I fail to fight a tear forming in my eye.

I wrap up my journal, leave the bottle for someone who needs it, and walk from the building with the renewed purpose of a leader. To bring about spring will be worth the terrible task.

* * *

Mr. Charles Botsford writes SFF novels and short stories. One of his SF short stories, *Homecoming*, was an award winner in the 2005 SouthWest Writers Contest. Mr. Botsford is a chemical engineer, with 45 technical papers published on energy, electric vehicles, and air quality. His website is www.abbotwriter.com.

Short Story SciFi/Fantasy/Horror - 2nd Place K. L. Wagoner

Soulkeeper

Catching a soul was a complicated matter, or so the witch had said. Melon and Rover needed courage and cunning and a shadow creature's favor to see it through. Two brothers, spells forgotten, spells spoken, songs sung—each with a part to play—and gold coin with its promise of full bellies and warm beds when it was over and done.

Melon's part now was to trust the witch and her plan, that he would remember what needed doing when it needed done. He did his best to tread through the depths of the midnight forest like one of the fae folk who followed no trail and left no track.

Only a fool set out to make noise in the forest of Evergreen, if such a fool wished a Shadow to hunt him down. Melon chose his steps, held his breath. He imagined himself a breeze that skims a field of grain, leaving only a whisper as it passes. No matter how careful his movements, his steps still seemed to shout his presence.

He searched the darkness for Shadow sign. Gnarled trees grew too close together here. Moonlight crept through the tangle of branches without reaching the deepest veiled parts of the forest. With every breath, the air weighed on him like a sodden cloak.

One more step, and something harder than the sponge of the forest floor gave under his weight. A twisted thing pushed up through decayed leaves at his feet and stared at him.

Melon screamed, jumped back. He slipped, crashed to the ground, and sunk into the muck. Without his weight to prop it up, the twisted end of a fallen branch slipped back under the leaves. He closed his eyes for a moment and let out a ragged breath.

The stench of black rot surrounded him, but he held off the overwhelming need to retch, and lay still where he fell. He didn't dare move or make another sound. Maybe the Shadows hadn't heard.

"For the love of luck," Rover's low curse carried in the silence. His steps made no more than a breath of a sound as he drew close. He glared down at Melon with arms folded across his chest. His eyes softened a bit, his mouth twisted up to one side.

"I hear whipmasters pay twice as much for the clumsy ones," Rover whispered. "Good thing I'm the one carrying the bottles, eh?" He snickered and returned to his near-silent course through the trees.

Melon's back made a sucking sound when he rolled over and the ground let him go.

Rover sidestepped a stump and picked his way farther into the forest. His pack, weighed down by two spell-cast bottles, swayed low on his back. Melon almost yelled for his brother to wait but stopped himself in time. Twice foolish, as Ma used to say, makes a one-eyed man a beggar.

Only luck knew if Rover would really turn Melon over to the whipmasters for his clumsiness, as he'd joked about more often than Melon could count. His brother didn't seem to care that Melon threw a knife sure and true every time. And hadn't he done a fine job steering them clear of traps set for grave thieves sneaking over the forest wall? Seeing in the dark came in handy on nights like these, but Rover had gone ahead without him, as if he didn't need Melon anymore.

Rover disappeared into the depths between a pair of trees that stood like sentinels with their upper branches twined together. Melon squinted at the darkness. No sign of movement among the ancient trunks. Cold oozed through the cracks of his worn boots and made his toes go numb. He chose his steps and stilled his breath, the way fae surely do, as he hurried after Rover.

This was no simple errand to dig for moonspur glowing among exposed roots or to gather tinder for the witch to cast in ever-flame. No, catching souls was a more complicated business than Melon was used to. Courage and cunning, spells and song. That's what it would take. Wind song…shadow spell…what had the witch said? He tried to push through the fog that captured her words. No use. He had to trust her promise to remember what was needed when the time came.

Through the tight tangle of branches ahead, a change in the ashen hue of night marked the end of the forest. Melon quickened his pace, drawn to the open air, and stepped onto the burial grounds.

Shifting waves of tall grass shimmered in the light of the moon. Nearby, paper lanterns rustled in the wind. A few lanterns still held the blinking halos of candlelight as they swayed on lines stretched over the smallest graves along the base of Paupers Mound. Would the children buried there cheer for him and Rover and what they were about to do?

And where was Rover? Only shadows hugged the run of newly-filled graves that bordered the Mound on the south. Ma was under one of those barrows, buried this day along with others taken by the plague. The witch said Ma's soul would still be there and Melon could speak to her, even catch her soul in a spell-cast bottle if she wanted to be caught. He shook his head. Maybe she'd rather stay in the field to comfort the children. She'd always been good at that.

A far-off solitary howl drifted on the wind. A dense shadow shifted in the middle of the row of new graves to reveal Rover kneeling on a long, low mound of earth. The shadow moved again, and half of Rover disappeared behind its bulk.

Rover's voice rose and fell on the wind as if he talked to himself. As Melon stepped close, the sound of two separate voices grew more distinct. With a rush of dread and a twist in his gut, he knew his brother wasn't talking to an empty shadow.

Melon had never seen a real Shadow but he'd heard plenty of tales. This veil of dark fog before him didn't look like a creature that would just as soon eat your soul as laugh—like the old stories claimed—and Rover didn't seem afraid as he knelt there talking and smiling.

"So, we came to get Ma," Rover said to the Shadow as he fidgeted with one of the spell-cast bottles. "And take her back with us."

Something pricked at Melon's mind. The same way light shifted into place to reveal the hidden traps of the forest. What if the old stories were true?

Melon drew a knife from his coat pocket, held it by his side as he stepped around behind his brother.

The Shadow leaned closer to Rover, its voice a low rumble that thrummed Melon's chest. "The catching of a soul is not as simple as one might think."

The creature's heavy gaze settled on Melon. Two darker, deeper points within the veil might have been the Shadow's eyes. An icy swell of air pressed in on Melon from every side. A pricking at his mind again. Emptiness from the void whispered...*Hunger.*

"Maybe you could help us." Rover held the corked bottle out to the creature.

The Shadow shifted. A part of it settled on Rover's shoulder, like an arm comforting an old friend. "Perhaps." It snickered.

Cunning was needed, the witch had said.

Melon bent down, watching the Shadow. "He can't help us," he whispered to Rover. "We can do this ourselves."

"But can you do it properly?" the Shadow answered for Rover. "And if your mother does not want to be caught, do you know how to change her mind?"

"The witch says—" Melon began.

"And who taught the witches, do you suppose?" The bottle drifted from Rover's hand and settled, half hidden, in the midst of the veil. "I shall show you how it is done."

The Shadow's gaze fell on Melon again. Cold crept into his bones. Truth spoke in the silent space between him and the creature. *Eternal. Emptiness.*

A sudden urge to flee gripped him, to race back through the forest and over the wall, to leave Rover behind and be safe.

The Shadow chuckled. "Call your mother."

"Rover, let's go."

"We came to do this, Melon. It won't take long."

"Call to her," the Shadow said. Though Melon couldn't see the creature's face, he heard the smile in its voice. The Shadow drew even closer to Rover.

"Ma," Rover said to the grave. He pressed his fingers into the loose dirt.

"Talk to her."

"Come to us, Ma. We miss you."

"More." Impatience edged the Shadow's voice.

Rover cringed, nodded. "Remember the songs you taught us? They eased our toil…and the storytelling and games by candlelight. We miss all of it. Come to us, Ma." He continued on, reminding Ma of the joy she'd brought to their family.

The wind took on the sound of Rover's voice. A prickle of static rushed down Melon's back. The same feeling he had in the presence of the witch. Magic.

In Melon's mind he saw Ma surrounded by scores of children, felt her need to care for them. A familiar, gentle embrace held him close. "Ma," he whispered.

Rover stopped talking. The wind didn't. It spoke of peace and joy.

The Shadow pulled the stopper from the bottle.

The wind continued its glorious song, for hours it seemed. Peace. Joy. Forever. Then Ma let go of Melon. Her presence fell away. He was alone again, but the vision of her with the children remained.

The Shadow fit the cork back in the bottle. "There," it rumbled, "could you have done that?"

"No," Rover said, the word filled with a quiet, faraway sound. He reached for the bottle, but the Shadow held onto it.

"How could you promise her peace and joy?" Melon said. He already felt Ma's unease as she waited, trapped in the bottle.

"And eternity. I will give her all three." *Once she becomes a part of me.*

"She doesn't want that," Melon said. "She wants to stay here in the field."

"She's made her choice," Rover said with that odd sound to his voice.

"No!" Why didn't Rover see the truth?

"Yes. You understand." A veiled arm swept across Rover's shoulder again.

Rover pointed to the bottle. "Maybe you could let her come to us one more time. Just to say goodbye."

The Shadow leaned in. "Of course. Come close." *And become part of me.*

"It's a trick." Melon tightened his hold on the knife. He wouldn't let the creature steal his mother's soul or his brother's.

The Shadow's gaze bore into him. A grip as strong as stone squeezed Melon's chest. He struggled to breathe.

"Come, Rover. Melon. Greet your mother."

Melon's back prickled again as the wind began to sing. Peace. Joy. In the arms of Ma. On and on, it continued until Melon believed the song. The grip on his chest faded. He breathed freely as he stumbled toward the Shadow and the bottle. Melon would live forever, at peace, with Ma. No hunger, no plague to threaten his body, no conspiring with the witch to earn a few coins.

The witch. What was it she'd said? Wind and song. Melon fell to his knees in the barrow's soft earth. The Shadow pulled the cork.

Courage and cunning. The spell still waited, and Melon remembered. He forced the witch's words to his lips and whispered, "Shadow song."

The wind sang anew in a softer voice that spoke of rest. Comfort. A forest renewed. Evergreen. The creature swayed, held the bottle close.

A wisp of love swirled around Melon. Ma touched him on the cheek and rushed away into the field.

Melon's knife lay in the dirt at his knees. When had he dropped it? He gripped the hilt, held tight to its cold comfort. The blade glinted in the light of the paupers' lanterns.

Rover shook his head as if to clear it and stared at Melon.

The song of magic continued. Harvests of honey fruit. Dancing in the forest. Forever.

Like an empty veil drifting on a dying wind, the Shadow floated down to the grave.

Rover grabbed the spell-cast bottle before it hit the ground. The cork rolled across the barrow. The song stopped.

The Shadow's voice bellowed from within the bottle. The veil began to fill again, beneath it a dark form rose from the ground. The head of a giant, shoulders as broad as a bear's.

"I can't find the cork," Rover yelled as he searched through the dirt.

Melon couldn't let the Shadow regain its feet. He jumped on the creature and drove the knife into the rising veil. The blade passed through a forever nothing, and finally sank into the firmness of muscle.

The Shadow bucked and screamed. Melon clung to it as it fought against him. He shoved the blade deeper and dragged it down, tearing through flesh. The blade bit into bone. The creature's voice raged again from the bottle, hollow now and faraway.

The cloak of magic that had hidden the Shadow's form vanished.

Melon lay on top of the dark mountain of the body of a beast, his knife sunk to the hilt between hunched shoulders. Coarse fur covered the creature, except for a mane along the edges of its face—a face of smooth skin that resembled a man's, though the nose was too wide and the ears pointed. Clawed hands gripped the barrow's dark dirt. Melon shivered and turned away. Whatever the Shadow had been, it looked too much like a man for Melon's comfort.

Rover still knelt on the grave. He held the bottle in one hand, pressed the stopper down with the heel of the other. "Quick, get the candle."

The last of the witch's words returned to Melon's memory. He fumbled in Rover's pack, past the second spell-cast bottle, and pulled out a broken candle. He ran to the line of lanterns, lit the wick, and returned to Rover, then sealed the cork with melted wax. Two brothers, spells spoken and forgotten, each with a part to play. The witch had told the truth.

He dropped onto the barrow beside Rover with the bottle between them. Melon wouldn't suggest they use the second bottle. Thinking of Ma's soul trapped in eternal darkness made his heart sick. He remembered her touch before she escaped into the field, but she comforted others now, and that was a better thing.

A howl rode the air, followed by another. Closer than the first?

"We should hurry," Melon said. He scanned the field for Shadow sign. Nothing moved nearby or along the forest edge.

Rover nodded and swayed to his feet. "We might make it back to the witch before she closes shop."

The bottle felt heavier now than when it waited empty and spell-cast. Melon held it out to Rover as they headed across the field.

Rover shook his head. "You carry it." He patted Melon's shoulder and continued through the cold grass toward the forest.

Melon tipped his head down to hide a smile. He slipped the bottle into a coat pocket and pressed it against his belly. He would not trip and fall. He would not.

The witch had promised two gold coins for each of them in exchange for a Shadow's soul. Hard won and worth it. Four gold coins would buy more bread than Melon could imagine, enough to keep both their bellies full for years. And when the coin ran out? He had no intention of coming back over the forest wall.

Maybe they should do something more with the coin than eat off it. They could buy a goat and sell the milk. They could buy a water-seller's license. Three gold pieces were enough for one of them to apprentice with the blacksmith.

A light rain washed over the field, but Melon didn't mind. No lightning, no thunder. He paused at the edge of the forest. For a moment he thought he heard the faint sound of children laughing.

* * *

KL Wagoner loves creating worlds of fantasy and science fiction. She's currently working on the fantasy trilogy **The Last Bonekeeper** and short stories in the same universe. Besides being an author, Kat is also a veteran, a martial art student, and a grandmother. Visit her at klwagoner.com.

Short Story SciFi/Fantasy/Horror - 3rd Place Caleb Castleberry

Deliver Us from Evil

Nicholas Thorne was an evil man. He drank and he swore and he gambled. If any woman had been unfortunate enough to wed him, he would have beaten her black and blue and left her for dead. But there were many men who had their vices and their violence, and yet they were not called evil. That title was reserved for Thorne alone among the men of the town. And why should the other men be called evil? They, after all, did not consort with the devil. The villagers would frighten each other with dark rumors behind closed doors, whispering about black masses and taking communion with demons, before crossing themselves to ward off Thorne's eye and ire.

Nicholas Thorne was a strong man. He towered over other men and was broader than all, save the village blacksmith. Despite the rumors (or perhaps to prove the power of the devil was still less than that of God), Thorne was asked to help with the construction of the new church. None of the other men could move the heavy marble blocks with the same ease as Thorne, with his bull's shoulders and bull's stubbornness. He took the job and drank his pay, laboring to raise a house for a God he had turned his back on.

Nicholas Thorne was a dead man. When the church was nearly done, he fell (or was pushed, the legends conflict) from the roof, snapping his neck when he landed. None grieved for his passing, yet they still gave him the proper rites. They were good Christians, after all. Thorne was the first lost soul to be buried in the new St. Anthony's churchyard.

But he was not the last.

As time marched on, as time is wont to do, the church of St. Anthony witnessed countless deaths and burials over the centuries. War, plague, famine, the silent stone saints saw all, and the victims of the latest tragedy would inevitably come to find their eternal slumber in the humble churchyard. The very air of St. Anthony's was heavy with the weight of loss and memory.

The plumes of incense escaping the censer Father Oswald swung as he made his way up the center isle of the nave mingled with that still and silent air. The only lights came from the candles on the altar he had lit earlier. The sun had set hours ago, and the church bell began to toll midnight as Father Oswald reached the altar. He set the censer aside, stepped behind the lectern, and turned to face the empty church. He made the sign of the cross and began to speak as the ringing of the midnight bells faded away.

"In the name of the Father, and of the Son, and of the Holy Spirit. Amen." He looked out at the dark pews before continuing. "The grace of our Lord Jesus Christ, and the love of God, and the communion of the Holy Spirit be with you all."

He waited for a reply that did not come before pressing on, making his way through the rituals of mass. As he sang the Gloria, he saw the first indication that he was not alone. The candles' flames flickered in the still air. Small pinpricks of light appeared in the dark, always in pairs, vanishing as soon as he looked at them. Through stolen glances he watched the dead press closer and closer as the mass continued. He could not make out individuals, only denser areas of shadow that swirled and billowed like fog. They seemed content to mill about the pews, none daring to come too close to the priest and his island of candlelight. What few details he could see beyond the candles' glow faded as his late congregation took their seats. It was as if the whole world had dimmed to nothing, as if all that was left, all that was real, was his tiny circle of light.

When he reached the homily, he faltered. There was no script for this, and his carefully planned words slipped away. Yes, he had performed funerals before, but this was no funeral. And even if it had been, though the funeral rites were intended to see off the deceased to their eternal reward, the true audience was the living. It was easy to preach to the living. The living could always strive for more, could change their actions and their futures. He could understand their wants, their needs. He could offer a listening ear to their confessions, congratulations for their joys, sympathy for their sorrows, and absolution for their sins. What could he offer the dead? It was too late to give them last rites. Their fates were sealed, and there were no more actions they could take. The living had a future. The dead were past tense.

He took a breath, the air thick in his lungs. "I want to thank you for coming tonight. I know this isn't our usual time for fellowship, but this does seem to be the time when you are most active."

He had been warned before arriving at St. Anthony's that many in the local community thought the church haunted. Nonsense, he had scoffed. Ghosts weren't real, and even if they were, surely the power of God would keep them away from the sacred grounds of the church.

At first, he was proven right. The church was an old building, constructed in the late 15th century, and like all old buildings it had its quirks. Doors that got stuck in their frames, creaking noises as the church shifted and settled, odd drafts from holes that needed repaired. Yet as the months went on, he noticed things that were harder to explain away. The sound of children giggling and playing late at night when he was locking up. The fact that no matter how many times they changed the lightbulbs or how many candles they lit, there were places that were always dark.

Then the visions began.

He was in the church kitchen the first time it happened. One of the ladies who had helped with a recent wedding complained about the refrigerator making an odd noise. When he had gone to check on it, he had seen an old woman dressed all in black out of the corner of his eye. He turned to apologize for not noticing her and ask what she needed, but she was gone, and no one knew of anyone who matched her description.

Another time, he had been in the confessional, waiting to hear the people's sins. There were the sounds of heavy, dragging footsteps and a thud, as if the confessor had thrown themselves to their knees. Yet he could not see anyone through the wooden lattice, not even a shadow.

Ignoring his unease, Father Oswald began, "In the name of the Father, and of the Son, and of the Holy Spirit. Amen."

"For..." a broken voice gasped. "Forgive..." it tried again before dissolving into a thick, gurgling wheeze.

"Are you alright?" Father Oswald asked, breaking the script. "Do I need to call someone? If you're sick, please go home. Your desire to come and confess is admirable, but we have a lot of elderly and don't want any diseases spreading through the congregation. I will gladly come to your house and take your confession there. Please take care of yourself."

"Home," the confessor whispered with such heart-breaking longing that Father Oswald pressed a hand to his chest. He pushed the agony in that voice aside and left the booth, intent on helping the poor soul who was clearly far too sick to be at church.

Yet, when he went to the confessor's side, it was empty. The only thing waiting for him was a spattering of brown blood, already dry to the touch.

Shaken from his recollection, Father Oswald forced himself to continue. "Jesus went out to meet people where they are. We see that in the stories of Zacchaeus, a reviled tax collector; the calling of Paul, who had persecuted the early church and yet became a great apostle; and the adulteress, who He forgave and would not stone and would not condemn. He showed these people, and many more, God's grace and love. The church and His followers should look to His example and do the same."

He moved on to the Creed, unable to think of anything to add, then began to prepare the Eucharist. He tried to not wonder about how the dead would take communion, if they should take communion, if they even *could* take communion. Would it be enough for them to be near the Host? Would it simply vanish from the communion plate? Why was he trying to force logic on ghosts when there was a decent chance he was hallucinating the figures swimming at the edges of his vision and having a mental breakdown?

"Blessed are those called to the supper of the Lamb," he recited. The silence where there should have been voices was not unexpected, yet this one was deeper than before, his voice oddly muffled in the cavernous space. He could no longer hear the soft crackle of the candles or the hiss of the wind blowing outside. Even the sounds of his own breathing were muted. He closed his eyes and took a deep breath, steeling himself to walk towards the edge of the protective circle of light and offer the Host to his congregation.

He opened his eyes and stared into two glowing embers of hellfire. The demonic eyes were set in the face of an impossibly large man, dressed like he had just walked out of an illuminated manuscript. Unlike the figures still hovering just outside the shine of the candles, this man was undeniably solid and undeniably unafraid of the light. If anything, the light seemed afraid of him. The shadows of his face did not match the shadows the candles should have been casting, the light shying away from him, unable or unwilling to touch him.

This was no hallucination, no stress dream. He towered over Father Oswald, glaring down at him. Father Oswald, for his part, was rather proud that he did not cry out in fear. He glanced down at his hands, as if to reassure himself that he hadn't dropped the Host and started. He could see through the hand, *his* hand, holding the communion-plate. Was he the ghost now, just another one of the unquiet dead? No. It must be a trick of the light or the being in front of him. Something to make him doubt and falter. He would complete the mass; he *must* compete the mass. He had a sacred duty.

"Is this the best you can do?" the demon rumbled. "You are alone priest, alone in the dark. You call to your God yet use the wrong words. This is not how an exorcism goes. This is not how you cast us out."

Father Oswald swallowed. "You are correct," he said, surprised at the steadiness of his own voice. "I am not here to perform an exorcism. I'm not even trained as an exorcist."

"A pity," the demon sighed, sounding genuinely disappointed. "I was looking forward to testing the faith of a true man of God. Instead, I get…" he waved a dismissive hand to indicate Father Oswald.

The insult stung, but he didn't rise to the bait. "My apologies for falling short of your expectations. If that is all, I would like to continue with my service, Mr. Thorne."

The thing that might have once been Nicholas Thorne grinned, the smile stretching beyond the corners of his mouth. "Don't you know that it is unwise to call a spirit's name? It draws our attention. And the attention of one like me is not something you want."

"To say someone's name is to remember them. After all, it is said that a man is not truly dead while his name is still spoken," Father Oswald replied. "And I made a point to find the names of all those buried here within church grounds. Including the very first. I may not know what words to speak to comfort the dead, but I can at least learn their names. It's only polite."

Thorne cocked his head to one side, then the other, examining Father Oswald. "What is your game, little priest? You come here in the middle of the night, not to exorcise the dead, but to preach to them. Why? How does this benefit you? You are no saint, forced to face trials to prove your faith. You do not have a lust for power, to prove yourself holier than your brethren, more deserving of advancement. I can taste your fear in the air, yet you do not feel like a coward desperate to prove his courage in the face of darkness. Why are you here?"

Father Oswald had asked himself these same questions before entering the church to enact his half-baked plan to address the hauntings. He looked towards the dead, still milling about in the shadows beyond Thorne.

"It is not a matter of faith, or power, or courage," he began, his words picking up steam as his thoughts came together. "It is a matter of duty. It is my sacred duty to care for and minister to all the souls who come to this church. Granted, all my prior experience is with souls that are still attached to their bodies, but it doesn't matter. These people are still souls under my care, and I will do right by them."

"You mean to minister to the unquiet dead?" Thorne mocked; his voice sickly sweet. "Evil spirits, monsters, demons, all those who come to turn the righteous away from your God? Why care for them?"

"How dare you call them evil!" The anger in Father Oswald's voice sparked between them. "Do you know who is buried here? Old women who caught a cold in their chest that never went away. Children that drowned in the river. Young soldiers who fought in a far off war and came home in a box. These aren't monsters, they're people. If I can bring comfort to even one of them, then my actions will not be in vain."

The demon changed tracks. "So kind you are to the dead, so generous. Do you show this same grace to the living? There are so many your church has decried as unworthy, unclean. If they dare step through your doors, would you be this welcoming? Or would they have to crawl on their bellies, begging for forgiveness for daring to exist before you would deign to look in their direction?"

"God's love is for everyone," Father Oswald said. "I will not deny that the church has not always had the most open of arms, but that is the church. All are welcome here, and anywhere I serve. I will not turn anyone away."

"Anyone?" Thorne asked.

"Anyone," Father Oswald repeated.

"The drug users, the alcoholics, liars, thieves?"

"Anyone," Father Oswald repeated.

"Gays? Divorcees? Unwed mothers? Those that would have been unwed mothers if not for a little procedure? There are so many unclean in the world. Do you expect me to believe you truly care about them? Don't you fear that letting in the filth will dirty you as well?"

"No. If they are filth, then so am I. We are all human, we are all sinners, we have all fallen short. I am not God. It is not my place to judge who is worthy to be saved and who is not. I will gladly welcome any who come here seeking God and I will do my best to guide them towards the light. Living, dead, sinner, saint, it doesn't matter. Anyone. Everyone," He looked up, directly into Thorne's burning eyes. "Even you, Nicholas."

Thorne's eyes widened in surprise, and he took a step back. "Me? Isn't that sacrilege? I am an evil, wicked man, after all."

"And who needs God's love more than evil, wicked men?" Father Oswald asked.

Thorne stood stunned for a moment, then began to laugh. As he laughed, the shadows lightened, and he shrank to the size of an ordinary man. The glowing hellfire of his eyes faded, revealing their true color to be a pale blue.

"You aren't a very good priest," Nicholas, a man once again, said. "But you are a good man. Those are far rarer to find and much more valuable. I wish you good luck in your ministries." He bowed his head.

Father Oswald blinked and he was alone in the candle lit sanctuary as the sun began to rise.

"Go in peace. Thanks be to God."

* * *

Caleb Castleberry was born and raised in Farmington, New Mexico. He now resides in San Francisco, California, where he works for San Francisco State University. He has written a variety of works, including poetry, nonfiction, and fiction, with his true love being fantasy.

Short Story SciFi/Fantasy/Horror - Honorable Mention **Mary Therese Ellingwood**

Retirement in Hell

Morte felt something behind him. Not in the physical sense, of course. He was a Death Angel after all and only those in action were gifted the physical senses to make their dealings with humans more compassionate. Empathy. In Morte's opinion empathy should be for the virtue-granting angels only. After all, they were the ones who must learn to forgive. But back in the beginning, in a world where time was left unmeasured, Hades had decided that the active Death Angels also needed this trait. In an effort to instill such an unnatural trait in the Death Angels, Hades had gifted them the five senses. Morte had shed them long ago when he retired, and he didn't miss them.

No, he couldn't physically feel the angel next to him, but there was an undeniable presence that hadn't been there before. It spoke to Morte's soul.

You are needed.

Morte made no effort to reply.

The Earthly population has grown unchecked and now their numbers are dying off.

Again, Morte ignored the pressure exuding from the presence beside him.

There are not enough of us. New recruits are forming. You will lead a contingent of them.

Morte sent a flare of emotions out to the other presence in a clear communication that he was not to be troubled. It left.

Morte was settling back into his eternal reverie when a new presence surrounded him in such a strong outpour of command that Morte's being itself was almost extinguished under its weight. Hades.

Morte. Go.

Hades departed as quickly as he had come but left behind the physical senses once again as Morte sighed inwardly. His new sight allowed him to see that, along with the senses, his physical self had taken form once again. Morte was no longer a solitary consciousness at the edge of the Underworld. He was back in command, and he had recruits to meet.

* * *

There were four types of angels that ran the Underworld for Hades. Death Angels and Receiving Angels were the first points of contact for a soul. The Death Angels were the only ones permitted transport to Earth, for they had to be present at each death to welcome a soul to the afterlife. The Receiving Angels assisted each soul received into one of three afterlife tunnels, which dictated the soul's eternal resting place based on their Earthly life. Gate Keeper Angels and Miracle League Angels ensured souls were granted opportunities of virtue. The Gate Keeper Angels protected passages between tunnels, barring the way until a soul's final judgement was complete. The Miracle League Angels could grant a human a *Miracle of Life* that would allow them to overcome an often-deadly traumatic event. Morte's recruits would have to learn how to work with the other angels, but first they would need to master their Earthly duties.

Ten of the more senior recruits gathered around Morte in the small confines of a room. It was stifling hot not just from the crowd of actual people, but from the fever which was palpable in the air. The woman before them, soaked in sweat with flushed cheeks and incoherent babbles on her lips, was dying. The living could not see the horde of angels gathered around them, nor could they hear as Morte droned on:

"Notice her breathing has turned ragged and her heartbeat has begun to sputter. What does this imply?"

The senior recruits just stared. One finally raised his hand and said, "Death is near."

A few of the recruits sniggered. "Death is always near when we're present," one whispered in a mocking tone. More sniggers.

"Yes. Thank you for the obvious, Demise." Morte sighed. "Anyone else have any keen insight for this situation?"

He was met with blank faces. A few of them shifted uncomfortably in the air as they hovered over the sickbed.

"At this stage we must be preparing. With death so near, the veil between the worlds will be thin. The sick may be able to glimpse the afterlife before her actual departure. And we prepare for this because..."

"Protocol states one on the edge of death's knife should not prematurely glimpse the afterlife."

"Good. And why is that, Ruin?"

The angel failed to give an explanation and instead looked around for help.

"Who's assigned the woman here?" said Morte.

A recruit named Tragic floated to the front of the crowded mass of Death Angels.

"Tragic, you're up. You should be monitoring the situation right now."

"I am, Angel Morte. I will not let her cross before it is time."

"And why must you not?"

Again silence. Morte mumbled under his breath, "well, this conversation is tragic." Then louder he said, "We do not allow the dying to first glimpse the afterlife because they may yet have enough life and energy left to either tell those around them of the experience or to make an appeal. Telling the living of what they have seen destroys their need for faith. Making an appeal can lead to a last-minute change in afterlife location – which, I remind you, is always a scramble and should be avoided so as not to add stress to the Receiving Angels."

A few of the recruits nodded in understanding while others were nodding to sleep. Morte let loose a wail that startled them into focus.

"Tragic. We leave you here to finish the job. The rest of you, take hold."

The angels closest to Morte touched his robe and they all vanished from the world to return to the Realm of Angels in the Underworld.

* * *

The small group of angels led by Morte appeared, suspended between time and space, to overlook the Tunnels of Passing. It was here that the newly deceased were routed toward the correct line and their spirit would journey through the appropriate tunnel to its eternal resting place. The angels felt comfortable here as it was made up of their own essence, without the physical restraints of Earth.

"Who knows where we are?" asked Morte. If one counted the Earthly hours, it was the third day of orientation.

"We are in the land of passing, overlooking the Tunnels," said an angel.

"Correct, Tomb. I believe you were here earlier with one of your deceased. And which way did they earn to go?"

"The Way of Light."

"Ah. An easy one. Though rare." Morte guided the recruits toward the entrance to the tunnels where they could see the opening.

A single pipeline stemming from Earth branched off into three distinct tunnels that veered farther and farther apart as they spread. Experienced Angels of Death could be seen leading new souls to the appropriate entrance and the Receiving Angels sent them on their way. One branch shined a brilliant gold light. The remaining two were deep in shadow.

"Perish, can you tell everyone why we are here?" said Morte.

Perish was trying to hide in the back of the group of recruits and mournfully came forward. Hanging his head, he said "If a soul makes it to the end of the Tunnel it will forever be trapped in the associated destination."

"Indeed. And recently did you not misguide a soul who is now suffering from an unjust fate of damnation?"

"I have dyslexia," Perish said.

"That's not a thing. Angels don't have maladies."

Perish complained, "The problem is that the Way of Judgement and the Way of Darkness are both cast in shadow. There is no way to tell them apart."

"Is that true, Tomb?"

"How would he know?" said Perish, "His charge made the Way of Light. That's the easiest gig ever."

Tomb floated in front of Perish and gave him a silencing glare.

"Any Death Angel worth his weight in souls knows that the Way of Judgement and Darkness can easily be distinguished by their location to the stem pipeline alone. But if you're too dim-witted to know that, you should have referenced the tunnels farther down to ensure you guided correctly."

Each tunnel gradually changed levels of illumination the further along a soul traveled. The shining Way of Light stemmed to the left and its golden glow intensified as the tunnel went along. The Way of Judgement branched down the middle. It started in shadow, but a soft glow crept in toward the end. This middle tunnel had several branches connecting it to the other two and Gate Keeper Angels, who protected these offshoots, ensured a one-way path for each soul. The Way of Darkness lay to the right. It began in shadow which deepened into tar-black until it was almost impossible to see the hardened souls within unless one knew how to sense such beings.

"Perish," said Morte, "You will shadow Tomb on probation until five and twenty souls have been successfully routed to their final resting place. Only then will you be granted permission to return to Earth's deathbeds on your own. The rest of you, note well the placement of the Tunnels and their destinations."

With that, Morte flashed open a fracture of spacetime and vanished from the presence of the recruits. One such blunder was too much. He went to plead to Hades on behalf of the misguided soul and did not want the recruits to witness his humiliation in the necessary act.

* * *

In Earthly hours, it was the tenth day of orientation. The recruits, minus Perish, had been on their own for several deaths and it was time for roll call and a report. Morte stood before the Death Angel trainees and said a word of command which produced a list of names in front of him as if they were written on air.

"As I call each soul's human name, please report if you covered the death and state the tunnel through which you gave guidance," Morte instructed. "Annette Shimly."

"Mine. The Way of Judgement," said Grave.

"Sean Ray McIntire."

"Mine. The Way of Judgement," said Loss.

"Yua Yamamoto."

"Mine. The Way of Darkness," said Ruin.

This continued as hundreds of names were read. As each name was read the list would produce a new one in its place. Some names were long, some pronounced in strange languages, but each Death Angel kept a prideful tally of their work and soon Morte was being interrupted before the names could be read in full. He didn't mind. It made the boring task go quickly as each name was mentally ticked off and vanished from the air.

"Mohammed Khouri."

"Mine. The Way of Light," said Decay.

"Muhamed Koury."

"Mine. The Way of Light," repeated Decay.

"We just did that one," mumbled Grave to Loss. "Get on with it so we can be done."

Morte scrolled through the last two names. "No. They sound the same but are of different spelling. One lived in the United States and the other was from Lebanon. There were two souls of this name."

The recruits looked at each other puzzled. Morte was speaking several words that caused the air to shift and report details appeared for the two souls in question. "Damn!"

"Yes?" came a reply from a young recruit.

"No. Not you, Damn. I was cursing! Decay, you were to guide Mohammed Khouri, but Repose was supposed to guide Muhamed Koury."

"Um…" Repose fumbled. "I thought it was a clerical error."

"Damn," said Morte.

There was silence.

"Damn, I wasn't cursing that time. Are you listening?"

Damn floated to the head of the recruits and nodded.

"Go track down Muhamed Koury on Earth. If we're lucky his illness has simply stalled its progress in death's pause. If we're unlucky, well…"

Damn left in a blink and almost immediately reappeared in front of the small group. He bore ill tidings. Muhamed had passed and turned into a ghost wandering endlessly the familiar paths of his Earthly self. Without a Death Angel to guide him, his soul had clung to Earth in despair.

"What happens now?" asked Repose.

"Ghosts are tricky," said Morte. "They are beings tied to Earth and until that tie is broken, they cannot move on. They are stuck between the planes of life and death. Repose, as this soul was your responsibility you will remain with him until he is ready for the transition."

"But that could take ages!"

"Indeed. However, since the soul is not directly in the plane of life your task is made easier. You can reveal yourself to Muhamed's essence. In time, as the human desires of his being begin to wear off, your presence will become a comfort and he will allow himself to be guided to the Tunnels."

Morte finished the list of deceased without further issue. After the reading of the last name, he reminded the recruits once more of their responsibilities to the souls on Earth. There was a review of the ban on reincarnation, an emphasis on the importance of communicating with the Receiving Angels in the Way of Judgement, and a reminder that all death times associated with children or those with terminal illnesses must be cross-referenced with the Miracle League Angels who many grant death immunities to those they deemed worthy. At the end of it all, Repose was dismissed to his ghostly babysitting and the remaining recruits departed for the next round of deaths.

* * *

Morte had less contact with the ten angels as their abilities to shepherd souls through their passing strengthened. There were still the occasional mistakes: two unapproved deaths were performed by overzealous recruits, another ghost was born of a neglected deathbed, a resuscitation which was slated for failure was accidently approved and the soul was granted additional years. But Morte was pleased with the overall results. Perish was confidently routing souls through the correct Tunnels and Repose had convinced Muhamed's ghost to surrender to the afterlife. The time of graduation for the Death Angel recruits was near.

Morte appeared before Hades to give final approval. He brought with him the long list of thousands of souls who had been directed through the Tunnels by his ten apprentices. Despite the mistakes his angels had collected along the way, they were each granted full Death Angel status and relieved of Morte's oversight.

Morte was shed of the five senses and his physical self-deteriorated. He gave a final sigh of relief and relinquished the last atom of his temporary body. It was glorious. He was nothing more than a retired mass of thought. A solitary consciousness at the edge of the Underworld devoid of space and time. It was liberating.

But being outside of time meant his rest was not only never-ending, but unfortunately never-beginning. For it seemed mere moments after he settled back into his peaceful reverie, a familiar voice was heard nearby.

Morte. Earth's population has spiked again.

* * *

Mary Therese Ellingwood lives in Albuquerque where she is a mathematics professor by day and a writer by night (or whenever she can find the time). When she's not reading to her three-year-old, she is lost in her own imagination until it can make it onto the page.

Flash Fiction – 1st Place **Mark Jones**

Don't Forget Us

It was a foolish effort to leave a note for those who might follow. If the flyboys miss, the destruction will eliminate our graves and everything else near the deadly mine's entrance. No matter. My headache and blurred vision made writing impossible. A nosebleed would signal my death within an hour.

The mining company questioned why I was the last of the twelve workers to perish. They promised to test my body for the pathogen and any linked antibodies I might have developed. Did they expect me to be flattered? I argued tests on Mars would be safer than transporting our bodies back to the Luna base, but despite the risk of three thousand deaths, the company refused to listen and cut our communications.

Apart from the human tragedy, we had lost nine years of development and construction. My team of four miners marked our first descent into the mountain five days ago, but it seemed we weren't the first. We transected a shaft already bored into the rock and caused its partial collapse. The shape of the ancient tunnel told us its purpose, likely the same as ours. We uncovered no alien materials, but the ice we found became our killer. The virus stayed frozen, waiting until we tested the tainted water. Illness came quickly, and eleven deaths followed.

The woman became the last before me. I dragged her body to the back of the sandsled for a final trip to the gravesites half a mile from the camp. It had been two days since the power generation system failed, and the woman and I had depleted the habitat's energy. If the sled's batteries faltered, it would become our headstone. Those worries became irrelevant after I directed the sled over a winding path to our cemetery.

A row of ten oblong graves marked the entrance into a nearby canyon. We had buried each dead miner under a pile of red and black basalt stones, with the owner's white helmet perched at the head of the grave. The swirling iron-red dust would paint the helmets orange until a gust of wind wiped them clean. Someday, the dust would win, and all would vanish.

I stopped near a pile of stones and tried to remember the woman on the sled. My distorted vision blurred the name on her helmet. A tender feeling flowed through me, and then a great deal of sadness. Could she have been more than a colleague? My strength failed, and I fell to my knees. Like me, the woman would remain uncovered in death.

Prayers? For what purpose? An omnipotent God knows I'm dying here alone, and God doesn't need a reminder. I leaned against the sandsled and stared at the pink sky. Something dripped on my lips and ran down my chin. Blood. It's my turn now. Ninety million miles from home. Don't forget us.

* * *

Mark Edward Jones retired after thirty-three years working in higher education finance. Since then, he has won multiple awards for his mystery/thriller, paranormal, and sci-fi stories. He grew up in Duncan, Oklahoma, and graduated from the University of Oklahoma. Mark and his wife will celebrate their forty-third anniversary in November.

Flash Fiction – 2nd Place Ivan Calhoun

Hung Up

Paul hobbled over to the kitchen window and coughed, spitting into the sink what had come up. He'd slept like shit and didn't know what he was going to do for breakfast. His prosthetic right leg was aching his stump again so he took three Advil and washed them down using one of the not so dirtied cups on the counter. Looking out the window he could make out something large struggling on the back fence even without his glasses. He yelled to his niece in the mobile home's front room, "Come in here Shelby."

The fifteen-year-old shouted back, "I'm doing something." Though she wasn't.

"Get your ass over here and tell me what's going on in back."

Shelby dragged herself into the kitchen and looked out scowling. "Heck. The neighbor's dog is hung up in the barb wire."

"Damn, probably been tryin' to get at the rabbits again." Paul muttered. "Should've shot that mutt long ago." He thought for a second.

"Well Shelbs, go get my cutters. We'll get that dumb ass dog freed."

* * *

Ivan Calhoun lives in Santa Fe, New Mexico and also cranks out a screenplay every once in awhile. Short fiction he's written has appeared in *Big Bend Literary Magazine* and in anthologies by the High Plains Writers and SouthWest Writers. He can be reached on Facebook and at www.clan-creative.com.

Flash Fiction – 3rd Place   Linda Triegel

Stay Put

The dark enveloped him, and he thought he heard his mother's voice.

Tommy, will you please stay put! Honestly, I can't turn my back for a minute!

He listened, but even as a kid, had always decided on his own way to do what she asked.

Stay in that chair and finish your broccoli!

He kind of liked broccoli, but it was funny to watch her get steamed up.

Stop fidgeting and fasten your seatbelt!

He'd have his own car some day and not have to go everywhere with his mom.

What's that burning smell? Can't you follow directions! The recipe says 10 minutes at three-fifty!

Anyone can bake cookies, he thought. How hard can it be?

Don't forget a corsage for Jenny's prom dress. Did you ask her what color—where are you going? Honestly, that boy...

He thought his eyes were open, but it was still dark. Then he realized he was wrapped in a blanket up to his head. He jerked up to a sitting position.

"Easy there, young man, you'll make yourself sick."

Sure enough, he felt woozy as he tried to get his bearings. What happened? Why didn't he have any clothes on under the blanket?

The man who'd spoken pushed him gently back onto some kind of cot.

"How do you feel?" he said.

"Cold."

The man chuckled. "I guess. You were lucky you didn't listen to the crew's instruction to stay in your cabin."

"Yeah, Mom always told me—Mom! Is she okay? Where is she?

"What's her name, son?"

"Margaret—Margaret Madison."

The man went off somewhere and came back with a list. He was smiling.

"She's fine," he said. "She was on deck when the ship was hit by the tsunami—arguing with a steward, apparently."

Tommy smiled and lay back, wrapping himself in the blanket again.

Probably telling him to stay put.

* * *

Linda Triegel states: "I'm a Connecticut Yankee by upbringing and moved to the Southwest in 2006. I'm a member, and newsletter editor, of Croak & Dagger, the New Mexico chapter of Sisters in Crime. I've published several historical romances as Elisabeth Kidd and am working on my second cozy mystery."

Flash Fiction – Honorable Mention **Helen A. Jack**

The Wingless Dragon and the Death of Honor

Honor didn't die overnight.

It receded, bit by bit, in the soft decay of forgotten orchards, in the crumbling mortar of once-packed banquet halls, in the tattered banners splotched with mildew and shredded by rats. It withered alongside the summer blooms and languished in the dry, cracked earth once buried beneath thunderous waves.

But now, as Syletheon lay in a sticky, fetid pool of his own blood, he cared less about when honor died and only that it had.

At the edge of the cavern above him, hand on one hip and a curved, blood-stained dagger in the other, Vyrith the Dragon King gazed down at Syletheon in exasperation – as though he were one of the poor, doomed humans who'd lost their way through the tunnels.

"I thought you'd learned, Sy. I really did." Vyrith flashed a savage smile. Crooked, predatory teeth inside an otherwise human mouth. Dragon's eyes glimmered from an otherwise human face, giving up Vyrith's disguise. A golden circlet rested on the Dragon King's brow amidst long, honey-colored hair, feigning civility while a monster raged within.

"When will you learn that we're not guardians anymore? The Ancient Ones left us – we're free now to do whatever we want. No longer bound to those pathetic humans out there. Idiots wouldn't find their way out of a shallow cave."

My wings…

Syletheon roared in agony and loss, his cry flooding the shallow cavern and threatening to shatter the very mountain above. Phantom pains seared, burrowing through the white-hot wounds in his back, his body not yet believing what his heart and mind knew. Sticky blood trails trickled over his silver scales and under his claws.

Vyrith shook his head and examined the curved dagger in his hand, unperturbed by Syletheon's pain.

"It would be best for all of us, Sy, if you stopped breathing." The Dragon King ran a languid finger along the dagger's blade. "You're the last one who gives a shit about this nonsense about us being guardians to the humans. We've been holding our breaths for years." A grin cracked his countenance and his emerald eyes flashed. "But I'd be happy to expedite the process."

Syletheon winced as Vyrith entered the cavern. A green robe, trimmed with gold and belted at the waist, lent a softness to the man's angular body that the Dragon King otherwise didn't possess.

Vyrith pressed the dagger to the side of Syletheon's throat, poised to slip between his scales and end his life with the faintest kiss of steel.

"Any last requests?"

Syletheon's mind recalled the stormy waters of the Norwegian Sea, where he'd taken his first breaths centuries before as a scaled infant ensnared in a fishing net.

Yet he'd no reason to fear. Ingrid had cut him from the net and bundled him against her breast, as real a son to her as her human offspring.

Syletheon closed his eyes. "Scatter my ashes to the sea."

* * *

Helen A. Jack is a literary crow and collects ideas and images as though they are shiny things to stow away and spin into stories. She lives in Albuquerque, New Mexico with her husband and three children.

Flash Fiction – Honorable Mention Janet Greger

Yellow

Ed's favorite color was yellow. Always was, but wow there was a lot of yellow at this funeral for his mother-in-law. Gladioli, lilies, and chrysanthemums. Either everyone had intentionally chosen yellow flowers, or the florists in this community had a limited selection. Probably the latter.

He had met his mother-in-law, Margaret, only once about two months before as she, his wife Judith, and Judith's brother, Jim, had argued about the sale of Margaret's house. Margaret looked better today. Her hair was combed, and her face wasn't contorted with rage at her children.

He wished Judith hadn't insisted on burying her mother in a yellow dress. The yellow seemed to emphasize Margaret's sallow pallor. But, no one had asked his opinion. He wasn't a real member of the family. He had married Judith six months earlier, and Judith seldom spoke about her childhood. He understood his role today.

Accordingly, he had dutifully stood next to Judith at the side of her mother's open casket during the viewing. About twenty people shook his hand and sniffed, when Judith introduced him as "Number Three." The rest of the attendees at the funeral had ignored him and only nodded at Judith as they gossiped with Jim and his wife. He wasn't surprised because Jim was a city councilman, who was running for re-election. Jim appeared to think his mother's funeral was a campaign opportunity, and he pumped the hands of everyone present.

Now everyone was seated. The minister started the service by saying, "Margaret was a loyal wife."

Judith snorted.

"And a loving mother of a son and a daughter."

Judith coughed as if she was choking. He patted her back and shoved his white handkerchief toward her.

"Margaret was a friend to many."

Judith's coughs turned into a caterwaul. People turned and stared. He wanted to appear to be an attentive husband, but he didn't know what to do. He put his hand on her shoulder.

"She was always willing to listen to the problems of others."

Judith was alternately panting and sobbing.

The minister continued to eulogize "this genteel woman."

Judith pushed his hand off her shoulder, shoved Jim and his wife aside, and rushed down the aisle.

Ed looked around. After offering apologies to her brother, he followed his wife.

He squinted as he left the darkened chapel and looked around the scorching asphalt parking lot. Judith was screaming as she kicked the tires of their car. He ran to her and drew her close. She panted and beat his chest with her fist. He swallowed hard. "I'm so sorry about your mother. I didn't realize the funeral would bring back so many fond memories."

She knocked him away. "What fond memories? I don't know the woman the minister was eulogizing. I wanted to shout: Lies, lies. The only good thing about this funeral was everything was yellow. She hated yellow, and everyone knew it."

* * *

J. L. Greger is a biology professor turned novelist. She includes tidbits about science, the American Southwest, and her international travel experiences in her Science Traveler Series. Her novels include: the *Flu Is Coming*, *Dirty Holy Water*, *Escape from a Dark Cave,* and *The Man Who Looked for Death*.

Section Three:

Opening Pages of a Novel

Painting the Chama by Rose Marie Kern

Published Novel - 1st Place Rosalie Rayburn

The Sunshine Solution

Chapter One

The fuzzy black-and-white picture showed a young teen, face wasted and body rail thin, pulling away from an older man. The man was tall, well-dressed, Hispanic. He looked as though he was trying to drag her down the street. The flier headline screamed, "Saturday night on Central Avenue: Orlando Garcia likes them young. Is this the man we want running our state?"

Orlando Garcia stared at the flier his aide had handed to him. She said she found it on her lawn that morning. His stomach churned. There had already been the rumors, the attack ads. He'd fought those off, but piece by piece they'd cut at his credibility. He knew now that the moment people saw this picture his political future would be over.

It didn't matter that the photo was not what it seemed, that he was not harming the girl but trying to stop her from another drug overdose. None of that would make any difference now. He wished he could make it disappear, undo its existence on this earth, roll back the clock. But one shredded flier made no difference. There were probably hundreds of fliers out there by now, and thousands of eyes would see them—HAD already seen them. That was how the political game worked. Your opponents would seek out a tiny vulnerability, something meant as a good deed in a dark world, and they would forge it into a deadly weapon. He could try to fight back, but he would always see the doubt in people's eyes. He'd seen that happen before to other candidates. You never got over a smear like that. It was over, everything he'd worked for.

He squeezed his eyes shut and felt dizzy, as if he stood at the edge of a cliff, hearing the voice inside his head praying to a god he no longer believed in to deliver him.

There would of course be no deliverance. When Orlando opened his eyes, the pieces of the poster still littered the floor; what had happened, had happened. He could see no way out. He'd failed them: his family, his supporters. He sat down at his desk, found a notepad sent to him in thanks for his contributions to helping the homeless, and wrote a note to his wife, pleading for her understanding. He wrote a note to his son and daughter, begging them to look after their mother. Then he went out to the garage, got in his car, backed out without looking, drove out of the city, and onto to the freeway, speeding south through a night sharp with stars, heading toward the canyon. Yes, that would be the place.

~~~~~

Chapter Two

Twenty Years Later

Snow had begun to fall shortly after two that afternoon—light, feathery flakes that floated teasingly through the sharp, thin, high-altitude air. Chris Lovington entered the Roundhouse, the seat of New Mexico's part-time legislature, which looked uncannily like a Spanish bullring, and was often the scene of verbal bloodletting. He stopped in the lobby and showed his ID card to the security guard, who checked the appointment book and frowned, Hmmm, the Governor doesn't usually see people up there.

"I know," Lovington nodded, "but he specifically asked me to meet him there." The guard shrugged. "Well, I guess he's the boss around here."

Lovington looked at his watch and opted to take the stairs rather than ride the elevator up to the fourth floor. He was apprehensive about the meeting, curious why the governor had asked for him, and puzzled as to why the meeting would be held in a room usually reserved for high-level discussions or critical announcements. When he reached the top floor, he expected to run into an aide who would announce him, but there was no one around. He knocked on the dark wooden door and waited; breath shaky, heart fluttering. A moment later a voice summoned him, and he entered.

Governor Joe Sheridan stood on the far side of a vast table. There were no lights on in the room and his face was ghostly pale in the low afternoon light. He was well over six feet tall, with iron-grey hair smoothed back over his scalp, deep-set eyes, and a long straight nose. Snide online Tweets sometimes called him "professorial" and today he looked the part, dressed in a gray tweed jacket over an oatmeal-colored V-neck sweater.

He pulled out a chair and motioned for Lovington to take a seat next to him. They sat silently, Lovington keeping his eyes on the polished surface of the table. Sheridan cleared his throat. "Thank you for coming at such short notice, Chris. I hope I didn't inconvenience you. I know things can sometimes be hectic on a Friday afternoon." His voice was deep and formal like that of an old-time newscaster.

Lovington shrugged. "No problem. My assistant Andy Whitaker can handle anything, and if he can't, he can always call me."
~~~~~

Sheridan nodded slowly. The skin around his deep-set eyes was dark and his lips were stretched tight, as if he were suppressing inner pain. Lovington knew Sheridan was in his late fifties. Today he looked much older.

"I'll get to the point quickly," he said, "I asked you here today because I'm going to be making an important announcement on Monday." He paused and looked directly at Lovington. "I've decided not to run for a second term."

Lovington's jaw dropped. Sheridan was popular and his poll numbers were good, the election was months away, and campaigning had barely started. Anyone in his right mind might say "Why this?"

"I know it's a surprise, Chris." Sheridan paused briefly as if gathering energy. "But I've had some news recently that's made this decision inevitable." He sighed. The murmur of air leaking from his lungs was like a slowly deflating bicycle tire. Lovington said nothing, waiting for the sound of Sheridan's lungs to re-inflate enough to fuel his next words.

"About three weeks ago my wife noticed some unusual pain. She'd been experiencing pain for a while. She always thought it was indigestion or something minor. But this time the pain was so severe she could barely stand. She went in for tests and a tumor was found on the liver…."

"Oh, but it's not…?"

"But it is cancer, and I don't think I need to spell it out for you. There are of course options for treatment, but she probably doesn't have long."

"Joe, I'm, so sorry, I …."

Sheridan held up a hand to ward off any further commiseration from Lovington. "I know, Chris, and thank you for your thoughts. Martha and I have been married thirty-three years. That sounds like a long time, but when you know your time is limited, there is never enough time. That's why I decided not to run. I want to be there for her as much as I can. I think you understand that from your own experience."

Lovington understood the reference only too well. He had lost his wife three years before to a brain aneurysm. They'd been married almost twenty-two years. Sheridan was peering at him now, and he sensed that another shoe was about to drop. He braced.

"That's one of the reasons I asked you here today," Sheridan went on, "I want you to know that I have been watching you as we've worked together during my term. I've been impressed by your integrity and your conscientiousness."

"Joe, I …" Lovington interrupted.

Sheridan held up his hand again. "I know. I know you had some questionable issues in your past. There was some ugly stuff, but the Chris Lovington I've gotten to know is not that guy. As State Land Commissioner you have a lot of responsibility. You're overseeing millions of acres, making sure the leases on those lands benefit our schools and colleges. I see how seriously you take your duties. I know you're under a lot of pressure from the oil and gas guys; especially because the state can make so much money from exploiting those resources. But since I've been governor, my major concerns have been water and climate. The hotter it gets and the more wildfires we have, and the poorer our state will become. I'm thinking about the long-term, and I think you get that."

Lovington nodded. He wasn't sure where the conversation was headed but he felt deep sympathy for Sheridan. The man had always impressed him.

"Anyway, the other reason I invited you here today is that I wanted to ask you to run for governor in my place. I think we share some of the same goals, especially when it comes to the environment. I've heard the way you talk about renewable energy. We need more of that, and that's why I believe you are the right person to carry on my legacy."

Lovington sank back into his chair. Relief flowed over him. Sheridan knew about his past, but he was willing to trust him. Still, he could never have imagined this. "I, uh, I don't know," he stuttered. "This is, uh, unexpected. What about Sylvia?"

Sylvia Sanchez, the Lieutenant Governor, who frequently appeared in evening news broadcasts, seemed the most obvious choice.

Sheridan shrugged. "Yes. I suppose everyone would think that, but I don't have the same confidence in her. My sense is she would take New Mexico in a very different direction and that would not be good for the land. So…well, I'll give you the weekend to think about it. Martha and I have managed to keep things quiet up to now, but it's going to get out. I'm planning to make a statement to the media this coming Monday afternoon. If you agree, I will use the opportunity to announce that I will be endorsing you for governor. So, I'd like your answer before then. Okay?"

Lovington knew the conversation was over. Sheridan had made up his mind. Now it was up to him. He stood up, thanked the governor, and left the room quickly, heart pounding.

Once outside the building, he stood for a moment staring at the street with its white dusting of snow. He looked at his watch and noticed it was just after four o'clock. It was Friday. The old guilt stirred within him, the dull ache of it had grown worse since Christine died. Shame. Deeds that could not be undone. He walked out to the street and turned left on Old Santa Fe Trail, heading for the Plaza. Because of the snow and the traffic, it took him longer than expected. It was nearly four-thirty by the time he reached the cathedral.

Entering the building, he saw that it was almost empty, with only a handful of tourists. They wouldn't notice him. Standing for a moment just inside the door, he let the familiar stillness settle over him like a comforting wrap. His feet took him towards the dark wooden structure where he could make his confession. Lovington was not Catholic, but he had discovered that this ritual soothed him more than any therapist's words. He saw no light glowing above the door, which meant it was available. He entered and knelt in front of the fretwork screen, shielded from the world, where his words would be heard in secrecy and safety. "Bless me Father, for I have sinned."

* * *

Rosalie Rayburn is a former journalist whose stories are inspired by reporting on corruption in city and county government. Her first novel, *The Power of Rain,* won a National Federation of Press Women award. She also had short stories broadcast on radio, and had a business guidebook published in Britain.

Published Novel – 2nd Place   Maralie Waterman

Running in Place: A Novel

MILE ONE...TRAVELING LIGHT

If relocation were a religion, my mother Erin would be the Pope.

A phantom of discontent settled over her with the aroma of chain-smoked Camels. She scratched numbers in blue ink on the backs of envelopes, the tattoo of her disappointments. A change of location created radiance in my mother as falling in love might in a simpler woman. Her pale complexion flushed healthy pink, and her eyes grew luminous with possibility. The glow lasted for as long as it took to unpack. Each difficulty from the previous location trailed Erin like a spurned lover, worsened by the costs of moving trucks and security deposits. Twenty-two moves in all, before I left for college.

By my teens, I refused to unpack more than clothes and necessities with each move. I put a few items in the closet. If no closet existed, I left clothes stretched out on top of a bureau. A silver boom box sat on a desk, then a milk crate. Sometimes the boom box rested on the floor beside my mattress. I collected the teen girl's standard arsenal of Clearasil and blue eyeliner. Running shoes sat by the front door. Erin's escape might be changing her address. Mine was the steady rhythm of my feet hitting pavement. I traveled light. The secret was to never unpack.

As an adult, I've moved six times in twenty-five years. It feels like too many. For three years in college and into grad school in southeastern Massachusetts, I lived in an older neighborhood slipping into decline. Gangbangers resided next door and their well-inked brethren riddled my house with bullets by mistake. It took me over a year to find a new place. I would rather be shot at than move.

* * *

Central New Mexico sun beat down on the soccer field. My daughter, Hana, every seven-year-old nerve fiber alert, stood ready to protect her goal. Blonde braids shook free in the melee and unrelenting canyon winds whipped hair across her face. I wondered if she had enough sunscreen on. My phone chirped from somewhere in my backpack and I dug through bags of gummies, goldfish crackers and frozen juice boxes.

Rare for me to have an address or a phone number for Erin. When she does contact me, most often there's been a crisis and I'm her last resort. I hit the call button though the number displayed as unknown. "Hello?" No response. I'd not heard from her in six months. "Mom, is that you?"

"Yeah," Erin expelled air into a poor connection. "It's me."

"Who?" my older daughter, Mel whispered as I rose from the blanket we shared.

"Erin," mouthing the word, my fingers to the microphone. I turned away from the wind but not before witnessing Hana block a goal with her face. I remembered her mouth guard this time. Mother of the Year, me.

I shifted the phone to the other hand and pulled my hat down to block the sun. "How're you doing?"

Erin was short on pleasantries. "There's no easy way about this, Corie. I've got throat cancer."

My mother's beaten Melanoma and bladder cancer. Emphysema has been the rottweiler nipping at her heels for years. A deep inhale and exhale wafted through the bad cell phone connection indicating a lit cigarette between her fingers and the worst brand of optimism.

"Corie? You still there, baby?"

Erin never called me "baby," until around my thirtieth birthday. After my grandmother died.

I've managed patients who use machines to speak and thought of highway billboards with the guy missing a throat. My feelings straddled heartbreak and hostility. Screaming at her for being as laissez-faire with her health as with every other aspect of her life would do nothing except ensure we didn't speak for another six months.

"I'm still here, Ma."

"Oh," she said. "Well, I'm starting radiation treatment next week."

"Do you have a surgeon? Can't they remove it?" I asked. She wouldn't respond well to sympathy. I was even more ill-equipped to offer it.

"It might spread. The radiation's safer -- for now leastwise."

"Where will Jamie go?"

Jamie was the teen son of my cousin, Robin. Erin's been raising him since he was an infant. My mother also cared for Ruby, her older sister, until Ruby's death several years earlier.

"Robin's better. She'll be here while I go back and forth to Flagstaff."

"Flagstaff?" I hadn't realized they were in Arizona. Last I knew, she'd been in the Texas panhandle. Erin's born-again, but a true believer in the Church of U-Haul.

"A'yuh. Been here in Holbrook since March."

Years earlier, Erin told me I needed to co-sign for a house in the middle of East Dust-Bucket-Nowhere, Texas or she, Ruby and Jamie would be homeless. I told her no. Pregnant with Hana; I couldn't afford to own land in Texas. Before that, she needed a few thousand dollars to buy a car so she could get to work. That time, I sent the money. A payroll loan company took the car, and we didn't hear from Erin for over a year. Still, I heard the words tumble from my lips and fall into the vast expanse that separated me from my mother.

"What can I do?"

Mel reclined on the blanket, long legs stretched before her, face to the sun. Her sister stood poised inside the goal, eyes bright, ready for battle. They were such different girls. They reminded me a little of Erin and Ruby.

"I haven't talked with Charlie since Ruby went," Erin said. "I wish he'd let me know he's okay. That's all I need."

Jesus. Was that all?

Charlie's evaded diagnosis, but like his half-sister, Robin, he had manic highs and devastating lows. Unlike Robin, he's managed to care for himself and stay away from law enforcement and the courts. Logical or not, I credited my grandmother.

While Erin was my mother, Gram created a home for Charlie and me. She cared for us, maintained emotional consistency, and fought with us when we were wrong. We always knew she'd love us no matter what. When she died, the fragile tendrils binding so many volatile relationships broke.

It's been two decades since her death, but my grandmother remains omnipresent in my life. "Corie," she'd say. "You're a smart girl with more opportunities than most. That means you have more responsibilities."

I should be able to manage this for Erin.

"Have you talked with Nadine?"

Nadine was Charlie's ex-wife, sort of. There was some question of whether a divorce had ever been obtained. She'd moved with him from New Hampshire and since then, threatened every few months to return.

"Bitch blocked me," Erin said. "Said she'd tell the cops if I kept calling."

There was, for sure, much more to this story.

"Okay," I said. "She's still in New Mexico though?"

"I don't know. That was a year ago," she replied. "That asshole she was hanging around with… what if they did something to my boy?"

"Nadine loves Charlie," I said, "but he was Dr. Jekyll when they married. She spent the next fifteen years with Mr. Hyde."

"He was okay before that whoring bitch."

Good lord. Charlie hadn't been anything approaching okay since he was about eighteen. Two decades before poor Nadine came on the scene.

A lighter clicked and my heart broke a little. Following a rattling inhalation, Erin said, "I wanna know he's okay. That's it. He doesn't have to come here or call if he doesn't want to. I just need to know he's alive."

Another point scored and a cheer went up from our side. Clutching the phone tighter to my ear, my attention shifted to Hana in the goal. She bounced up and down and pumped her arms in the same "Woot! Woot!" gesture her father used for Bruins games.

At the blanket, I settled beside Mel. She leaned over to rest her head across my knees. The sun turned the scarlet strands of her hair to firelights. She closed her eyes, and I rested my free hand across her face to shade her. I existed for her comfort in the way Gram once existed for mine. I wasn't sure what Erin was entitled to, but I owed Gram everything. I would always be my grandmother's child, and now, I would also try to be a good daughter. I asked the question, not thinking about how I might put a plan into action.

"Where was Charlie the last time you talked to him?"

MILE TWO...FAMILY RITUALS

Moving was my family ritual, a process we undertook more often than we put up a Christmas tree.

The places we lived in for a month, or a year, were always uninhabitable at the beginning. My childhood was an endless cycle of painting, wallpaper, laying linoleum over floors that had never seen it, installing portable toilets and lugging water. Adult me has never lived anywhere that could be condemned, yet a sensation of the terminally unsettled remains. The boxes of this era, a natural byproduct of moving, are my personal form of cancer. They go into remission, but they always come back.

Currently, they sat in the garage of the home I shared with my husband, Keith, and our daughters. The papers were signed years ago. I knew this was my final move. Still the boxes lined the wall of my bay, spreading into the area where I should be parking. I opened the garage door each morning and afternoon and walked deliberately past them. My half-dead SUV collected pollen in the driveway. I'd adapted to scraping frost from the windows in the winter and burning my hands on the steering wheel in summer.

I've promised on a regular basis to address the pile. Still the boxes sat. We're at zero hour. A new truck would arrive from the dealer in two weeks.

"You can't park a new vehicle in the snow, Corie."

"It's not snowing," I speared a carrot as though it had personally done me wrong.

"Yet." Keith raises one thick blond eyebrow.

"I'll take care of them."

Mel, our fifteen-year-old expelled a single deep sigh. She sliced her meatloaf into smaller and smaller pieces.

"When will it snow?" Hana asked. Her eyes grew large, round, and hungry with the possibility of snowmen and ice skating.

"No snow," Mel said. "Not for months. And we live in New Mexico, so maybe never."

"We had a foot a few years ago," I reminded her. It was the last time I bought boots for the girls.

"That's a long time," Hana said, as she rested her head on her hand and gazed at a piece of meatloaf.

"When?" Keith said.

"When what?" I asked.

"When will you take care of the boxes?" Keith had a good voice. Calm, deep and deliberate. He spoke as if this were a benign request akin to asking me to drop off dry cleaning or pick up milk on my way home. My stomach muscles tightened, and cold panic seeped into the fibers of my t-shirt. My fingers grew slippery with sweat.

"This weekend," I said. My voice was level and not at all a reflection of how I felt.

"We're going to dinner on Sunday, remember."

"Okay, then. Saturday."

"Promise?"

"Yes."

"It would be a waste of new paint to park that truck outside."

"I promise."

"Jackie Buford got a new yellow Mustang for her birthday," Mel said while stabbing an innocent green bean into mush. "Can I have a Mustang on my birthday?"

"I want a horse, too," said Hana.

"Not that kind of Mustang, Hon," her father told her.

"We're not Jackie Buford's parents," I said. My voice was a bad recording, played too often and at a low rpm.

"And," Keith said and grinned sideways at me. "We have nowhere to park a new Mustang, because your mother hasn't cleared out her side of the garage."

MILE THREE...THE BEAUFORT PLACE

My grandmother called our house the Beaufort place for the old man to whom Erin paid twelve dollars in rent each month. Earlier that year, a state welfare worker told Gram we needed a room for 12-year-old Charlie, or he couldn't live with us. There was a recently constructed second bedroom large enough for his single bed.

When Ruby married, Gram expected Charlie to live with Ruby and the new husband.

Gilbert, the new husband, was having none of it.

One afternoon, the summer before I turned five, Charlie and I peered out the front window into the dooryard. Gilbert sat in the car. A neon orange hunter's cap covered hair the yellow of egg yolks. He stared out across the open field, chain-smoking Pall Malls.

Ruby was settled in a kitchen chair with my cousin Valerie curled onto her lap. Gram cradled chubby Robin, who still wore diapers. Erin moved up and down from her chair. She paced the limited floor space with a cigarette between her teeth, pausing to glare out the window at her brother-in-law before returning to the table once more. Up and down, Erin repeated the pattern until Gram ordered her to sit.

My aunt was forty, but still the beauty of the family. Her eyes were the same clear, pale blue as my mother's. Shiny coal-black hair hung down her straight back in thick waves. Her olive skin was unmarred by time and worry, though she'd seen her share of both. Gram said her older daughter took after my grandfather's mother, also "Ruby," and rumored to be a Mohican from northern New York.

Erin was Gram's youngest child, named for my Uncle Ray's twin sister, a stillbirth. Where Ruby was voluptuous in every sense, my mother had the lean, hardscrabble look of Gram's nineteenth-century German ancestors, fresh off the boat, but with none of their optimism. Long-limbed and rawboned, she never filled any piece of clothing. On a first name basis with unrequited expectations, Erin played the drone to Ruby's queen and grew unhappier with her lot each passing year.

Charlie and I were exiled to back bedrooms that smelled like the musty comic books my brother favored and the closeness of several bodies in a small home without indoor plumbing. A single thin curtain separated living and sleeping areas. The adults spoke in hushed tones to maintain the illusion of privacy. The gulf of a few inches between the jamb and the fabric ensured that Charlie and I could hear every word of the exchange. From my vantage point on the bed, Ruby's broad shoulders concealed Erin, but my grandmother was visible in silvery profile.

Gram's neck muscles corded beneath skin like crinkled parchment paper. She disliked Gilbert. Her opinion was not improved by this conversation with my aunt.

"I can't take Charlie, Ma. It wouldn't be good for him or for me an' the girls."

"He's your boy, Ruby. He's been thinking you needed a place big enough and he could come be with you. What'll you say to him?" Gram asked.

"Don't you know what this'll do to him?" my mother hissed through a cloud of cigarette smoke. "Dumpin' him all over again?"

"That's not fair," Gram said to my mother. She turned to Ruby, "Good Lord, didn't that man out there hidin' in the Buick know you'd want your little boy with you?"

"He don't care 'bout what I want or you or anybody. Doesn't want Charlie and says he won't feed him."

A moment of silence was broken by Gram's shocked response, "Won't feed him?"

"Gilly says he ain't responsible for Charlie. He thinks you oughta' keep him on accounta' you had him this long."

"Ain't isn't a word." Gram took a long drag of her cigarette and narrowed gray eyes at her eldest daughter. "What do you think?"

"He's jealous," Ruby said with a shrug. "Gilly'd be like there was another rooster in the coop."

"Piss-poor excuse for a man," Erin said.

"I don't know. Makes him 'bout like your dear Roy, I 'spect. He's stayed through and didn't tryta make me get rid of that one." Ruby inclined her head toward Robin. She continued in a hiss, "so I guess I might've done you one better."

"Shut your smart mouth," Erin said, her voice fell above a whisper. "You don't know what you're talkin' about."

"I do. So do you. The reason you ain't where I am's on accounta' you always had Ma and Daddy and they favored you."

"I didn't get myself in the family way to catch a man." Erin's tone dripped with disgust.

"I didn't neither and you got no call to talk to me like that."

"Do I need to knock your heads together?" Gram asked. "I can still do it."

Bitterness was pungent as cigarette smoke in the air and would last long after Ruby was gone. Charlie curled at the end of the bed. Flattened wet ringlets stuck to the side of his grimy, tear-streaked face. He clutched one of Ruby's discarded sweaters, a nubby black-and-white knit.

We listened to the crunch of the Buick's wheels pulling out of the driveway and down the dirt road.

"She didn't even say good-bye," Charlie whispered into the sweater.

I crawled into Gram's empty lap. A wet area on the front of her cotton dress smelled of Robin's milk. Gram kissed the top of my head, rocking me forward and back while soft strands of her hair brushed my cheek. The curtain shifted and Charlie strode past us. He walked out into the backyard, letting the screen door slam behind him.

My mother moved to go after Charlie. Gram wrapped gentle fingers around Erin's thin wrist and shook her head. "Let him go for now."

* * *

Maralie Waterman moved over 25 times before she left for college. Each location had texture, personality, and occasionally, ghosts. Her fiction moves from crime to horror to family dysfunction and the abstract. She lives in New Mexico with her children and a chihuahua familiar, blogging occasionally at https://rednetpress.wordpress.com/

Published Novel - 3rd Place Jeff Otis

Raptor Lands

Chapter 1

Touching the Past

That's one magnificent hand," Doctor Cantor Hoffman commented, pushing his brown hair out of his eyes. He marveled at the fossil from the 2027 dig in Utah.

Alex, a grad student at the Berkeley paleontology lab, carefully removed the rock from around the dark fossil with a small grinder. The semi-circular table held several other specimens at various stages of completion.

"It's bigger than anything I've seen from a *Utahraptor*," Cantor said. "I think the animal must have been at least 1100 pounds."

"And deadly as hell," Alex said, brushing off some of the dust his grinder made.

"Yeah. Quick and powerful. There isn't a predator on earth today that could stand up to this. How long before the foot is ready, Alex?"

"Another month I figure."

"Sweet."

Alex held up the partially prepared fossil foot. "As you can see, I've already freed the foot's sickle claw. It's one for the record books, 9.4 inches long."

"Seeing that must have made some dinosaurs very uncomfortable," Cantor replied, shaking his head.

"How are you going to feel when you get to see the real deal?" Alex asked, tapping a finger on the claw's sharp tip.

"Thrilled! But only if Kumiko can pull it off."

~~~~~

Chapter 2

Innocent Beginnings

In 2029, an oddity was born of an idea. In 2030, humans reverse-engineered the oddity further, gradually bringing back a life form from the distant past. In 2031, its arms unfolded.

* * *

Doctor Kumiko Chen sat in her U.C. Berkeley office, scanning student test grades. She wished the grades had been a little higher.
~~~~~

Her face flushed as she glanced at the two letters on her desk. When she heard the sound of her husband's squeaky shoes, her mood lightened.

"Hey, sweetheart," Cantor said, grinning as he strolled into her office, then draped himself over one of her leather chairs. Despite winter coming, he wore a blue T-shirt with an orange silhouette of a *Tyrannosaurus*. The pockets of his brown cargo pants bulged with papers, pens, and a crunchy oat bar.

She shook her head at the coffee stain on his shirt.

Running his finger along the shiny wooden surface of her desk, he said, "How do you find time to keep your desk so well organized?"

"How is it you don't?" she replied, wondering when he'd last even seen the surface of his desk.

She noticed him looking at the tall wooden bookshelf behind her, filled with genetics papers, journals, and books. Then he picked up the framed photo of her, himself, and their son, George, at a fossil dig in Utah. She remembered how new it was to her and young George, being among the first humans to recover and admire the remains of a creature entombed for millions of years.

"Well, we're making progress," she said as she hit a key on her keyboard, sending the student grades into cyberspace. Pushing against the arms of her chair, she stood up, grabbed one of the letters, and walked around her desk. "Look at this letter I found in my mailbox."

She watched his expression as he read.

"Why can't people understand we aren't interested in selling the dinos?" he said with a grimace.

"This is becoming a problem," Kumiko replied. "This is the second letter I've received from this individual. They even hint at legal action!" She held her hands out, shaking her head, allowing some strands of straight black hair to escape from behind her ears. "They're claiming we can't possibly provide a proper habitat for the animals."

"That's twisted," he said. "I'm no expert about the law, but wealthy jerks like this can take us or the university to court. They can drag this out for years."

Kumiko took the letter and tossed it in the trash. "Habitat indeed! I'm betting the habitat they'd prefer is a circus." She picked up the other letter from her desk. "Here, look at this."

Cantor opened the envelope and read: *Your Frankensteins shouldn't exist. You don't belong in America. Go back to China. You are playing God. Stop what you are doing now! There are consequences!*

"That pisses me off," he said, crumpling the paper in his hand.

"Me too. It's frightening."

"What an ignoramus."

"Cantor, he's threatening us!" *My given name isn't even Chinese! Nor was my mother!*

"Have you notified campus security?"

"Yes. What can they do? This will just go into a folder with the other twisted letters."

Without a word, Cantor took the first letter out of the trash and uncrumpled the second. Then he held her hand and looked into her dark eyes. "I'm sorry, Kumiko."

She shook it off and held her head higher. "Before we look at the C4s, I've got something more uplifting. Look at this C5 diagram." The computer displayed the expected appearance of the next iteration of proto-dinosaurs.

"Beautiful," Cantor said. "Those arms look just like a *Utahraptor's*. Wow. How soon?"

"Not for at least a year." Kumiko knew her husband dreamt of coming face to face with a real dinosaur. It was this boyish part of him that attracted her. He lacked all pretensions.

"Finally, we're going to understand dinosaur behavior," he said, rubbing his hands together.

"Not so fast, Cantor. It's going to take many iterations. The C5s will only be halfway to being real dinosaurs."

"Yeah, I know. When will we have the real deal?"

"I don't know," she said. "I'm puzzled by the C4s. When we created them, the only genetic changes we made involved improvements in the hands, tails, and arms."

"So, what puzzles you?"

"Their bodies are bigger. They're growing faster than their C3 mother did," she said, hands on her hips.

"I'm not worried," he said. "It shouldn't affect my research on their behavior. Things happen. It's a significant achievement."

Kumiko shook her head and sighed. "Let's go look at the C4s in the lab. They're vaccinated and out of quarantine. You're going to love them."

Cantor rose from his chair and followed her down the hall, past offices, and inquiring students.

In the lab, two Golden Eagles studied him from their large cages near the windows. Several grad students looked up, smiled, and returned to their work. He sauntered over to the two-foot by three-foot wire cage sitting on a metal table where a mother from the previous iteration tolerated her playful children. Several tanned-colored chicks with green eyes snapped at one another or squabbled by grasping their opponent with arms and hands while using their tails to keep balance.

The chicks checked each other out and the surrounding humans, pecking at anything they found at the bottom of the cage. If someone made a sudden move or a loud sound, they ran to their mother.

It was a little warmer in the lab than other parts of the building. All for the good of the chicks. The smell of birds, straw, and cleansers hung in the air.

"These animals look nothing like chickens now, Kumiko. They're amazing. The hands are there and the tails aren't so wobbly. You're so good."

"Don't forget how good Arthur's computer simulations are. It's like solving a genetic puzzle," she said, smiling and pushing her bangs off her brow.

He continued to study the chicks. "I see the flight muscles are smaller. No need for them now. The feathers are nice." He stuck his finger into the cage. "Ow! Damn, the little guy bit me!" he said, holding up his damaged index finger for Kumiko to see. An arc of little red beads appeared where each tooth had penetrated his skin.

"I'll get you a bandage," Kumiko said, examining the small cut. "I'm not sure who in the family is more injury-prone, you or George. We'd better put some antibiotic on it just to be safe." She pulled a tube from her lab coat pocket.

"You carry this stuff around with you?" he said, trying not to look at his finger.

"I figured someone would get bitten eventually," she said, also retrieving a small box of bandages.

"I'm the first human to be bitten by a dinosaur!"

"Be glad it's a baby."

"It's like being a time traveler!" Cantor said softly. He took Kumiko's hand and raised it to his lips.

"Cantor, not in the lab!" Kumiko whispered, noticing the smile on a grad student's face. But she didn't pull her hand away.

He smiled as he picked up a chick from the backside, avoiding the little snapping jaw, and examined the three fingers on each hand. They were clawless and pointed in odd directions. "Definitely incomplete. We have a lot of work to do before those fingers can bend properly. Nevertheless, I don't think any roosters are going to want to tangle with this guy when he matures." He gently placed the wiggling chick back in the cage.

"Nor paleontologists. How's your finger?" Kumiko asked.

"No worries," Cantor replied.

Kumiko knew when it came to blood, his stomach often went into boa mode and squeezed itself, pushing out whatever he'd last eaten.

The latest high-tech equipment surrounded the chicks. Usually, one to three graduate students worked the machines, fed the animals, or took notes.

She watched as Cantor gazed at all the glinting hardware. Paleontologists, like himself, rarely used most of these things. There were gene-splicing machines, cell analysis machines, DNA sequencing machines, and more. All with flashing lights in green, red, and yellow. "I'll never understand how these contraptions work."

"No problem, I do. You know, we have a lot more work ahead of us," Kumiko said. "The genes that control diet are so complicated, I'm thinking it'll take at least one more iteration before I can change these dino-chickens into pure carnivores." She turned and looked at him. "I still wonder if we shouldn't try to reproduce a plant eater instead. I think you'd relate to them better."

"Good vegetarian joke. Thanks a lot. As for vegetarian dinos, it ain't going to happen. Even the chicken's ancestors loved their steak. Deep down inside – really deep – chickens are yearning to be predators."

"Oh? Did you take a poll of all the local chickens?"

"As a matter of fact, I did. They all want to rebel against the junk the farmers feed them and yearn to be masters of their domain," Cantor said, trying to pick up another chick. "Anyway, all birds came from meat-eaters similar to *velociraptors,* as far as we know." Gradually, his hand approached another chick.

"I'm aware," Kumiko said. "Honey, you're going to get bitten again. Please put on some gloves."

Cantor continued, "So, when do you think you'll be able to start work with the eagles? Are you up for that?"

"I love a challenge," she said, toying with her dragon necklace. "Since they're already genetically programmed to eat meat, it might be easier to devolve them into dinosaurs. I'm still waiting for Arthur's recommendations."

He began doing a two-step with her, holding her close, then twirling her in a circle. "I don't know how many more iterations we'll need, but we're going to make a real dinosaur. You are the only one that can do it," he whispered in her ear.

The grad students stood and clapped, which only encouraged Cantor.

* * *

Kumiko loved to enhance her class lessons with real examples of creatures or vivid visual aids. The next morning, Kumiko discussed her research with her sophomore genetics class. She didn't adhere to university norms and wore a yellow blouse and a flowered orange dress. Using a laser pointer, she discussed the images on the large wall screen. The classroom lights were off and the blinds closed.

"Today, I have a surprise for you. But first, let me lay some groundwork. Scientists have long known that the body structures of ancient ancestors often appear and then disappear during the development of the embryos." She clicked the remote in her other hand and a new photo appeared.

"For example, whale embryos have tiny buds for hind limbs, all of which disappear as the embryo develops further, and the associated genes are turned off. Well, scientists like myself are turning them back on," she said, her eyes sparkling.

Kumiko handed out a sheet of paper titled *Devolution* as students stopped writing and socialized with one another.

"Everyone got a copy?" She waited for the chatter to fade away. "You can follow the outline as I cover the next topic. Today I want to talk about my own research. I call it Devolution, basically running evolution backward starting with an existing organism, in this case, a bird. It's like reversing evolutionary time.

"Because of the publicity around my research, you may know I work with a scientist named Arthur Saxton, at Los Alamos, New Mexico. We are turning chickens and eagles into dinosaurs." The slide showed a cartoon mother chicken chasing a dinosaur youngster, three times her size, out of her kitchen.

"Los Alamos provides the quantum computer simulations of genes that work out their hypothetical expressions. I apply the results in the lab by altering the genes in the previous iterations to produce a new animal closer to a dinosaur. The latest iteration is called C4. Please turn on the lights." A student flipped the switch on the wall.

"And here is a C4." Kumiko put on a set of leather gloves and put the cage on her desk. When she took off the cage's cloth covering, the room erupted with 'oohs' and 'ahhs'. Carefully, she pulled the young eleven-inch-long C4 out of the cage and held it in her extended arms.

"As you can see, it's a bird-like animal, but with teeth and hands. What makes this guy different from my previous version, the C3s, is he has the neural 'knowledge' to use them. He will chase mice and anything else that moves, including my husband's finger."

The students laughed as they strained to get a better view.

"And the tail doesn't just stick out and wobble. It is now used expertly for balance while running."

Many hands were in the air.

* * *

Later that day, Cantor and Kumiko attended a meeting with members of the Board of Supervisors as well as city and federal representatives. The board members insisted they could not allow any of the animals to be housed near Cantor's home, despite its semi-rural designation.

"We don't allow lions, or hippos, or elephants to be kept in residential areas as pets. We certainly don't allow these things you say are proto-dinosaurs," a city councilman said, as if that settled the issue.

A federal lawyer responded, "Sir, can you show the city ordinance that says people cannot own dinosaurs?"

"Don't be ridiculous."

"Look, Berkeley's facilities are strained as it is," Cantor said. "The pens I'm proposing will be sturdy and subject to your inspection. We don't exactly live in a residential neighborhood; my nearest neighbor is a half mile away."

"It doesn't matter," the city councilor said.

"It does matter," the federal lawyer added. "These animals, even in their current incomplete state, are a national treasure. Dr. Hoffman and Dr. Chen are qualified to give them the best care, albeit only temporarily. Someone will find a better habitat, eventually. Is that correct, doctors?"

"Yes," Cantor and Kumiko said together.

"Given their value, it would be advisable for no one, other than those directly involved, to know of the whereabouts of the animals. They are priceless," the lawyer said.

The councilman objected. "They belong in zoos."

"We must resolve this issue soon," the president of U. C. Berkeley reminded them. "No one is better equipped to study these wonderful creatures than the professors here. There are no other facilities where they can do their studies of dinosaur behavior. It is too important in the minds of the public for red tape and ordinances to stand in the way of this research."

* * *

Finally, approval for the construction of dinosaur pens near Cantor's house was granted. The pens would be built ten feet outside his backyard wall.

"I think we can learn a lot if the animals roamed freely in an enclosed setting," Cantor told Kumiko in his office later that week. He had his feet up and a coffee mug in his hand. Outside, the rain pelted the window and students ran to their classes. It made him glad his next class was over an hour away.

"I suspect you are talking about your backyard," Alexander Petrov added with a grin, his Russian accent apparent. His friends and colleagues knew him as Alex. For his doctorate, he'd switched from the study of fossils to the new field of experimental and behavioral paleontology under Cantor. Alex was almost a foot taller than his mentor, with gray eyes and a perpetual five o'clock shadow.

"Every paleontologist on Earth would give their big toe to watch dinosaurs in the flesh," Cantor said, looking at Kumiko eagerly.

"Our knowledge of dino behavior will grow exponentially," Alex said, rubbing the stubble on his chin.

"Are you suggesting you'll let them out of the pens?" Kumiko asked. She sat with her legs crossed, one hand cupped under her chin. "I don't think the administration agreed to that. And what will you do about cats and hawks?"

"Our backyard will be fine. Once the animals have grown a little larger, no cat will want to fight a 'chicken' that can fight back," Cantor said with a grin.

Kumiko replied, "Don't get too cocky, sweetheart."

* * *

Jeff Otis

His first book, *Raptor Lands*, was published in March 2024. His short stories appear in *A Diversity of Expressions, Woven Pathways,* and *Holes in Our Hearts.* He loves writing stories that involve romance, adventure, suspense, conflict, science fiction, fantasy, sometimes horror, and humor.

UnPublished Novel – General - 1st Place Russ Gritzo

Expiration Date

Prologue

Darkness.

Wait – no – there is a light, faint. Am I imagining it? No! It's really there.

Now it's gone.

Silence. Random images, flashes, blurry.

I'm in pain. I hurt everywhere! I want to cry.

Glimpses – fleeting and then they are gone.

I'm struggling. I can't move my arms. Something is wrong!

Choking! I can't get my breath!

Darkness again.

As she started to wake, Roxy tried to open her eyes. *"I'm too tired to open my eyes. I will just rest and try again. Maybe a bit more sleep..."*

Then she was awake, blinking in the harsh light of the room. A woman with a kind but age-lined face in a mask was staring down at her. Her eyes were a pretty green but showed a mix of worry and happiness.

"Hello, Roxy! Can you hear me?"

Roxy nodded and tried to speak, but all that came out was a hoarse croak.

"Shhh..." the woman said, touching Roxy's shoulder gently and speaking slowly, "Just relax until you are a bit more awake. I'm Mary. I am your nurse. You are in Centennial Regional Hospital, in the Intensive Care Unit. You have been in a car crash, and you have some pretty serious injuries, but you are through the worst of it. You are recovering now. Just nod if you understand what I said."

Roxy nodded slowly, still trying to process everything, but at least that explained why she felt so groggy and disconnected, and it explained the pain and the strange surroundings.

"We were pretty worried about you," said another voice to Roxy's right. She tried to turn to look at the new voice and winced in pain as it felt like needles were shooting through her neck and head. Roxy groaned and closed her eyes until the pain passed.

"Let me come around," said the new voice. When Roxy opened her eyes again she saw a shorter, darker-skinned woman in a white lab coat standing next to Mary.

"I'm Dr. Martinez. I am your surgeon. You suffered a pretty serious head injury. We performed a couple of surgeries on your head to relieve the pressure and repair your skull. We induced a coma for a few weeks so that we could give your brain time to heal. The surgeries went well, and now all we need you to do is rest and recover!"

Roxy took all this news in silence before trying to speak. It took her several tries to speak. Mary helped her by tilting the bed up to raise her head and giving her a sip of water. After a few moments, Roxy was able to form the words and get them out.

"I don't remember an accident!" she whispered hoarsely.

"That is completely normal in situations like this," Dr. Martinez assured her. "Some patients never fully recall their accidents; others do, but it may take some time. Let's test your memory a bit right now, though. Can you remember your full name?" Dr. Martinez asked.

"Roxanne Kristen Ternelle, but I go by Roxy," she said.

"And your birthday?"

"November 28th, 1990," Roxy replied slowly, finding it hard to think but sure of the answers.

"Good, good!" said Dr. Martinez. "And do you recall who we are?"

"Nurse Mary and Dr. Martinez."

"Good! That is good news for all of us. I am going to leave you to rest, and Mary here will be checking in on you. Feel free to sleep as much as you need, but when you are awake, try to do some mental exercises, like the alphabet forward and backward, listing the states in the US and their capitols, and things like that. Do you understand?"

Roxy nodded gently, leaned back in bed, and let herself drift off to sleep again as Dr. Martinez and Mary moved away from the bed, chatting quietly between themselves.

Blurry

Over the next several days Roxy continued to improve, spending more time awake each day. Mary was working with Roxy to slowly bring her into a routine, waking in the morning, staying awake a good part of the day, then sleeping primarily at night.

Although the pain in her head, neck, and side was terrible at times, the pain medication was effective. The bandages on her head were itchy, though, and Roxy wanted to get them off.

"Can we please take these bandages off? They are seriously irritating, and it makes me feel like I am sicker and weaker than I actually am," Roxy asked one morning in a pleading tone.

"OK, I think we can do that, just promise you won't pick at your stitches. Promise?"

Roxy would have promised almost anything at that point just to get the bandages off. As she looked at Mary to reply a small blurry rectangular spot appeared, seemingly floating above and to the left of Mary's head. Roxy blinked a few times, thinking it was some cruft in her eye, but the spot stayed, and for an instant, Roxy thought she saw numbers forming inside the spot. Just as she was going to say something about it to Mary, the spot went away.

Over the coming days Roxy's parents and friends came and visited. Roxy was relieved when her parents brought her laptop and the charger for it. She felt much better getting back online and trying to resume some normalcy: checking into work, answering emails from well-wishers, catching up on X and Discord, and generally getting re-connected to the world.

Roxy thought nothing more of the blurry spot.

10220 15 43

Roxy looked up from her laptop as Dr. Martinez came into the room.

"I need to examine your head wound, and I need to test some motor reflexes again," Dr. Martinez said as she leaned in to brush Roxy's hair aside and look at her head.

10220 15 43.

The numbers appeared slightly blurry, but clearly distinguishable above Dr. Martinez's head, slightly to the left.

Roxy gasped and drew back, blinking.

"What's wrong?" Dr. Martinez asked with a quizzical look on her face.

"I… I don't know!" Roxy replied hesitatingly. "As you came closer, all of a sudden, I thought I saw numbers – white numbers against a black background – appear above your head. 10220 15 4.. something. I don't recall the last number."

Dr. Martinez's face gave a moment's flash of concern before she could restore her 'medical professional' face. She paused for a moment and asked, "Are the numbers still there?"

"No, Roxy replied slowly. "They came, were clearly there, and then they went away. They are gone now."

"Has this happened before?"

"No. Well – kind of. I thought I saw something a couple of days ago when Mary was taking the bandages off. But it was just a blur."

"Hmm. Well – you have had a serious injury, so perhaps this is just your brain working through the healing process. Let's not be concerned about it, but let me know if it happens again." Dr. Martinez replied with a long-practiced medical professional assertive voice, curated to inspire confidence. The rest of the exam was conducted briskly and clinically, leaving Roxy feeling uneasy. To Roxy, Dr. Martinez seemed worried about something – she just wasn't going to let Roxy know that.

00002 12 14

As Roxy continued to recover, she started taking walks down the corridor in the morning to build her strength. Despite the ever-present pain, her walks were manageable if she stayed on her medications. Still, she was happy to get out of bed and move around, her quickening pace down the hallway tangible evidence that she was getting better.

Often she encountered an old man whose room was at the end of the hallway, walking about the same time she did. Roxy later learned that Frank was his name. Bent and frail, he moved in slow, shuffling steps, using a walker, with a nurse by his side. At one point, Roxy learned that he was in hospice care with stage 4 cancer.

That Wednesday morning Roxy made it all the way to Frank's room before seeing him. She was starting to get a bit concerned, but just as she arrived at his room Frank appeared at the door, trembling, leaning heavily on his walker, with a nurse standing at his side steadying him.

Then it happened again.

00002 12 14.

The numbers appeared clearly above and to the left of Frank's head, as if they were one of those infuriating flashing popups on a computer website, unbidden and unavoidably distracting. Roxy gasped out loud and felt a shock through her core like she had touched a live electrical wire. She jerked her gaze away from the numbers, tried to focus on Frank's eyes, and to give him the reassuring smile she thought he needed.

"I know," Frank replied haltingly, his voice weak and raspy. "I must look like shit. I feel like shit." he said.

"No, no – I just... I was just worried about you!" Roxy stammered, trying to force herself to exude a cheerfulness she definitely did not feel. "I thought... I am glad to see you are up; I look forward to seeing you on our walks."

"Thanks. I like seeing you too," Frank replied with a weak smile, his voice trailing off at the end.

Roxy and Frank exchanged light conversation for a moment, but Roxy could see that each sentence was taking its toll on him, with his words coming out ever more haltingly. After a few more moments Roxy made her excuse and turned around to return to her room. Taking several steps towards her room, she paused to look back to see if the numbers were still visible, but Frank and his nurse had returned to his room.

The trip down the rest of the hallway to her room seemed like a waking dream. The squeak of her shoes on the polished floor, the antiseptic smell in the air, and the soft beeping of monitors, as she walked past open doors, hovered in the background like a fog, there, but not really there. Even Mary's gentle and precautionary hold on her elbow and Roxy's ever-present pain barely registered to her. As she lay back down in bed, her heart racing, Roxy's mind was a tumbling mess of thoughts, and she couldn't focus on any one of them before another one intruded.

It happened again. What is that? Why the number 00002 12 14? That is much smaller than the other numbers I saw before. Or that I think I saw before. What does it mean? Maybe I'm imagining it. Maybe it's nothing. No, I'm sure I saw them. I saw them clearly this time. But didn't Mary see it? Or did she, and she is just not saying anything?

Roxy's thoughts were interrupted by Mary.

"Are you OK?" she asked.

"Yeah, yeah, sure. I am fine. I guess." Roxy said slowly, avoiding Mary's eyes as she tried to decide if she was going to tell Mary what happened. She wanted to know if Mary saw the numbers as well but was afraid of what the answer might be. After a long delay, Roxy continued, "I'm just—I just worry about Frank. He did not look well." Roxy was partly truthful but mostly trying to deflect Mary's attention.

"Yes, he did not look well," Mary replied as she straightened the blankets on Roxy's bed with practiced efficiency, "but he, and all of us, know the end is near for him. Try to not let it upset you, you have your recovery to focus on now."

Mary fussed over the bedclothes a bit more, making occasional eye contact with Roxy. Roxy sensed that Mary was doing this hoping she would open up more. Instead, Roxy sat in silence staring at the tent her feet made in the sheets, trying to tame her jumbled thoughts. She felt slightly relieved when Mary eventually left the room, but a part of her still worried that she should say something.

A Theory Emerges

The next few days and nights went by in a haze. Every beep, every door closing, every hushed conversation, every sound in the hospital echoed throughout her head and blurred in with her dreams. Her semi-wakened mind was rolling the same thoughts over and over.

"*What's happening to me? Why do I see numbers sometimes but not always? Am I losing my mind? Will this go away? What do I do? Do I talk to somebody? What if they think I'm crazy and lock me up?*"

Saturday dawned bright and sunny, with the morning sun streaming in the east-facing window. Although she woke a couple of times during the night, Roxy was definitely feeling better, and the pain was not as bad this morning. She still needed the pain medications though, and without them, Roxy felt horrible. Not just pain, but her stomach hurt, and she was shaky and weak. Today she felt stronger though, so when Mary arrived, Roxy was eager for her walk.

As they approached Frank's room, the door was open, the curtains were drawn back, and the room was light and airy. Letting go of Mary's arm, Roxy swung into the room to say a cheery hello to Frank but stopped in her tracks. The bed was empty, and the room was clean. There was no Frank.

"What happened? Where's Frank?" Roxy asked Mary.

"Ahh," Mary replied. "Frank passed away last night. I'm so sorry. I know he was your friend."

Roxy just stood in the doorway, frozen in place.

"When?" She asked.

"Last night sometime."

"No – When – Exactly When?" Roxy snapped at Mary. "I need to know exactly WHEN he died!"

"I…. I don't know." Mary stammered a bit, her eyes widened at the intensity in Roxy's voice. "But – I can find out. Hold on. Alice? What time did Frank pass away?" she asked, addressing the nurse in charge of that area.

"About 15 minutes after 10:00 PM last night," Alice replied, after looking at the paperwork on the clipboard on her desk.

Roxy stood rigid in the doorway, hands clenched, trembling. In her mind she was engaged in a raging personal war. She knew instinctively that she did the mental math quickly and correctly. Still, a part of her did not want to confirm the conclusion she arrived at, so she tried to deny that she did the calculation properly and to even deny what the other part of her brain was thinking. She tried to force herself to not repeat the calculation, but her subconscious did anyway, without her conscious brain's consent.

She had done the math right. She struggled to try and believe that this was really happening.

Frank had passed away 2 days, 12 hours, and a handful of minutes after Roxy had seen the number 00002 12 14 appear above his head.

The inescapable conclusion was that the numbers she saw were how much longer Frank had to live at the time they appeared to her. She had seen his "expiration date".

As Roxy stood in the doorway, staring into the empty room, the uncontrolled thoughts inside her head tumbled over each other like the cacophony of thunder in a violent storm.

This clearly happened as a result of my accident. But how? How could this have happened? Why did this happen? What does this mean? What do I do now? Do I tell someone?

What

the

actual

hell?

Roxy had no answers.

"Are you OK?" Mary asked. She had to ask a couple of times before she got Roxy's attention.

"Huh? Yes... Yeah... I'm... I'm fine." Roxy said slowly and haltingly as she turned away from Mary and started down the hallway towards her room without waiting for Mary. Mary followed closely behind Roxy on the trip down the hallway, watching her carefully. Where earlier Roxy had held her head high, shoulders back, her stride exuding a renewed physical strength and confidence, now Roxy's shoulders were slumped and her steps halting and uncertain.

The trip back down the hallway was a blur in her mind. Inside her head she wanted to scream, cry, rage, and hide all at once. The implications of what she had just concluded were shattering, but as she walked down the hallway, a more profound fear took hold of her thoughts. She had looked at herself in the mirror many times since the accident of course, as she watched the healing progress of the scars on her head, gently stroking the prickly stubs of hair that were growing back from where her head was shaved. Never did the numbers appear in the mirror, but now that the realization of what they meant was becoming clear, would her own number appear?

Arriving back in the room, Roxy made her excuses to Mary, assured her she was fine, and went into the bathroom, closing the door behind her. With her trembling hands on either side of the sink, staring down at the white porcelain and the dull metal of the drain she silently argued with herself.

"I have to look. I can't not know. But what am I going to see?"

Roxy continued staring into the sink, arguing with herself. Suddenly, like mentally ripping a band-aid off, she jerked her head up and looked her reflection straight in the eyes. Nothing. No numbers. She stood there for several minutes, looking away, and then back in the mirror. Still nothing. It wasn't until she said the words out loud several times that she convinced herself there really was nothing there.

"There are no numbers. I don't see my own 'expiration date'. There is nothing there."

After saying it to herself out loud several times, she opened the door, turned the bathroom lights out, and returned to her bed, relieved somewhat but still trembling and numb with shock.

* * *

Russ Gritzo

Russ has had a creative streak for as far back as he can remember but spent decades in science and engineering. Russ has reached the point in life where it is time to let the creative side out into the light of day.

UnPublished Novel – General 2nd Place Michael Grady

The Angel of Tolleson Gap

Prologue: The Capsule

September 24, 2017

Klieg lights framed the square in a buzzing tungsten white when Police Sergeant Raella Washington pulled to a stop on the Tolleson Pike. Eleven p.m., and the crane's massive boom was already poking into the sky. Rae blew into her hands and looked around.

A black cop, an iron soldier, and a median lit for night baseball. *Should be fun,* she thought, as she headed for the Bobby T.

"The welders are over in the van," Officer Gibbs caught her in stride. "They're firing up their torches now and – watch …" An oversized flatbed was backing up to the pedestal. "We're waiting on the boom guys. When they're ready, they'll cut 'round the base of the statue while the Stuart boys secure harnesses up top."

Rae looked up at the arm overhead. "That'll be enough to lift it?"

"They say so," Gibbs shrugged. "No one's an expert on this sort of thing."

She nodded, glancing down the side streets. "See any friends?"

"Friends?"

"White Pride? Aryan Nation?"

He shook his head.

"Okay. HEY!" She shouted to the welders. "Yes, you! Let's get this party started!"

* * *

Six weeks ago, Charlottesville, Virginia's city council voted to pull down a Robert E. Lee statue in one of its parks. The decision drew white supremacists out of the woodwork; who, in turn, drew liberal counter-protestors. Sleepy Charlottesville suddenly became a battleground for the Southern soul. A protestor and three law enforcement officers died.

Three days later, Tolleson Mayor Louis France convened a meeting with Rae's chief and the city council. "It could happen here." He warned. "Richmond and other cities are removing their statues at night, when no one can fuss about it. We should do the same."

"Mr. Mayor, I'm confused." Chief Simpkins broke the silence. "Are we talkin' about Bobby T, here?"

"Robert Taggert was a Confederate general."

"And a local hero," one of the councilmen added. "He fought here, Louis. At Tolleson Gap. He's a part of our collective history."

"You'll chap a helluva lot more hides takin' him down than leavin' him up," the Chief was trying not to smile. "Look, I know the liberals got their back up since the election. But they got hundreds of Lee and Stonewall statues to tear down first. How far …?" He began to laugh. "How far down the outrage tree d'ye think they gotta get before they even gon' care about Tolleson and Bobby T?"

But the mayor was not smiling.

* * *

"Damn shame, if you ask me." Officer Gibbs said.

They sipped coffee at Rae's squad car, watching torches on the pedestal spit cinders and light. General Taggert shuddered under the sparks, but the hero of the Confederacy would not come free.

"Give 'em hell, Bobby T!" Gibbs raised his cup. "Don't blame him one bit. How is a 150-year-old statue suddenly a problem?"

Rae sipped, keeping an eye on the side streets.

"I grew up with them, you know. Both of 'em: Bobby T and the Tolleson Angel."

Rae nodded.

"S'what put us on the map."

I know the story, Rae told him. But he told it, anyway: Theresa Danforth, the Tolleson Angel, standing between the armies to keep the peace on Christmas Eve. And Robert Taggert, who led his outnumbered soldiers into history the following day. "Learned it all in kindergarten. Did pageants on it and book reports and such. Now suddenly, it's like asbestos."

"Lost me there, Gibby."

"Remember asbestos when it was a good thing? When it was fire protection? Did the job, too! My dad was a contractor. They used to brag about putting asbestos in schools."

Rae looked at him. "You know it causes cancer, right?"

"If you disturb it! If you get right up on it, and— " He took a deep breath. Rae watched the square as the welders cut neat molten lines around the hooves of Bobby T's horse. "Just sayin'. Most things are fine if you just let 'em be."

She looked at him: "Again. Cancer."

"So maybe that's a bad example. But who is Bobby T hurtin'? He's … what, now? A symbol of oppression?"

Rae said nothing.

"They'll come after the Angel next. Mark my words. One day someone'll be 'offended' by the way Theresa Danforth stood down the guns. 'She didn't do it quickly enough,' or 'she didn't stop the whole war' or 'she shouldn't have stopped the Union guns' or some damn thing."

Bystanders poked out, in ones and twos, as arc light flickered on the storefronts. Gibbs talked about growing up, when the Bobby T statue presided over the whole roundabout. "Little boys would climb to the horse's leg. In middle school, you had to touch his gun. See? Hangin' from that forearm, that was braggin' rights. Then in high school, if you could crawl up on the saddle with Bobby T—"

"You got a drunk-and-disorderly?"

They laughed. Then Bobby T's bolts started coming off in a series of loud bangs.

"You don't find it racist." He said it uncertainly, asking for confirmation. But Rae didn't bite. "Right? I mean, as an … African-American woman?"

Rae crossed her arms. "I always found it an interesting one-two punch. Here, you got Theresa Danforth, coming out of the woods, saying 'put down your guns! It's Christmas Eve,' then … "

"Then Bobby Taggert kickin' Union ass the next morning?" Gibbs chuckled. "Well, that's just the South. We're very devout. But don't fuck with us."

The noise drew a few drinkers out of The Alibi. Over on Turnbull Street, people collected on the sidewalk to watch the show.

Rae said "The statue isn't 150 years old, you know."

Gibbs insisted it was. "Tolleson Gap was fought on Christmas 1864."

"But if you ever read the pedestal you were trespassing on, you'd see the statue wasn't dedicated 'til 1894."

Above them, the Stuart boys had run enormous slings under the belly of the horse. On the corner, Sergeant Dixon was in discussion with several men.

"Why did they wait 30 years for a statue?" Gibbs asked.

Rae thought: *Or what happened in 1894 that made them want to put a giant, armed white man in the middle of town?*

The corner discussion was getting animated. Several men were talking over each other. Sergeant Dixon raised his hands gently as the conversation took on an edge.

Rae palmed her nightstick. "Wanna take a walk?"

But it escalated before they got there.

"BOBBY T!" A gangly kid ran loose into the square, waving his arms in drunken grief. By the time Dixon chased him to the statue's base, about a dozen others had poured in: snarling at the police and the welders and shouting for others for join them. A few were talking on phones.

Rae, hoping to walk it all back, caught up with gangly kid, now prostrate near the statue. He was actually crying.

"How're you tonight?"

"I can't believe you're takin' Bobby T!"

"You been drinking tonight, sir?"

"The fuck is it to you?" One of the voices behind her said. She turned to it. "He ain't drivin'."

"No," Rae replied. "But he can't stay here."

"Free country – last I looked!" Another voice said.

"WHAT THE FUCK ARE YOU DOING TO THE STATUE?" Another was straining against his friends. "IS THIS 'CAUSE OF THIS …"

"Charlottesville—"

"—THIS CHARLOTTESVILLE SHIT?!"

"We all gotta be pussies, now."

People were suddenly streaming into the square. Two more officers had joined them, but they were already outnumbered. Rae caught Gibb's eye, as he quietly called for backup.

"Did you CHECK WITH ANYBODY?!" Screaming guy pointed at Rae, then at the statue. "'CAUSE I DON' REMEMBER VOTING…"

"Gotta be mulatto pussies."

Rae spread her hands. "Decision of the town council. This is not me, fellas—"

"No, but you're lovin' this, aren't ya?"

She bent down to help gangly kid up. "But right now, this is a work site …"

"Hey, don't touch him!"

"… with hot cinders flying —"

"I SAID 'DON'T TOUCH HIM!"

"— and you can't. Stay. Here."

They were all shouting now, sending the officers back a step before they grabbed their nightsticks and drew a line. Rae stood her ground, trying to connect with anyone in the flailing mass now shouting profanities her way.

The flat-bed driver honked his horn. "I'm not gonna stay!"

Rae asked one of the welders to fetch a bullhorn from the nearest unit. Above them, she could hear the Stuart brothers screaming that the statue was almost free. Cherry-tops were flashing their way up the pike as windows lit on every side and streetlights caught more people rushing toward the commotion.

"Folks. Listen to me, please." Her voice was tetchy and nasal through the horn. "The statue isn't being destroyed, okay? It is just being moved."

That just poked the bear. The jeering grew louder. A toxic cloud of accusations, racial epithets and white pride jargon poking out here and there.

"This is fascist bullshit!" A young man at the back was taller and more verbal than most.

"Liberal establishment bullshit chipping away at the heritage of the white race!"

He stepped forward on a tide of "Hell yeah's." Rae had seen him around before. Not to speak to. But she knew he wasn't an outside agitator. He was homegrown.

"This is what they do in Russia, man! When the- when the New World Order moves in? What's the first thing they do? They tear down the FUCKIN' STATUES!" He threw his hands like a rapper, and Rae wondered how many angry young white men modeled their moves from Compton.

"This is our HISTORY!" He had the crowd listening now. "Y'all are so quick to go to the courts or the media when a precious piece of your mongrel history is in danger—"

Dixon stepped forward: "Y'all can shut yer damn mouth—" But Rae froze him with a look. *Let him talk.*

And he did: About white pride, and the creeping corruption of the race. As his anger fanned out – to politicians, welfare queens and "people who hate us" – Rae could see the steam bleeding out of the crowd. No one who agreed wanted to interrupt, and no one bent on violence had the guts to go first.

Then the statue broke free, swinging lazily on the trusses beneath the crane. It stole the young man's thunder, as everyone stopped to watch a local landmark give way to the tide of history.

"You can tear down the statues," the young man pointed at Rae as three squad cars slid into the square. "Go on, sneak 'em away in the dead of night. But the truth is still here. The truth will out."

"YOU ARE INSTRUCTED TO DISPERSE BY ORDER OF THE TOLLESON POLICE." She recognized Chief Simpkins' voice through the bullhorn. "LEAVE THIS AREA NOW."

They didn't comply at first. But as more officers got out the crowd flaked off in twos and threes; talking tough and gesturing defiantly while walking backwards to their cars. The officers drew tighter around the statue, steadying it for the flatbed.

Once the stragglers dispersed and the tie-downs were done, they sent General Taggert on his very last ride.

Rae turned to Gibbs. "Give me a boost."

To the great amusement of Dixon and Gibbs, she pulled herself up on the pedestal plaque then crawled atop the ragged, empty plateau.

"Not gloatin' up there, are you?" Dixon asked.

She wanted to see Bobby T reach the highway. His stolid profile merging onto the 431 and sailing, bravely, toward its warehouse would be a sight to see. She didn't spot the capsule until she kicked it and sent it rattling across the pedestal.

It was some sort of canister. Scuffed and covered with dust, it did not explain itself under Dixon's flashlight. "No markings at all," he observed. "This was under the statue?"

"Maybe it's the warranty," Gibbs joked.

Dixon tucked it under his elbow and worked one end like a stubborn jar. "Dix, we don't know what this is," Rae said. "Maybe we shouldn't—"

Then the end squirted into the darkness, and a sheaf of yellowed papers slid to their feet.

Rae picked one up. It crackled under the light.

"If you're reading this, the statue has fallen. It's time to know the truth about the Battle of Tolleson Gap."

* * *

Michael Grady

Mike's first novel, *Breaking Ball*, debuted in 2021. His plays include *Dancers*, winner of the American College Theatre Festival's National Student Playwriting Award; and *Harmony Codes*, staged at the Sundance Playwright's Lab. He won multiple writing awards as a features writer/humor columnist for *The East Valley Tribune.*

UnPublished Novel - General 3rd Place Sarah Kotchian

Bodies of Water and Dust

Chapter 1

Emily slowed at the western edge of Moorhead as her car approached the I-94 bridge over the Red River. The dividing line between Minnesota and North Dakota, the river bordered the adopted homeland of her immigrant ancestors, a place almost mythic in her imagination. When she reached Fargo on the other side of the bridge, she thought, she would be in new territory, at the end of one journey and the beginning of another, much like her great-great-great grandmother in the 1870s.

She was grateful that her inheritance from Great Aunt Minnie had coincided with her sabbatical in the fall from Massachusetts University, which meant no money worries while she traveled. She figured the semester away would help her sort out lots of things – her collection of poems that had gotten bogged down over the last two months, for example, and her new status as "not in a relationship." Recently emerged from the breakup of a long romance, she had decided it was the perfect time to explore the land of her ancestors. She also wanted to see the family homestead and surrounding land in Southeastern North Dakota she had inherited from childless Aunt Minnie, the last remaining Jahoda descendent of the early homesteaders. She could give herself a much needed new horizon, research some of her family history, and take stock of the property before she arranged to sell the house and land.

Emily was an Easterner, and North Dakota sounded like a place of extremes: blizzards, droughts, grasshoppers. She was fascinated that her people had traveled all the way from Germany and England to settle here, but then, they hadn't been told about the climatic conditions. They had just seen the advertisements by railroad companies for fertile soil and free land through the Homestead Act, and that was enough to convince them to make the journey to escape conscription, poverty, and to make a better life for their children. She had read about their long journey across the Atlantic and then overland, and the difficult years eking out a living before they could file a claim, build a house, plant crops. They had been made of tougher stuff than she was, she thought.

After the spring semester ended a few days ago, she had packed up her Honda SUV and pointed it west with a duffle bag of clothes, a cooler with some homemade dinners that she could reheat, and her computer. She hoped she might be able to stay at the homestead, but if not, she could find a small place to rent for the summer and fall. A planner by nature, Emily felt very brave coming out here without a plan and trusting that what she needed would turn up. North Dakota could have very hot days and very violent thunderstorms, sometimes on the same day. At least she was prepared for weather. Looking back on it, it turned out that was about the only thing she was prepared for.

Emily filled up the gas tank in Fargo. Needing a few fresh groceries, she used her smart phone to locate a grocery store and found the address for Hagerman's, a local store on the west side of Fargo. She preferred to shop at family owned businesses whenever she could. So many of the small town businesses were forced out by the huge corporate retailers like Bullmart and internet giants who promised short term convenience and cheaper goods but didn't put down community roots. She stepped out of the car and stretched her legs for a moment, stiff from the long ride across Minnesota. Inside, the cashier greeted her, "Welcome to Hagerman's," and actually looked at her and smiled.

Emily picked up some bananas, blueberries, sliced turkey, two cans of soup, whole grain bread, a quart of milk, cereal, a bag of salad and an orange-tinged cantaloupe from the produce section labeled "local," as well as some chocolate chip cookies, two chocolate bars, some paper plates, a small bag of plastic utensils, and a bag of ice. She looked longingly at the local sweet corn, its tassels still a fresh pale yellow; she wasn't sure when she'd be able to cook it, but she put two ears in her cart just in case. She had brought a small camp stove with her, and with the stove and the cooler in her car, a few plates and bowls, a serrated knife and some simple eating utensils and kitchen implements, she had food for dinners and breakfasts if it turned out there weren't places to eat where she was going. She paid the friendly cashier and loaded the cold items into the cooler in the back of the car, making space next to the hard-sided file box in the back seat. The box held copies of the documents that her aunt's estate lawyer had given her – the dates and locations of the homestead claims and a set of keys to the house, the birth and death dates of four generations of grandparents and great-grandparents, a copy of her great aunt's will, and, most interesting of all, the small key to a safe deposit box in the Prairie Bank in Richland. She could hardly wait to see what might be inside that bank box.

It was late afternoon as she drove towards the southeastern corner of North Dakota where she had reserved a place for the evening, a working farm bed and breakfast. She parked in the circular gravel drive and took her duffle and computer bag from the car. She'd leave the cooler and files and ask her hosts for more ice in the morning. She stood for a moment, breathing in the smells of the countryside, the faint whiff of mown grass, the damp smell of the willow and cattails that lined the pond with the chairs and little rowboat on the bank. They must sit out here on an evening, she thought; how wonderfully peaceful. The white farmhouse was inviting, with a porch that stretched the length of the front, rocking chairs, hummingbird feeders and hanging baskets of red and salmon colored geraniums and trails of green and white ivy. She could hear the sound of farm machinery in the distance and the hum of trucks a few miles away on the interstate. Overhead, a meadowlark with a velvety black vee on its deep yellow chest warbled into the warm early evening air. She smelled the aroma of fresh bread as she stepped up to ring the bell next to the screen door.

In a few moments, Sandy, who owned the farm with her husband, John, appeared, drying her hands on her muslin apron stenciled with rose buds. "You must be Emily," she said, "welcome to Horizon Hill Farm."

She held the screen door open for her as Emily stepped inside, admiring the polished banister, the oak floors, the living room with its easy chairs, modest television, side tables with craft and farm magazines, and soft curtains that framed the pond and the fields beyond.

"What a beautiful spot you have," Emily said.

"Yes, it's been in our family now for over a hundred years. We've seen a lot of changes, but we've managed to hold onto it. I'm not sure for how much longer, with the economy the way it is. So many of the young people, including our two boys, have left to find work elsewhere, and it's getting too much for John to manage by himself. Some of our neighbors have already sold out to larger corporate farms."

She looked wistful for a moment, but then returned her attention to her guest.

"You've had a long day, let me show you to your room."

She led the way up the stairs to a room marked "Kestrel" over the door.

"I hope this will be all right for you," she said.

Emily looked at the spacious square room, the queen sized four poster bed with its hand sewn sunbonnet quilt, the vase with fresh roses on the side table, and its claw foot bath tub on the side of the room.

"All right?" Emily said with a grin. "I'm not sure I'll want to ever leave!"

"Have you had a chance to get some supper?" Sandy asked.

When Emily said that she had brought some things with her, Sandy said,

"I've made some baked chicken and potato salad, you're welcome to join us if you're not too tired."

How unusual, Emily thought, and how generous! She accepted with pleasure. It would be a treat to unwind with such nice company and home-cooked food, and she could learn more about Horizon Hill Farm and the local area.

* * *

The next morning, Emily slowly drifted awake, listening to the nonstop conversation of the house finches, the mourning dove cooing, and a dog barking. Sandy had offered to have breakfast ready at 8:30, although the farm couple had been up long before that tending to farm chores. She pulled on a white short-sleeved tee, some clean khakis and her trainers and went downstairs. In the breakfast room, she found a carafe of coffee and a pot of hot water with a selection of tea bags. Emily chose the English Breakfast tea. She loved strong coffee, but it always made her hungry again in a few hours and she had lots she wanted to do this morning before stopping again to eat. Sandy came in with a plate of two fried eggs and whole wheat toast. The crystal jar of marmalade and a little plate with butter were already on the table.

"This looks delicious," Emily said. "I don't know how I can be hungry again after that wonderful meal last night. Thank you again for inviting me to join you."

Sandy smiled in return. "It was nice to visit with someone new for a change. We haven't had many visitors from New England here. I'm not sure they know where North Dakota is on the map – somewhere out beyond Chicago, probably."

With that, she smiled and left Emily to enjoy her breakfast. Emily gazed out at the green fields, already hazy with the growing heat of the day. From their conversation the evening before, she knew they raised soybeans and sugar beets, a change from the wheat that her ancestors had grown. She wondered what she would find today as she visited the town where her family had homesteaded more than a hundred years ago. North Dakota had changed in so many ways. The reservations had built large casinos; out-of-state agribusiness had bought up much of the land; fracking had introduced another boom and bust cycle to the economy. North Dakota was used to boom and bust – it had experienced it multiple times with the arrival of railroads, extended drought, bonanza crop years. There were always environmental consequences for any development as well– groundwater and stream contamination, disruption of green spaces and flyways, hazardous wastes, light and noise pollution. She wondered how she would find the little town of Richland after all of the changes.

She finished the rest of her tea and went up to the room to pack her things. Sandy met her as she came downstairs, and Emily settled her bill and thanked her for all of her hospitality. Sandy handed her a bag of ice from their icemaker, and said she hoped Emily would stay with them again some time if she were back in the area. Emily started the car, putting the windows down as she left the property. She decided to take back roads to Richland rather than getting on the highway again. She wanted to enjoy the freshness of the morning pouring in and was not eager to be swapping lanes and exhaust with tractor trailers on their way to Sioux City, South Dakota. She drove south again, paralleling the Bois de Sioux River that emptied into the Red River. Green fields stretched out on both sides of the road, broken occasionally by a row of trees or a farmhouse.

At Fairmount, she turned west on state road 11, the road that would take her all the way to Richland. White cattle egrets lined the ditches and water glinted off the sloughs that interrupted the rolling grasslands. She passed over the Wild Rice River, winding its way northeast. She saw red winged and yellow headed blackbirds, and overhead a red-tailed hawk circled. She had expected many small farms, but instead she passed miles of fenced crops with corporate logos and the brand names of the seeds being grown. Things had changed so much since her ancestors' time.

She thought about what this country looked like a hundred and forty years ago when her great-great-great grandparents traveled here by horse and wagon in the 1870s, crossing the Red River, pulling the few belongings they had into unknown territory. She pictured the men going into the claims office, learning what land could still be claimed, filing for a homestead, promising to farm and to build a dwelling within five years. She wondered whether they had camped along the way at night, whether the women stayed at the camp with the children while the men went to file the claim. Perhaps the women and children had stayed back in Minnesota or Wisconsin, waiting for the men to return to tell them where they were going to move. Either way, she could hardly imagine the life they had had to hew out of this land with its black dirt, blazing sun, and exposure to the raw elements.

She passed through Harkinton, another small town that had been founded in anticipation of the Canadian Pacific Railway that still ran through it. There were few cars on the road, but she passed one small white pickup coming from the opposite direction with a green and blue state government logo on the side – maybe agriculture or fish and wildlife, she guessed. The driver, a young man, drove slowly, looking at the water in the ditches alongside the road, and raised one finger off the steering wheel in greeting as he passed.

She saw a sign pointing south toward the South Dakota border: "Dakota Casino; Feeling Lucky?" That was certainly a change from her ancestors' time, she thought. Taking advantage of nation sovereignty, many indigenous nations had started casinos in the last two decades to provide income and jobs. *What a strange thing in the midst of farmland*, Emily mused, *farms as far as the eye could see, then suddenly a huge casino, parking lot, bright lights*. She wondered whether the local people liked it, tolerated it, patronized it, or disapproved but appreciated the benefit to the local economy.

The sign just west of Harkinton indicated thirteen miles to Richland. All the roads in this part of the country were laid out in a grid pattern. Life wasn't that way, though, was it, she thought. Not so many straight roads; more detours left and right, with only a few straight patches. She wondered now whether her life was on a detour or a straightaway. In the distance she saw the water tower of Richland, painted with its name and an eagle's head, the symbol of the Warbirds, Richland's high school mascot. Yes, she thought, this is truly a land that had seen its share of warbirds, and most of those in the past century had been the new European arrivals.

There was only one business street in Richland, and she easily found the bank. The town didn't look as deserted and dilapidated as she had feared; there were several shops and a diner, and of course, the fact that there was still a bank here meant that there was at least some economic activity. She pushed open the glass door of the bank, whose brick exterior looked much as it must have in her ancestors' day. The bank wasn't busy at mid-morning on a Monday. At the information desk, she provided her driver's license and trust paperwork and said that she was there to look at the contents of the safety deposit box. A bank representative led her to the vault. Inside were a table and two chairs, where box owners could sit in privacy as they removed or placed items. He slid out a long metal box with the number 201 which had belonged to her Great-Aunt Minnie. The box rattled as he moved it, as if there were a marble rolling around inside. He placed the box on the table and left her to her work.

Now, Emily thought to herself, we shall see what else Aunt Minnie left me. She was curious but also strangely anxious about opening the box. What was inside? What might she find that she might not wish to know, learn that she could not then unlearn? She slid the key into the lock and turned it. She heard the lock release, and she held her breath as she carefully unhinged the lid. The box was almost empty – except for a small round brown object. She pulled it out and set it in the palm of her left hand, touching the small, knobby cap with her right index finger. An acorn. She sat, dumbfounded. She slipped the acorn into her pocket, locked and replaced the box, and exited the vault, signaling the bank attendant that she was finished. She stood outside on the paved walk, blinking a bit in the bright noon sun, and staring into the trees and sky beyond the buildings of Main Street. What had Aunt Minnie been trying to tell her? What on earth did an acorn have to do with her past – and perhaps, with her future? What now?

* * *

Sarah Kotchian's poetry collection, *Light of Wings*, was published by the University of New Mexico Press in 2024. Her book *Camino* received the New Mexico/Arizona Book Award and Seven Sisters Book Award. A contributor at the Bread Loaf Writers' Conference and Pushcart nominee, her work has appeared in numerous journals.

UnPublished Novel - Mystery/Thriller - 1st Place Rodney Walther

Spirit of the Gazelle

CHAPTER 1

Zelly Chadwick always believed that Leon would kill her.

She stood in her musty bedroom closet on the foggiest morning she could remember since they moved back to Kansas. After sliding a handful of wire hangers down the rod and brushing a lock of auburn curls behind her ear, she stared at the open gun safe.

I've dreamed of this moment.

She'd grown so tired of listening to Leon's rants, tired of fetching his next beer, tired of ducking to avoid his slaps and punches. Maybe she should just snap the magazine into the semi-automatic pistol, wheel about, then fire off a round—or six—into his chest. He deserved it, not just for last night but also for the cumulative pain he'd doled out during their long marriage.

Zelly lifted the components of the Smith & Wesson from the safe. *Just like the movies. Snap, squeeze, boom, thump.*

For years, she had felt like a zoo animal, scrutinized by a surly, cruel keeper whose sole purpose was to make her life miserable. This pistol was the key to her cage.

Beneath the smell of gun oil and the sweaty stench of a police uniform hanging from the rod, she allowed herself to imagine a sweeter fragrance: the scent of freedom. She exhaled slowly, a low whistle escaping her lips. As she examined the cold metal in her hands, she suddenly understood she couldn't confront her controlling husband, couldn't drop his pasty, doughy body with one shot, couldn't kill the man Dylan called Dad.

Because she didn't know how to load and fire a gun.

"I'm gonna be late," Leon growled. "Stop screwing around and help me."

Zelly's emotional cage door clanged shut. She shuddered and turned, her face cast downward, and surrendered the service weapon to him.

Leon laid his gun and its clip on the bed, then leaned over and fastened an empty ankle holster over his sock, his only clothing except for a pair of white briefs which fit his rolling gut like a size-sixteen shirt on a size-eighteen neck. Thick hair covered his chest and back, making him appear Neanderthal.

"I'm expecting a package," he said.

"Oh, right. Something came yesterday."

His nostrils flared like a predator scenting the wind. "Why the hell didn't you tell me?"

Zelly held her tongue. "It's from that hunting catalog place. Probably your new jacket." She pasted on a false smile. "Didn't you order some stuff for Tornado, too?"

Their male Chesapeake Bay Retriever had arrived earlier this spring, when Leon showed up one day with the dog on a leash. Of course, Zelly was expected to look after the day-to-day needs of "Nado," as Leon called him, but she didn't mind so much. Her heart was ready for someone else to love.

At the mention of Tornado's name, Leon's grim face melted for a moment. "Did I tell you that I'm getting him ready for field trials in the spring?" Without pausing for an answer, he added, "Gonna be a great hunting dog. Can't wait to bring home a trophy or medal or whatever they give out."

He flashed a wide, confident smile. It was the same smile that had once convinced her to go out with him and later to sleep with him, to believe his boasts and fall for his apologies.

Leon stood and slid on the dark-gray trousers of his uniform. "Where are my shoes?"

Swallowing hard, Zelly remembered that one of those polished, black shoes had flown across the bedroom last night and struck her above the left temple, punctuating an argument and momentarily dulling her consciousness. She pointed to the carpet where one shoe lay, then to the dresser across the room.

"You get off at six?" she mumbled.

"Yeah."

"I'll have dinner ready." She had no intention of repeating the events of yesterday, when Leon's complaints about cold burgers and limp, greasy fries had escalated into rants about her poor mothering abilities.

"Make something decent for once," he grumbled.

His words from last night...*You're worthless*...echoed in her mind.

Sure, she was an imperfect parent and a disappointing wife . . . especially in Leon's eyes. Yet Zelly had done one thing right. She'd prevented Leon from training his rage on their son. Dylan never knew the feeling of emptiness after a scathing rebuke, the pain of a knobby knuckle twisted between the ribs, the taste of blood from a busted lip.

She wanted to prove Leon wrong. *I'm not worthless.* She could cook a nice dinner. Yet with the budget he'd established, she could barely afford the cheapest ground beef.

"How about meatloaf?" she suggested.

"Not again."

"I could make it with brown gravy instead of tomato sauce. And mashed potatoes."

"No."

When Leon said *No*, that ended any conversation. He told Zelly what he wanted, and she complied. So, tonight she needed to create the perfect meal, because she keenly understood the lesson learned early in her marriage. *Failure has consequences.*

A bark sounded from the doorway, and their chocolate-colored dog bounded in. His entire backside wagged rhythmically, his tail whirling like a conductor's baton.

"Nado, come," Leon called, his voice suddenly warm and loving. "Give me a little kiss."

It's just a dog. When did I stop deserving affection?

Leon crouched, and Tornado loped into his open arms and nuzzled into his hairy chest. Rubbing the dog's head and giving him a peck on the ear, Leon said, "You're a good boy, aren't you, Nado? Yes, you are. We're gonna kill us some quail this weekend. You ready to hunt?"

Nado barked.

"Hunt!" Leon repeated. Nado spun three tight circles and barked twice, wagging his tail in a helicopter motion.

Leon laughed so hard that he farted.

Zelly stared at her husband in stony silence. The selfish asshole who drenched his skin with Old Spice and his liver with Jack Daniel's, the penny pincher who wouldn't pay for vacuum cleaner repair or TV streaming services, was the same man who had shelled out fifteen-hundred bucks for a puppy.

"I didn't know you were going hunting this weekend," she said, trying to keep accusation and complaint out of her voice.

Ignoring her, Leon rose and tugged his shirt on, then strapped the Smith & Wesson to his waist. Finally, he turned to Zelly, the harshness returning to his face. "Season opens tomorrow."

"Aren't you taking Dylan to the KU game?"

Leon inspected himself in the mirror, licked his fingers, and matted down a cowlick. "Like I can afford football tickets on a cop's salary. Me and Dylan already have plans. He's coming with me."

She wanted details but knew better than to ask.

"Don't give me that judgmental bullshit," he snapped. He stomped away, shouldering her as he passed, his holster brushing her hip.

Zelly pictured the gun safe. *Next time, I'll be ready.*

Leon reached for the doorknob, then hesitated. "Tell me what you're doing today."

"I gotta go shopping—"

"You don't need nothing."

"Just groceries." Zelly lowered her eyes. "For tonight."

"Twenty bucks. That's all you get. And speaking of tonight. It's been two days. Wear your fishnets. Maybe that nurse outfit. I'll bring handcuffs."

She recoiled inwardly but forced a smile, managing to complete what qualified as foreplay in the Chadwick household.

Zelly followed her husband outside through a soupy fog which obliterated everything, then watched him crawl into his beat-up Chevy truck. The engine roared to life with a throaty rumble. Strains of hard rock vibrated the truck's glass. Leon rolled his window down, and the unmistakable screeching sounds of AC/DC—both guitar and vocals—split the morning silence.

"I'll see you later," he said.

His words hung like a threat.

~~~~~

CHAPTER 2

Zelly kept herself busy all morning by cleaning the house and doing laundry. She spent thirty minutes watching the news at noon, which she multitasked with nibbling on a tuna fish sandwich. It may have been boring to others, but in her life, boring was wonderful.

Chaos would soon reenter her world, with Dylan coming home from middle school in a few hours. She still needed to go grocery shopping and cook their dinner—*what the heck am I going to make?* Sometime around seven, Leon would make his appearance, with an attitude that could range from detached and surly to loving and apologetic.

She'd deal with him when the time came.

A garbage truck rolled down the street, and Zelly turned at the sound. Peering out through fog that seemed unwilling to dissipate, she saw the truck clip the corner of their trash bin, knocking it over. A crew member hopped out and righted the bin, then signaled the driver, who used the truck's magic arm to pick the bin off the
~~~~~

ground and dump its contents. The man jumped back in, and with a rev of its engine, the truck drove away.

But they'd missed something. A partially torn bag had fallen out of the bin and landed on their driveway.

Oh, no. Leon won't like this.

It didn't matter that she was barefoot and still wearing sweatpants and an old t-shirt, she threw open the door and dashed to the end of the driveway. Garbage littered the concrete. An old pizza box drenched in grease drippings, wet paper towels, some unopened junk mail, a shattered foam egg carton. A light wind was blowing the foam fragments around in little eddy currents.

No, no, no. The trash bin stood against the curb, its lid agape, and she began tossing everything into it. Tears welled in her eyes, the too-familiar panic setting in.

"Hi, Zelly!" a cheery voice called.

The voice belonged to Betty Losenkopf, her next-door neighbor, who was noisily dragging her own garbage can from the curb. Although she wore nondescript clothing over her average, forty-something frame, Betty stood out in a crowd, her makeup liberally applied with trowel and paintbrush, possibly a caulk gun.

"You're supposed to let the trash guys do that," Betty said.

"It's okay," she replied, pushing down the panic. "I like to think of it as the highlight of my day."

"You're funny. Hey, we haven't seen you guys around much."

Well, I have a cage. "We stay pretty busy," Zelly lied. "Sometimes we get away for the weekend."

"Ooh, speaking of weekends. Did I tell you about what happened?"

Zelly stared blankly.

"Alex and me?" Betty was married to Alex Losenkopf, a professional of some sort, an accountant or computer whiz, a guy you'd order out of a *Perfect Husband* catalog. "Last Saturday, we celebrated our tenth anniversary. He gave me a huge bouquet of red roses and one of those half-day spa treatments. He's so romantic." Betty moved closer, her voice dropping to a conspiratorial level. "We spent all weekend in bed."

"Good for you." Zelly's weekend had gone differently, as Leon had enjoyed two hours on a barstool and, later, two minutes in the sack. She hadn't enjoyed anything.

Tornado barked and nosed Zelly's leg. Reaching down and rubbing his head, she said happily, "Did you follow me out here, boy?" His tail thumped against the trash can. She hugged him tightly, swept up in his boundless affection.

Then she sighed. "Betty, I need your help."

"Whatcha need, sweetie?"

"I want to cook a nice meal tonight. Bit of a tight budget, though. I'm at a total loss."

"You're so sweet. You know, I have a recipe for chicken spaghetti that's simply amazing. There's a drawback, though. Stuff works like Thanksgiving turkey. One big plate of Betty Spaghetti, and your man'll just drift off to sleep." Betty cackled. "But that won't be any fun."

Zelly pondered a moment. "So, can I have the recipe?"

* * *

By afternoon, the fog had finally relented, thanks to a cold front blowing through. The cloudless sky was now a rich cerulean. Zelly chopped mushrooms on a butcher block cutting board and peered out the box window above the sink. Her gaze slid past long-forgotten aloe vera plants and miniature cacti imprisoned in garage-sale crockery, past the window's burglar bars, and toward the concrete intersection of their aging subdivision.

Kansas is so different now. Back when she was a little girl known as Giselle to her family, back before she became a rebellious teenager and changed her name to be "edgier," Zelly used to sit in her momma's lap and watch the wheat stalks wave like grasses of an African savannah.

Zelly set down the knife and moved to the stove, where penne pasta cooked in a dented pot. Onions sautéing in the skillet filled the room with a pleasant, pungent aroma. A three-pound roasted chicken cooled on a plate at the kitchen table, next to a grocery bill for nineteen dollars and forty cents.

The back door opened, and Tornado padded in, followed by Dylan. Her son looked sullen, as usual, dark hair hanging low over his eyes. His denim jacket was covered with patches of Metallica, Foo Fighters, and My Chemical Romance. Dylan had the temperament of a high schooler, but he wouldn't celebrate his thirteenth birthday for another six months.

"I'm hungry." Dylan scowled at her and threw his backpack on the floor.

"We'll eat in a couple hours. I'm cooking dinner."

Dylan made a sour face. "You? Forget it." He retreated to the adjoining room and fired up *Call of Duty* on his gaming console.

Zelly followed, almost tripping over the dog. "Your dad said he's taking you hunting this weekend."

"That's the plan," Dylan said, slipping on a pair of wireless headphones.

"You like hanging out with your dad?" When he didn't respond, she tapped him on the shoulder. "Dyl?"

He yanked off his headphones. "What the hell, Mom?"

"Sorry, I was . . . How was your math test?"

"It's a stupid class. I hate school." He rushed away, toward the stairs, then stopped and scrunched his nose. "What stinks?"

Zelly looked back to the kitchen. Thick smoke rose from the stove.

"Oh, no!" She rushed to the skillet, where now-black onions threatened to burst into flames. Water from the pasta foamed over and vaporized with a hiss. When she turned off the burners and lifted the pot of boiling water, steam scalded her hands and arms. She yelped and dumped everything into the trash.

Tears rolled down her cheeks as she ran cold water over her reddening palm. The burning pain spread deeper. Then an image of Leon filled her mind, laughing at her in one moment, yelling at her in the next.

"I gotta make this work," she mumbled. "Dig up money from somewhere and go to the store again." She turned to fetch her purse, then gasped.

Tornado stood atop the kitchen table, paws splayed across the surface, his face shoved deep inside the chicken. He gnawed furiously, nudging the plate to the table's edge, where it crashed to the floor.

"No!" She pushed the dog off the table, and he scurried across the room. "Dammit. Now guess who he's gonna blame." Throwing open the door, she thrust an angry finger. "Get out!"

As Nado slinked into the back yard and gazed mournfully through the window, Zelly couldn't help but feel sorry for him. He hadn't done anything out of malice. "It's okay, buddy, I forgive you," she said softly as she opened the door and tossed the partially devoured bird outside. "All yours."

As she watched, Nado attacked the carcass again, making guttural noises as he ripped meat from bone, gulping without chewing. Bones cracked as his jaws tore apart the chicken.

Then Nado suddenly stopped and hunched over, attempting to cough something up. He fell onto his side, convulsing as if in the throes of dry heaves. His eyes bulged in panic.

Oh, my God.

"Nado? Nado!"

She raced outside and shoved her hand down the dog's throat. As his jaws clenched on her wrist, she swept her fingers to dislodge what was choking him. She withdrew her hand. Blood seeped from two puncture wounds.

Zelly dropped to her knees and pressed on the dog's chest. *Is this how you give CPR?*

Minutes passed as she tried to revive him. Exhausted, she collapsed to the concrete. Beside her was Nado. She stroked the dog's fur and wept.

"I'm so sorry, Nado. I didn't mean it."

The door opened. Dylan poked his head out. "Dad's on the phone. He wants to—oh, shit."

"Nado just—"

"Mom! What did you do?"

"Nothing. I—"

"Dad's on the phone."

Her breaths came in rapid, shallow bursts. "This can't be happening."

Dylan held his forehead with both hands. "What did you do?"

Zelly stared at the dog. Leon's dog. The one she'd failed to save. *Failure has consequences.*

Dylan handed her the phone when she came inside. "I didn't say anything," he whispered.

"Um . . . Hi, Leon." Blood droplets fell from her hand to the floor.

"Good news. Got off early. Be home in half an hour. What are you making?"

Zelly gaped at the dead dog and ruined kitchen. In a shaky voice, she said, "It's a surprise." Then she hung up.

What now? Stay home and get beaten half to death—maybe worse? Or take the step she'd only dreamed about? Her cage door was ajar.

"What's Dad gonna do?" Dylan asked, his eyes wide with fear.

She ran to her purse. "You've got five minutes. Grab whatever you can. We're leaving."

* * *

Rodney Walther is the award-winning author of two bestselling novels. In his books, he explores themes of loss, regret, and second chances. The winner of seven writing awards across the country, Rodney now spends his retirement days driving a tractor, playing with grandkids, and making up stories. ~~ RodneyWalther.com

UnPublished Novel - Mystery/Thriller - 2nd Place Michael Avery

Mama's Boy

Chapter 1

The roar of a shotgun blast echoed through the apartment, ripping William Jackson from sleep. He bolted to a sitting position in his bed, clutching a wool throw close to his chest. The boy crouched forward, listening for something, anything, to explain what was happening. Silence. Then the sound of running feet slapping the floor in the back of the apartment. A door opened and was slammed shut.

William called out, "Dad! Dad, are you all right?" No answer.

He cautiously stood up. He was fully dressed, sneakers on his feet. He hadn't meant to fall asleep. He was supposed to be at a friend's house, watching a Celtics game. His mother had gone out, he didn't know where. He shouted again, "Dad!" When he heard nothing, he crept to the living room where he'd left his father watching TV.

Ralph Jackson was splayed against the couch, a gaping hole in his chest. His mouth hung open. Blood had gushed from his body to the floor. William gasped and erupted into tears. A shotgun lay on the floor near the door to the hallway that led to the kitchen. William ran down that hall. A window gave the boy a view down the street. A figure ran to the corner. It made the turn and disappeared around the block. William continued to stare out the window for a couple of moments. No one else appeared.

William stumbled back to the living room. His father was beyond help. He picked up the shotgun and examined it. It was an alien device. He'd never held a firearm in his hands before. *I need to call 911*, he thought. His phone was in the bedroom. He took a step to get it. With a loud crack, the front door burst open. The door hung awkwardly on its hinges. Two uniformed police officers, guns in their hands, charged into the room.

"Drop the weapon!" one screamed.

William let the shotgun fall from his hands. One of the cops grabbed him and took him down to the floor. He yanked the boy's hands behind his back and cuffed him. The officer rolled him over and looked him up and down.

"It wasn't me!" William shouted. "I didn't shoot him. He's my dad."

The policeman looked at Ralph Jackson's body. "Sure as hell looks like you did," he said. "You had the gun in your hands. You're under arrest."

The cop took a card from his pocket and read, "You have the right to remain silent. Anything you say can and will be used against you in a court of law. You have the right to an attorney. If you cannot afford a lawyer, one will be provided to you. Do you understand these rights?"

William couldn't believe what was happening. He nodded dumbly and started to cry. While the first officer was cuffing him and reading his rights, the other had swiftly cleared the apartment. He returned.

"Nobody else here," the cop said. "Back door is closed and locked. No signs of forced entry. Put him in the cruiser. I'll call it in. We'll wait for backup to secure the scene until detectives arrive."

The officer led William outside to the cruiser, sobbing. The flashing blue lights of the police car produced a surreal spectacle in the dark night as a crowd gathered. A girl shouted out, "William, what happened?" He looked in the direction of the voice but couldn't see anyone. Everything was a blur.

The policeman eased the boy into the back seat, holding his head as he slid under the door frame. When another cruiser arrived, the arresting officers took William to the station at Roxbury Crossing. They booked him, promised to call his mother, and put him in a cell, still crying.

~~~~~

Chapter 2

The early Saturday morning phone call from her boss, Jane Friley, was the last thing Susan Sorella needed. She'd been looking forward to getting things done at home. The apartment was a mess, she was out of groceries, the laundry basket was overflowing, and she needed a haircut. All that would have to wait. Jane, who was skiing in Vermont, wanted Susan to see someone at the jail.

Susan's eyes were red, and her face was lined. She'd spent every day of the past week taking depositions in a police brutality case, and four hours every evening working on a brief for the Court of Appeals. When she wasn't thinking about how to get the cops to admit that fourteen slugs were fourteen more than they'd needed to pump into the unarmed body of her client's husband, she was mentally sorting through the cases in her brief to explain why the search of another client's house was illegal. She'd thought the brief was finished last night but woke up this morning thinking about a counter argument the government would make. Back to square one. In November 2023, she was eight years into her career as a lawyer and had little time for anything else.
~~~~~

She made a cup of coffee and looked down from her third-floor window to the park across the street. She was shocked by the dramatic transformation the early morning had brought to the city as it turned from a dull gray to a glistening white. Snow was still falling. A carpet of five inches dappled with angels made by neighborhood children covered the ground. What in Buffalo or Minneapolis would be but a minor inconvenience had choked the traffic on Boston's city streets. If it was a school day, they'd close the schools.

There's no snow day at the jail, Susan thought. She sat down at her computer and found Jane's email. The client was William Jackson, an eighteen-year-old Black kid from the Roxbury neighborhood, charged with first-degree murder. Although Massachusetts had recently raised the jurisdictional age for Juvenile Court to seventeen, William turned eighteen three days before the crime. He'd be tried as an adult. *That's bullshit,* Susan thought. He's still a child, a senior in high school with little experience of life and an undeveloped prefrontal cortex. In her mind, they should have put the age for Juvenile Court even higher.

She downloaded and read the police report attached to the email. Neighbors had called 911 when they heard a shot from William's house. The dispatcher radioed a cruiser on patrol nearby. It responded immediately. Within moments, cops burst through William's front door and discovered him standing over his father's body, a shotgun in his hands. No one else was in the house. They put cuffs on the boy and hauled him away. He made no statements other than to claim he hadn't shot his father.

Murder. It appeared the client had been caught red-handed. Susan tried to withhold judgment, but she found the case depressing. Making the point that things weren't always what they appeared to be was her stock in trade as a defense lawyer. The D.A. couldn't convict someone based just on a police report. This, however, looked bad. She wondered what William would say.

Susan got dressed, donned her boots, and slipped into a warm down jacket. She examined herself in the mirror located in her front hall, mostly pleased with her appearance. Her deep set dark brown eyes and long lashes created a sense of mystery, particularly given the faint inch-long scar on her left cheek. She stroked the scar, caused by a flying shard of metal when a suspect's car she was tailing exploded. She winced, remembering the pain. In the puffy coat today, she looked like a light blue grenade herself. The outfit wasn't flattering, but everybody would be bundled up.

She plowed through the snow to the T station. Only a few shopkeepers were out to shovel their walks. The cold weather and fresh snow were invigorating. Susan wished it would last but knew it wouldn't. Boston snow quickly became slush. The white blanket on the ground would melt and get dirty. It would stay nice in the suburbs north and west of Boston, but Susan was a city girl. Her heart was in the North End, the Italian section of town. That's where she'd grown up and still lived near her father's restaurant, Gabriella's, named after Susan's mother, who'd died when she was a child.

Susan rode the T to the jail. The oldest subway system in the United States, it had opened in 1897. The grimy trains looked and sounded like it, screeching as they went around curves, the system plagued by frequent service interruptions.

She met her client in the attorney visiting room. William was a handsome kid, dark skinned, tall, and muscular. He wore the standard orange jump suit. Butterfly bandages covered two cuts on his forehead. The fright in his eyes betrayed that he was out of his depth.

"What happened to your forehead?" Susan asked.

William touched the bandages with the fingers of his right hand but didn't answer.

Susan frowned. "You're talking to your lawyer, not one of the guards. You can tell me what happened. If you don't want me to, I won't say anything about it."

William shook his head. "It was nothing."

Susan sighed inwardly. Eighteen-year-olds in the adult jail were preyed upon by older and harder men. Everyone in the system knew it, but very little was done about it.

"Did your mother tell you that your lawyer would be coming to see you?"

William nodded.

"You can be completely honest with me." Susan said, "Without your permission, I can't repeat anything you say, except to my boss and anyone working on your case for our office. We keep everything confidential. We'll defend you, whether you did this or not. You need to know, though, that if you tell me you shot your father, I can't put you on the witness stand to deny it."

William's head was down, looking into his lap. "I didn't shoot him," he mumbled.

Susan didn't want to dive into that yet. "I'd like to know something about you. Do you have any brothers or sisters?"

"No."

"What about school? Where do you go?"

"Jeremiah Burke."

"What year are you in?"

"Senior."

"Do you like school?"

William shrugged. "It's okay."

This is like pulling teeth, Susan thought. She hadn't talked to a teenager in a while.

"Do you have any problems at school?"

"Not really."

"What do you mean, not really?"

"High school is, you know, something you gotta go through. My grades are good, but it's not easy."

Susan nodded. "I remember. I couldn't wait to get out. What bothers you about it?"

William ran his fingers over his buzz cut hair. "There's pressure. Gangs. Drugs. Grades. The whole social thing."

"How do you deal with that?"

"I mind my own business."

Susan realized it would take a while to establish a relationship with this boy. Better get on to the case. See what he says about that.

"To defend you, I need to know your side of the story. What happened that night when you got arrested?"

William described how he'd been awakened by a shotgun blast, found his father dead in the living room, and seen someone running down the street from the kitchen window.

The "some other dude did it" defense, Susan thought. She leaned forward in her chair. "What did the person running away look like?"

"It was dark. They were wearing pants and a jacket, that's all I know."

"Were they white or Black?"

"I couldn't tell."

"A man or a woman?"

"Couldn't see."

Susan made some notes. William's description of the killer wasn't much to go on. And who knew if he was telling the truth?

"Do you know what time it was when all this happened?"

"When I got up, the clock next to my bed showed eight o'clock."

"What did you do after you saw the person running down the street?"

"I ran back to the living room to check on my dad. He was dead. There was nothing to do." William closed his eyes and shook his head. "Blood was everywhere. On him, the floor, the couch behind his body. A shotgun lay there. I picked it up."

"Why did you do that?"

"I don't know."

"Were you afraid the person who shot your dad might come back? Did you pick up the gun to protect yourself?"

William didn't take the hint. "I just picked it up."

"Then what happened?"

"The cops came through the front door, waving their guns and shouting for me to drop the weapon. I did. They threw me to the floor and handcuffed me."

"Did you tell them about the person who ran out the back?"

William hesitated, then spoke haltingly. "No. One cop read me my rights. He made it sound like I shouldn't say anything. I didn't know what to do. They said I was under arrest for murder. I was scared. I just said I didn't shoot my dad."

Susan didn't buy it. If he was telling the truth about the killer going out the back and running down the street, he would've wanted the cops to chase them. She could already hear the prosecutor cross-examining William: "You didn't tell the police about this mystery killer when they arrived? You didn't tell them about the person who shot your father when they still might have had a chance to catch him?"

Susan knew it wasn't wise to take everything her clients said at face value. They'd do a neighborhood canvass to see if anyone saw someone running down the street in case William was telling the truth. She doubted anything would show up.

The boy was shaking. "Can you get me out of here? It's scary. I'm afraid something bad will happen."

Susan put her hand on his shoulder. "Why don't you tell me what happened to your forehead?"

He looked down into his lap, then up at Susan. "Some guy who knew my parents had a liquor store figured I'd get money in my commissary account. He wanted me to buy some stuff for him. I said no, and he smashed my face into the wall. Lucky for me a guard came along."

"What did you tell the guard?"

"I said I tripped and fell. Please don't tell them what really happened, or things will get worse."

"Don't worry, I won't. Do you have any friends in here from outside?"

"There's a couple of kids from Burke. I'm a little friendly with one of them, but they deal drugs and I'm not into that."

"You're a big guy. That might help. Try to get some friends—guys who don't need anything from you."

"Can I get bail?"

"We'll try our best, but it's rarely granted when the charge is murder," Susan said. "I'm sorry, but you'll probably have to stay here until your trial. Don't talk to anyone at the jail about your case. There are a lot of snitches in here. You don't want somebody showing up at your trial, lying and saying you admitted you were guilty. That happens too often, and we don't want it to happen to you."

Susan left and headed home. It had stopped snowing. She walked across town instead of taking the train to give herself a chance to think about William's story. Jane would want to know if Susan believed their new young client. If he was telling the truth, she couldn't understand why he picked up the shotgun or why he didn't tell the police about the person running down the street.

* * *

Michael Avery
Education: B.A. and L.L.B., Yale; M.F.A. Bennington
Profession: Civil Rights and Criminal Defense Lawyer; Law Professor, Suffolk Law School, Boston; Writer
Book Publications: *We Dissent: Talking Back to the Rehnquist Court; The Federalist Society; Police Misconduct: Law and Litigation; The Cooperating Witness; Murder in Blue*

UnPublished Novel-Mystery/Thriller - 3rd Place **John Riley**

Deadrun

CHAPTER 1

Pasadena, California Thursday, June 15, 1977

The last thing he wanted to see was more dead men.

As Rescue Team One sped along a closed section of the new Foothill Freeway, Training Officer Dru Barlow, age 36, glanced at his rookie partner, Janis Carson, the city's first female firefighter. If they could save lives today, their tomorrow together would be a double celebration.

They swerved around retreating cement mixers and halted at a Maginot Line of construction barriers. Dru radioed the dispatch center; "We're on the scene, topside, as directed."

The duo sprinted to the canyon's edge. The forms and shoring for a new bridge had collapsed as the concrete was being poured, leaving a mammoth gap in the unfinished expressway. Earthy odors of wet cement and shredded lumber drifted up from the chasm.

"Stay with me," Dru called to Janis. "We caught a big one."

From high above he surveyed the destruction. Miniature-looking engine companies, arriving Code 3—all red lights, sirens, and air horns—disgorged rescue workers in full turnout gear. They skirted mounds of fresh concrete and clambered over torn timber. Twisted I-beams and rebar punji stakes added to the war zone impression. Something bitter assaulted Dru's mouth, as if he were back in the jungles of Vietnam. He pinched the old bayonet scar under his shirt.

He radioed Captain James "Toots" Tooshaz, a guy with walking-around sense and the balls to use it. "Rescue One to Engine One: Status report?"

"We're in the bottom of the canyon. Six men buried, no sign of life. The concrete foreman says that's all of 'em. You and your partner stay up there on lookout."

"Ten-four." Dru jammed the portable radio back in his belt holder.

Saving lives today would have made Janis a favorite for rookie of the year and contributed to her acceptance by holdouts on the crew. Now, they'd have to wait for the next big one. He liked accolades too, but to narrow the gap between lives he'd ended and lives he'd saved was even better.

Noise from working men and equipment funneled up from the canyon bottom. The partners strode to the edge of the precipice. A helicopter circled overhead.

Only rebar remnants of the collapsed bridge remained, high above the crews working below. Like bony witch's fingers clawing the air, the concrete-coated, dangling bars projected out from the ends of the new freeway on both sides of the canyon.

"Danger from falling material," Dru shouted to Janis. "Call Dispatch and confirm all choppers are kept away from the site."

"Will do." Janis wiped the palms of her hands on her pants and grabbed her radio. The heavy turnout gear hid a bronze, toned body that confirmed an off-duty surfing obsession. Sun-bleached hair peeked around the edges of a dark helmet, her blue eyes barbed arrows piercing his heart.

Since they couldn't save anyone on this call, staying up top was best for Janis. Still a rookie, she'd be spared the ugliness of multiple-body recovery this early in her career—lifeless eyes and gaping mouths—the dark spirits that haunted his nights. She'd now have time to further settle in before confronting mass casualties, where the best intentions got overwhelmed, life-saving training went unused, and daydreams of heroism were put on hold.

"Keep your guard up, Janis. Be ready for anything."

Rising air carried whiffs of desert sage mixed with the stench of summer smog. He rubbed his stinging eyes, then squinted in the strong sunlight.

"Looky-loos, ten o'clock high," Janis shouted as she gestured across the gorge at homes clinging to the steep hillside.

A gaggle of young people in speedos and bikinis, all hoisting beer bottles, crammed a narrow deck. Some gestured and bellowed down at the wreckage, like they'd discovered Farrah Fawcett on location. Others yipped and howled at a pair of displaced coyotes advancing up the steep embankment.

"Tragedy as entertainment," Dru said. He reached to hug Janis but dropped his arms. She smiled back, mimicking his crooked smile. How'd he get so lucky? She often told him she adored his robust good looks and quirky sense of humor. And who was he to argue?

So far, their year-long relationship was known only to their closest friends, but that was about to change. At Malibu tomorrow—after she'd surfed and they'd frolicked—he'd ask her to marry him. Flush with big-wave success, he was sure she'd coil around him like a slightly mad mermaid and accept his proposal. Then, in three more days, after her probationary period ended, their unlikely pairing could finally go public.

But, enough of this. Something seemed off.

The partners looked over the edge of the cliff. A cement-coated length of rebar dipped lower than the others, half obscured by a patch of smaller bars cross-wired in a grid. He beckoned Janis to follow. They skirted the edge of the abyss to get a better angle.

"Man impaled!" Dru yelled. "Close, but out of reach." He pointed to Janis's radio. "Tell Toots what we've got. Have him clear out everyone below us."

Next, he shouted to the injured laborer. "Don't move! *Tranquilo. ¿Como se llama?"*

"*Gustavo*," came the barely audible reply. The man's dark, glossy hair and olive skin contrasted with his white, sunlit T-shirt. "I have . . . *esposa y hijo."*

"We'll save you."

But how? One thing for sure, losing this guy was not an option—he'd lost enough men in 'Nam.

The laborer's torso was suspended face up over the canyon, like a victim of Vlad the Impaler. His legs drooped and his arms dangled in space. The end of the thick rebar penetrated the crotch of his work pants and passed under his shirt and tool belt. Blood trickled down one arm, gathered on his fingertips, and surrendered to gravity.

Dru machine-gunned through a mental checklist and ruled out nearby heavy equipment as unworkable. What about the crane trapped in the debris in the bottom of the canyon? He radioed Toots and learned the operator was in the cab, ready if needed.

Janis was Dru's first choice to help in a rescue. She was smart and capable and had mastered fire service operations and procedures. She lacked experience in large-scale rescues, but so did everyone else on the crew.

He scanned the shaft impaling the laborer and confirmed the bar's size: a number eight, an inch thick. Plenty strong enough to hold him and Gustavo.

"Five men lost, Janis, but this one's ours. Ready to earn your stripes?"

"Absolutely." She followed Dru's lead and shed her bulky turnout coat.

"Call Toots. I need him and his radio in the cab of that crane down there. Gonna make you a lifesaver, partner."

"Shall I alert the Battalion Chief?" She pointed to her radio.

"Negative. Only call Toots."

"What if the boss-man jumps me later? I'm still on probation."

"Refer him to me."

"But he's . . . he's in charge."

"We need action, not over-thinking the problem. I want the Chief busy in the bottom of the canyon as long as possible."

"Also, radio Toots to have the operator boom his cable up here," Dru said. "Then have Wade Jenkins sent to me on the double."

"What? Why that guy?"

"I'll tell you tomorrow over lunch. Now grab three rescue belts off our rig. Chop-chop."

He ran to the cutting torch in the back of a nearby utility truck. After confirming the cylinders were full, he checked the hoses were long enough to reach the victim. He raced back.

"Progress report?"

"Got the belts, cable's coming, and Jenkins is on his way up." Beads of sweat dotted her face.

Dru drummed his fingers on Janis's helmet. "Now listen up. I used to work the high iron before I joined the department. I want you to mount the cable tension weight—the headache ball. It's safe but scary. Some iron workers ride it without a safety belt. I'm even guilty of that."

"You want me to stand on what?"

"That round iron mass with a hook on the end. It keeps the crane's lifting cable hanging straight down. Looks like a giant plumb bob."

"Oh, that."

"I'll climb out on the same rebar the guy's skewered on. Together, we're going to set him free. We'll both be in safety belts. I'm confident I can do my part. You have to decide now if you're up for this. If so, I'll go over the details. No one will fault you if I pick one of the guys instead."

She looked into the deep canyon, then stared at the victim. "Let's do it."

"Copy that. But know this: My first priority is your safety." He pointed to the rescue belts in her hands. "Buckle yours on gut-busting tight. Rotate the D-ring to your rear. Back up to the cable and snap the hook in place before you step onto the ball. That way you're free to use both hands while you lean forward. Once I'm out on the bar and headed toward you, strap the second belt on Gustavo. Make sure you trap the rebar against his body. Hook him to the cable between your legs. Use your radio to direct the crane operator. My hands will be full, so I won't be able to respond. Move slowly, don't out-hustle your head."

"Task saturation leads to accident investigation," Janis said. "But seriously, I'm a bit scared." She cracked her knuckles.

"That's okay, so am I. Try to think excited—a similar emotion. Like when you bust that giant surf. Ride the cable the same way."

"Right. And tomorrow we'll walk on air instead of sand, on our way to the waves." She tightened her helmet's chin strap.

"Stage yourself behind Gustavo's head, but not too close. We don't wanna spook him."

Dru used his radio to issue a command for the crane operator to hoist the headache ball into position.

Once hooked in place, Janis thrust her hands behind her back and clutched the cable. She nodded like a rodeo rider ready to leave the bucking chute.

Dru radioed the operator. "Take her away!"

He saluted Janis as the crane powered her off the roadway. But, at times like this, he wished he still believed in prayer.

CHAPTER 2

No turning back now.

The crane swung Janis toward Gustavo. Dru felt like peeing his pants, always a good sign when the stakes were so high. Plus, adrenalin kept his mind alert.

Wade Jenkins came running up.

There were times to use this man's vast knowledge of tools and rigging and to ignore his boorish personal opinions for the sake of the mission.

"Jenkins, I need a torch-wrangler I can trust. I'm heading out on the rebar. Feed me the hose with only a little slack. Soon as I burn off the bar, I'll ditch this thing and you shut 'er down at the cylinders. Can't have a brush fire on the canyon walls roasting my ass."

"Not so fast," Jenkins said. "Once your gal's got Poncho gift-wrapped, just whack that steel boner off back here. That's a lot safer."

"No can do. There'd still be a long length of cantilevered rebar ripping him up inside. This way, only a short hunk of bar will remain for the doctors to remove. And his name's Gustavo. He's got a wife and kid."

"Whatever." The man's frown made him look like a shelled walnut. "Level with me now. Is your gal up to snuff?"

"Firefighter Carson outscored everyone at the Fire Academy. I requested she be assigned to my rescue squad. She's more than ready."

Jenkins raised his hands over his head like he was held at gunpoint. "It's your story and you're stuck with it."

Dru shook his head. Gotta jump on this shit early. Firehouse scuttlebutt implied Janis was the department's token woman, but only half a real firefighter.

"What pressures you want?" Jenkins asked. He didn't make eye contact.

"Gas at ten, forty-five on the oxygen. Now hand over your Bic."

Jenkins produced a disposable lighter. He peered over Dru's shoulder. "All hail the Chief!"

"What is going on here, Barlow?" The raspy voice carried a familiar bureaucratic cadence.

Dru didn't respond.

"Well?" The Chief made one syllable sound like two.

Battalion Chief Hillard was short and beefy with powerful arms and lots of practiced poise. His graying hair gave him the look of experience without a loss of vigor. He had a habit of standing too close to anyone he addressed. The stink of cigarettes was always present.

"We are rescuing a man."

"Better elaborate. And drop the attitude." The Chief's pupils sparked like a chisel held to a bench grinder.

"I'm heading out there to join my partner and save a life."

"Too risky. Miss Carson is our first—"

"Time is running out here, Chief."

"I'll call for a second crane. And quit interrupting me." He poked his badge with a stubby finger.

"It's rush hour. And there's long setup time. We have to consider worsening shock, internal injuries, and the victim could freak out."

"What we have here is a textbook example of the risk-benefit ratio." The Chief sounded like he was narrating a training film for the State Fire Marshal's office.

"He's dying while we debate."

The Chief sucked in his gut as he hiked up his pants. He stared at the Channel 5 News van parked behind police barricades. "Even though this is a question of policy . . ." He spread his legs wide, drew in a deep breath, and coughed. "Look, Barlow, I know you make good calls, but—"

"Always have."

The Chief again glanced over his shoulder. "Okay, okay. I won't order you to stand down, but I *could.* If this thing goes sideways, my reservations are so noted. I'll go give the news crew an update before I head back down."

Dru keyed his radio. "Janis, go! Over and out."

"Ten-four."

His thoughts sped like a wind-driven brush fire. He'd blown too much time dicking around with the Chief. Same for trying to convince Wade Jenkins to listen up.

Final assessment time: Dark glasses? Check. Gloves? No, grip was key. Rescue belt? Yes. Janis? In position. Gustavo? Calm, survival likely. He again confirmed the cliffside end of the rebar was firmly embedded in previously cured concrete.

Dru cracked open the acetylene valve and lit the sweet-smelling gas. A long flame roared from the tip. As he added in the oxygen, he adjusted the blazing tail to a hotter, pointed one. Got to protect the flame. Can't relight out in space balanced on a knobby steel rod, holding on with one hand, clutching a heavy industrial torch with the other. He draped the hoses over his right shoulder to lighten the weight on his arm and for a clean castoff when the time came.

He eased down on the bar and clipped his rescue belt to it. Wiping his free palm on his shirt, he took a deep breath and clamped his hand around the rod.

Tugging himself forward, he thrust his legs out and back in a herky-jerky rhythm. His boot strayed near the flame. He smelled burning rubber and angled the torch away.

The bar lurched lower. He teetered off balance and fought to right himself.

Leaning out, Janis reached the rescue belt toward the impaled man.

As Dru edged closer to the victim, sweat blurred his vision. He tasted brine. His arm trembled as he advanced the bulky torch. He'd have to work fast once the guy was secured.

Gustavo awoke from a shock-induced torpor, lashed out at the air, and slid forward on the rebar.

"*¡Alto!*" Janis shrieked. She snatched back the safety belt.

Dru lowered the loud, hissing torch as much as he dared. The hoses slithered off his shoulder. His arm burned and he stifled a cry of pain.

The rod bounced under the weight of both men. Gustavo slipped closer to the end of the rising and sinking bar.

Straining against her rescue belt, Janis yelled something to the victim. He stopped flailing his limbs and raised his head.

She again extended the belt. Her hands shook.

Gustavo craned his neck and clawed at her.

Dru hurled the cutting torch into the void. He jerked the radio from his belt. "Crane operator, bring her in now!"

Gustavo howled and seized her wrists. Janis jolted away reflexively, yanking him the rest of the way off the bar.

The heavy victim whipped Janis forward and down. Her feet flew off the headache ball and her inverted body slammed down on it. The unused rescue belt streaked out of sight.

The hanging pair resembled trapeze artists who'd switched places—the smaller, lighter person being the catcher. At least Janis was anchored to the cable. But could Gustavo hold on? The laborer flexed his arms, like he was doing pull-ups, head-butted Janis's helmet, and kicked his legs like a man being lynched.

The crane operator started moving the dangling pair toward safety.

On the canyon's bank, Wade Jenkins leaned out, waving his arms. A police officer held the back of his pants.

Janis flung her legs wide apart.

Dru's eyes locked on her rescue belt. Too low on her body, around her hips instead of her waist! And Gustavo controlled her hands.

The victim's heavy body wrenched Janis's slim hips through her belt. Only her V-shaped legs stopped the pair from plunging into the void.

"Fight, fight!" Dru cried. *Please, God, please—anything!*

Janis raised her head. Her wild, pleading eyes met his.

* * *

John Riley
"I'm a former Fire Captain and NASA coordinator with a B.A. in Anthropology and an M.A. in Fine Art. I'm also a notorious bull-running survivor, once featured on network TV for saving my twin brother's life. In addition to writing, I enjoy creating welded metal sculptures."

UnPublished Novel – Mystery/Thriller Honorable Mention **T.K. Sheffield**

The Infinity Thieves

The Chronicles of Dr. Bonnie Law, Vigilante Veterinarian
"I could do terrible things to people who dump animals by the roadside."
~Dr. James Herriot

Chapter One

Bonnie Law stole plenty in her life: hearts, glances, second base in softball. Candy from her sister's Halloween stash.

Sissy had it coming. That girl never learned to share, not even one piece of fruit-stripe gum. Fifty years later, she still couldn't.

But Bonnie Law never stole ideas. Or horses. That kind of thievery was wrong, plain and simple. She was driving a one-ton dually in pouring rain. Two hundred thousand miles on it. The truck, not the rain.

A trailer with a living quarters and box stall was hitched behind the truck. As Daddy used to say, "It was a waste of a dually's time and engine for it not to pull 161omething'."

The trailer was packed with Bonnie's stuff, like, all her stuff. Its one closet had her clothes, softball mitt, and her good pair of boots, Luccheses with rhinestones. When Bonnie pulled those on and started two-stepping, a man's heart didn't stand a chance.

An older man's heart. Fellow in his prime. Sixty and above. A hottie with wrinkles and age. They were smart and cute by then.

The trailer's medicine cabinet held what was left of her vet career: A stethoscope custom-fit for her ears and a tricked-out First Aid kit. (Her other kit, the Last Aid one, was hidden. Its location was Need-to-Know basis only.)

Way in the back was—drumroll, please—almost a ton of horseflesh. Eighteen hands of muscle and sass. Clyde, a bay gelding with snow-white stockings and kohl-rimmed eyes, seduced his share of looky-loos.

Clyde kicked sometimes. No one should approach him without asking first.

Bonnie was aware she and Clyde, the Clydesdale-mustang cross, were alike.

The truck's wipers slapped back and forth. Sheets of rain pooled like oil, then slid across the windshield like grease. She gripped the truck's wheel. Dusk in a rainstorm. Worst time to drive. No contrast between the gray road and the sky.

Fourth of July traffic, too. People drove too fast for the conditions. Even the backroads of southwest Wisconsin were jammed with summer travelers.

She passed a sign: House on the Rock, two miles.

The place was Bonnie's destination for the weekend. She'd always wanted to tour the southwest Wisconsin attraction. She learned about it decades ago while growing up in Oklahoma. It was a cross between a house and a James Bond film. Rooms of weird stuff: Galleries of jewels, doll houses, and firearms. Also, a two-story circus carousel and a giant sea creature fighting an octopus—all under one roof!

To tour it would be a dream.

No, a nightmare.

What wasn't to love about that?

Bonnie also wanted to walk the Infinity Room, an enclosed walkway attached to the House on the Rock, and live to talk about it. Innocents walked a glass plank suspended over the Wyoming Valley. It was like striding over a pine-tree-filled Grand Canyon without a net. Rumor was half the walkers made it. The other half, well, no one knows, and the locals wouldn't talk about it.

Bonnie smiled, relishing the adventure ahead. She and Clyde would ride in Dodgeville's Fourth of July parade, too. Clyde had heard about the parade somehow. (Horse campgrounds can be gossipy.) Before leaving their site in Illinois, he'd refused to load and pawed like crazy.

Bonnie had to figure out what the horse wanted. Of course it was to wear his blingy parade saddle and silver bridle to prance for a crowd. Clyde could be a real diva when he wanted. *She rarely argued with him. The horse's Clydesdale half was reasonable. The Mustang half, well, it depended on the day.*

She looked in the side mirror. A convertible sports car had been riding her bumper like a burr to a sock. The smart alec flashed his lights, then pulled out to pass.

Idiot.

She took her foot off the gas. Her rig slowed, the heavy trailer dragging her back. Idiot sped by in his two-seater, then swung back to her lane. Up ahead, a minivan making a left turn stopped on the road. Idiot was going too fast! He braked to miss the minivan but fishtailed, hydroplaning on the slick pavement—*rats, he was gonna rear-end 'em!*

Sure enough, the little stinker's fancy hood emblem kissed the mini's "Tommy Bartlett Water Ski Show" bumper sticker. Not in a soft, sweet way, but in an ugly way that caused dents and blaring horns.

Bonnie flipped on her safety flashers, her rig a safe distance behind the accident. Idiot pulled onto the gravel shoulder. So did the minivan.

When the minivan got hit, its tailgate popped open. Bonnie spied a black Lab. One second, he was minding his own doggie business, dreaming of snacks—or his blingy parade outfit, maybe—then pop! Everything was different.

From her truck, Bonnie watched the Lab. He'd been closed in, and the next there were muddy fields to run in.

What's a dog gonna do?

"Don't jump don't jump don't jump," Bonnie said.

Out he went, leaping onto the pavement and bounding from the van like a kangaroo. Big dog, but still young. All legs and ears.

She saw an oncoming car. "Please no please no please no!"

The car honked, then swerved and slammed its brakes. The dog shied and then ran—like, sprinted for the next county. Bonnie watched the Lab go up an embankment and down a side road like a coyote after a rabbit.

Bonnie glanced at the roadside. The minivan people were out, yelling at Idiot. She flipped on her turn signal. It was noisy in the cab with the wipers swishing and the blinker clicking.

She eased her rig onto the gravel side road.

Time to rescue a runaway dog.

~~~~

Chapter Two

Bonnie rolled down the side road eyeing Blackie Lab. She'd given him a nickname already. The light was dim. The dog was in a field, zig-zagging between knee-high cornstalks like he was in a pole-bending race.

Uh oh.

A milk tanker barreled toward her. Dairy cows didn't quit; thus, neither did milk runs. Bonnie flashed her headlights, hoping to alert the truck's driver. He'd need an airport runway to stop. If the dog ran in the road and he slammed his brakes, the stainless-steel monster would jackknife and crush Bonnie and Clyde.

"Stay over there, Blackie," she warned. She saw him slow to a trot, sniffing the ground, then the air. He halted, then looked toward the road—no, at her.

Crap, he smelled the horse trailer!

"No," Bonnie begged.

The tanker was coming fast.

The dog took a step, then another.

"Please don't!" she cried.
~~~~

The ground rumbled. The tanker was a sixty-mile-an-hour bowling ball. Bonnie felt like she was in an earthquake. Blackie Lab stepped closer to the road, nose in the air.

"Stay!" she yelled.

WHOOSH!

The tanker blew past like a 747 lifting off a runway. Bonnie's rig shuddered from the force. She stared in the side mirror—Clyde hated tractor-trailers. She looked toward the corn.

Rats.

Blackie Lab had disappeared.

* * *

Bonnie had zero time to find the dog. Another tanker could be coming. Or a speeding truck. Or a holiday partier driving wildly. She scanned the gravel road for fur splotches. Bonnie was a vet. She'd seen lots of those, sadly.

She looked to the cornfield.

There was Blackie, fifty yards off.

He must have shied from the noise. Bonnie cracked the window, then her horse whinnied. Clyde probably anticipated that a campsite was close by after hours on the road. Bonnie braked and felt the horse stomp in the trailer. Not to get graphic, but Clyde did what most horses do when trailers stop. He took a potty break. Dogs were thrilled by that "perfume." Especially goofy ones like Labs.

Bonnie watched Blackie Lab approach, nose in the air. The dog cantered toward the truck, then crossed onto the gravel, trotting toward the wheels like they were magnets.

She threw the truck in "Park," then eased the door open and stepped out. "Here, Blackie," she said.

"WOOF!"

"You're handsome." She scratched the damp gravel with her fingers. "Got hot dogs on the trailer."

He started walking in a half-circle, eyeing her but giving himself an escape route.

Chasing him would be disastrous. He'd bolt off into the farm fields as night fell.

She had to move fast. Bonnie crab-walked to the trailer's door, then unlocked it with the key around her neck. "Stay with me, fella. Don't run," she said.

She flipped on the light, opened the fridge door, and rustled plastic bags, the universal signal for "food was coming." She figured the sound would register on

Blackie's antenna. Sure enough, a face appeared in the doorway. Dark eyes, velvety ears, wet nose twitching.

"C'mon in, fella. Let's have a hot dog," she said.

"RUF."

"Don't worry. They're organic."

"Ruf."

"Gluten-free."

That did it.

He jumped in, sniffing crazily. She opened the hot dogs, allowing the animal to inhale the smell. He stepped toward her, keeping his head and body low, tail tucked.

"Hey, handsome," she said. "Hungry?"

His tail wagged slowly.

"I won't hurt you."

He looked up at her, his eyes soft. He had a collar with a tag.

Bonnie smiled at him. "What's your name, good lookin'?"

* * *

The dog's name was Blackie, sure enough, according to the jingly ID on his collar.

Bonnie called his family, leaving a message. They were still dealing with the van accident, she figured. She dried off the dog and gave him nibbles of food, interspersed with water, as he cooled down.

She checked his vitals. "Nice, healthy dog, aren't you?"

She'd moved the truck and trailer to a lay-by, out of the way of traffic. An hour passed, then Bonnie heard a knock on the trailer door. Blackie woofed. Bonnie put the knocker through her security protocol—never know who could knock on a trailer door at nine-thirty at night. "Who is it?"

A man's voice. "The Petersons. We're here to pick up Blackie?"

"What's the password I told you?"

"Bart Starr, the Packer quarterback."

"What was his jersey number?"

"Fifteen, I believe."

She peeked out the window. The trailer's porch light was on, as were its running lights. In the drizzle, she spied a tall man standing with a tall boy. It appeared the Norwegian apple hadn't fallen far from the Norwegian tree. The boy was all joints and lanky like Blackie. The dad was the person who'd been yelling at Idiot.

She called out, “Spell Ashwaubenon.”

“I could; I know its history related to Lambeau Field and the Packers football team.” He tapped again. “But was spelling part of the password?”

She unlocked the door. “C’mon in.”

Blackie recognized them and bounded over.

“Hey, I missed ya,” the boy said. The dog tackled him, and they rolled toward the gooseneck, becoming a ball of joints, fur, jingly collar, and a plaid shirt.

Dad Peterson said, “Thanks for catching him.”

“No problem.”

“That was scary.”

She nodded. “How’s your minivan? It didn’t run off, too, I hope.”

He sighed. “Just a dent. There’s a good mechanic in town who’ll fix it.”

“I like a town with a good mechanic. Says a lot.” There was a flash of light, then thunder. “Guess that storm’s here.”

Dad P. pulled out his wallet. “I’d like to pay you—”

She shook her head. “No way, no money.”

“But this rig—”

“Isn’t big enough for more. No matter what you pay, I’m not keepin’ the dog or the kid. I’m a sixty-year-old woman livin’ in a trailer with a horse that orders hay like he’s at Starbucks. I got enough trouble.”

The boy piped up. “You live in here? Are you on the run?”

Bonnie preferred it when children didn’t talk. There was a reason why she’d gone to veterinary school and not medical school.

“I might be.”

She winked at Dad P. He pulled out a bill and tried to give it to her.

The kid said, “That’s cool, but my dad’s a parole officer—he’d catch ya.”

Again, Bonnie preferred the child to be silent. She’d been holding a cast iron frying pan, just in case. She held it up. “No, he wouldn’t.”

Dad P. looked around, taking in the gooseneck bedroom, the galley kitchen, and the seating area. “You live in this, Ms. Law?”

She set the pan on the mini-stove. “Sure do. Well, I exist here. The horse does the real livin’.”

Bonnie had left her stethoscope and First Aid kit on the Formica table. The kit had the name of a vet clinic on it.

The boy saw it from where he was on the floor. He lifted to his knees and picked up the stethoscope, letting the rubber cord dangle. "Are you a vet?"

"I was." She squinted at him. "You need one? You're lookin 'a little pale."

The boy smiled. "You're funny, kinda."

"Thanks, kinda."

He crawled up on the bench seat, then patted the cushion. "C'mon up, Black. Hey, lady, I can spell Ashwaubenon. Lambeau, too. Been there, like, with Dad, for a game."

Bonnie smiled. "How about a Wisconsin city like Oconomowoc?"

He reached for his phone.

"From memory, no phone," Dad P. said. "Sound it out, son."

"Use your fingers. That's what I always do." Bonnie held up her hands.

Both guys laughed. Blackie even looked like he got a kick out of that one.

"Ms. Law, are you staying for the holiday weekend?" Dad P. asked. "The parade, the softball tournament, and the amusement park rides? It's a huge festival. Draws folks from everywhere."

"Yeah, I thought we would." She nodded toward the back. "Clyde is crazy for the Tilt-a-Whirl. Can't keep him off of it."

"Clyde is, like, your horse?" the boy asked. "You guys are Bonnie and Clyde?"

She nodded. "You guessed it. Just like the outlaws."

"So cool. I read about you guys, like, in school."

Dad P. scanned the interior again. "Where will you park, Ms. Law? Unless you have a reservation in Governor Dodge Park, and it was made weeks ago, you'll never find a place."

Bonnie wasn't one for reservations. "Well, I—"

"I have a little farm with an old dairy barn with a stall and corral for the horse. You're welcome to stay the weekend."

"I don't know. Clyde's a handful."

"Please, I insist." Dad P. moved closer and lowered his voice. "There's been chatter among law enforcement. I can't believe horse theft is a modern-day problem, but it is. It's like the old west out there—horses, tack, even their hair—are being stolen. We think a ring is working this area."

Bonnie gasped.

Clyde could be at risk?

Thunder rolled again. Rain poured harder on the roof, making a *rat-tat-tat* noise. It sounded like hail. The clatter jangled her nerves. She thought about her personal motto: Use a cast iron skillet first, ask questions later. But a gang of horse thieves—*wow*. That meant a lot of frying pans she didn't have yet.

Bonnie envisioned a dry stall for Clyde. That would be excellent. He'd be out of bad weather and could rest his legs after a long day of travel. He'd also be safe while she toured the House on the Rock. Clyde was too big to be smuggled in. She'd have to leave him for a few hours.

Bonnie wondered if the barn had electricity. She could hook up and not use the generator.

Heck, if thieves were in the area, they'd walk off with that if she parked somewhere random.

She looked at Dad Peterson. "I'll take you up on that offer, sir. Lead the way."

* * *

T.K. Sheffield writes stories for readers to laugh and escape. Her comic cozy mysteries, The Backyard Model Mysteries, are funny whodunnits, mysteries served with a brandy old-fashioned and side of cheese curds. TK is on the board of the Wisconsin Writers Association, and a member of Blackbird Writers and Sisters in Crime.

UnPublished Novel - Mystery/Thriller **Aiden S. Clarke**
Honorable Mention

Sunriver Heart

The iron door shut with finality, an all-too-common metal ka-chunk and a judge's gavel sound playing in her mind made famous on police detective shows. This is why they called it "the slammer", she mused, except it wasn't funny.

Catherine exhaled, turning to face two bone-white cots secured to the wall by chains. Calling them beds would be far too generous, as she wasn't planning on sleeping, nor letting any part of her naked skin touch against the asylum grade sheets if she could help it. Or using the toilet for that matter. Not here.

She wiped her nose on the sleeve of her orange jumpsuit. The joint was empty, dark and smelled like bleach—preferable to the pee smell in the rest of the building.

"This is bullshit," she squeaked to no one. "Can't get any worse though."

Her thoughts turned to her dad. Pastor Cookson loved to preach almost any bad job or unlucky circumstance could be made more enjoyable by re-orienting one's mindset, making it a positive. And sure, when she was a child, she believed it, as well as most any tired axiom her father spouted. The upshot of him being deceased, at least he wouldn't have to endure this latest embarrassment of his daughter's making.

The jail had a row of windows, high-up, barred of course and smudged like shower curtains. Or was it blurry vision? They glowed silver-white, a summer moon the only natural illumination. Speaking of the season, it was boiling hot. Beads of sweat glistened on her forearms and chest. She pushed back her dishwater blonde hair, a tangled flat mess and she had no brush to fix it. Didn't matter. Not like she expected someone pleasant to come visit.

She wished dearly she could blame it on a mis-understanding. At some point during the afternoon, a hot streak of insults escalated into an all-out shouting match. Her intelligence and character had come into question, or she perceived it. And the result: she assaulted a customer with a dinner plate. The snotty rival had taken a sizzling plate of enchiladas to the kisser. Retaliating, the female aggressor slapped Cathy across one cheek—rather weakly—and Catherine clocked her. After this, Miss Cookson stormed out the back, had a smoke under a palo-verde tree and got handcuffed when the cops arrived.

Everyone witnessed it. Just thinking about it made her run her open palms across her face. Was this a prison cell, or was life itself a prison?

Of all the indignities she'd suffered, perhaps the most humiliating, ending up in a police cruiser wearing a waitress uniform. Now that wins first prize. Getting arrested in your stupid work attire introduced a new level of shame.

The root of it all, a combination of rum, high temps and not eating for ten hours.

She put up a hand, breathing onto it and attempting to sniff her own breath. It smelled like garbage. A doctor recently informed her the bloodwork he ordered indicated worsening liver function; she'd kept this grim news to herself.

No use calling anyone now, her pop couldn't rescue her. Perhaps even if he were still kicking, he would refuse; long ago claimed he'd bailed her out for the last time. Said she needed to straighten up. Instead, she leaned her head against the wall, let her knees buckle and gradually slid down until she was in a squatting position. Then she started sobbing.

From there Catherine lost track of time, falling into a light sleep, succumbing.

Hours later ...

"Hey there cowgirl, tell me what happened?"

A compassionate voice, sounding like an angel, whispered to her and roused her from the world of western landscape dreams. She opened her eyes, seeing a ghostly Melinda Martinez—weird old-lady pixie cut hair with a pink headband—kneeling on the hard floor outside the jail cell. An admirable dose of kindness shown in her eyes, and at this odd hour she somehow looked lovely. Lovely in the way of a sixty-year-old who aged remarkably well.

Yet they weren't exactly on the best terms. Hadn't spoken more than a sentence or two in 20 years.

"What're you doing here?" Catherine replied sourly. "Come to see the circus freak?"

Lyndy never had braces yet possessed a killer smile, another thing Cathy resented. The smile remained on her face.

"I'm here to bail somebody outta county jail," stated Lyndy.

"So then, official business?"

"Nope. Here for a friend actually."

Cathy sighed, rolling her bloodshot eyes and folding her arms. "F-you."

"Okay-doke. Wanna stay here and get doused by a firehose, then risk being pricked on a bedspring and catching an incurable disease? Sounds pleasant."

Cathy scowled, muttering a curse word.

Lyndy continued, "Already finished the paperwork cause I'm a pro! You owe me like four-hundred seventy bucks by the way."

"Oh, swell," said Cathy. "Put it on my tab."

"So, what the hell happened?" Lyndy repeated. "You attacked someone?"

Catherine sniffed, staggering to her feet. Then she walked diagonally to the front of the cell while burping. "What's it to you?"

Lyndy frowned. "You sound like you're repeating lines from a renegade biker movie."

Cathy chuckled. A smiled curled on her lips. "Thanks for coming anyway. You're a good enabler … but you're still a bitch."

Thirty minutes later she'd made it back to the free outside world, for the time being.

Cathy exhaled, squinting painfully at the gleaming sun, like a fiery ball of judgement in the morning. She stumbled on her pumps in the gravel. Next, her blurry vision caught sight of the vintage automobile. How was it possible? The same crappy white mustang? Still running? Oh, for god sake! How she once hated that obnoxious car.

Lyndy squeezed on Cathy's shoulder, steadying her. In the back seat waited a young stranger engrossed in a romance novel. The dark-haired girl with purple eyeshadow seemed oddly familiar in many ways.

"Hey. Who's the twenty-year old chick with … like the same haircut and awful fashion sense as you? Someone else you bailed out?"

Lyndy smiled. "Catherine, I want you to meet my daughter Maribel."

Catherine's jaw dropped, her expression morphing to one of utter disbelief.

"I've heard a lot about you," Mari commented, putting down her book. "You worked at The Vanishing Point roadhouse. It was the place to be seen in the eighties."

"Holy crap," said Cathy. She looked at Lyndy with one raised eyebrow. Without words, she was asking many questions.

"Her father is Kyle Ellis," replied Lyndy, twirling the car keys.

"The … the … guy …" Cathy faltered, attempting to overwrite the thoughts which were on a scrolling marquee in her brain: "*your boyfriend whom I slept with behind your back!*" Cathy fumbled awkwardly and finally something sensible and less controversial blurted out: "The guy … with the lake house?"

"Yup," answered Maribel cheerily. "My dad has like five vintage boats."

Lyndy chuckled, shoving rose-tinted sunglasses over her nose.

"Mom constantly reminds me I'm an Ellis, not a Martinez," added Maribel. Then she tilted her chin down to continue reading her paranormal romance book.

Ducking into the front seat, Catherine felt like her whole world order had upended. Not only was her hip, carefree image diminished, now people whom she felt superior to had kids. It was strange to be envious of something The Spitfire had that she didn't. Lyndy was always broke. Yet here it was.

"Lyn, I'm sweatin' like a you-know-what in church. Guessing your old clunker doesn't have AC," complained Cathy, who already felt so overheated she was ready to faint.

"Nope," Lyndy replied.

"Where are we going?"

"You'll see," said Lyndy, sliding into place behind the wheel.

"I hope it's not one of your trailers. Lyn, no offense but your places are all dumps." A long pause. "No offense."

"You're right. Excuse me while I go pick a couple hundred thousand off my money tree. Buy a better house." From the back, Maribel giggled. She knew Kyle had offered to buy her a house, but Lyndy was too proud or stubborn to accept it.

"Fine." Cathy pressed her temple against the A-pillar, then closed her eyes. "Just don't take me to an AA meeting. I beg you."

* * *

Lyndy Life Observation: Here's one of those classic redneck jokes: You might be one if your to-do list includes bailing a friend out of jail today. You know who you are.

If one were prone to migraines, the metal stands of a dirt track might be one of the last places on earth you'd pay to visit. Pandemonium didn't begin to cover this place—made a rave party seem tranquil as a koi pond.

Currently they were running the figure eight rallies. Junkyard cars were racing and meeting in the center, having to honk and feather the gas pedal to zoom their way across a treacherous intersection. Minor collisions happened every thirty seconds. However, in many ways it was the perfect venue to keep Catherine occupied. Lyndy wanted to drag her by her ear to an AA meeting, however in her current state of mind, she'd have more luck getting a feral cat into one of those pet carriers.

Seated a row behind and a yard or two down, Lyndy kept an eye on the dour waitress while she munched on nachos and sipped Mountain Dew. Clearly something deeper was going on. Miss Cookson had battled alcoholism for decades, but she'd never been known to have a violent bone in her body. The idea of her assaulting someone was unthinkable.

A fellow in a giant sombrero and a beer cooler strapped to his chest was picking his way through the stands. Business here was good.

Was discouraging to see her same-age friend like this. Cathy wasn't fat per say, but up til now she'd always maintained an enviable figure. Not anymore. Now the waitress appeared bloated around the mid-section and flabby in the arms; must have gone up several dress sizes. By comparison Lyndy was feeling trim and healthy.

One never wants to tell a friend they look bad, but *damn* girlfriend.

Of course, looks were deceiving. From an amber bottle, Lyndy shook loose a white blood pressure pill, popping it onto her tongue. She washed down the bitter medicine with another sip of cold Mountain Dew. Then she undid the topmost button of her snap cowgirl shirt, which kept things modest but helped cool her torso considerably.

Maribel was here too somewhere, just not in the stands. She'd been keen to make the rounds. Lyndy accepted the fact Mari had become a minor celebrity at the dirt track. Car guys loved talking to her—there were seldom issues of social class, or even race here. And to witness young Maribel interacting with such confidence and grace made Lyndy a proud momma. Would be better if she had the same attitude on the college campus.

Meantime Lyndy continued to search the crowd, having a premonition this night was about to get interesting. Seconds later a confirmation, as her eyes fell upon the stranger. This fellow in a black hat and business suit seemed out of character in the hot-rodder crowd. He had the look of a casino executive, but not the Vegas kind. The ones on Indian land.

He only sat down for a minute or two, as he pretended to watch the races. But she knew he was here for other reasons. He made a sharp turn at the middle aisle, then ascended the steps toward Lyndy's position. Casually, Lyndy set down her tray of nachos.

As he brushed by, he set a business envelope on the empty seat next to her, tipped his hat, then sauntered away. Lyndy's heart began to pound.

She shifted, eyes darting about, wondering if anyone else witnessed this odd event. No one had. Surreptitiously The Spitfire clawed the envelope under her thigh, waiting until the next really loud boom from a crash to distract the crowd. When it finally happened and folks leapt from their seats, she unfolded the letter impatiently, resting the creased note across her lap. Luckily it was in enormous type, as it was nighttime and her eyes were crap. But she could read this one sentence: Miss R. Thurgood requests your presence. Meet at trailer number-19 in ten minutes. Lyndy shoved the paper back inside and folded up the envelope. Good. Lyndy needed money.

Meantime from her purse, Catherine pulled a five-dollar bill. Waving it in the air at the dude selling beers she shouted: "*Senor! Senor! Un tecate por favor*." The Latino man smiled, enthusiastic to pass her the can.

Oh, here we go. Lyndy hopped up out of her seat, diving across and grabbing firmly onto Catherine's wrist with the money to stop her. "She doesn't want it," warned Lyndy, pushing the can away, shooing off the disappointed vendor.

"*Ay caramba*!" said Lyndy, scolding Cathy.

"Sheesh!"

"Come on. Follow me. We need to make our way to the pits."

"What? Why?"

Lyndy shot Cathy a look that said: Just move already.

Catherine gripped the railing, then trotted down the creaky metal stairs moving like a robot—the awkward gold c3po one in Star Wars. Lyndy shook her head, chalking it up to a combo of her shoes, the blue dress she was wearing and the fact of being really inflexible.

"Lyn. Do you think we can stop at a Target to get me a hairbrush and some new clothes?" Cathy complained. "Cause, I feel totally ridiculous."

Maybe don't punch people then!

Circling the crowded pits area, where fatty food trucks intermingled with macho dudes wrenching on cars, Cathy continued to complain. A group of unsupervised kids were toying with dazzling sparkler fireworks and smoke clouded the scene. The whole area smelled of this. The slots were numbered with 12-inch-tall stakes and in large fonts like a fairground. Peering through the fog she was able to locate trailer-19, a non-descript white fifth-wheel style one might find on a movie shoot. Only one outdoor light.

She felt confident in her choice, as a man with long black hair, looking like a nightclub bouncer waited by the door. She glanced back to check on Catherine, though dragging, almost there. "I miss the twentieth century," she was muttering to no one, like a crazy person.

"You wait outside," Lyndy ordered, then she turned her attention to the bodyguard.

He made a motion for her to lift both her arms and be ready for a pat down.

Lyndy objected with a scowl, stating: "No touch! Pal, I'm near sixty years old. What am I gonna do?" Still, she opened her purse so he could see she had no weapons and then smoothed the pockets of her jeans using the palm of her hand. They were empty.

He nodded, pushing open the door for Lyndy as she climbed the set of two stairs.

Cathy turned to face the stands. She glanced to the bodyguard, pointing to a colorful tilt-a-whirl, the only amusement ride on scene, brought in to keep children occupied and out of trouble. "See that?" she queried. The tall man set his gaze toward the ride. "When I was fifteen, I was on one of those, upside down at the highest speed and both my shoes flew off to outer space. I never found em. My dad was P-Od." Then she pulled a vape pen out of her purse to have a puff.

Inside the trailer, Lyndy recognized Miss Thurgood seated at a fold-out dinner table, typing furiously on her laptop. Nearby was a mountain of receipts from ticket sales or her motel business. Across from her, eyes focused on a gritty western TV drama, a younger man she presumed was also a bodyguard. He barely seemed to notice Lyndy.

Rhonda, who'd been born on the Navajo Nation, was all of thirty years old with curly light-brown hair and pink lipstick. Her inch-length fake nails caused her to type in that bad-for-you fingers lifted in the air style. A string of vintage pearls rested upon her dainty collar bone. Completing the ensemble: a fashionable cheetah print headband tamed her "Flashdance" hair.

"Have a seat," Rhonda commanded, not looking up.

Lyndy eyed the bodyguard, who wore a decorated gun holster on his waist. Then eased her way to the fabric couch, a kind with no meaningful back support. Lyndy checked her watch. 9:30. An uncomfortable minute elapsed as no one spoke, giving her time to worry. She clenched one fist around the other, trying to stop herself from fidgeting.

At last, Rhonda pulled herself away, slamming the lid of her Apple computer and locking her green eyes upon Lyndy. "You have impressed us greatly Miss Martinez," Rhonda paused, adding emphasis. "...with your many talents. The praises heaped upon you by The Lovelace Corporation have been found well deserving."

Lyndy always did poorly with compliments. She opened her fist, stared down at her curled fingers. "Yeah, but what you didn't know. I also knit beanie caps and sell them online at a craft website." She waited for a response.

"Wait. Really?"

"No way. Just kidding. That's stupid." Lyndy laughed at her own bad joke.

Rhonda coughed, seeming to politely suppress a chuckle.

"I hear your talents include use of black arts," grumbled the young bodyguard, suddenly switching his attention from the TV to Lyndy. "Witchery."

Lyndy glared back at him in a steadfast, challenging manner. She made no denial. What did he think? She was cheating at a life and death occupation nobody in their right mind wanted to do anyway, and didn't pay very well considering. And who the heck were these people to judge? Come to think of it, who the heck were the "us" in Rhonda's language?

"It doesn't matter how the jobs get completed," asserted Rhonda. "Only that it's done cleanly. And don't use any of that on us."

Rhonda offered a sheet of paper to Lyndy. "This man is wanted by the Marshal Service."

* * *

Aiden S. Clarke was inspired to become a writer after experiencing the wonders of the Mojave Desert on a class trip. He has been actively involved in conservation efforts throughout the Southwest region. His characters represent the blending of unique cultural identities and the resiliency found within all of us.

UnPublished Novel - Romance 1st place T.K. Sheffield

The Valentine Lines

Chapter One

23 December, Mineral Point, Wisconsin

The problem with bakeries that tempt patrons with coffee, a cozy fire, and a goddess-like proprietor resembling Aphrodite and Audrey Hepburn was … nothing, honestly.

Monet's Café was heaven on earth to Cupid. Not that he had the nerve to enter the place. His life would change forever if he did. Cupid, minor god of love, purveyor of arrows, had been struck with one—oh, the irony!

He shuddered, and it wasn't due to the cold temps of Wisconsin. His Aunt Hera, CEO of Mt. Olympus, Inc., would be furious if she knew he'd fallen for the mortal inside the café. Hera once tried to chain her husband to a tree for eternity. What she'd do to Cupid Bartholomew Apollo McGee, junior god, forever stuck in middle management, was frightening to consider.

Cupid stood near the entry door of Monet's Café, peaking inside. For the umpteenth time, he realized his Mediterranean wardrobe was *not* suitable for the wintery conditions of the Upper Midwest. He hadn't planned on staying in Mineral Point, a quaint burg that reminded him of the Cotswolds, yet he'd lingered for two weeks. During the holidays, no less.

He watched a genial-looking fellow select truffles from the bakery case. Monet—she was Eve in a garden of baked goods—placed the chocolates in a gold box and gave them to the man. He paid, then ambled to the exit, approaching Cupid, who stood outside.

Cupid opened the glass door. "Allow me, sir."

The fellow tipped his cap. "Thank you. Merry Christmas."

"Happy Val—er, Holidays, I mean," Cupid replied.

Heavens to Zeus. He must get his greeting straight if he were to reside with mortals as he'd planned.

He pressed against the building, its cold brick stinging like needles through his lightweight jacket. For eons as a relationship engineer, Cupid visited shops like Monet's to inspire romance. He'd enter stealthily, ignoring lattes and cheesecakes while hunting couples to zing with arrows. Sadly, Hera had restricted his travels during the last century due to financial problems at The Firm. Plus, Cupid's job kit was hopelessly outdated—how could a brittle bow and dull arrows compete with dating apps?

Another patron exited. As the door whooshed closed, the aromas of coffee, cinnamon, and vanilla drifted to his nose. *Delicious.* Cupid peered inside, hoping to appear nonchalant while gazing at the display case brimming with goodies. All baked by Monet, of course, a woman with Botticelli-like beauty and the confidence of a lioness.

He watched customers purchase treats and then stream out past him. He guessed the temperature was thirty degrees Fahrenheit and about twenty per hour—gold boxes flying out of the café, that was.

Cupid wanted to grab the door handle—vintage brass, wet with snowflakes—and stroll inside, but he knew what would happen: His life would change as soon as he entered the bakery in the middle of nowhere.

He'd fall in love. His Aunt Hera would have a meltdown. The goddess-CEO forbade fraternization with mortals. Hera controlled Cupid's paycheck and job kit, obsolete as it was. All the handmade chocolates in the world—he *always* brought them for his performance reviews—wouldn't put Hera's temper back in her primal lower cortex, where her leadership skills resided.

Wrath and a drawer filled with Zeus's thunderbolts were how she kept her employees in line.

Cupid glanced into the shop again. Monet mesmerized him, melted his heart like chocolate simmering over a double-boiler.

He *needed* to enter the café.

Despite the risk to his life and livelihood, Cupid Bartholomew Apollo McGee felt ready for love.

* * *

Cupid sat at a table, his hand wrapped in a bandage, a mug of tea near him. He'd grabbed the door handle and entered, all right.

At the same time, a woman wearing overalls and boots stomped out. She'd smelled faintly of horses and wrenched the door from his hand like a tractor towing a car from a ditch. The action ripped skin from his fingers.

"Flying chariots!" Cupid cried. "Ouch!"

Monet heard him scream. She'd grabbed a towel and started over, but then an older woman jumped from her seat. "Let me handle it, Monet. You get back to your customers," she'd said.

Thus, Cupid ended up sitting by the fire, his hand tended by Mrs. Bradshaw, a seventy-year-old charmer wearing a Santa hat and a sweater festooned with reindeer.

She examined his injured paw through half-glasses adorned with crystals. "You'll be fine. Just keep an eye on it for a few days. And, please don't mind Deirdre, the horsewoman you met."

"A horsewoman?" Cupid shook his head. "Surely, the gal is a prizefighter. Must have loads of wins under her belt."

"Deirdre isn't herself. She and her fellow broke up."

"I'm sorry to hear it."

"Would you like more tea? Or another cinnamon roll?"

"No, thank you, Mrs. Bradshaw. I'm fine."

"Call me Mrs. B." She smiled. "You're new here, correct?"

"Indeed."

"Are you single? What's your name?"

Lots of questions. Cupid paused, inhaling to collect his thoughts, then: "I'm Bart. B-Bart McGee."

He always used his middle name with mortals. A bit awkward otherwise. But this time, it felt strange, like it was his real name. Like he'd adopted a new identity.

Yes, as soon as "Bart McGee" walked into Monet's café, despite injuring himself, he felt like he'd changed.

~~~~~

Chapter Two

Christmas Eve Day, 24 December, Mineral Point

Cupid, er, Bart, hadn't played hooky in December in centuries. After Valentine's Day, the holidays were—or had been—his busiest time. He disliked admitting the seasons of good tidings and romance weren't what they used to be.

Dating apps changed everything.

Bart stood in the lobby of The Palace Hotel, a lodge across from Monet's café. It was seven o'clock in the morning, still dark. Vintage lamps on the street flickered like firelight. He wanted to dash over and chat but would *not* act like a lovesick puppy. Overeagerness, or slip-ups like forgetting his new name, could end his plan of romancing the baker and relocating to the village.

He moved to the hotel's front window and observed the shops lining the street,
~~~~~

their windows decorated with evergreens. It was a very different scene from his studio apartment on Olympus. Bart's closet on a cliff overlooked the Olympus chariot yard and an angry sea. It was like living over a cauldron of rock soup. Nothing but flashing landing lights and the crash of waves slamming into boulders.

Bart had wanted to relocate for centuries and live beyond the tentacles of Hera while assisting mortals. He must provide for himself, though, so he devised a plan: establish a matchmaking firm in a small town. Counsel mortals one-on-one. They needed it. *Desperately.*

Bart knew about mortals' dissatisfaction with romance. He witnessed it. The online world promised roses and chocolates. Reality often resulted in shriveled petals and sugar substitutes that caused intestinal distress.

He was unable to help. His snap-on wings were shredded, and his job kit of ancient bow and quiver of arrows was worthless. The bow had dry rot. The arrows were dulled by too many encounters with mortals' hardened hearts. Bart tried to update his tools. Get a new bow. Stronger arrows.

You-know-who rejected his requests.

He'd fill out a requisition form in triplicate and hand it to Hera. She'd cackle in his face. "Your tools have worked fine for two thousand years!" she'd laugh. "If they ain't broke, don't fix 'em!"

"That's just it, Hera. They *are* broken," he'd argue.

She always pretended to not understand, then stamp the form with a fat, red "DENIED."

Bart shook his head at the memory.

No negative thinking. Look where that got Prometheus—a bird pecking his liver for eternity.

He glanced around the lobby. He'd never seen anything like it. Old World charm meets America's Dairyland. Cream-white walls with plaid curtains draped huge windows. Bovine sculptures were everywhere and decorated for the holidays. A seating area near the check-in desk featured velvet-covered furniture with black-and-white pillows.

Bart inhaled, noting scents of roses, lilies, and paperwhites. Flowers were for sale at the front desk. He stepped over to purchase a bouquet.

A clerk, "Hope," by her name tag, assisted guests.

Bart smiled at the young lady. "Do you have anything in 'Secret Admirer?' A bouquet that says, 'respected from afar?'"

The woman grinned. She was fresh-faced, early twenties. "Sure do. Not roses, though. It sounds like it's too early in the relationship for those."

He nodded. "Excellent observation."

"How about Narcissi?" She pointed at daffodils in a vintage crock. "We're just starting to get those in."

"Lovely flower. A decent god, also, until vanity took over." Bart winked, then glanced toward purple stems. "Those look perfect."

"Irises, my favorites. They're a symbol of hope. That's my name, too."

"Sold, Hope. You're an excellent saleswoman. Will you wrap a dozen?"

"Sure thing. What brings you to town?"

"I've met someone. I'd also like to open a business here."

"That's great. Congrats."

"I'm looking to rent a place. A storefront and apartment—"

Hope held up a hand. "Say no more. My grandpa, Ed Bradshaw, is a real estate agent. He knows every available space."

She reached into a drawer, pulled out a business card, then handed it to Bart.

He read it. "Is your grandfather's better half a dynamo with gray-pink hair? Sort of Tinkerbell meets Florence Nightingale?"

"Great description. Yes, that's grandma."

"Will you wrap a dozen of her favorites and give them to her? She assisted me yesterday, and I'd like to say thanks."

Hope beamed. "Yes, I will, of course. Whom shall I say they're from?"

"Bart. Bart McGee."

"What's your line of business, sir?"

"Romance," he answered. "I help people fall in love."

* * *

The problem with bakeries with a goddess for a proprietor was … everything.

Bart entered Monet's Café, stage right, carrying a bouquet. It was just after eight. Golden light streamed through the windows, and aromas of coffee and chocolate tickled his nose. Monet stood at the counter wearing a candy-cane print blouse and an apron, a beret covering her dark curls.

Bart estimated her age at forty, give or take a few years. Not that it mattered. She had wisdom lines decorating her eyes and lines around her lips. Great revelations of character, he believed.

For the first time in his life, Bart wished to be mortal. He and Monet could age together, then. Bart began life as a sprite, a flicker of light no larger than a fireplace ember. That's how pin-on wings had worked for so long, but centuries of nutrition and exercise gave him size and weight. His stature was moderate, admittedly. If he were a boxer, he'd be a welterweight. Not a heavyweight like his friend Hercules.

Bart thought he resembled a tallish Leprechaun.

Monet saw him and waved. "Hello again. How's the hand?"

He lifted the flowers. "Works perfectly. No problem carrying these."

She smiled. "They're lovely."

He stepped to the counter. "They're for you. Er, the shop. You put flower buds on the tables, I noticed." He handed over the bouquet. "Thanks for the help with my injured wing."

"I didn't do much. It was mostly Mrs. Bradshaw."

"The tea and roll were a vital part of the recovery."

Bart peered at the apron Monet wore. It featured heart-shaped cheese and cursive lettering. He read it out loud: "*Brie mine.*"

"Excuse me?"

"It's your apron. Funny, I have one at home that says *Brie My Cheddar Half.*"

She smiled again, and his heart melted. How could this woman, a goddess if Bart had ever seen one, be real? Her dark eyes shined like black diamonds, and the lines on her olive skin looked like engravings on a sculpture.

She buried her nose in the stems. "Flowers are a beautiful way to begin a friendship. What's your name?"

"Bart. Bart McGee. Out-of-towner for now, but I plan to relocate."

"That's wonderful news. I'm Monet LeFleur." She gestured toward the fireplace and seating area. "Welcome to my café."

* * *

TK Sheffield, MA, writes stories for readers to laugh and escape. Her comic cozy mysteries, **The Backyard Model Mysteries**, are funny whodunnits, mysteries served with a brandy old-fashioned and side of cheese curds. TK is on the board of the Wisconsin Writers Association, and a member of Blackbird Writers and Sisters in Crime.

UnPublished Novel - Romance 2nd Place Barb Simmons

The War Zone

Prologue

Kandahar, Afghanistan

Stark light crept through the missing boards in the roof, casting blinding streaks across both their faces. Choking dust and debris sifted over them with every blast.

Hunkered down in the back corner of what was left of a tiny house, Nash held Ray's back to his chest tighter. He hoped to God the increase in pressure on his body armor would somehow slow his bleeding. They were stuck right where they were until their platoon got there. They'd been out on point and unexpectedly run into a shit-storm.

"You have to make sure Danni gets this back, man. She has to," his best friend demanded in a hoarse whisper. His heavy wheezing a very bad sign. Ray had torn the little Zia pendant from his neck, holding it in a death grip.

Ray had been hit in the chest as least twice, maybe a third. The bastards managed to shoot him just so the rounds got in through the arm hole of his Kevlar. It had all happened so fast.

Nash struggled to keep his tone calm, in spite of the amount of blood seeping through his fingers where he held onto Ray. "Hang tight, Ray. We'll get out of here."

They waited.

Heavy machine gun fire continued in intermittent blasts, while grenade and mortar explosions rocked the ground beneath them.

Choking, acrid smoke drifted through the fissures in their battered shelter. The only reason their platoon hadn't come for them was because it must be too hot to get through.

Waiting for back up with five measly rounds in the midst of all the noise and confusion was worse than hell. Nash had taken a couple bullets in the upper arm and was bleeding pretty bad himself, but it was nothing he couldn't handle.

Exhaustion hit him like a freight train. He must have drifted off. Because when he regained consciousness, it was dark and quiet and Ray lay heavy and cold in his arms.

Chapter 1

Albuquerque, New Mexico
One year later

Nash stood on the front stoop of Ray's widow's home--sweating, anxious and painfully ambivalent. Yet, there really wasn't any choice about him being there.

He eyed the cheery garden flag welcoming him, along with a bunch of clay pots holding flower mixes and several interesting kinds of cactus.

As he reached up and rang the doorbell, he heard voices from inside. A woman's, probably Danielle's, even-toned, patient but firm, and a male voice, louder than hers, commanding. Their words became clearer as they neared the door.

"Vince, I don't want to talk about it anymore," she said as the door came open.

She was tall, probably five-ten. Her dark hair pulled back in a high ponytail, no make-up, wearing an armless fitted sweatshirt and knee length workout tights. She was barefoot and her toenails were painted black.

Stunning.

The guy looked a lot like Ray, only smaller and had a bunch of tats on his neck and arms. Didn't look all that friendly either.

He offered his hand to Danni. "I'm Nash Santana."

She took it, shaking his hand with comfortable strength. She didn't smile, but her bright green eyes were warm and welcoming.

"Hello, I'm Danni, and this is my bother-in-law, Vince." Vince stepped up, put his hands on his hips and maneuvered himself just a bit in front of her. This whole situation was awkward enough without this fool adding his macho crap to the mix.

A huge brindle Pit Bull sauntered up beside Danni, nudging her hand. "Sit, Lulu." The dog immediately dropped to her butt. Nash's anxiety went up another few notches, but as long as Lulu sat there looking disinterested, he'd let that go.

He put his hand out to Vince, but the guy made no effort to reciprocate.

Nash refocused his attention back on Danni. "As I said on the phone, I thought I'd just take a look at the kitchen to see how far Ray had gotten with the remodel."

Vince took another step toward him. "Just how are you gonna' finish that kitchen with only one arm?" asked Vince with a patronizing snort. He crossed both of his arms over his chest, tilting his head to the side to get a better look at what was left of Nash's left arm.

Danni gasped, her cheeks turning red. "Oh my God, Vince! I can't believe you just said that." She stepped forward. "I'm so sorry."

"Don't worry about it." He'd been wondering the same damn thing, ever since he'd received Ray's letter. Their CO had forwarded it to him, while he was in the VA Hospital. Ray had requested he finish Danni's kitchen remodel along with a few other appeals he was definitely uncomfortable with. "I'll manage."

Danni stepped aside and motioned Nash to follow her toward the kitchen. When they entered the room, Nash felt his eyes widen, barely keeping himself from blurting out, "*Oh, shit*!"

The room was completely dismantled. The only things that looked operational was the stove and the original base cabinet sitting next to it. A large cutting board spanned that cabinet.

Had she been doing dishes in the bathroom all this time?

The new granite counter top leaned against the side wall of the kitchen. Wall cabinets lined the back wall.

The laminate flooring, still in boxes, was stacked in the corner. Nash's sense of impending doom almost made him sink to his ass on the floor. An odd sensation pulled him from his spiraling thoughts. Lulu had sat down next to him, and licked his hand. Looking up, she gave him an encouraging doggie smile.

"O-K, looks like everything is here. I'd like to take inventory of any other supplies. Where are the rolls of sub-flooring?"

He followed her toward a door in the back of the kitchen leading into the pantry. One area of the pantry was devoted to an array of hardware, several rolls of white sub-flooring, a good-sized tool box and what looked like a lifetime supply of Hostess Twinkies. He'd forgotten about Ray's jonesing for those things.

Aside from the Twinkies, it looked like he had most of what he'd need to get started.

"When would you like me to start?"

The calm Danni had exuded so far, faltered. "Ah, I don't know…Friday?"

"You want me to *start* on a Friday?" *Unbelievable.*

"Yeah." She stepped backward.

"So, you want me to work through the weekends?" *That wasn't going to happen.*

"Oh, no. I'll need my weekends to myself."

Good, me too. He needed some in-between time to figure out how he was going to hang wall cabinets with one arm. Already a two-man job, in this case most likely three. "OK, Friday it is," he said, clearing his throat.

* * *

Later that afternoon, Danni huddled in her window seat reading nook, clutching the plush wiener dog Ray had won for her on their first date, the New Mexico State Fair.

She watched Lulu chasing and leaping at a butterfly as it fluttered around the back yard. She smiled. Ray had been a little disenchanted when their Lulu hadn't turned out to be the proud, fierce Pit he'd imagined. But he'd loved her anyway.

Danni was thrilled Lulu had turned out to be a sweetheart. Who ever heard of a Kindergarten teacher with a big scary dog?

Sadness overwhelmed her, and she hugged the stuffed dog tighter. Tears welled and fell. She and Ray had planned to start a family when he came back from this last tour. Now, a year after he'd been killed in action, she still hadn't cleaned out his closet. All of his tools were right where he'd left them, and no one dared touch his Twinkie stash.

When Ray's friend Nash was at the house today, she'd felt incredibly disloyal allowing him to disturb any of Ray's things.

All the remodel stuff was exactly where Ray had left it. His deployment had been so fast he hadn't had a chance to put anything back in order before leaving. For sure her world would go even more out of balance, if any of his things were messed with.

Danni looked over at the huge pile of multi-colored silk flower petals lying on the bed and sighed. They were the basis for this week's Mother's Day project. Her students were to make cards to take home.

As she put down her stuffed dog, the real one came ambling in, panting. "That butterfly too much for you?" Danni got up from her perch and scratched LuLu's neck. Her dog had this uncanny ability to seek her out when the sadness built to critical mass.

"Let's go, Lu." She stood, dropped the stuffed dog to the bed, and they headed out to the backyard together. Once outside, she grabbed up her dog's favorite squeaky and threw it a long pitch. LuLu took off after the prize. Danni sank down into her lounge chair and watched as Lulu took her time, meandering back to her.

Commotion at her side gate stole her attention. She sat up. The gate opened and Vince entered the yard, two of his friends following.

Lulu dropped her squeaky and trotted over, settling beside her chair.

The three self-imagined bad-asses marched toward her.

Oh, what now? Vince was coming over without calling way too often. *That* was beginning to get on her nerves. She knew he was trying to stand in as the man of the house, but that too, was getting old. They would have to have a talk.

Vince walked up to her chair. "I need Ray's truck."

She almost asked him if he was out of his mind, but stopped herself. "For what?"

"We want to go out to the Manzano foothills."

"You're going hiking?" That would be positive thing for him to do.

"Not exactly."

The guy right behind him piped up, "We wanna' go shooting."

Oh, great. She didn't have any problem with target practice. She had a problem with the fact that Vince's sense of responsibility had never been all that reliable.

"The keys are on the hook by the dryer." She grabbed his arm, stopping him. "Please be careful."

"I will," he said, easing his arm from her grasp.

~~~~~

Chapter 2

Danni stood at the front of the classroom holding up a folded piece of construction paper.

"Everyone!" She waited until all eyes were on her. "Peanut, peanut butter," she sang out to her students.

"And, jelly," they all sang-shouted back, settling into their chairs.

"Remember. Glue your petals to the front of your card, *only*, OK?"

Most of her students gave her their full attention, but there were three boys at the back table who insisted on trying her patience pretty much every day. They were currently pasting the rose petals all over their faces.

"Matt, Estevan and Pedro! Please come up to my desk, *now*." She and Sylvia Duran, her teacher's assistant, exchanged glances--their silent communication. Sylvia took over the class.

The boys ambled up to her desk, their eyes cast down. Looking flakily contrite, as they always did when getting caught at something. She opened a desk drawer, pulled out a hand mirror, and held it up in front of the boys.

Pedro's horrified expression indicated he was appalled, and he immediately began yanking the petals away from his face. Matt laughed, but removed them as well. Then Estevan, cracking a giant smile, turned his head back and forth, admiring himself. He then began a little song and dance, "I'm the flower ki-ing, I'm the flower ki-ing," in a conga cadence.

No matter how much irritation the guys ignited in her, she often found humor in their antics. She stood, took Estevan's hand, and danced him back to the table. The other two walked behind.

Estevan sat in his little chair grinning up to her.

"Enough, OK," she advised, using *the tone.*

He nodded, then pulling a petal from his chin, he glued it to the white construction paper in front of him. Matt and Pedro took their seats as well, and commenced working on their cards.

Danni went back to her desk put a Green Chili Jam Band CD in the old boom box she'd gotten from her mom. "Toothless," one of the kids' favorites filled the room. Some started singing along while they worked.

She noticed the afternoon sun pouring through her classroom windows. A butterscotch glow illuminated her students, giving her a warm feeling all over. She hadn't felt that particular sensation in a while, and it made her smile.

Pulling out her planner, she checked tomorrow's schedule.

Friday.

Ray's friend Nash would be starting work on the remodel. In reality, he'd gotten stuck with pretty much the entire job. Ray had just started when he'd been deployed. She guessed the friendship between them must have gotten really tight during
~~~~~

combat, for Nash to be willing to do this. She should feel grateful but all she felt was huge resentment for Nash being here, when Ray wasn't.

Rising from her desk, she walked among the tables dividing up her students. "Please start putting your supplies away. The bell is going to ring in ten minutes."

Maisy, her most fretful student, raised her hand. "Miss Danni. I'm not done." She held up her card and waived it. Three petals fell off, floating to the floor. Danni walked over, snatched up the petals and placed them back on the fresh glue spots.

"Maisy, Mother's Day isn't until this weekend. You can finish up tomorrow, OK?"

"Thank you, Miss Danni," Maisy said, noticeably relieved.

"Class, please leave your cards out on your tables. They will dry fine overnight. We can put in our messages, and finish them up tomorrow."

After Sylvia came back from taking the kids to the bus, she sat down and changed out of her sneakers and into her new red pumps. They went surprisingly well with her red and black work outfit. "You know it's your turn to take them out to the bus tomorrow, Danni. Don't even try to sneak out of it just because it's a Friday."

"Don't worry, I won't. I'm going to take my time getting home tomorrow. The work on my kitchen is starting up again."

"It is? Didn't that remodel start right before Ray went..." Sylvia's voice trailed off.

"Yeah. It has been a while. I guess it's time to have my kitchen whole again. I need to get things cleaned up tonight. The guy's going to be there before I leave for work." If only she felt the enthusiasm she expressed.

Danni gathered up her Super-Girl lunch box, her Y*ou can't scare me, I'm a teacher!* tote bag, and backpack purse, and headed out to the parking lot. She grimaced, thinking about having this man roaming around her house, invading her privacy, and messing with Ray's stuff--for who knew how long.

It was going to be horrible.

* * *

Nash sat at the dinner table with his parents. He'd given up his place when he'd last been deployed, and it looked like he needed to find another soon.

Being around people constantly, grated. Especially people who loved him, who tried way so hard to help him. They were only looking out for him, but it didn't help.

"So, what're you going to do with yourself, now that you're a civilian?" His dad, again, was trying to get him to be conversational.

"Not really sure yet, Dad." Nash stabbed at the already cut up pieces of steak on his plate. Back only a month and they kept asking him that. *Jesus.* He needed time to think. Things were moving too fast and too slowly at the same time.

"Your father was talking about how maybe you could help out around the shop."

Nash felt his face heat up, his blood pressure rise and he almost came up out of his chair. He'd risked his life, lost a damn limb for his country, and they wanted him to be a lackey for the family contracting business?

Feeling both insulted and pressed by guilt, Nash pushed away from the table and rose. "I've got things to do."

"You've hardly touched your dinner," his mother said, concerned.

"Christ, Mom, I'm not five years old. I'll eat it later."

"Ok, Nash," she said looking back down at her baked potato. It made it worse that she was being so damned reasonable.

Nash grabbed his plate and headed out to the kitchen, stepping through his parents' palatable frustration and bewilderment. He still hadn't figured out plastic wrap with one hand, so he covered his plate with a bowl. After stowing it in the frig, he headed out to the garage.

He'd take inventory of his tool box. Make sure he had everything he'd need to work on Dani's kitchen. The prospect of the job was absolutely frightening. Another demeaning opportunity to demonstrate he was no longer a whole man. Yet, he was compelled to go through with it, because Ray had asked. Because Danni deserved her kitchen back.

Ever since he'd met her, he couldn't stop thinking about her. In just a few days she'd become some sort of pure, glowing beacon in his gray world. *Crazy.*

The first woman that stirred him since his injury, and she was completely untouchable. He hadn't been with a woman since he and that cute Lieutenant from the motor pool drank too much Jack together, just days before he and Ray got trapped in that damn house.

That was a year ago last month. He hadn't been celibate this long since he'd lost his virginity in the 10th grade.

His loneliness and fear of wanting made him vibrate with anxiety. He needed to relax. Needed to do something that would calm him down. He needed to go for a run, he decided--giving thanks that he still had two good legs.

* * *

Barb Simmons is an award-winning writer of romantic fiction. She and her husband, CJ, live south of Albuquerque, enjoying a quiet life in the country. They make regular forays out and about, to discover the magic of the great Southwest. Her first book, *The War Within,* was a winner in the 2020 SWW writing contest.

UnPublished Novel – Romance 3rd Place Dita Dow

Cuffs & Kisses

Chapter One: Love on the Run

Chloe Monroe stood at the edge of the bustling Trenton farmers market, clutching a crumpled photo of her latest target. The warm breeze carried the mingled scents of freshly baked bread, ripe strawberries, and sizzling street food. Colorful stalls overflowed with produce, flowers, and handmade crafts, creating a vibrant tapestry of sights and sounds.

"Okay, Mr. Carlos DeLuca," Chloe muttered to herself, glancing at the photo of a middle-aged man with a thick mustache and a guilty-looking smile. "You're about to have a very bad day."

Chloe adjusted her sunglasses, then tucked a loose strand of auburn hair behind her ear. She moved through the crowd with the ease of someone accustomed to blending in, her eyes scanning the throngs of people for her quarry. As she weaved through a group of giggling teenagers, she nearly tripped over a toddler chasing a rogue balloon.

"Sorry, kid!" she called out, regaining her balance just in time to spot a familiar mustache disappearing behind a stand selling artisanal honey.

"There you are," Chloe whispered, her pulse quickening. She picked up her pace; the soles of her sneakers were silent against the cobblestones amid the noise of the market. As she rounded the corner of a large produce display, she nearly collided with a man carrying a stack of wooden crates.

"Whoa! Watch it!" the man exclaimed, sidestepping to avoid disaster.

"Sorry!" Chloe darted around him. Carlos DeLuca was in her sights, browsing a table laden with jars of homemade pickles. She slipped her hand into her bag, fingers brushing against the cool metal of her handcuffs.

Just as she was about to make her move, a strong arm wrapped around her waist, pulling her into the shadows of a nearby alley.

"What the—" Chloe started, but a hand clamped over her mouth.

"Quiet," a deep voice whispered in her ear. "You're making a scene."

Chloe's heart raced as she struggled against the grip, but her captor's hold was firm. After a few tense seconds, the hand slid away from her mouth, and she spun around to confront her assailant.

"Who the hell do you think you—" Chloe's words died in her throat as she found herself staring into the deep blue eyes of a man who was decidedly not Carlos DeLuca.

Tall, dark, and infuriatingly handsome, the man raised an eyebrow at her. "Nice to see you too, Chloe."

"Ethan Blake?" Chloe's surprise quickly turned to annoyance. "What are you doing here?"

Ethan leaned casually against the alley wall, a smirk playing at the corners of his mouth. "I could ask you the same thing. Last I heard, you were supposed to be tracking down a skip."

"I am tracking down a skip," Chloe retorted, glancing back at the market. "And you just made me lose him."

"DeLuca?" Ethan nodded toward the market. "Don't worry, he's not going anywhere. I've been watching him for the past hour."

Chloe blinked, flustered. "You've been here watching me watch him?"

Ethan shrugged. "I was curious to see how long it would take you to find him. Besides, I've got my own reasons for being here."

"Which are?" Chloe crossed her arms, tapping her foot impatiently.

Ethan's smirk widened. "Wouldn't you like to know."

Before Chloe could respond, a commotion erupted from the market. Shouts and the sound of breaking glass echoed through the alley.

"Looks like DeLuca's on the move," Ethan said, straightening up. "Our resident five-finger-discount connoisseur just made off with another tip jar. Shall we give chase to the walking calamity?"

He nodded towards a lanky figure in a ratty jacket weaving through the crowd, clutching a glass jar to his chest like it was the Holy Grail.

"I swear, that man's sticky fingers could teach an octopus a thing or two," Ethan muttered. "Think this is attempt number what? Fifty-seven at reforming the irreformable kleptomaniac?"

Chloe shot him a glare but knew she had no choice. "Fine. But stay out of my way."

They emerged from the alley just in time to see Carlos DeLuca sprinting down the street, knocking over a display of tomatoes in his haste.

"Stop! Bounty hunter!" Chloe yelled, tearing after him.

Ethan was right beside her, matching her stride for stride. "Nice to see you're still as subtle as ever."

"Shut up and run," Chloe shot back, her eyes fixed on DeLuca's retreating figure.

They dodged pedestrians and leapt over obstacles, their footsteps pounding in unison. As they closed the distance, Chloe felt a surge of adrenaline. This was the part she loved—the chase, the thrill of the hunt.

DeLuca glanced over his shoulder, his eyes widening when he saw Chloe and Ethan gaining on him. In a desperate move, he veered into a narrow side street, likely hoping to lose them in the maze of alleyways.

"Split up!" Chloe commanded. "I'll take the left."

Ethan nodded and veered right without a word. Chloe pushed herself harder, her breath coming in quick bursts as she followed DeLuca into the labyrinthine alleyways. She could hear Ethan's footsteps echo nearby, and Chloe felt oddly comforted—a sentiment that hit her like a rogue shopping cart in the produce aisle. Since when did Ms. Lone Wolf start appreciating backup?

DeLuca's panicked breaths were loud in the confined space, and Chloe knew she was close. She rounded a corner just in time to see DeLuca clambering over a chain-link fence.

"Oh no, you don't," she muttered, grabbing hold of the fence and hauling herself up. She swung a leg over the top and dropped down on the other side, landing with a grunt.

DeLuca was only a few feet away now, his escape route blocked by a dead end. He turned to face Chloe, his eyes wide with fear.

"Stay back!" he shouted, brandishing a piece of broken glass like a weapon.

Chloe held up her hands in a placating gesture. "Easy, DeLuca. Let's not make this harder than it has to be."

DeLuca's grip on the glass tightened, his gaze flickering side-to-side as he searched for another way out. But before he could make a move, Ethan appeared behind him, silent and imposing.

"Game over, DeLuca," Ethan said, his voice calm and steady.

DeLuca spun around, his eyes darting between Chloe and Ethan. Realizing he was cornered, he let out a defeated sigh and dropped the glass shard.

Chloe stepped forward, pulling the cuffs from her bag. "Smart move. Now, let's get these on you."

As she cuffed DeLuca, Ethan leaned against the wall, watching with an amused expression. "Not bad, Monroe. Not bad at all."

Chloe shot him a look as she secured the cuffs. "You know, I had this under control before you showed up."

Ethan chuckled. "Of course you did."

Ignoring him, Chloe turned her attention back to DeLuca. "Alright, let's get you to the station."

She guided DeLuca out of the alley and back toward the market. As they walked, Chloe couldn't help but steal a glance at Ethan. Despite his infuriating attitude, there was something about him—something that made her heart race in a way that had nothing to do with the chase.

"By the way," Ethan said casually, "you owe me lunch for ruining my stakeout."

Chloe rolled her eyes. "In your dreams, Blake."

Ethan's grin was maddeningly charming. "I'll take that as a maybe."

As they escorted DeLuca to her car, Chloe felt a strange mix of irritation and excitement. She had a feeling this wasn't the last time Ethan Blake would complicate her life.

~~~~~

Chapter Two: A Date with Danger

The Trenton police station was a hive of activity as Chloe marched a handcuffed Carlos DeLuca through the bustling bullpen. Phones rang incessantly, mingling with the clack of computer keyboards and the low murmur of conversations. The air carried a heady mix of stale coffee, sweat, and the faint tang of desperation that seemed to cling to the wanted posters plastered on every wall.

"Well, if it isn't Chloe Monroe," drawled a familiar voice. "Looks like you caught yourself a big one."

Chloe turned to see Detective Jake Hanson leaning against a nearby desk, a smirk playing across his chiseled features. With his tousled blond hair, piercing green eyes, and a jawline that could cut glass, he looked more like a movie star playing a cop than an actual officer of the law.

"DeLuca here is small potatoes, Hanson," Chloe said, giving her skip a little shove. "I'll be back with a real catch soon enough."

Hanson chuckled. "I don't doubt it. You're like a dog with a bone when you're on a case. A very attractive, very single dog, from what I hear…"

Chloe rolled her eyes. "Down, boy. I'm not here to play fetch."

She handed DeLuca off to a waiting officer and turned to leave, but Hanson stepped into her path, his grin widening.

"What's the rush? I thought maybe we could grab dinner, discuss the finer points of bounty hunting… among other things."

"As tempting as that sounds," Chloe sidestepped him, "I have plans."

"Plans?" Hanson quirked an eyebrow. "With whom?"
~~~~~

As if on cue, Ethan Blake sauntered into the station, drawing every female gaze like a magnet. In his fitted leather jacket and dark jeans, he looked more like a bad-boy heart breaker than a private investigator.

"Blake," Hanson said, his voice cooling several degrees. "I should've known."

Ethan flashed him a grin. "Hanson. Always a pleasure."

The two men stared each other down, the air practically crackling with testosterone. Chloe resisted the urge to roll her eyes again.

"If you two are done measuring your manhoods, I have another skip to track down," she said, brushing past them.

Ethan fell into step beside her, ignoring Hanson's glare boring into their backs. "So, about that lunch…"

"I never agreed to lunch," Chloe said, pushing through the station doors and out into the hazy Trenton afternoon.

"You never said no, either," Ethan pointed out, his grin widening.

Chloe shot him a look. "Has anyone ever told you you're insufferable?"

"Many times. I choose to take it as a compliment."

Despite herself, Chloe felt a smile tugging at her lips. There was something about Ethan's easy confidence, his devil-may-care charm, that was hard to resist. Not that she'd ever let him know that.

"Fine," she said, coming to a stop beside her battered old Honda. "One lunch. But only because I'm starving and you're buying."

Ethan's eyes sparkled with mischief. "I wouldn't have it any other way."

~~~~~

Chapter Three: Lunch and a Showdown

The neon sign flickered above the diner's entrance, casting a garish glow across the cracked pavement. "Eat at Joe's," it proclaimed in sputtering red letters, looking more like a threat than an invitation. Chloe eyed the peeling paint and greasy windows with trepidation, then turned to Ethan.

"Seriously?"

Ethan grinned, holding the door open with a flourish. "Don't be fooled by appearances, Monroe. This place has the best burgers in Trenton."

"It also probably has the best chance of giving me food poisoning," Chloe muttered as she stepped inside.

The interior was a time capsule straight out of the 1950s, complete with checkered floors, vinyl booths, and a jukebox in the corner playing a scratchy rendition of "Earth Angel." A bored-looking waitress in a pink uniform popped her gum as they approached the counter.
~~~~~

"Well, well, well," she drawled, eyeing Ethan appreciatively. "If it isn't Mr. Tall, Dark, and Troublesome. And who's your girlfriend?"

"She's not my girlfriend," Ethan said quickly, just as Chloe snapped, "I'm not his girlfriend."

The waitress smirked. "Uh-huh. Heard that one before. Lemme guess, the usual for you, heartbreaker?"

"You know me so well, Darla," Ethan said, flashing her a wink. "And my not-girlfriend here will have the same."

Chloe shot him a glare as they slid into a booth. "Do you flirt with every woman you meet?"

"Only the ones who can kick my ass," Ethan said, grinning. "Which, now that I think about it, is most of them."

Chloe fought back a smile. "So, what's the deal with you and Hanson? I could practically see the sparks flying back at the station."

Ethan's grin faded. "Let's just say we have a history. The guy's a good cop, but he's got a stick up his ass the size of the Empire State Building."

"And you're the picture of professionalism?"

"Hey, I get the job done," Ethan said with a shrug. "I just don't like people telling me how to do it."

Their burgers arrived, and Chloe had to admit they looked delicious. She took a huge bite, closing her eyes in bliss as the flavors exploded on her tongue.

"Oh my god," she mumbled around a mouthful of beef and cheese. "This is amazing."

Ethan grinned. "Told you so."

They ate in companionable silence for a few minutes, the only sounds the clink of utensils and the steady hum of conversation from the other diners. But the peace was shattered by a sudden commotion at the door.

"Nobody move!" a gruff voice shouted, and Chloe looked up to see a man in a ski mask brandishing a gun. "This is a robbery!"

Across the booth, Ethan tensed, twisting to see what Chloe had spotted at the door. His hand crept towards his holstered gun, but Chloe was faster. In a flash, she was up, trusty stun gun already in hand.

"Hey, ski mask!" Chloe called out, brandishing her stun gun. "Drop the gun, or you'll be doing the electric slide in about five seconds!"

The robber turned, his eyes widening behind the mask. "Stay back! I'm warning you!"

Chloe smirked, taking a step closer. "Ooh, I'm shaking in my sneakers. Whatcha gonna do, shoot me? Please. I've faced scarier things in my morning coffee."

As she advanced, the stun gun crackling menacingly, Chloe caught Ethan's reflection in a nearby mirror. His face was a comical mix of horror and fascination. She almost laughed when he hissed, "Chloe, what the hell are you doing?"

Chloe ignored him, her focus entirely on the robber. "Last chance, buddy. Drop the gun, or you'll be twitching on the floor like a fish out of water."

The robber hesitated, his grip on the gun tightening. Chloe didn't wait for him to make up his mind. With a sudden lunge, she jabbed the stun gun into his chest, the air filling with the sizzle of electricity and the robber's pained yelp. He crumpled to the ground, his gun skittering across the floor.

Ethan gaped at Chloe, his eyes wide. "Are you insane? You could've been killed!"

Chloe shrugged. "Hey, someone had to do something. You were just sitting there like a deer in headlights."

"I was assessing the situation!" Ethan protested.

"Well, while you were 'assessing,' I was taking action," Chloe said, giving the unconscious robber a nudge with her foot. "You're welcome, by the way."

Ethan shook his head. "You're crazy, you know that? Absolutely certifiable."

Chloe grinned back. "Yeah, but you love it."

As sirens filled the air, she caught a flicker of reluctant admiration in Ethan's eyes. He might not admit it, but Chloe knew her brand of crazy was growing on him.

Moments later, a familiar figure strode through the door. Detective Jake Hanson surveyed the scene, his eyes widening as he took in the unconscious robber and Chloe's still-crackling stun gun.

"Why am I not surprised to find you two in the middle of this?" Hanson shook his head, motioning for his officers to secure the scene. "You know, Monroe, when I said I wanted to see you again, this isn't quite what I had in mind."

Chloe grinned, holstering her stun gun. "What can I say, Hanson? I like to keep things exciting."

Detective Hanson approached Ethan with a smirk on his face. "Gotta say, Blake, I'm surprised to see you sitting on the sidelines while Monroe here takes down the bad guy. Losing your edge?"

Ethan scowled, crossing his arms over his chest. "I'm a PI, not a cop anymore. It's not my job to take down armed robbers."

Hanson chuckled, turning his attention to Chloe. "Well, then, it's a good thing we've got Monroe on the case. Looks like she's still got those academy reflexes, even if she never made it to the force."

Chloe rolled her eyes. "Hey, it's not my fault I shattered my knee and wrecked half the ligaments in my leg."

"And look at you now," Hanson said as he turned back to Ethan. "A hotshot private investigator, taking on cases the police won't touch. Must be nice to be your own boss."

Ethan shrugged. "It has its perks. Like not having to deal with pencil pushers like you all day."

Hanson clutched his chest in mock hurt. "Ouch, Blake. You really know how to wound a guy." He turned back to Chloe, his smile turning flirtatious. "What about you, Monroe? Ever regret not joining the force? We could use a tough, beautiful woman like you on our side."

Ethan cleared his throat loudly. "If you two are done flirting, some of us have a burger to finish."

Hanson held up his hands in mock surrender. "All right, all right. I can take a hint. But if you ever change your mind about that date, Monroe, you know where to find me."

As the police took over the scene, Ethan leaned in close to Chloe. "Next time, maybe we should just get takeout."

Chloe grinned, punching him lightly on the arm. "Where's the fun in that?"

Ethan sighed, but he couldn't quite hide his smile. "Yeah, yeah. Just try not to get us killed before dessert, okay?"

As they watched the robber being loaded into the back of an ambulance, Chloe smirked, mulling over Ethan's words. Crazy, he'd called her. Well... Dangerous? Probably. Unpredictable? Definitely. More than a little crazy? Always. Boring? Never.

* * *

JJ Sinclair, (aka Dita Dow), a New Mexico-based author, crafts hilarious love stories inspired by her own rom-com worthy life. A former police detective, her Hawaiian wedding misadventures set the tone for 31 years of a laughter-filled marriage. When not writing, JJ travels, attempts gardening, dotes on cats, and explores quirky coffee shops.

UnPublished Novel - Scifi/Fantasy/Horror - 1st place Charles Botsford

Essex

Chapter 1 – The First Day of the Rest . . .

It's 2 am, my fingers fly through the office holo-vid projection, and my heart pounds like a bass drum. A sliver of moonlight shoots through the window at my back and lands on the far corner of my desk. I had to come back to do this one last act.

A text alert pops up on my holo. To: Emma Chung, NexCon Senior Program Manager: "Emma, stop."

It's MacPhearson, NexCon's CTO. He's gotten our IT department to try to halt my data run and called security. He's too late, too arrogant, too inept. I hate him, but don't remember why.

"Emma," MacPhearson says, his face appearing in the holo. "Stop. We've got complete backups of every file, and every version of every file that every NexCon employee has ever produced. You're not accomplishing anything. It's late. Let's get a drink. I'll call off Security."

"Screw you," I say to myself, not answering him. The data never resided on the company servers.

I'm finished, in more ways than one. My fingers still and my hands shake. My mind hunts for more to do, but finds nothing. The office, where I've slaved for so many hours, is dark, surreal. Tears flow. It hurts so much to delete my work, which now exists only in my head. The desk picture of Daddy and me at Yosemite, when I was very young, reminds me of better times.

The wall monitor shows four security guards exit the elevator and run down the corridor towards my office. Crap.

They'll be here soon.

I've done my damage, they've done theirs.

I could run, but where? I have nowhere to go. I'm broken.

I have perfect recall, or had perfect recall, but now I have gaps; like the MacPhearson gap and why I hate him; like the gaps about Raman and Fox and others. The distressing gaps lie just beyond my reach. I've never had gaps, and now I have two months of them. I know only that I can't allow my work to fall into their hands, whoever they are: yet another gap. I'm a week past twenty-seven and my life might as well be over. I saw it coming, though not so swiftly or viciously. Bastards. They tortured my mind . . . my freaking mind!

You got yourself into this mess. Think yourself out.

A face replaces MacPhearson's inanity in the desk holo. It's familiar, evil.

"Emma," John Fox, NexCon's CEO, says. His voice is full of mock tragedy. He's trying to help. "You don't have to answer. Security has arrived and will take you into custody. I'm sorry it had to go this way."

I'm glad I disabled the surveillance cams. Fox can't see what a mess I am. The face disappears, leaving me in peace. I don't need an office anyway. I can work anywhere, though a park bench will challenge even my skills.

Voices outside. I rise from my chair.

The office door bursts open.

"Stop right there, Chung."

The lead security guard, overweight and with bulging eyes, rushes in at the head of the squad, and stoops over to catch his breath. He thinks I'm a dangerous criminal. Little does he know. I stop, frustrated, glancing out the door and down the corridor, and edge forward. He points a taser at me.

"Stop!"

I don't.

My shoulder stings and a cramp immediately takes control of my body and shoots lightning through my organs and limbs. My head wants to explode and I shake from top to toes.

"Sonofabitch!"

I slump to the floor, crying from the pain and humiliation.

The early morning has not ended well. I seize again and bang my head on the floor . . . can't seem to focus . . . hurts so much . . .

* * *

"Chung," my least favorite guard, Mad Maddy, yells.

I ignore her.

"Hey, everyone." Mad Maddy yells even louder. "Our celebrity criminal has a visitor. As if our geek thief wasn't famous enough, now she's pregnant. It's a miracle. Get your ass over here, Chung."

Mad Maddy makes me cringe. I don't want anyone to know I'm pregnant. I don't want to know I'm pregnant. Crap.

Sitting in my lower bunk, careful to keep my head below the bottom of the top bunk, I've got the left leg of my blue scrubs rolled up. I continue to pluck short black hairs stub by stub from my left shin. Tweezers would be nice, but they don't supply those in this particular institution. It's a disorder, trichotillomania, disgusting. Gets worse when I'm stressed.

It's also an excellent way to count time. At my current plucking rate, in two days, three hours, they'll allow my weekly visit with Miss BlackBerry to work unofficially on my design.

"Chung!"

I sigh. Our cell stinks from sweat and other disgusting odors. This is not a nice place. Oddly, I'm beginning to settle in. After three weeks here, I've finally stopped crying myself to sleep every night, which is good. Crying seriously impedes my coding efforts.

I code in my head. It's not like I write in assembly language. How primitive would that be? I could, though. When I'm frustrated, I play in assembly language. It's pure, mystical, therapeutic.

For everyday work, I code in blocks, groups, and rings—nothing fancy, just functional. I don't have a computer here, so I use my brain to design and code. However, my brain is slow and not all that reliable, especially when I softsave, which I do by dividing what I've worked on into discrete chunks, and then using a mnemonic to tag each chunk for later retrieval. Chunk and tag, chunk and tag. Repeat. The process takes forever. Apparently, my ability to softsave is an anomaly. People just look at me when I try to explain it. They think I'm kidding them.

The project is all. My creation, my monster, my Essex. I have hope for my monster, just as Frankenstein had hope for his monster. I hope my monster doesn't try to kill me. I deleted his electrons from my computers, which is what landed me here. He was too dangerous to let fall into those bastards' hands.

"Stop it, you OCD bitch!" The opposite lower bunk cellie slaps my hand away from my shin. She's returned the three steps from staring out the tiny rectangular hole in our cell door. "If I have to listen to you another second, I'll strangle your scrawny neck."

She could try, but she's a Latina and even smaller than I am. She murdered her girlfriend, self-defense supposedly. Her tats and vacant skin holes accentuate the imperfections in her body. She normally doesn't watch me, preferring to lie facing the wall on her lumpy bunk mattress. She claims she can hear my activity, but that's just ludicrous. Plucking hair is as silent as one hand clapping.

My other two cellies occupy the top bunks and mostly bitch about their pimps and dealers. Both are redheads, one black, one white. Somehow, the prison admin shoehorned two sets of bunk beds into a cell that would have been crowded with one. Our tiny cell is typical, but the tiny space allotted me is plenty for the requirements of my coding and design work.

"Mad Maddy's calling you. Are you deaf?" She yells in my face hoping to get a reaction. I ignore her like I ignore Mad Maddy. I can't give her or Mad Maddy control.

I might have a visitor, though the universe of possible visitors for me is very small. None of the people on my list are ones with whom I wish to visit. I'd love to see Daddy, but Mom threw him out ten years ago. In fact, if she weren't dead, Mom would be my pick for the person who somehow got me pregnant. She always wanted a grandkid. She would not be on my wanted visitor list, dead or alive.

I heard Mad Maddy, but my activity provides me with a much greater sense of control than giving Mad Maddy a portion of my valuable attention. Besides, the sadistic guard enjoys whacking me every chance she gets when I'm out of the cell. The long walk to the Infirmary yesterday was sadistic fun for her.

"Chung," Mad Maddy shouts. "Visitor. Am I gonna have to shove my stick up your tight Chinese ass to pry you out of there? Hands in the door."

Daddy is second generation Chinese. Mother was Indonesian. Growing up in Seattle, I never much thought of myself as Chinese. I don't know Mandarin from Cantonese. I guess the name and looks fool people. I like to imagine I could be a white girl from the Valley, except of course when my cellies call me an Asian bitch. They're bigoted city hillbillies.

I've come to something of a stopping point in work, anyway. I softsave my last three hours' work. How nice it would be to have a brain implant in which to hard file data. Unfortunately, implant tech is many years away and my neurons will likely be too old to accept the bio-interfaces necessary for an implant, or so they say. So, I softsave.

The management here doesn't let me near a computer, let alone a network. They're afraid of my skills. But once a week they let me play with an ancient thing called a BlackBerry, with actual keys I get to punch. A few of them stick. Miss BlackBerry, I call her. She doesn't have a sim chip. That would be way too useful. She also doesn't let me program her. She would if she could. My first time with her was four days ago. I had no expectations, no hope. They obviously think I can't do any harm. I spent my two hours exploring and then five minutes downloading my brain through my thumbs. What a revelation. This was much better than softsaving.

I rise from my bunk, walk to the cell door, and slowly push my hands through the rectangular slot, imagining without much effort a sword lopping off my hands at the wrists. Instead, Mad Maddy slaps on heavy-duty shackles. I pull my hands back, hear the clank of the door lock disengaging, and watch Mad Maddy pull open the door.

She slaps me. "Don't ever make me wait again."

She whacks my shoulder as I pass her. Shit. I don't wince or moan.

She whacks me three more times on the way to Visitor Control, always just under my shoulder. Maybe she thinks no one will detect the bruising. Hurts like hell, but I don't flinch or cry out. Nothing she does affects me, or so I want her to believe. If this is what it's like in county jail, I can just imagine prison. I want to cry, but bear the pain instead. I can't give her the satisfaction. After the long walk, we finally reach visitor control.

I've been here one other time, two days after they arrested. I met my public defender. She seemed competent, if a little fatalistic. No hope from her.

After we pass through countless control stations, a guard opens the heavy door to the bank of glass cubicles. Mad Maddy stays behind and scowls at me. I sit.

On the other side of the glass, in walks a scruffy white guy with a week-old beard, tall and skinny, looking maybe ten years old if not for the beard, and wearing jeans and a polo-shirt that looks like he's slept in it for days. He works for Fox.

He punches the button and moves his mouth close to the microphone in the middle of the glass. I mimic his movement on my side and punch my button.

"You my new public defender?"

He doesn't nod or say anything, just sits.

"Emma Lai Chung?" he says into the mic. His squeaky voice makes my heart sink along with my false sense of control. He flashes an ID. "I'm Dave Madsen."

I remain silent and watch him. He looks familiar. Have I met him before? I don't know a Dave Madsen. Fox must have sent him to replace the lady defender. Maybe he's really a serial killer who likes the grungy look. He can't really be a public defender. If Fox sent him, I'm screwed. If Fox didn't send him, I'm screwed. Who is he really? I clench my toes so hard they cramp. I wonder if I will ever recover the holes in my memory. I know him.

Dave, the grunge boy, observes my disapproving stare and adjusts his slumping posture, running a hand through his slick, unruly black hair. His self-conscious action doesn't help his appearance, but does make me think Fox might not have sent him. I continue to stare.

"I'm older than I look," he says, shifting in his seat. I'm older than I look, too. I look like I'm sixteen. What's good for a girl must be hell for a guy. "I need to prepare for your court date in two months, but we have only fifteen minutes today. After reviewing your file, I'm mystified. Tell me about—"

"I'm guilty," I say, interrupting him. His eyebrows rise. What does he expect me to say? I really am screwed. I suppose I could have played innocent. Maybe I should play innocent and give him a sense of purpose. Why bother? He can't free me. He won't free me. "I did it."

His eyes narrow and he smiles the smile of understanding. Maybe he has a brain after all. Unfortunately, that increases the probability he's Fox's agent. Either way, I can have fun with him. I smile back.

"Honesty. I like that. The county med staff reports you're seven weeks pregnant. By the time your trial finishes in a few months, and I get you released, you'll have a nice baby bump showing. Too bad your public defender couldn't get your bail reduced. Someone in your condition shouldn't have to endure jail. Has your boyfriend visited you?"

Clueless, or playing dumb. At least he doesn't ask if I'm *the* Emma Chung, which means he's invested at least thirty seconds Googling me . . . failed pianist, failed artificial consciousness researcher, and now apparently, felon.

"I don't know who the father is."

"Oh." He has to think about that. "Then you volunteered for the new Re-Pop program?"

"Nope."

"Wow." He has to think about that again. No way is this guy Fox's agent. He's too naïve, or playing naïve. He's nervous, but he's a good actor. He sits back in his chair, plainly not believing me. Then he scrunches his eyes in disbelief. "What do you mean?"

"I have a blank spot in my memory." I smile at him, though I want to cry. He tries to play tough with me, even if his acting sucks.

I don't tell him it was Fox's crew who detained me . . . Fox's head of bio-research directed them . . . I think . . . I don't know . . . foggy. Raman . . . bastard. They screwed with my mind! Even now, what seems crystal clear, fades to fog. They drugged me. They definitely screwed with my mind. I think I might have gotten pregnant before then, but my memory says nothing.

If only Mom could see me now. She would smile her wicked smile.

"Sorry." He almost looks sorry. I don't tell him the full story, what I remember, or don't remember, of it. "Can we get back to your case? The DA's office said they might recommend leniency if you return what you stole. Otherwise, they won't deal, which means they must think their case is solid. They're willing to drop the assault charges."

"The what charges?"

"You don't remember? You clocked one of the guards when you broke into NexCon. He's out of the hospital. Apparently, you pack quite a punch for someone so small."

I did not. My memory has been perfect since the bastards released me. I don't let Davey-boy see my confusion. However, I now see the extent of how they've played me, and how I waded right into their plans. Due process? No process.

Plus, I can't return what I stole. It's in my head and I destroyed every other fragment of it. I frown at grungy boy. Do I play him back? No, not worth letting them know that I know.

"The news didn't provide details of your sabotage," he says, fishing, trying to make light. He's curious. He's wasting his fifteen minutes, now down to five. He tries too hard to appear studious, taking notes on his wrist pad, nonchalant. "Your employer, NexCon, Inc., develops artificial intelligence products and plans a product release later this year for something called the ST system. Was it software?"

"Fox did send you." I frown again. I find no humor in this. ST is smart, but she's nowhere near conscious. Essex could have helped with that, but that would just be wrong. "Are you even an attorney?"

"Yes, and yes," he says with no shame at all. His disguise as a poor, overworked, disheveled public defender suddenly seems thin. His eyebrows converge, making him appear puzzled. "Look, you're screwed, but you can be out of here this afternoon if you cooperate."

I try to affect an expression of concentration, as if I actually consider the offer. Of course it's bogus. If I give up, I'm dead in a heartbeat. They can't kill me, yet, not if I hold out. I have a plan. It's a long shot, but it's all I've got so far.

"Your fifteen minutes are up," I say. "You work for the devil."

I move my face away from the microphone and watch him speak into his wrist pad as he stares back at me. Then he rises and leaves the visitor cubicle, smiling.

* * *

Mr. Charles Botsford writes SFF novels and short stories. One of his SF short stories, "Homecoming", was an award winner in the 2005 SouthWest Writers Contest. Mr. Botsford is a chemical engineer, with 45 technical papers published on energy, electric vehicles, and air quality. His website is www.abbotwriter.com.

UnPublished Novel - Scifi/Fantasy/Horror - 2nd place **Neal Holtschulte**

Tall Boy Sun

Chapter 1

Sol Linocass tripped on the walkway leading up to the house of his ex-wife and kids. He should have anticipated the crack in the pavement, but he'd been distracted by the holographic video playing in his palm.

He fell. His Personal Interactive sailed from his hand, tumbling the ad for the space show through the humid morning air. Palm-sized starfighters arced in tight formations, armor gleaming, nose-mounted coil guns cackling. Then the PI hit the ground and the advertisement winked away.

Sol belly flopped hard enough to knock his wind out, but there was no time to hurt. He scrambled forward to rake the dew-soaked grass for his PI. The rectangular device, smaller than a "fun size" chocolate bar, was merely *water resistant*, and not so cheap that he could afford a new one.

"Come on, come on," he muttered around the shuddering of his diaphragm.

He should have sprung for a sturdy belt buckle interactive or one of the ear studs that communicated with smart gloss, which fashionable people painted onto their fingernails, but Sol worked with his hands, hands that burned from the slap of the fall.

He spotted the black device amidst the green and carefully plucked it from the grass. He rolled the PI against his shirt to dry it, then gave it a tentative shake. The advertisement sprang into the oily air, banners appearing alongside dueling starships.

Tour a Frigate-built MKIII Destroyer! (Including bridge access!)

Performances by the elite Solar Flair Stunt Team! One Week Only!

Sol swiped through the display. Three holographic tickets appeared, admittance to the space show for one adult and two kids. He swiped again. The tickets were replaced by a wing-bracketed medallion, a contestant badge for the Plutonium Cup tournament.

He sagged with relief, but his heart was a drumming reminder that he wasn't as young as he used to be.

"Thirty-five isn't that fucking old," he told the concrete.

In his mother's voice he heard, *It is if you don't treat yourself well.*

Sol ran his hands over each other, checking his fingers and wrists for tenderness. Everything seemed to be okay. He could still manage a flight stick and throttle.

The space show hosted an annual, amateur pilot contest, a dogfight in simulation for the coveted Plutonium Cup, bragging rights, and fifty-thousand in cash. Sol pictured himself lifting the trophy, his ex-wife Kimberlynn throwing her arms around him while the kids latched onto his legs. It was a beautiful fantasy and it filled him with a fire considerably more pleasant than the lingering acid burn of the hot sauce on last night's rice-and-beans dinner.

If he didn't win, he wouldn't be able to make rent. There wasn't enough overtime at work. Maybe if he scored a hot find at the scrapyard he might get by, but if not, he could end up on the streets, homeless and choking on smog. Kimberlynn could get his visitation rights revoked.

Borrowing future trouble is weakness. That was his father's voice.

Sol stood, grunting only a bit. He steadied himself with a variant of Hook Breathing, a technique pilots used to stay conscious during high-g maneuvers. A tang of polluted air slipped into his mouth and puckered his tongue. He adjusted his expired air mask and took in the neighborhood.

The horizon swam with dawn's citrus colors. Grizzled roach pigeons, adapted to the harsh air, cooed from the power lines. Sol stood in front of a two-story duplex, not much different from its neighbors. Crabgrass besieged the sidewalk. The roof showed its patching in a calico pattern of varying materials. The walls, Sol knew, let every sound through. He missed the place dearly.

One more breath to push back the longing, then he stepped up to Kimberlynn's door and rapped his knuckles across it. Inside, a child squealed. Someone was banging silverware. Dishes clattered. The refrigerator *whumphed* open, then slammed shut.

Sol knocked harder. "Honey, it's me. It's Sol."

Footsteps approached. The latch slid. The security mechanism beeped. The door screeched as Kimberlynn yanked it open. The poorly installed hinges weren't taking the weight properly. Factor in humidity and the door might as well have been rated to keep the vacuum of space at bay.

Kimberlynn squinted into the morning sun. Dimples pinned her cheeks and the bright light turned her brown eyes to honey. Her blonde hair had been hastily tied back, a style she never wore in public due to self-consciousness about her button ears. She was still dressed for bed: faded pajama pants and one of Sol's baggy t-shirts. A lump rose in his throat. He wondered if she'd thought of him when she'd put it on.

He smiled. "Hi, honey."

Kimberlynn brushed away a loose strand of hair, put her hand to her forehead as a shield against the sun, and looked up at Sol bewildered.

"Sol, what are you doing here?"

He lifted holographic tickets up next to his face. "I'm here to pick up the kids. I bought tickets to the space show."

Kimberlynn tilted her head and pursed her lips around an unspoken question. One of their children banged a spoon. She cast a glance back into the house then shook her thoughts free of distraction. "Have you been drinking? It's not your weekend," she hissed.

The irritation and pity in her voice doused him in cold water. He started to gesture at his PI for the date. "I could have sworn… I promise I'm sober."

Kimberlynn's shoulders slumped. "You had the kids last weekend."

Sol scratched his neck. A pleading whine slithered into his voice. "Kimber, babe, I'm sorry, but I've already got the tickets. I'll get the kids out of your hair. What do you say? It's going to be great. We're going to ride the space elevator and everything."

He had pleaded so much leading up to their divorce. He hated himself for not breaking the habit.

Kimberlynn shook her head "No," but with a wobble that meant she was casting about for a reason.

Advice from his father arose. *Make it seem like a win for the other guy.*

That advice was supposed to apply to business, not family. Not like Dad had ever made a distinction.

Sol pulled his mask down and put on a grin that Kimberlynn had once called "cute and boyish." He said, "You'll have the kids off your back all day."

Kimberlynn emitted a small, disbelieving cough. "No, Sol. No. That's beside the point."

He held on to his grin for dear life. "Honey, can you let it slide this one time? You used to let things slide."

Kimberlynn's eyes snapped into focus. "No, I didn't. I kept track. Every time."

"But-" Sol tried to get a word in.

"But nothing. If I did let something slide, that was immaturity. I confront things head-on now, like an adult. I've grown up." She snapped her mouth shut, leaving Sol to wonder if the question "Have you?" was trying to slip out.

"Just this once, please?" His grin collapsed. He was pleading again. He couldn't help it.

"The kids have Starspeak lessons," she stated plainly.

"The pin… The refugees came here." He didn't think. He just said it. He barely stopped himself from using the pejorative "pinheads."

"Don't be like that. They make up sixty percent of the population."

The urge to double down pulled Sol toward its thorny, well-trod path. He knew the shouting, screaming, fury at the end of that road. It still appealed. "Only in the metro area," he blurted.

Kimberlynn turned back inside, her hand on the doorknob. "It's not even eight a.m. I can't do this right now."

Dangerous words tried to come up Sol's throat. He pulled in a deep breath, and made an effort to strip the pleading from his tone. "Peace! Peace. Please. I'll be good, I promise." He put his hand over his heart. "Can I at least come inside to say 'hi' to the kids?"

Kimberlynn chewed her lip.

Part of Sol wanted to fly away to some other planet where he couldn't foul up and hurt people just by existing, but his feet were planted. He wanted to be a good father and a good husband, if only he knew how.

"I won't fight in front of the kids. I promised that before and I've done it, haven't I?" It wasn't much, but the accomplishment was a life preserver he clung to in choppy waters.

"Sure, come in," she said, attempting a polite smile. "But hide that." She pointed at the hologram, where tiny starfighters with unrealistic contrails orbited splayed tickets.

Sol turned off the PI with a fist closed gesture and pocketed the device. He followed Kimberlynn into the house. The door begrudgingly squeezed shut behind him.

"Daddy!" Gav exclaimed as he and Kimberlynn entered the kitchen. The seven-year-old pitched toward Sol. The stool beneath him tilted dangerously. Sol rushed forward to avert disaster. He gave his big-headed boy a side hug and tousled his mop of brown hair.

Hope, his little blonde girl, had been shoving food into her face. She took her fingers out of her mouth and spread her arms wide. It was important that if her older brother got a hug, she got one too. "Me too!"

Sol hugged her. Little wet hands dabbed his shirt sleeve. She was a perfect mess.

Sol beamed at his children.

Hope had Kimberlynn's blonde hair. She wore her googly eye T-shirt, printed with the tongue-out smiley face. One googly eye bounced as she wriggled in her booster chair. The other eye had fallen off, but Kimberlynn had drawn on a less-dynamic replacement with permanent marker.

Gav's hair was darker and would darken further, like his dad's. Gav wore kid jeans and a tight-fitting white T-shirt. He'd fixated on a cartoon about dinosaur construction workers who sported the style as they drove their big trucks around, protecting Earth from giant, evil rat-men.

Hope turned to Kimberlynn, her expression confused. "Whaddabout lessons?" she asked.

"You still have lessons. Your daddy's just here to say 'hi.' He has to leave soon." She shot Sol a look, shining bright with the message, *You do have to leave soon.*

Sol picked up his cue. "That's right. I'm just stopping in."

"Awww," Hope whined. "I don't want lessons. I wanna go with Daddy."

Gav pushed a 'Breakfast Bro' biscuit around his plate as if it was a hovercraft. He offhandedly commented, "Last week Dad took us to the junkyard."

Kimberlynn's voice dropped to a whisper but both children were well within earshot. "I thought we agreed that was dangerous."

Sol winced and addressed the kids. "That's right. We agreed. No more scrap trips."

Gav frowned at his mother. He understood who was making the rules. "Aww, come on."

Sol jumped in. "We'll do something else fun, I promise."

Gav swiveled his big blue eyes to his dad. "Like what?"

Sol looked down to the PI in his breast pocket, but when he looked up, Kimberlynn had one eyebrow arched and her stare was a fully charged disruptor beam.

"We'll think of something."

"There's nothing to do at Dad's place, besides watch him play video games. That's booOoorrring," Gav whined.

Kimberlynn frowned a question at Sol.

He tried to change the subject. "Why don't you teach me some of that Starspeak you've been learning?"

"Vack, vack, vack," Hope chanted, glee filling her chubby cheeks.

Kimberlynn made a fierce face.

Gav howled with laughter, crumbs spraying from his mouth.

Sol looked around confused. "I'm missing something."

"It's a naughty word–" Kimberlynn faced Gav. "–and I asked you not to encourage your sister to use it. If I hear that word out of *her* one more time I'm taking away *your* toy privileges for fifteen minutes this afternoon."

Gav's laughter turned to indignation. He pounded his fists on the table. "That's not fair!"

Hope opened her mouth to speak, devilish delight stretched across her cherub face.

"No!" Gav shoved a biscuit in her mouth.

Pandemonium erupted, full of shrieking and biscuit crumbs. It concluded with laughter, though Sol figured that was due to luck more than any particular parental tactics.

Sol and Kimberlynn relocated both children to the living room before more mess could be made. Sol ended up with Gav on his lap, telling his son in his best fatherly voice, "Your sister looks up to you. You have to set a good example."

It sounded like a good thing to say, though he felt like the slipperiest fraud as he said it.

Gav fidgeted. Hope dropped her mirth and picked up her earlier complaint. "I don't like lessons! Teacher's stinky!"

"That's a very rude thing to say," Kimberlynn said, polite, but stern.

Gav wrinkled his nose. "The aliens smell like glass cleaner."

"They aren't aliens," Kimberlynn pointed out, but her reasonable observation was lost on her son.

Sol made a show of sniffing Gav. "You're stinky too!" Tickles and shrieking ensued.

Sol ran out of breath before his son got tired of the attention. He lifted Gav and set him on the floor. Gav was getting too big to sit on his lap anyway.

"Take your sister and go finish your breakfast," Sol instructed.

"I don't want to." Gav clung to his shirt, then something caught the boy's eye. He yanked the interactive out of Sol's pocket. "Can I play PI?"

"That's Daddy's," Sol said, trying to keep his voice bland as if he was talking about taxes, but it was no use. Sol had a habit of distracting the kids by letting them mess with his PI whenever they got restless and acted out.

Gav shook the PI. The space show advertisement flashed alive, as eager to receive attention as Gav was to give it.

"Whoa!" Gav crooned. "I wanna go! Are we going!"

"Not until later," Sol said.

"Sol…" Kimberlynn warned.

"Much later, like when you're older. You can even see your dad fly one of those ships one day."

Gav wrinkled his nose. "You're too old."

"Am not!" Sol protested, realizing too late that Gav was parroting words he'd overheard his mother use, words that had gotten an oversized reaction out of Sol the last time they'd been spoken.

"You're too old and Mommy won't let you," Gav said with a giggle, delighting in his father's wide-eyed expression.

The truth hurt, but his son's transparent ploy for attention showed Sol his own desires in a new light. He relaxed his face and arched a stern brow at Gav. "Mommy won't let you either, not unless you and your sister finish breakfast. Now give back Daddy's PI."

"Can I keep this?" Gav asked.

"Sure."

Gav closed a fist over the hologram and pitched it toward the ceiling, copying the advertisement to the house network. Then he led his sister to the kitchen.

Sol and Kimberlynn were left alone, Sol on the fold-out sofa, Kimberlynn on the shabby recliner.

"They learn so fast," Sol mused, considering both Gav's manipulation of the hologram and his son's readiness with words that exposed Sol's deep-held inadequacies.

"I wish you hadn't done that," Kimberlynn said softly, eyes on the steaming mug she held.

"Done what?"

"Let him copy the ad. It's all he'll talk about for days."

Her tone didn't suggest an argument. He needed to do his part to steer clear of a fight. He teased back, "I noticed the new food printer in the kitchen. I recall you saying, and I quote, 'Those things print out bland, processed crap, and I will never let one in my house.'"

She looked up from her mug. A smirk curled her lips like she'd been caught with her hand in the cookie jar, but already eaten the cookie. "It's really convenient."

He chuckled.

She went on, "You wouldn't believe. You just pour the powder in, then the kids choose the color and shape. There're flavor options." She threw her head back against the recliner. "That's how they get you. The flavor packs cost a fortune."

Sol laughed harder. Kimberlynn smiled, but tension crimped the corners of her eyes.

"I appreciate your understanding."

"About?" Sol started, taken aback.

"I dunno, the food printer, the expense of it. Work's been stressful. It's fundraising season. If I don't hit my targets, the nonprofit goes under, I can't help anyone, don't get a paycheck… if you can call what I earn a paycheck." She let out a massive sigh. "I don't have the energy to fight with our picky eaters."

Sol's thoughts flopped like a fish out of water. Did she want him to offer her money above the usual? He literally could not. He'd spent everything on the space show tickets and entry fee for the Plutonium Cup tournament.

"If there's a way I could help…" he tried. "Maybe house repairs? How's the new filter fan working?"

"Great, thank you for fixing that. Gav's cough cleared up."

"Outside air will do that."

"It will," Kimberlynn agreed.

A lull descended. Sol tried his luck. "I could still take the hellions off your hands today. The kids could miss lessons this one time."

Kimberlynn's smile cracked. "No, and don't make me the bad guy."

Sol surrendered, hands up. "I didn't say anything bad about the lessons."

"You didn't say anything good either." She inhaled deeply, shoulders lifting and falling, as if bracing herself. Sol felt tension mount, defenses rising on both sides. "Piloting is your dream, Sol, not theirs."

* * *

Neal Holtschulte is a computer science instructor and distance runner. His short fiction has appeared in *Amazing Stories* magazine, *Ghostlight: The Magazine of Terror*, and *THEMA Literary Journal. Crew of Exiles* is Neal's debut novel. This opening excerpt is from his second novel.

UnPublished Novel - Scifi/Fantasy/Horror - 3rd Place **Helen A. Jack**

The Thorn King

Chapter 1

LYRA

Moans of hunger had become commonplace in exile. Nevertheless, Lyra blinked back tears at the soft cries of hungry children that echoed through Rissing Stronghold. She ignored the stabbing emptiness in her own gut and tried to focus on each stitch as she wove ragged wool into something worth wearing.

Beside Lyra, baby Alby rolled over on the stone floor. He'd bunched up his worn blanket in pursuit of mobility, and Lyra managed a faint smile as her infant son grasped a spoon in his small fist.

"He's smaller than he should be at this age." Viola picked Alby off the floor and pressed a hand to his belly. The infant squirmed in the healer's arms, reaching for the spoon that had slipped from his grasp.

She inspected Alby's eyes and laughed when the infant grasped the end of her purple headscarf, unravelling the cloth and sending Viola's black hair spilling out over her shoulders.

"Yet he seems overwise healthy, despite everything." Chuckling, Viola placed Alby back on the floor and retrieved her headscarf, securing it around her head. "Is he still nursing all right?"

Lyra's back ached from where she leaned against the stone wall. She shifted, straightening the threadbare sleeves of her dress, and continued knitting. By some miracle, the women had managed to spin coarse goat hair into half-decent yarn.

"I'm not making enough milk," Lyra admitted. "I feed him mashed grain mixed with water from what's left in our stores, but it isn't enough." She stabbed the bone-hewn needle through the loops.

"You haven't been taking the witchgrass." Dark eyes stern, Viola crossed her arms over her chest.

Though only five feet tall, the Saramore master healer had mastered the art of appearing benign and formidable all at once. In the prime of her life at one hundred fifty years old, Viola had the wisdom of middle years, but the vitality of youth. Often keeping her black hair tied back from her face with a wrap, Viola's fine-boned features and faint spray of freckles lent her a pixie-like countenance. Paired with the almost luminescent ivory skin that all Saramore shared, her large, dark eyes shone like polished stones.

"How can I," Lyra replied, "when there isn't enough to go around? I'm not the only nursing mother here, Vi."

As if on cue, Alby crawled towards his mother and pulled at her dress. She unbuttoned her bodice and scooped him in her arms, relieved as frothy milk bubbled at the sides of his mouth.

"That may be true," Viola sighed, tightening her faded headscarf, "but you *are* the only mother raising Valyron's heir."

Lyra exhaled at the mention of her brother. *If Valyron would only marry again*...the thought narrowed her eyes and pursed her mouth, *he wouldn't need to claim his sister's son as his successor.*

Across the hall, Lyra watched Vitany throw another pellet into the fire. She wrinkled her nose and tried to ignore the smell. Goat dung kept the fire burning, though not without filling the bare castle with the cloying odor. Sixteen years hadn't been long enough to completely eradicate her sense of smell.

Lyra changed the subject. "I saw the fires burning this morning."

Viola closed her eyes and bowed her head. "Ermendy's daughter didn't make it."

Lyra's breath caught in her throat, and she tightened her arms around Alby.

"Poor Ermendy. First her husband, now her daughter." Looking around in the vast hall, at all the women taking advantage of the fire's warmth, Lyra didn't see the grieving mother.

Women and children sat in groups around the bare hall, women carving tools from bone and knitting blankets from yarn spun from goat hair. Mothers darned their children's clothing, already worn from countless mending. Children played in the empty areas, drawing with charcoal on the stone and rolling marbles carved from bone. Tansy, Lyra's five-year-old daughter, played among them.

Sated, baby Alby began to snore softly. Lyra bundled her infant in furs and laid him on the floor.

"I'm going outside to collect more fuel," she said, wrapping her ragged cloak around her shoulders. Once lined with thick wolf's fur, the cloak had shed patches over the years, the remaining fur ragged and worn.

"Tulla already collected the pellets this morning."

"Goats shit more than once a day, I've heard." She managed to get a smile out of Viola before adding, "besides, I need some air. Can you watch Alby? I won't be long."

Lyra made her way through the Great Hall. While a place for communal meals and mutual congregation for the remaining members of the Saramore tribe, the cavernous hall was also a center of industry for them. Not a single hand was idle.

Women sewed, cooked, and prepared tools from the bones of marine life scattered across the island. Bottles of goat milk lined the high windowsills to keep them chilled. She passed the entrance to what Valyron called the Garden Hall – a rather pretentious name for shabby, makeshift greenhouses full of half-wilted vegetables.

A blast of icy air blinded Lyra as soon as she stepped outside. Her eyes watered and she pulled her cloak tighter around her body as the wind assaulted the exposed skin on her hands and face.

The goats bleated loudly, some of the billys aggressively shaking their heads to display their horns. Lyra quickly snatched up a whalebone club and shook it. "Don't even think about it, ugly. Or you'll find your way into a soup."

Lyra had been right. The goats had dropped pellets – piles of them – along the ground. Lyra collected them into a bucket. They were easy to spot against the bleached white ground.

The entire island was a barren wasteland of bone and black obsidian, without a single sapling or patch of grass in sight. Shortly upon arriving to their gods-forsaken exile, the Saramore had dubbed the island "the Bones." The gods had been unanimous when they'd created such a land: nothing could live out here.

Lyra smiled wryly as she could already hear Valyron's reply, defiant and sharp: *But we can.*

To which she'd reply, *what we do can hardly be called 'living.'*

Squinting, Lyra could barely make out the silhouettes of the men near the shore, milling along the barren banks. Her brother was out there, King Valyron of the Saramore, toiling side-by-side with his guards and the other men to find food.

He has to find food, Lyra thought, gritting her teeth and tilting her head to the sky in silent prayer, despite years of unanswered pleas. *He just has to.*

~~~~~

Chapter 2
VALYRON

"Anything yet, Your Grace?"

Without lifting his eyes from the damnably still water, Valyron replied, "No. If we can't find anything near the shore soon, we'll have to row out further."

Byrd nodded and grew silent, scanning the water for movement.

Makeshift spear in hand, Valyron crept through the calf-deep water. The chill seeped through his boots and his eyes strained to detect the slightest movement. The
~~~~~

previous day's catch had been so meager that he and the men had gone without food, saving what they had for the women and children.

In the tense silence, Valyron's growling stomach seemed to echo. He pursed his lips. It had been four days without a decent catch, and the autumn's early snowstorms had kept them from venturing out into deeper waters.

But now, with clear skies above and desperation in their eyes, Valyron refused to return to Rissing without their nets and buckets full. The cold no longer deterred the Saramore men. Nearly two decades in the Bones had taught them to value anything that prolonged their survival – even the dry, bitter meat of the ice carp.

While Valyron usually grimaced at the thought of picking bone splinters out of his teeth, his mouth now watered at the prospect of quelling his nagging hunger.

A movement on the shore caught Valyron's eye. He lunged from the water, plunging his spear towards the flash of red that emerged from between two clusters of onyx. The spearhead didn't penetrate the large crab's tough shell, but it knocked it onto its back, and Valyron shoved the shaft of his spear into the crab's pincers before it could clip him.

But as Valyron quickly bound the claws with twine, it released the spear shaft enough to clamp down hard on his thumb. The king swore as blood bubbled up from the wound.

"Bastard," Valyron seethed, and dropped the bound crab into the rusted pail. A desperate attack from a doomed creature, refusing to give up even in the face of its own extinction.

"Send out the rafts!" Valyron called across the water, his teeth chattering.

The Saramore men looked up from their roaming along the shoreline and jumped into action. Valyron joined his men as they hoisted one of the rafts from the ground, their malnourished muscles straining, and staggered beneath its weight to the water.

"Three will be enough," Valyron panted, the exertion providing brief relief from the cold as sweat seeped through his wool tunic. He retrieved his black fur cloak from the ground and wrapped it around his shoulders to drive out the chill.

"Tallon and I will take one, Modrane and Byrd the second, and Lysander and Emery will man the third. As for the rest of you –" he gestured to the remainder of shivering, shabbily-dressed men, "keep combing the shoreline. We're not returning empty-handed again."

The men on the shore nodded and headed off, spears and nets in hand, their threadbare clothes and patchwork boots barely held together by stitches.

Valyron crouched over the side of the raft as they sailed away from the shore, the bleached white bones fading from view as the waters grew deeper. The colorless sun had chased away the mists, making it the safest time of day to hunt. Beyond the island, the gray sea stretched almost endlessly in every direction. Glaciers dotted the distance, hulking blue phantoms moving interminably towards the horizon.

"We always find a catch out here," Tallon said, his voice light and reassuring. "The snows just kept us from fishing out this far until today."

Valyron set his jaw. "And how many snows will keep us from food this coming winter?" he asked, bitterness serrating his words. "Four days and we can barely lift a raft. How do you think we'll manage once the snows are too high to leave Rissing?"

Valyron thought of the sparrow that had arrived early that morning with a message tied to its foot.

A royal wedding between Cinderone and Skyryn, the message had read. *Reducing their attention to the north coast.*

Tallon didn't miss a beat. "The same way we've managed for the past sixteen years."

"Your optimism makes me want to punch you."

Tallon only grinned, running a hand through his auburn beard that hid half of his boyish face. "That's one of its many benefits, yes."

Valyron was about to reply when flashes of silver glinted from the waters around the raft. He gripped the edge of the raft, his knuckles white. "Get the net!" he cried.

It was almost too heavy for both men to pull back onto the raft as hundreds of squirming silver spears wriggled and writhed against the confines of the net. Tallon waved towards the other two rafts, whooping in triumph, directing them to the catch. He waved his spear over his head as though it were a flag in battle.

"We'll eat well tonight!" he cried as the rafts approached, and the other men scrambled to cast their nets. "Saros has blessed us once more!"

"Thank you, Saros," Valyron whispered, kneeling beside the squirming mass of caught fish. Tears sprung to his eyes as he clasped his hands together. "I knew you'd never forsake us."

On their return to Rissing, the rickety handcarts strained beneath the weight of the catch. Most of the fish had gone still, but crabs still scraped desperate claws against the pails, their frantic scratching mingling with the groan and clatter of carts over uneven ground.

An icy wind gusted across the land, making the Bones howl like damned spirits. Valyron adjusted his black deerskin coat and pulled the fur-lined hood up around his head. It was a cruel wind that threatened yet another early winter, this one harsher than the one before.

Valyron spotted Lyra as soon as they hauled the nets of fish inside. She bounded into the kitchens, laughing wildly as she threw her arms around Tallon and then Valyron.

Unshed tears glinted in her wide gray eyes, which matched Valyron's own. "I knew you'd be successful," she said, clutching her brother's hands.

Valyron didn't answer. Tallon grinned and spun Lyra as though in dance.

"Of course, we were!" Tallon laughed, kissing his wife's mouth. "We weren't going to return without a catch."

Others funneled into the vast kitchens, their relieved exclamations echoing off the stone. Valyron's head ached as he thought of the sparrow again, and the message it had carried.

It was time to share the message with the others.

"Tallon, Simeon, Byrd, Emery…a word?"

He pulled the four members of his Crimson Guard aside, leading them down a nearby corridor where they could talk in private. None of the men spoke as Valyron found an empty room and closed the heavy door behind them.

"Is everything alright?" Tallon asked. He and Simeon exchanged worried expressions.

Valyron exhaled as his eyes fell on the only piece of furniture in the room: a mirror nailed to the stone, patches of rust eroding the shimmering surface. He tried not to grimace at his sorry reflection.

"I heard from Maya and Kalthar today."

Each of the guards' eyebrows shot skyward at the mention of their spies in Cinderone and they all leaned in, listening with bated breath.

Valyron's fingers played along the hilt of the dagger at his waist as he averted his gaze to the vaulted ceiling. "Cinderone is preparing for the royal wedding of their princess to Skyryn's crown prince. Both nations will be vulnerable, as all attention will be averted to Scorchfall. Cinderone and Skyryn's northern borders will be unguarded."

He fingered the large ruby at the dagger's hilt. "We can't turn down an opportunity like this for a supply raid. Especially not now, when winter is well on its way, and we've nearly depleted our stores."

Simeon took a deep breath. Aside from Valyron's sister Lyra, Simeon was the last relative Valyron had after the Red Solstice.

"We lost Brennan on our last raid," Simeon said, his gray eyes sorrowful.

Valyron dug his fingernails into his palms. "I know," he said, his voice like a blade. "But we don't have a choice."

Simeon paused and stared out across the sickly gray sea. "I know."

"We'll leave at dawn," Valyron continued. "In the meantime, we're in desperate need of a meal and some rest to prepare for the journey. I'll be out soon to deliver the news."

Valyron's men filed back out into the corridor. In their palms were the knotted scars that ensured Valyron of their loyalty. Like the Saramore kings of old, Valyron had chosen the members of his Crimson Guard just days after his coronation. The memory of their oaths brought Valyron a solemn joy, recalling the silent reverence as each of the sixteen candidates stepped forward and offered a drop of their own blood to the Vessel.

Because the Sight had been with Valyron that day, he'd known who would lay down their lives for him if necessary. The deep scars across theirs and the king's palms had solidified the blood pact. Once a man became a Crimson Guard, there was no turning back. Betrayal of one's vows to the king was punishable unto death.

"Come out soon, Val," Tallon said as he stood in the doorway. "Or else Lyra will worry."

"She always worries." Valyron attempted a smile, but the weight of their coming supply raid yoked his shoulders like heavy stones.

"For good reason," Tallon said. "Someone has to worry about you."

Alone in the bare room of Rissing Stronghold, Valyron turned a wary eye to his haggard reflection. The Saramore king stood tall, his height exacerbated by his lean frame, the long lines of his body rigid and unflinching. His eyes shone like molten silver from a face thin with chronic hunger. His skin, like all Saramore, seemed as though carved from ivory, its pallor almost luminescent.

While one half of his face was smooth and comely with youth, the jagged scar running from hairline to jaw on the other side testified of the horror most Saramore hadn't survived.

A second scar encircled Valyron's throat – like the shadow of a noose – and trailed up behind his left ear.

Despite the scar's age, it burned red and angry as it had in the early days of exile. The mark from Balthazar's poisoned blade snaked down beneath the privacy of his high-collared tunic, and few eyes had seen the similar scars that wound across his shoulders and back like tributaries of a cursed river.

He brushed haphazard fingers through his hair, which hung to his shoulders in cream-colored waves, though grime muddied its natural color. Knots snagged against chipped fingernails and refused to relent. The sleeves of his threadbare wool tunic fit snug against the lengths of his arms and hung down to his knees. His wool trousers and deer skin boots were still damp from fishing.

All their years in exile hadn't been long enough to banish the memories of royal life from memory. But now, tattered furs and threadbare wool replaced regal garments of silk and dyed linen.

Not a king, but a pauper. Valyron grimaced at his reflection.

No, worse than a pauper – a thief, reduced to stealing to survive.

Valyron exhaled and straightened his tunic. In rags, he would address his people – and try to convince them there was still something to believe in.

* * *

Helen A. Jack is a literary crow and collects ideas and images as though they are shiny things to stow away and spin into stories. She lives in Albuquerque, New Mexico with her husband and three children.

UnPublished Novel - Scifi/Fantasy/Horror - Honorable Mention KL Wagoner

Sundog

Chapter 1

Captain Brand never tired of the view of Jupiter from the top of the massive mining rig. The consortium might complete its plans to alter the surface of Io. Engineers could form rolling hills from the landscape of igneous rock and fill the moon's valleys with high-rises that mimicked the biggest on old Earth. Surface biospheres might one day bring rain to fields of golden grain and send a manmade river flowing through its little bit of heaven, but Jupiter would still rival anything man could create or imagine.

He sat against the base of the rig's swivel arm, stretched his legs, and rested his feet on a crossbar. Storms raged across Jupiter's surface, seemingly at his feet. The eye of the maelstrom was just coming into view. Such a vast planet, impossible to see the entirety of its shifting mass all at once. It was as if eternity passed below him in that dance of dense gas. The storms raged in silence while the monotonous drone of the oar diggers rose up from the base of the platform below him.

"Hey, Cap," Reko's voice crackled from the comm in Brand's helmet. "Two updates. One, we got the new wanted postings. And two, Nail might have found us."

"How sure are you?" It was about time the bounty hunter caught up to Brand and his men, just as he'd done a dozen times in the past decade. The man was tough and unrelenting, but he was slow and never quite hit the mark. They didn't call him The Hammer or The Chisel, or even The Nail. Just Nail. The nickname sounded so much more adversarial than Maurice Allgood.

"I'm still verifying. But I'm betting we can count his nose hairs by end of shift."

"On my way." Brand watched the black sky beyond the curve of Jupiter, waiting for a glint of movement. Twenty space platforms and production satellites orbited Io, all automated stations. Most sent scheduled speeders to the surface to retrieve tanks storing natural outgases from the moon's active volcanoes, or collectors holding energy produced by the ion stripping between Jupiter and Io, or mining cars full of a dozen different ores depleted on Earth over fifty years ago.

A silver speck zipped across the horizon heading in the direction of the landing pad on the moon's largest settlement. Up until a week before, a visual check was the only way to discern between a satellite and an approaching ship. But Reko and Tulip had done their magic and found a way to filter the magnetic waves disrupting normal instrumentation, making Nail's inevitable visit less of a surprise.

"Sorry, Cap," Reko interrupted again. "Data confirms it. No doubt it's Nail."

With luck, Nail might only be on Io chasing down a lead, or maybe he'd come to enjoy the view.

Unless Brand could erase the mistakes he had made ten years before or the government gave up the chase, he and his men would be on the run until the day they died. The mining camp had been home for nearly a year. Now that he knew Nail was near, a strange relief flooded over him. At least he wouldn't waste another ounce of worry wondering when the bounty hunter would find them. Odd that Nail was always one step behind—slow enough to give Brand and his men the time they needed to slip away. Maybe Brand was just that lucky or Nail was really that slow.

He climbed over the crossbar and slid down the outer braces of the long ladder with his safety line detached. Some might say he was too reckless, and maybe he was, but not with the men under his command. His crew had the best safety record on Io and he intended to keep it that way. Now that orders had tripled for the new ore dubbed Living Rock, the need for safety was even more important.

Original plans for the Io settlement hadn't included mining on such a huge scale. The ice cap needed tapping, of course, for the good of the settlers, and iron ore was in abundance for its many uses. But mining the rest of the moon's riches for shipment to Earth was impractical for the travel time and financial outlay. There wasn't enough backing for a large commercial venture because there simply weren't enough people left on Earth to bother with. All that changed with the discovery of Living Rock below Io's surface. Pliable in its natural state, the new "ore" became harder than any known substance when exposed to oxygen. Absent O_2, the Rock slowly returned to its original form as if it had a memory. Possible uses counted in the hundreds. No doubt the military already had plans to weaponize the stuff.

Brand let go of the ladder and dropped the remaining few feet to the pockmarked surface at the rig's base. A wisp of yellow sand scooted out from under his boots, and the faint odor of sulfur pricked his nostrils. Time to check his suit's filters again.

He followed a narrow path carved into the rock leading down between the rig's feet. The booming of the ore diggers grew in intensity the moment he stepped through the gaping entrance to the central mine. Overhead lamps flickered on at his approach, revealing the rough-walled tunnel in a halo before him.

A fork on the path led him to a six-seat mag-car parked at the entrance to the service tunnel whose length ended in dense shadow. He climbed into a rear-facing seat, put his feet up again, and pushed the start button. The open car whined as it crept down the tracks. There were only two controls for the thing—start and stop—and only one speed, slower than the dead. Tulip still hoped to skew the mag sensors. Bets had been made on how long it would take to override the safety controls. No question of "if" he could succeed. Tulip never gave up, and he never lost a fight.

The mag-car slowed in painful increments as its forward sensors detected the end of the line where a second car sat on a parallel track. Brand jumped out before the car stopped. He took the snaking path farther underground. At its end waited pressure locks and more safety protocols. He followed the routine to move from the weightlessness of Io to the filtered air and heavier gravity of a sim-Earth environment. He concentrated on the checklist in each lock. One mistake could mean the death of his men waiting in the underground biosphere beyond the fourth lock. He shut the last hatch behind him, climbed out of his suit, and hung it in a locker marked "pressure test."

As soon as Brand left the sanitary locker room, the subtleties of order faded by degrees. Smooth surfaces and prefabbed archways gave way to uneven angled walls and floors, both encountering intermittent barriers the original builders had given up on trying to move. The passageway narrowed then widened. The ceiling dipped, eventually jutting down at a sharp angle until one side of the passage joined with the other, one wall becoming the ceiling.

The mining company had invested so much on digging equipment and the camp's immense grav-stabilizers, there wasn't much left for esthetics or convenience. When the transport had dropped Brand and his men on the surface, the pilot forgot to mention the camp wasn't finished. They found a working biosphere crammed into a dome-shaped cavern, and only empty trans-containers and basic supplies. Nothing to be done about it. A ship wouldn't return for another six months—not for the death of a crew member or the imminent destruction of the biosphere, not even for the loss of the mining operation.

His men knew the odds. They had faced death alongside Brand a hundred times in a dozen wars the government had deployed them to. Good soldiers made the best of what they had and moved on. That's exactly what they'd done in the decade since the Settlers War ended—worked together and watched each other's backs through whatever circumstance needed a tough skin and a hard edge. When this job ended, they would move on to the next with no guarantees. Wanted men had little choice when it came to how they lived their lives.

Brand ducked and stepped out from the crazed passageway. The camp spread out before him built on a foundation of hardened Living Rock the size of a football field. Empty trans- containers marked living quarters, a welded-together doublewide held their galley and comm center. Harsh lights hung from a grid overhead, defining the upper edge of the biosphere.

He passed five go bags waiting at the midpoint along the path, packed and ready to be grabbed when Brand gave the order to haul ass off of Io.

He'd given the squad a few days break after the new order for Living Rock came across the comm. No use working his men until they dropped. There would be time enough for that in the course of the next few months, if Nail moved on. The bounty hunter might just do that. Tulip was an expert at covering their digital tracks.

Brand turned at a Frankenstein-conglomeration of shipping crates and into the comm center. Reko sat at a terminal on one side of the space. The galley's empty table and chairs, and the shelves of crates stuffed with dry meal packets, reminded Brand he hadn't eaten since breakfast. He didn't have much of an appetite right now, and might not until this business with Nail got sorted.

Wanted postings flickered on Reko's screen. One-dimensional photos and genetic markers of criminals, conspirators, and political activists cycled across one of the two consoles. The other console held a grid noting the crew's standings among the rest.

Reko lifted his cap in salute, brought it low over his eyes once more, and handed Brand a digi-pad.

"Who's on top?" Brand ignored the wanted postings and glanced at the results of the latest atmospheric scan. Tulip had tapped into several satellites and turned their vid-screens toward space. A hotspot in the northern hemisphere revealed a ship's engine burn heading for the main settlement.

"Looks like Malcolm's still the king."

"Looks like? Maybe you need your eyes checked." It wasn't like Reko to be so reserved on posting day, the highlight of his week. He'd been betting Malcolm would keep his spot ahead of the rest of the squad for months now, and winning a pint of homebrew every time.

"Gotta collect my winnings." Reko shuffled out through the doorway, heading for Newley's still on the other side of the dome.

Brand searched the listing for names he might recognize from his days in service to the war department. There were still a lot of good men out there who had been part of the Settlers War, who turned against the government in its attempt to control the colonization of the solar system. Good men that Brand wouldn't mind adding to the squad.

He checked the deceased roster first before moving to the Most Wanted section. His own name marked the top of the list. He'd taken himself out of the contest long ago. Didn't seem right to keep taking the squad's money. Msgt Malcolm's name held steady farther down the list. The rest of the crew was spread out in positions of importance that varied weekly with the strength of opposition to the government and the number of political dissidents caught and executed.

He set down the pad, picked it up again. Something about his listing didn't look right. Two genetic markers flashed next to his name where there should have been only one. A coder had made a mistake and would probably lose his job over it.

Tulip stepped into the room carrying a box heaped with salvaged parts. His biceps flexed as he set the container on the table, making the inked flowers and vines ripple like living things growing around his forearms.

"See the posting?" Tulip said.

"Same as always."

"That's what I thought at first. Look closer." Tulip sat at the monitor. "See the two markers on your posting?"

"Yeah, some poor kid's going to lose a stripe or two over that."

"Not a mistake, Cap. Not a duplicate."

Brand maneuvered the two genetic strings until they lined up side by side. He turned them 360, checked the coding.

"They're almost the same," Tulip said, "but..." He pointed to the printed code and then to the corresponding section of the twisted DNA ladder.

"Doesn't make sense," Brand said. "I don't have a brother. And my father's long dead."

"What about a son?" Tulip raised a brow.

"No, no son." Not anymore. The reminder sent a spasm across his chest.

An alarm sounded from the monitor.

Tulip toggled to a new screen. A warning flashed, and a real-time scan shifted to follow an arc across a grid overlaid on Io's landscape.

"Nail?" Brand asked.

"Gotta be."

Brand nodded and stuffed his hands in his pockets. Reko stepped through the doorway, a laser rifle strung over one shoulder. Malcolm, Newley, and Tito filed in one after the other, each with a favored weapon of choice in his hands.

"So what's it gonna be this time?" Tulip said. "We going or staying?"

They had set everything in place for either scenario within the first few days of landing on Io. Now it was a matter of deciding what risks they were willing to take.

"Anyone feel like a hand of poker?" Brand said.

* * *

KL Wagoner loves creating worlds of fantasy and science fiction. She's currently working on the fantasy trilogy The Last Bonekeeper and short stories in the same universe. Besides being an author, Kat is also a veteran, a martial art student, and a grandmother. Visit her at klwagoner.com.

UnPublished Novel - Scifi/Fantasy/Horror Honorable Mention **Carol Potenza**

Moonlit Skies and Canyon Lies

The Figure

The missile came from the wrong direction, so it couldn't have been launched from the White Sands Proving Grounds. The base and its testing range lay due east of Francie's Capitan Mountain ranch, and the missile originated from, well … straight up.

Atop her palomino, Orion, Francie clutched the reins, shading her eyes with her free hand. She followed the downward streak—a brilliant lavender teardrop against the powder blue of a cloudless morning sky. No contrail, so no fuel burn, something she'd expect if another V-2 rocket had gone off course. Maybe a meteorite plummeting toward the New Mexican plain southeast of Corona and northwest of Roswell.

An odd coincidence since an unknown object had recently crashed in the same area, although that object wasn't so unknown anymore. While newspapers initially trumpeted the alien flying saucer nonsense—she wrinkled her nose at the absurdity—the military retracted the story and quickly settled on the crash of a perfectly boring weather balloon. Too late, though. The military's first story tore off the lid to an extraterrestrial Pandora's Box. Flying disk fever swept the United States like any bold outrageous lie, the truth still putting on its shoes to catch up.

Orion shifted underneath her and heaved a side-swelling sigh. She dropped her hand and patted his neck, wishing she'd brought a wide-brimmed hat, before shading her eyes again. Whatever it was was too small and fast and too … *purple.* Like nothing she'd ever seen before.

But the war had changed the country, put it on an aggressive offense against threats. No more playing catch-up, like they had at Los Alamos. It could be a new kind of weapon powered by a new kind of fuel. Still, unless its trajectory changed, Francie could count on one known against the unknowns: it was going to crash into the ridge north of her, right in the middle of her land.

Worrisome, since the military had forcefully taken so much private land to test new weaponry. Francie's throat dried. Would the government expand the forfeitures and take her ranch, too? She lifted her chin. Not if she could help it. This was her refuge, where she'd been born and raised, where she'd fallen in love. And where she'd retreated to heal her wounds.

The bright object in the sky sped closer and closer. The violet light jumped, flickering back and forth over the straight line of its path. It flared as it approached the ridge, Francie tracking it with eyes narrowed against the final burn, and disappeared behind the trees. She tensed for the explosion and flash of impact, tightened her hands on the reins to control Orion, and …

Nothing.

Orion dropped his head to snatch a quick mouthful of grass. Francie tugged at his reins and stared at where she was sure the object had impacted. She furrowed her brows. How could nothing have hap—

Suddenly, Orion's ears perked. He tossed his head over and over, his body quivering. Anticipation twitched his skin as if he'd sensed some power, some unseen force.

And within a blink, an electric surge slammed into Francie.

The hair on her neck stood as vibrating pulses passed through her body, expanding, then rushing away in all directions. All sounds ceased, only to flow back as the vibrations diminished. She pressed a hand against her head, her breathing ragged.

What on Earth?

Both Francie and Orion shied as sparks soundlessly exploded into the air like a swarm of purple fireflies on the ridge above. A rumble started as the tallest of the pines lining the sky shivered and slowly toppled down the cliff, tumbling and rolling, branches snapping and trunk splintering as it fell.

She caught a silvery flash and her gaze jerked upward to the fresh cut of sky between the towering pines. Her breath caught. A figure stood where the tree was once anchored. She was too far away to take in details other than it was human—wide shoulders, two arms, two legs—his whole body encased in a puffy white body suit. The head was round and white except for a dark glassy shell covering the face.

The tree crash landed with one final crack in the gully. Orion sidled sideways and threw his head, tugging on the snaffle. The figure's black shining faceplate turned slowly as tense seconds ticked before the figure turned and bounded behind the ridge line, dropping from sight.

Had he seen them? She didn't think so but—who was he? A pilot ejected from some experimental aircraft out of White Sands? Or closer. Roswell Army Air Field had a flight training program.

But what she'd just seen was almost … unbelievable.

Orion danced beneath her. Francie unconsciously controlled her horse and stared at the opening in the line of trees. Her mind screamed to retreat, to run away. To contact someone to help.

Except she'd learned the hard way she couldn't rely on anyone but herself.

Francie reached with trembling fingers to touch the rifle sheathed in the scabbard next to her leg and set her jaw. No one would take her land.

Digging her knees into Orion's sides, Francie pointed him to the trail that led up to the ridge and to the person who'd fallen from the sky and trespassed on her ranch.

~~~~~
~~~~~

Chapter 1

She—Francie Pearl Cortez—was a nobody. They wouldn't believe her. Wouldn't believe what she'd witnessed. Why should they?

Doubt had grown during the precipitous drive from her mountainside ranch to the city of Roswell. Doubt had made her drive past the Roswell Army Air Field gates, past the Sheriff's office, and turn into the quiet turn of the century neighborhood. Doubt ran heavy through her body as she sat in the cooling cab of her pick-up truck. Her eyes burned with it, her vision blurred. With effort, she pried stiff hands from the steering wheel and brushed the pad of a gloved finger across her lashes to clear away the moisture.

The two-story Victorian, painted a pleasant sky-blue with a surfeit of bright-white gingerbread scrollwork, housed the man she'd called her mentor. Retired now, he and his wife lived a cozy, quiet life, their past accomplishments aspirational to Francie. Because of his help, she'd once believed with all her heart she'd been on the right path.

But she hadn't been strong enough.

Francie shook away her bitter thoughts. No use dwelling.

She unlatched the truck's door, extending a stockinged leg, her foot shod in shoes she'd purchased in Albuquerque two years earlier—patent black alligator-grained calf with a pyramid heel. Serious but with laced with a bow. She'd been worried about that bow. Worried whoever she spoke to about … about what she'd seen would dismiss her story as just one more crazy flying saucer sighting. But they were all she had left of her college wardrobe, along with the blue shirtwaist dress and wrist length matching gloves.

Stepping off the running board into onto the street, Francie breathed deeply, an attempt to slow her racing heart. She stared at the sunny yard surrounded by towering trees that acted as a living wall surrounding three sides of the house keeping the outside world out. The box hedges lining the sidewalk appeared a little ragged, as if they hadn't been trimmed. Francie frowned. Dr. Baer, an enthusiastic gardener, normally had them manicured to within an inch of their life. He told her it was how he relaxed his mind, how he worked out tricky solutions to even thornier problems. At Los Alamos, he'd used tiny Bonsai trees as his gardening outlet. They'd dotted the desk and table-tops of Francie's office and the Baer's home in the compound.

Francie negotiated the short steps to the narrow walkway that led to the veranda, her frown deepening. Sunny, bright, and too warm, the day sparkled around her, but the windows were dark except for glints of refracted sunlight on dusty panes. Like the glassy-eyed death she'd seen in an animal's eyes up on the ridge. The shadows under the veranda roof were hard and sharp, not a welcoming respite from the sun's heat.

She stopped and stared at the home of her friends. Was everything alright? Or had what happened that morning shaken her so badly that she was emoting her worry and unease on the world around her.

The ornate front door, stained glass woven around it in a colorful arch, opened. Dr. Baer slipped through, hunched in a black summer-wool suit. His thick white hair was mussed as if he'd just awakened from napping in the pair of matching chairs he and his wife sat in by the veranda window to watch the world go by. He squinted at her before his wonderful smile blossomed on his face.

"Francie! My dear. So unexpected yet so welcome." His faint German accent brought each syllable to a crisp end.

The world seemed to lighten around her. Her shoulders relaxed, and she dashed up the wooden steps onto the veranda to be enveloped in a hug, her nose pressed into the wool of his jacket, breathing in menthol and root beer. The man was addicted to Horehound candy.

Stepping back, Francie tugged Dr. Baer's spectacles from his shirt pocket, opened the thin wire arms, and tucked them over his ears and nose.

"Always forgetting," she said.

"At least they weren't perched on top of my head this time. An anchor is what they are, pulling me down to the depths of an age I don't wish to face." He waved a hand for Francie to proceed him inside, eyes twinkling behind the lenses. "You've come at the perfect time, my dear. Willa Mae has fixed us some tea and engelsaugen, which, I know are Christmas cookies, but Adelaide would have them now."

Dr. Baer led her into the foyer and left to the parlor when she found Adelaide Baer sitting in her cushioned chair, hand beckoning, and a lovely tray set with a silver teapot and paper-thin china cups arrayed next to a plate of Angel Eye thumbprint cookies, the jam center filled with either peach or apricot jam.

"Apricot," Adelaide said, as if reading Francie's mind. "From your trees at the ranch."

Francie's smile faltered a little as she bent to kiss the woman's papery cheek. Taller than her husband by half a foot, Adelaide appeared diminished, weight loss showing on gaunt cheeks normally apple round and pink, the color now owing to a heavier hand with powdered blush. But her eyes were still lit a bright cerulean blue and sparkled with life. She, as Adelaide had reminded Francie many-a-time at Los Alamos, did not need spectacles as her vision was perfect.

Francie perched across the low oval table on a green velvet settee, gloved hands tugging her dress over silk-stockinged knees before she accepted a cup of tea, one lump of sugar, a cookie tucked on the saucer.

She caught up with small talk and gentle gossip and sipped tea. The cookie was delicious, Francie's stomach reminding her that she hadn't eaten much of anything that morning because she'd been so keen to ride up to the … crash. If that was what she'd found. She stared pensively into her cooling tea, only vaguely realizing the conversation had lulled.

"And to what do we owe this visit, for you are dressed for success," Dr. Baer said, eyes behind his specs curious. "Not in your usual dungarees and boots, charming as that is."

Francie bit her lip. She flashed a glance at Adelaide, who seemed to understand without words.

"Ah! You need to speak to Eitan. Top secret." Adelaide smiled, but her eyes sharpened. "I'm used to it. I will speak to Willa Mae about dinner in the kitchen."

The Baer's housekeeper appeared as if by magic at Adelaide's side. Dr. Baer stood. Francie, rose too, breath catching as the two gently guided Adelaide to her feet and steadied her.

Adelaide clasped Willa Mae's arm, her smile still in place, but her face white and strained. "Would you join us for dinner, Francie?"

"I-I can't. I need to get back to the ranch tonight."

"Your animals." Adelaide chuckled. "How is your father's horse? And does that skunk and the other creatures still appear in your backyard?"

"Orion's as arrogant as ever and has added a few more tricks to his bag of 'let's mess with Francie'. The skunk shows up almost every night. The doe still comes—her fawn has lost its spots—and the ringtail cat family. And someone new. A pretty red fox, who showed up a few weeks ago."

"A red fox? Interesting. Well, let me disappear so you can have your talk. Please don't leave before I get to say goodbye."

The kitchen door closed behind the two ladies.

"Dr. Baer?" Francie gestured after his wife, but he shook his head.

"I'm afraid Adelaide wishes her health to be top secret for now. Just know she is getting the best care available." He sat across from her and clapped his hands on his knees. "Now, what can I help you with?"

The faded blue eyes of the man she'd deemed her mentor and supporter for the last five years probed her gaze. She hadn't lived up to her promise to him. Why would he believe her? Her shoulders slumped.

"Francie? What is the matt—"

"I saw something," she blurted. "This morning. In the sky. A-A bright light, but there was no contrail. I thought, maybe a missile from the bombing range. It dropped out of sight behind the ridge—the one close to where dad disappeared." She swallowed, unable to continue for a moment. "And then ..."

How could she explain the silent vibration? The purple fire-fly sparks? The fallen tree?

"You think a missile crashed on your land?" His brows pulled together. "Possible. Two have gone off course badly from the bombing range. Perhaps—"

But Francie shook her head violently. "But there was no crash, no sound. I rode up to the ridge to find it, and instead ... Instead ..." Her voice had dropped to whisper.

"What do you think you found, my dear?" His expression held pity.

He knew. He knew where she was going with her story. Knew because with time and distance, the same doubts had run through her head over and over on her drive to Roswell. Doubt about what she'd seen, what she'd experienced, her constant companion since she'd abandoned her degree and dropped out of college. Doubt that amplified her humiliation and the pity in the eyes of students and friends. Doubt that drove her to hide on the ranch.

Her stomach burned. Maybe she shouldn't have come to Dr. Baer. She'd only wanted to tell someone she trusted, to run the astounding story by someone who wouldn't dismiss her.

Francie stared at her knotted hands, afraid to look up in case his pity had morphed into derision. Gathering a seed of courage because *she knew what she'd seen*, she plowed ahead anyway.

"I think I found something not of this world. Something I can't explain." Francie met Dr. Baer's eyes. "I think I've found an extraterrestrial landing site."

~~~~~

Chapter 2

Dead silence, except for the ticking of half a dozen clocks hung around the room. It went on so long Francie squirmed in her seat. She felt a familiar sting behind her eyes.

"Oh, my dear." Dr. Baer shook his head, distress shadowing his gaze. He stood and shimmied around the coffee table to sit by her side on the settee. He picked up one of her hands and patted it.

"It's just a manifestation of anxiety. The war is over, but the world has changed so fast. And that bomb."

She'd seen it. Watched the detonation at Trinity. Had come down from Los Alamos with Dr. Baer. The fear and awe she'd buried deep inside emerged sometimes—dreams morphing into horrendous nightmares waking her in the middle of the night such that sleep didn't return. She'd get up, make coffee, and head to the barn and the comfort of her animals.

"Every day there is a new sighting," Dr. Baer continued, "or someone coming forward to report something odd in the skies. Oregon, Washington … Even this incident to the north with the weather balloon—"

"Do you believe what crashed on the Brazel ranch was just a weather balloon?" Francie had. Until that morning.

He raised his eyebrows. "No, but military secrecy runs deep. I do believe what crashed was top secret, and that they made a mistake saying it was a flying disk to cover it up. Yes, they corrected themselves the next day, but it just added to the craze. But I never thought you, of all people …"
~~~~~

Francie tugged her hand away and stood, humiliation complete. She was glad she hadn't gone to the military first and been laughed off the base, sneered at as just another stupid girl who couldn't handle her hysteria.

Dr. Baer stood slowly, brow and lips puckering. "Francie, I am sorry. I did not mean to hurt your feelings, not after what happened last year at university. I know you are sensitive. But to survive in this man's world, you must stiffen your upper lip, as the British say. Take the criticism thrown at you and learn from it."

"There was a spear," Francie said. "Like nothing I've ever seen. I-I took it and hid it in some rocks."

The phone in his office off the parlor jangled loudly. "Of course, of course! But you did not bring it with you? Excuse me, my dear, if I answer this." Dr. Baer hurried through an open door.

Francie stared after him, the crushing weight back in her chest. If he didn't believe her about the artifact, then he'd never believe her about the alien.

* * *

Carol Potenza taught biochemistry before transitioning to a full-time mystery writer. Her first novel was the Tony Hillerman Prize winner, *Hearts of the Missing*. She sets all her books in the beautiful state of New Mexico, where she lives with her husband, Leos. Please visit her at www.carolpotenza.com

Section Four: Writing for Children and Young Adults

Busted Artwork by Deborah Ranniger

Young Reader (Ages 8-12) – 1st place **Mary Therese Ellingwood**

Mrs. Weakly's Weekly Challenge

The school bell was minutes away from announcing the end of school. However, Nick and his classmates had one more important assignment left before they could pack up their bags for the day. It was time for Mrs. Weakly's Weekly Challenge.

"This week's challenge," said Mrs. Weakly, "is to go without screens. No phones, video games, TV, tablets. All screens must remain off."

There were a few groans, but most of the class was too shocked to even make a sound. No screens? Whatever would they do with their time?

"Remember to write down your experience each day in your Challenge Journals. See you tomorrow!"

The bell rang and everyone got ready to leave. Nick saw a classmate turn off her phone. He didn't even know phones could be turned off! He watched as the screen went dark and was shoved into a backpack.

On the bus ride home, Nick was still wearing his smart watch. It could probably be turned off, but was it really considered a screen? He could send and receive texts, but nothing else. Surely it wasn't part of the challenge. Besides, the challenges were technically optional. He knew some of his classmates were making up things to write in their Challenge Journals. But Nick was proud to have accomplished each challenge so far: a week of spending more time outside each day (he had taken the family dog, Barkley, on walks), a week of no sweets (that had been tough), a week of new desk-partners every day (not much of a challenge, but he got to know his classmates better), and a week of brainteasers to start each day (he found these pretty fun). But this was the hardest challenge yet!

When Nick got home, his older sister Valerie was already there. Her bus dropped her off from high school a half hour earlier. She was painting her nails and watching a show. He grunted a "hello" and went into his room. What was he going to do all week? He was bored just thinking about the possibility of no screens.

He threw his backpack in the corner of his room and stared around at the mess. There were clothes lying everywhere. Some were clean and some were dirty, all strewn about in a hurricane of colors. A few unread books were in a corner with a slightly deflated basketball leaning against them. Pillows and blankets and the rare stuffed animal were scattered on the floor, resting where they had landed when he flung them off the bed to get ready this morning. His desk was buried under mountains of art supplies, paper, rocks he had collected from his walks with Barkley the month before, and other stuff. It made sense to start his screen-free afternoon by cleaning. But replacing fun with cleaning? Ugh!

His watch pinged a text alert. Nick sprawled onto his unmade bed and tapped the tiny screen on his wrist.

Ping *Gonna do the challenge?*

It was from his best friend Garret.

He texted back: *Dunno*

Ping *Gotcha!*

Nick imagined the goofy grin on Garret's face. Garret was one of those who hadn't completed any of the challenges. He bragged to Nick and others about what he had written in the Challenge Journal and how clever he was to make stuff up while not doing any work.

But Garret could get away with that kind of thing. He was almost always alone since he had no siblings. His dad had left when he was little, and his mom was lucky to come home and make him dinner before heading out to her second job. Garret liked to talk big about how easy he had it with no one hounding him about school, but Nick suspected it got lonely.

Nick, on the other hand, always had family dinners where his parents asked what he and Valerie had learned at school each day. After dinner, they had to show their completed homework before they could go back online for the evening. And, to top it off, his mom was in the same Saturday morning yoga class as Mrs. Weakly. She always knew what Nick was supposed to be doing in class, so there wasn't much Nick could do to slack off without getting caught. Besides, he had actually enjoyed the other challenges. Maybe this one wouldn't be so bad.

Ping *Time to level-up*

Garret and Nick played Diablo online most afternoons. A whole week without playing would really set his character back.

Nick didn't reply.

Ping *Get'n on*

Nick wondered if he should take off his watch. It felt like cheating even if he didn't respond.

The text pings kept coming. Nick switched to vibrate mode in an attempt to ignore them, staring up at the boring ceiling instead. Finally, his watch went silent. Now all he could hear was muffled dialog from his sister's show floating though the air. He wondered where Barkley was.

Time passed slowly as he continued to loaf around on his bed. Eventually Nick heard the first car arrive in the driveway followed by a cheery, "I'm home" yell from his mom.

Maybe I should start my homework early, thought Nick. But, again, not fun. He didn't move.

About a half hour later Nick heard the second car pull up and then his dad's voice drifted in from this kitchen, "What's for dinner?"

Nick perked up. Food had a way of bringing him back to reality and the realization that he'd been starving for the last hour.

"Pork chops," came the response.

The warm smell of apple-marinated pork drifted over him. Nick felt very relaxed. Just lying in his room doing nothing actually felt pretty good. He would just wait for food to be ready and then he could decide what to do with the rest of his boring night.

Sitting down for dinner, Nick knew exactly what topic his mom would bring up.

"So," she looked eagerly at him, "what is Mrs. Weakly's weekly challenge this week?"

The sentence always made Valerie chuckle. Doubtless, his mom already knew and was waiting for him to say it.

"No screens."

"Seriously?!" said Valerie, stunned. "Wait. How come you're still wearing your watch? Skipping out on this one?"

"It's a watch. I'm just using it for the time."

"Sure. Cheater."

"Well, I think that is an excellent challenge," said Mom.

At her tone, Nick began to wonder if it had been his mother's idea to begin with. Maybe a list of chores was about to come his way. You know… to fill his time. He sighed.

"What are you going to do instead of playing video games?" asked his dad. Right on cue. "You could go back to walking Barkley after dinner if you like."

Barkley was sitting at his usual spot under the table. Nick felt his head perk up at the sound of his name and the word walk. A small whine sounded from under the table.

Nick had enjoyed walking Barkley, but he didn't want his parents deciding what he was going to do. He just shook his head.

"No. I have a lot of homework tonight," he exaggerated. "And there's lots of things I want to do since Garret and I can't play our game."

"Well, if you're done discussing Nick's life, I'd like to remind you that I need to get more driving hours in before Saturday," said Valerie.

Thankfully the rest of the meal's conversation was hijacked by Valerie discussing her upcoming driver's ed exam, a wish-list for the car she thought she was getting (which she definitely was not getting) for her sixteenth birthday, and then all things Semi-Formal related. Nick helped himself to seconds and pondered his undesired freedom and what he'd do with his time. He still had no idea.

"How was your first day of the challenge?" asked Mrs. Weakly. "Anyone want to share what they did?"

There were a lot of grumbles and whispers that passed through the room. Some took the opportunity to privately chat with their desk mates. Awkward silence grew as Mrs. Weakly waited. Then a few hands went into the air.

"I started a new book," said Tiffany. *Sure*, Nick thought. *She was probably going to do that anyway*. Tiffany was a bookworm who thought the eBook format was a travesty to education.

"I helped my younger brother with his homework," said Josh. Josh was a teacher's pet and never wasted a moment to stress his rule-following efforts.

"I held an extra jam session with my band," said Pete.

Garret caught Nick's eye and winked. Then he raised his hand. "I helped my mom clean the basement."

Garret's house didn't even have a basement. But Mrs. Weakly just smiled and said, "wonderful!" Then she put 'cleaning' on the board next to 'reading,' 'homework,' and 'practice and instrument.' So far, the list of things looked dismal.

Nick wondered if anyone had actually done anything fun with their time. He certainly hadn't. He had lounged around in a bore for the afternoon and after dinner had done his normal homework in record sloth-mode, while scribbling doodles in the margins.

Mrs. Weakly then asked for a show of hands of which students hadn't started the challenge yet. A few brave students, and those who simply didn't care, admitted this fact. She encouraged them to at least try it for one day while Garret shook his head knowingly at all the slackers. Suddenly Nick's backpack vibrated. He stole a peak as his hidden watch lit up.

Games 2nite?

Nick hid a smile.

Arriving home that afternoon Nick was determined to find a way to fill his time with fun. He thought back to his childhood. He must have had some way of entertaining himself before screens took over. Sweeping aside space on his desk, Nick made a list of things to do. Walk Barkley was at the top. Necessary chores filled most of the remaining space. Where was the fun? Valerie was yet again watching TV in the living room, this time while scrolling on her smartphone. Man! Two screens while he couldn't even have one.

Finally, when Mom came home and announced she was starting dinner, Nick had a plan.

"Mom, can I help make dinner?" Nick asked.

"Well, sure! That would be great."

Nick only knew how to make sandwiches and microwave meals. Tonight, Mom was cooking breaded chicken with roasted vegetables and homemade macaroni and cheese. She showed him how to peel the carrots and he got to pound the chicken into thin strips. That part was a lot of fun! The kitchen smelled amazing as the chicken fried on the stove and the veggies baked in the oven.

While the rest of the meal cooked, Mom taught him how to make the macaroni sauce. But he wasn't watchful enough and the milk quickly boiled over. What a mess! Cream streaks caked the side of the pot, and the burner was surrounded by a puddle of milk. Starting over, Nick asked if they could make it spicy and his mom added a pinch of cayenne pepper to the cheesy sauce. When her back was turned, Nick added a tad more. *Nothing wrong with bringing the heat*, he thought.

When they finally sat down to dinner, Nick felt proud that the meal turned out great, but the mac sure was spicy! Valerie took a big bite without realizing it and tears came to her eyes. Nick laughed hard.

"Well, if you don't like it maybe you can help with dinner next time," Mom said to her.

Dad loved Nick's take on the meal and decided to call the spicy macaroni and cheese Nick's Fire Noodles. That sounded cool!

After dinner Nick ended up taking Barkley on a walk.

* * *

The next day, Nick not only helped make dinner again, but he got to choose the meal – spaghetti and meatballs with garlic bread.

After dinner, he took Barkley on a new path to the park. Some kids around his age were starting a pick-up basketball game and asked him to join. Barkley was happy to sit in the shade and watch. Nick met Tony, Lamar, and Dion. They went to one of the charter schools in town and met up every Tuesday for a game of ball. Nick helped even out the teams and they played three short games before it got too dark. He was invited to come back next week for a rematch.

By Thursday, Nick was starting to enjoy his screen-free time. He had almost forgotten about his smart watch, which was sitting neglected at the bottom of his backpack. He was officially Barkley's new walker, much to his dad's delight. He also had some awesome ideas added to his list of things to do, which extended beyond chores: earn money by helping around the neighborhood (maybe he could start a dog-walking service), consider joining an after-school club, Basketball Tuesdays, dust off his guitar skills and get playing, try some art tutorials on YouTube (because, well, heck. The challenge wouldn't last forever).

For a week that started off as a complete nightmare, Nick was surprised at how quickly Friday arrived. At school, he turned in his Challenge Journal detailing his screen-free week. The weekend opened up, and Garret was insistent that Nick get back to their online game. Garret had completed six quests without Nick and was eager to show off all of his character upgrades and new loot.

Nick was looking forward to the return of screens, but he had enjoyed his break despite it all. He didn't want to go totally screenless again, but maybe less time playing video games and scrolling online would have its benefits.

* * *

The following Monday, as the day came to an end, Nick sat awaiting the next challenge with the rest of the class.

"This week's Weekly Challenge," said Mrs. Weakly, "will be to make or cook your own meals at least once a day. You could make breakfast, pack your own lunch, or help a parent make dinner."

Now Nick definitely knew the truth! At yoga his mom obviously talked to Mrs. Weakly about the class challenges. But he had to admit, he was looking forward to cooking more with her and learning new recipes. Maybe they could even do some baking this week. Cinnamon rolls for breakfast sure sounded good.

* * *

Mary Therese Ellingwood lives in Albuquerque where she is a mathematics professor by day and a writer by night (or whenever she can find the time). When she's not reading to her three-year-old, she is lost in her own imagination until it can make it onto the page.

Young Reader (Ages 8-12) – 2nd Place **Rosie Kern**

Joe and the Princess

In the kingdom of Jasra near a large lake, lived a family of German Shepherd dogs. Kaiser Shepherd was the Chief Palace Protecter.

His troop protected the King.

Chief Kaiser was very proud of his family. He and his mate, Jarlene had many puppies. Kevin, Karl, Kasey, Karla, Kethry, Kelly, Kerry and Joe.

As all the puppies grew, they dreamed of being police dogs, rescue dogs, guard dogs and guide dogs.

All except Joe.

Joe dreamed of dancing and making people smile.

Kaiser taught all his children to defend themselves and others. He taught them when to attack and how to tell a friend from foe. All of them excelled in training.

Even Joe.

But Joe did not want to train in fields or get his fur all muddy. Joe wanted to dance and leap and play in the sun with a buddy.

One day Kaiser took his family to the palace. All the puppies padded along in perfect formation with heads and tails held high. They went to see the King and Queen.

All except Joe.

Joe loved the big open halls and stairs. He fell behind because there were too many places to look.

Kevin, Karl, Kasey, Karla, Kethry, Kelly and Kerry bowed before the King and the Queen. Kaiser barked a command and they all sat in perfect formation.

But where was Joe?

Joe was upstairs walking down a hallway when he heard crying. He poked his head in a door. There was a little girl sitting in a big room by herself. She was sad.

Joe did not like people to be sad.

Joe walked up and poked his cold nose on her cheek. The little girl was startled. She looked at Joe and sniffled. Joe cocked his head. The little girl's eyes were wide.

Joe did not want her to cry, so he began to dance.

Joe spun around and pretended to snap at his tail. The girl giggled.

Joe jumped to the side of a bed. He pulled a small blanket off and started tossing it up then slapping it down on the floor. The little girl laughed and laughed.

The King and the Queen thought Kaiser's kids were wonderful. The Queen said to the King "My dear, Princess Janelle has been sad and lonely of late, perhaps she would like to see Kaiser's children parade."

Kaiser and the King went up the stairs. The Queen and the pups stayed below. The King looked for Princess Janelle.

Kaiser looked for Joe.

The King and Kaiser opened a door. They found Joe and Janelle playing tug of war.

The King looked at Kaiser. Kaiser thought he was in trouble. Then the King looked at his daughter and his laughter rumbled.

"Kaiser, my boy, if this is your son, I would give him a job. The Princess needs a companion."

Kaiser gave him a nod.

So, Joe guards Janelle and sleeps by her bed.

They dance, and they play, and she never is sad.

* * *

Rosie Kern

This story was inspired by my crazy German Shepherd, Joe. He loved to grab his leash in his mouth and jump around when we went walking. For more information on Rosie's books go to: www.rosemariekern.com

Young Reader (Ages 8-12) – 3rd place **Mary Therese Ellingwood**

Chasing a Wish

Chase couldn't wait for his party to begin. It was his tenth birthday and he had spent months dreaming about the wish he'd make when he blew out the candles. Chase had always wanted a dog.

After a day full of fun at the zoo and dinner at Pizza Palace, the family was at last back home for cake and presents. Everyone sang Happy Birthday as his mom placed a huge chocolate cake with sprinkles in front of him. Ten candles were a lot to blow out, but he had been practicing. Chase knew the wish would only come true if he blew them all out in one go.

"… and many more," they finished singing.

"Make a wish," said his dad.

Chase took a deep breath, closed his eyes, and blew as hard as he could across the ten tiny flames.

Everyone erupted in cheers as he opened his eyes. He had done it! All ten candles dripped with wax but not an orange flicker of light in sight. Score!

"What did you wish for?" asked his older sister Lilly.

"I can't tell you or it won't come true," Chase said, digging into the cake.

He ate his slice quickly, glancing at the presents on the table. They were sure to be great, but none of them was big enough for a dog. He looked around on the floor and craned to see into the living room, checking for any hidden gifts.

Once the table was cleared it was time to open presents. One by one, he tore off the wrapping paper. He got a new video game, some books, a large brick-building set, a pair of squirt guns and a remote-controlled robot that could walk and move its arms. He tried not to look too disappointed. They were all fabulous gifts, but none of them was a dog.

"There's just one more," said Dad.

Chase looked around but didn't see any more bags or boxes. Where was it?

"Why don't you check the front door?"

Chase's face lit up and he raced to the door with everyone trailing behind him. He tugged it open…

On the front steps was a shiny new bike. Lilly ran over to it and looked at the gears.

"No fair! His new bike has twelve speeds! Mine doesn't even have gears."

"Now, Lilly," said Mom. "Let Chase enjoy his new bike. Why don't you kids get on your bikes and ride around the neighborhood?"

Chase had to admit, the bike was pretty fantastic. He, Lilly, and their older brother, Drew, spent over an hour racing down the empty streets. They biked past a friend's house so Chase could show off his prize. It was a lot of fun. But Chase knew it would have been better to be racing with a dog than his two siblings. Would his dream of owning a dog ever come true?

The next morning at breakfast, Chase had an idea.

"Mom, is it true that you can make a wish if you blow on a flower?"

Lilly chimed in, "Only if it is a dandelion and you get all the seeds off in one blow."

"Oh. Are there other things we can wish on besides birthday candles and dandelions?"

"Sure," said Drew. "You can wish on lots of things. Shooting stars, ladybugs – but only the red ones – a fallen eyelash, the time at exactly 11:11, four-leaf clovers, wishbones…"

Chase was getting excited.

"I'd like to try my wish again, since it didn't come true on my birthday. Is that allowed?"

"I don't see why not," said Mom. "I doubt I can find a turkey this time of year. But I can make a whole chicken tonight so you can have the wishbone."

"Dibs! I want to do it with you!" Lilly said, raising her hand. "Remember, only the one who breaks off the biggest half gets the wish."

There sure were a lot of rules to wishing, thought Chase.

That afternoon, Chase's mom took him and Lilly to the park. Drew went over to a friend's house to play in their pool. Instead of running around on the playground, Chase went to the open field and hunted for dandelions. It was hard because Lilly was there, too, snatching many of them before he got a chance and blowing on them fiercely while shouting, "I wish for money. I wish for purple hair. I wish for s'mores for breakfast. I wish for a unicorn. I wish…"

Her wishes seemed to get louder and more ridiculous. Chase found many dandelions himself, but he was having trouble blowing all of the seeds off at once. They were much harder to blow than birthday candles. Lilly offered to help, but he had a feeling that one of the rules was that he had to do it himself. Finally, on his fifth dandelion, it worked! All the seeds blew into the air in a rush of white fluff that drifted lazily back down to the ground.

Chase made his wish silently. Then he went to play on the swings. He didn't want to jinx his wish by being too greedy. He suspected that none of Lilly's wishes would come true because she was overdoing it.

That evening his mom made a delicious roasted chicken. She even made green bean casserole and rolls to go with it. It reminded Chase of a mini-Thanksgiving, but instead of focusing on being thankful he was focused on his upcoming wish. He'd be thankful when it came true. There was just one problem – Lilly.

After dinner, he stood with his thumb pressed against the top of the wishbone looking into Lilly's determined face across from him. He couldn't bear to have his wish stolen by someone who wanted purple hair! What a waste that would be.

"Ready?" Mom started the countdown. "Three, two, one!"

They both pressed and pulled mightily before a loud *crack* snapped through the air. Chase did it! He had the bigger bone! Silently he made his wish again.

"Well, at least I made lots of other wishes today," said Lilly. She didn't seem too disappointed.

"Mom, can I stay up late tonight?" asked Chase.

"Why?"

"I want to make a wish when the clock shows 11:11 *and* I want to wish on a shooting star."

"But you've already made two wishes today. Don't you think that's enough?"

Chase shook his head.

"I think staying up may not be the best idea," said Mom.

Chase was disappointed.

When his parents said goodnight to him that night, his dad pulled him aside and winked. "I have a plan," he whispered. "Good night, Champ!"

Chase lay in bed and tried hard to stay up anyway, but eventually his eyes closed, and he was pulled into a wonderful dream about a genie and a magic lamp. Then he felt a gentle nudge on his shoulder pulling him out of his dream. Waking, he saw his dad pointing to the clock in his room.

"Almost time," Dad whispered.

The clock read 11:10. Chase rubbed his eyes clear and stared without blinking. The red glow seemed to pulse with energy until finally the zero blinked out and was replaced by a one. Chase silently made his wish. He turned to go back to sleep, but his dad shook him again and motioned for him to follow.

Outside of his room Drew was waiting with a flashlight.

"Let's go find a shooting star," he whispered.

Chase filled with excitement. They tip-toed out of the house. Drew led him to the back, and they raced to the very edge of their yard. Plopping down on the cool grass they gazed at the sky. His brother turned off the flashlight and they were plunged into darkness.

"What are you wishing for anyway, Chase?"

"I can't tell you or it won't come true."

"Maybe if you tell me I can help it come true."

Chase just shook his head, his gaze never leaving the sky. After a pause he asked Drew, "Have you ever seen a shooting star?"

"No. I think they are quite rare. But then again, I've never really looked."

The stars twinkled above but there was no movement other than a few bright lights signaling the path of a few airplanes into the night.

"If we don't find one can we try again tomorrow?"

"Tomorrow I'm staying over at Jason's," Drew replied.

"Oh."

"But maybe we can try another night."

Chase smiled with promise, his eyes still fixed on the sky. Tonight there just had to be a shooting star!

As they waited and searched, Drew pointed out some constellations. Chase had heard of them before, but he'd never seen them. The Big Dipper was his favorite and Drew said it could be used to find the North Star, but he couldn't remember how. They chatted about the summer and what sports Chase might play once he got into middle school. Chase hadn't spent much time alone with his older brother because they liked to do different things. But it was nice to talk to him secretly out in the yard under the stars. It made Chase feel older, somehow, and valued.

Suddenly, a spark sped across the open sky and winked out just as quickly.

"Did you see it?!" asked Drew.

"I did! I saw it!"

"Let's make a wish."

Chase silently made his wish. Glancing over at his brother he saw Drew's eyes were closed. He was wishing too. Chase thought wishes were only for younger kids, but the sight of his brother sending a secret hope into the night made him smile.

"That was really fun," said Chase, as they walked back to the house under the guidance of the flashlight.

"It was. I hope your wish comes true."

"I hope yours does, too." Chase had the feeling his brother had wished for something more important than purple hair.

Back in bed, Chase went to sleep with dreams of wishes coming true.

The next day began with the usual routine of family breakfast and then freedom. Drew left for Jason's house on his bike. Lilly went into her room to practice her make-up skills with help from an online tutorial. Chase decided to start building his new brick set and dumped the colorful pieces onto the floor of the living room. A cell phone buzz interrupted his concentration and then he heard his mom's muffled voice chatting with the invisible caller.

"Lilly, Chase, get your shoes on," called Mom's voice a few minutes later. "We're going over to Jason's house."

"Why?" shouted Lilly from her room, "Did Drew forget his toothbrush?"

"No. Drew didn't forget anything. There's a surprise over there."

Chase climbed into the car with Lilly wondering why Jason would have a surprise for them. When they arrived, Drew and Jason were playing in the front yard inside a fenced off circle that was full of…

"Puppies!" yelled Chase as he ran over to meet them.

"Drew talked your father and I into getting a family dog. What do you think?" said Mom.

Lilly and Chase leaned over the makeshift wire fence to pet the squirming, jumping litter. Four golden labs barked in delight at all the attention. They were so cute!

Drew leaned over and whispered to Chase, "Was this your wish?"

Chase nodded.

"Mine, too. Jason told me about the puppies a month ago, but they weren't big enough to meet yet."

"We didn't come earlier because it was your birthday, Chase," said Mom. "And this won't be just your dog. It's the family's. So, which one should we get?"

"I don't care. They are all so cute!" said Lilly.

"I think Chase should pick," offered Drew.

Chase looked back at the four adorable pups. Two were tripping over themselves trying to get the most pets, one was sitting and panting on the grass, and one simply tilted his head back with one floppy ear covering an eye. He whimpered at Chase.

"That's the one," he said.

Chase thought about all of the wishes he had made over the last two days.

"Can we call him Wishbone?"

Lilly laughed.

* * *

Mary Therese Ellingwood lives in Albuquerque where she is a mathematics professor by day and a writer by night (or whenever she can find the time). When she's not reading to her three-year-old, she is lost in her own imagination until it can make it onto the page.

Young Adult (Ages 13-17) - 1st Place E.A. Rickman

Brena the Brave

PART I

A fisher young will find
the rainbow bridge to anchor.
Then cure a monster-maker
so peace will come to kind.

Chapter 1

I will. I will. Stop, Gran," bent over and panting, Brena Fisher put out her hand toward her grandmother. Another scream pierced the dark, wet night. Pain was evident in the woman's cry. Whoever was torturing that woman wanted Brena, too.

She looked around the corner of the rain-slicked building. She wanted to know who and why she was being hunted. Huge black wings of an otherwise invisible predator flapped across the street above the empty town square. She pulled her head away from the street and back into the alley. Where could she go, who could help her?

The windows were dark on the upper floors of the buildings along the alley. No one looked out to help her.

She felt a familiar pressure on her forearm and heard a loving voice, "Remember, save Henry," her Gran insisted. She nodded and mouthed, "I will, Gran."

Brena's brother Henry was three years younger and "clueless," which probably was the reason Gran wanted Brena to protect him.

She felt Gran squeeze and pat her arm. Brena's attention recoiled from the street and town square. Her Gram would know what to do.

She turned to where she had felt her grandmother. No one was there. With a shudder she remembered that her grandmother had died the previous year.

Brena stood alone, shivering.

As close to the wall as possible, she walked to the opposite opening for the alley and peered out onto the larger street.

How long had she been running? Her feet were bare, cold on the rain-slathered cobblestones, her pantlegs drenched. In the shadows of the night, she pulled close her hooded cape and dashed alley to alley, across the deserted road.

The drizzle pelted sideways.

She heard the distant baying of hounds. Closer still, she felt the batting of those large wings that broke up the horizontal droplets. Dim streetlights flickered as if a colony of bats swarmed them. Shadows formed and disappeared.

A high-pitched screech pierced her heart. Was that a woman in pain or a bird of prey? She had to go faster.

Too wet, too deserted. She ran full-out down the alley.

Not good, she thought. Another shriek ripped the night. She slowed.

"Remember, save Henry," her Gran pleaded.

"Yes, yes, I will," Brena mouthed as she tried to melt into the slick stone wall. Hands on her knees, she panted and listened. Were they close? She heard the hounds, straightened and ran again.

"Remember," her grandmother's voice returned and surrounded her even as talons attached to a hand too claw-like to be human began to materialize over Brena's head.

"Come, little witch, all of you Fishers soon will be mine."

That wasn't Gran's voice.

The talons reached for her.

"Gran? Granlo? Where are you? Brena twisted but could not raise her arms. Ropes tightened around her as she squirmed.

She rolled across a firm smooth surface, away from the talons.

"Wake up. Remember." That was Gran.

Where was... Brena strained to come fully awake. Horror lingered.

The crash was enough to shake Brena from her nightmare and spin her out of her bed sheet.

She bounced to her feet in a fighting crouch. Birds chirped outside.

Birds chirped? There'd been no chirping birds. She looked around at her radiantly yellow bedroom. Night had disappeared. No storm. Instead, the day's brilliance cascaded in. She almost collapsed in relief.

Silly me. Brena of the Fisher Clan swung her head to shake her hair out of her eyes before remembering that she no longer had waist-length hair. She was no longer a child, she was a woman now, and she was alone in her own bedroom.

Safe. No boogeymen. No Gran. Despite or maybe because of the closeness of Brena's family, Gran's death had been a major loss for all of them, and had been particularly hard for Brena.

The clock read six-thirteen. She shut off the alarm that would have roused her and Henry in two minutes. She stood before the mirror. Looking ahead and behind her, something *felt off.* Nothing seemed out of place, but there was that *feeling.*

She shook herself. The nightmare was like a lingering tangible odor that covered her body, crawling around under her skin.

What had her grandmother told her to remember? What was it? The claw, I remember the claw, the dark, and the creepy wet streets, and Hobo.

"Henry," Brena bellowed and dashed into the hallway and her brother Hobo's bedroom. Hobo was Henry's "birth name," the name he carried until his naming ceremony when he was six. After he received his naming ceremony, his birth name became a nickname. Her birth name had been Bluejay.

"Henry, are you all right?" She faced a mound on a bed.

Puddles gurgled merrily from his bassinette across the room. He pulled himself up to stand. Gripping the bars, he bounced up and down. He released the bars to put out his arms to her. With a plop, he fell back onto his bum. After blinking and looking around, he beamed up at her.

"Good one, Puddles." She turned back to the inert object. "Henry, wake up," Brena shook the heap.

"Huh" came a muffled grunt from the mass of sheets and blankets.

"Are you okay?"

"'Course I," and the answer ended.

Brena turned back to her baby brother, "Keep an eye on him, okay?"

Puddles gurgled his response.

"Love you, Puddles."

The baby nodded vigorously again grasping the bars of his crib.

"Time for school, Hobo," Brena swatted Henry's bulk, more bed linens than boy.

* * *

Something's missing, she thought. She showered, dressed and towel-dried her hair. Her hair's texture was soft and, just like her mother, aunt and grandmother, like all of the women in the Fisher family, curly bordering on frizzy. When dry, her "Fisher hair" resembled a shiny new penny, her mother's gleamed black as obsidian. She mentally went through the morning's checklist—*room's good. Everything's picked up, but there's still something missing.*

"Earbobs," she said aloud and rummaged through her box of pretties. Aunt Geri had told her that Gran called earrings "earbobs." "Yes, the green glass droplets that look like emeralds." They would bring out her hazel eyes.

She inserted the earrings and looked carefully at herself in the mirror. "Sun sprinkles," commonly known as freckles, dusted her nose, shoulders and the tops of her arms.

Next time, I'm choosing Hobo's complexion, she thought. She did not know if reincarnation existed, but she knew that Hobo's complexion was less trouble. Even with sunscreen, her skin turned from "peaches and cream" to painful lobster red and peeled.

Without sunscreen, after a day in the sun, his olive skin turned pinkish tan and then golden, the hue deepening daily until his skin became the same bronze color as his hair, which perfectly set off his blue eyes. *Yep, next time.*

"Breakfast is ready," her mother called up the stairway. "Let's shake a leg."

"Another magnificent day," Brena pronounced her beginning-of-the-day mantra then stopped to wonder, *Had I said the phrase quickly to anchor the delights of a new day or ward off something else?*

She pinned aside her still wet auburn bangs to better see the world.

Opening her bedroom door, she snagged her feathery knit boa and shouted, "Coming."

More softly, she pronounced her new word, "Panache. That's what I have." But this morning, it was not what she felt.

Something is in my house that shouldn't be here, something I can't see or hear, but can feel. She refocused her sight, looked around and shrugged again. *My imagination.*

"Nightmare forgotten," she pronounced. At fourteen Brena often spoke aloud to herself. As Gran said, Brena was her own best counsel.

She jumped two at a time down the stairs, her backpack bouncing with each leap. She deposited her bag and boa next to the backdoor and swung into the kitchen.

"Good morning, Mamá," Brena said. She kissed her mother's cheek, and received a steaming bowl of cereal and cup of cocoa with marshmallows.

"You look lovely this morning, my dear," Glenda said, assessing her daughter. "But, is that skirt just a bit too short?"

"Thank you, Mamá, but you'll find that I am one-quarter inch inside the rules." Brena smiled triumphantly before blowing on her cocoa.

Her mother winked, "That's my girl. Stay within their rules. I don't want you sent home for dress code violation, and you *do* look wonderful." Humming softly,

Glenda checked the kitchen clock, and turned back to the stove where she stirred simmering cocoa.

Brena was in the second week of the tenth grade. She considered her friends as wonderful, but her classes were not yet what they should be. According to Brena, the school's administration listened to parents but not to students, whom they considered children without the right to advocate for themselves.

Her family and the rest of their Fisher clan saw her differently. To them, Brena was an adult, and had been for over a year.

From her stool, she stretched out an arm and snagged a discarded section of newspaper from the kitchen table and flopped it onto the island counter. She glanced at the front-page headlines, skimmed the photos and stories.

"How's Henry?" she asked her mother while she ate and read.

"Hmm, let's see how our Hobo fares." Her mother winked at the kitchen corner's TV screen. It came on seemingly by itself. Henry was struggling into a navy-blue pullover sweater, nearly dressed.

"Remember your shoes, Henry," Glenda said softly.

"I got it, Mum, no worries. Did Bren tell you she accosted me this morning?" Henry fell onto his knees to look under his bed. He pulled out one of his shoes and looked around his bedroom. "Dang, where's the other one?"

"Your other shoe's in your other hand. Hurry along. Cocoa's waiting."

"Thanks, Mum, I'll be right down."

"Good morning, Puddles," Glenda crooned. "I'll be up after the big kids are off to school."

"Want me to bring Puddles?" Henry asked as he looked for his comb.

"No need, just remember your backpack, okay?"

"Backpack, check. Guys' room out."

Brena's mother blinked again at the television screen that went blank. "Tell me about accosting Henry this morning?"

Brena turned to the newspaper's astrology section. "Sure." She looked up. "I had a weird dream. Gran kept telling me to save Henry."

"Granlo or Granbe?" Granlo would be Grandmother Louise, Glenda's mother. Granbe would be Grandmother Beatrix, her father's mother.

"Granlo. When I woke up, I went in to check on him. He moved, but who could tell with his pile of blankets. Henry sleeps like a burrowing critter. So I kept poking until he told me he was okay."

Brena deposited her empty dishes into the sink and retrieved her lunch and Henry's from the refrigerator. She placed Henry's lunch sack on the counter.

As usual in the morning, Bob sat at the kitchen table. Bits of eggs and toast remained on the plate in front of him. He was sitting back, reading the sports page, and occasionally sipping his cup of coffee. They had a truce. Unless in public, he took no notice of her, and Brena appeared to ignore him.

As always, she told herself, *It's not Bob's fault.* She named the real problem, *He looks too much like Pa.* He looked like her father, sounded like him, walked like him. In fact, Bob was a perfect duplicate. He was the golem magically created to stand in for her father so their neighbors would not question his absence. When Normals were around, she called him "Pa" and acted like he was her father, but he was not her father.

Someday, we'll all be together again, was her frequent refrain. *I will* not *be upset,* she quietly repeated and stood straighter. *I'm in charge of my own attitude. This is going to be a wonderful day.* She glanced at the clock.

"Where's Henry?" Brena asked, perhaps too pertly, as she folded the newspaper.

Ladle in hand, her mother softly muttered a familiar spell. The television again came alive.

"Henry's still in the bathroom, working on his hair. The baby's sound asleep in his bassinette."

Brena pointed her index finger and flicked her wrist. Instantly, her emptied bowl and spoon were washed and resting on the drainer.

"Thank you, my dear," her mother said.

She seems preoccupied today, Brena thought.

"Will Hobo be ready on time?" she asked as she inserted her lunch in her backpack.

Her mother swept her hand clockwise at the television screen. A chronometer in the screen's corner rapidly advanced 10 minutes but Henry still was in the bathroom.

"Not without help," her mother said. She blinked and the television screen darkened. "Henry," she called loudly. "Get ready."

"Ah, Mum," he called down. "I can do it, really I can."

"Here it comes," she replied, snapped her fingers and flicked her wrist.

Instantly, Henry appeared in the kitchen, book bag in hand, hair combed, fully and neatly dressed, shoes tied.

She squeezed his book bag. "I remembered your lunch," his mother commented and smiled. "Did I include breakfast as well?"

"Don't think so," he answered as the clock struck seven.

"What would you like?" she asked.

"Eggs and cinnamon waffles, please," Henry answered perking up. His mop of sandy brown hair began to slide down his forehead.

His mother patted his shoulder. The slender young man belched.

"I like the cinnamon, but I thought they were going to be on a plate," he lamented.

"If you're on time tomorrow, they will be," she smiled.

"Right. Thanks, Mum," Henry said looking a bit disconcerted.

Brena flicked her pinkie. Her book bag transported onto her shoulders and her boa to her hand.

"Remember, you two, magic in the house, not outside." Their mother smiled. She blew Brena a kiss before turning back to Henry. "As for you, my young man...." She squeezed his nose, patted his tummy, and kissed his cheek. "Have a great day and keep the magic capped."

He nodded solemnly.

"Come on, Hobo, or we'll miss the bus," Brena said. She opened the door and pushed Henry through. "Love you, Mamá. Bye all," she called over her shoulder.

She followed him through their side yard, under the trees, and across their neatly trimmed front yard. A breeze tousled her hair interrupting her thoughts. The accompanying energetic tweak informed her that this was another magickin, not an ordinary breeze.

Good morning, she sent telepathically to the invisible magical being who played with her.

Good morning to you, Brena the Brave, the air current sent back to her.

Gosh, I like the title, though undeserved. What's your name?

Sophie, the voice answered, *and your title will be deservedly earned.*

Uncertain of that comment, Brena asked the name of Sophie's Group, *What kind of Current are you?*

Watcher, the breeze replied.

Are you watching anything in particular today, or just visiting? Brena asked.

We're watching you, Sophie answered with a twinkle in her voice. A giggle rose from what sounded like several young people.

Me? I'm honored, but think you'll be pretty bored watching me go to school. You must have seen this millions of times, Brena said.

Today's special, Sophie replied.

Special how? she asked.

Beware, another voice said in a rushed whisper.

What? Brena began a question, but the Currents were gone. Only stillness and sunshine surrounded her.

"You coming, Slow-poke?" Henry called to her. The large, marigold colored school bus rounded the curve two blocks away.

She smiled at him, "Not to worry, young-un."

"Don't *Speed.* You know what Mummy says," he called back to her.

He was right. To Normals, magic was silly tricks or the stuff of madness. After all, what normal person would ever chat with the wind?

The Dexter boys ran around the other corner nearing the bus stop. If she did *Speed*, she would have an audience, which required rearranging memories to forget what they had seen.

"Hardly worth the bother," Brena muttered to herself. Instead, she ran to the bus stop in the normal way, greeted the Dexter boys, and took her seat in the back. Feeling another energetic tug, she looked out the rear window and heard tingling laughter. All was still and calm in her neighborhood, except the dust devils trailing the bus.

* * *

E. A. Rickman has lived in and around Albuquerque since well into the last millennium. Dr. Rickman favors reading, writing, travel, and myriad community projects, including being a life member of La Montañita Co-op, and involvement with the Innovation Academy at the University of New Mexico.

Young Adult (Ages 13-17) - 2nd Place **Hayley Nations**

Inheritance

Prologue

Rain pattered on the windowpanes one night. Most of the exterior walls were made of windowpanes in the penthouse, the double mirror kind, in which the occupants could look out but no one could look in. The effect was mostly pointless, as the penthouse was higher up than any other building in a one-hundred-mile radius at least, but it gave a feeling of safety and isolation. The sound was calming, carrying the family into a deeper and deeper sleep. Or perhaps that was the effect of the drugged beverages from dinner.

The king and queen slept, lightly snoring, deeply in the dark, rainy night, blissfully unaware of the danger that was now breaking into the penthouse. The emergency exit, built to only be used as an outward door, was being opened from the outside. This should have been impossible.

The assassin sneaked in, feet silent on the soft floor. The killer already had the floor plan memorized and knew exactly where to go. First the parents, then the daughter, then the son. The whole royal family wiped out in one fell swoop.

The king and queen didn't stir as their bedroom door was opened. The assassin stepped over the still forms of the bodyguards, some dead and some drugged, and walked closer to the bed's occupants. No reaction from them. The assassin slid a knife from an inner pocket and across their throats, no fanfare, no theatrics, just alive and then dead. The king and queen were not awakened and never would be as their blood streamed onto the bed and soaked in.

It was on the way to the oldest child's room, the heir, that the assassin started getting followed. A shadow in the darkness, the royal guard followed behind the intruder.

Sensing prying eyes, the assassin stopped, waited a heartbeat, then whipped around in time to dodge a punch that would have landed on the back of the neck. The assassin back tracked, made room, then leaped forward, knife in hand. The royal guard, who had missed dinner, pressed forward, feinting and throwing blows. The assassin lashed out with the knife, but was disappointed to find it couldn't penetrate the guard's armor. They continued to fight, the assassin slowly leading the guard down the hall and towards the emergency exit and the fire escape.

Once at the straight hallway that lead directly to the exit, the assassin turned and sprinted towards the fire escape, grabbing a leather satchel from a hidden pocket.

The guard gave chase, enhanced muscles and augmented joints increasing his speed. The assassin was through the exit and turned to the door but didn't have enough time to fulfill that part of the plan. Instead, the guard tackled the murderer at full speed, jetting the two off the top floor fire escape and hundreds of feet towards the cold, hard ground.

Even with the armor and augmentations, the guard didn't have a chance at survival. The two crashed into the ground, becoming a horrifying and mangled pulp. The heads-up display on the guard's face screen flashed red, warning of broken bones, smashed organs, and a fading heartbeat. The armor tried multiple times to restart, but the damage was too severe. The guard would die soon, but he already knew that before the jump.

A young man walking by, down on his luck, hands in pockets and head down, was startled by the sudden crash. He quickly jumped out of the way, back behind a dumpster. After a moment, he peeked around to stare at the two bodies. Both men were obviously dead.

He approached, finding one hand clutching something tightly. Kicking gingerly at the arms and legs, he was able to see it and snatch it up. Opening the satchel, his eyes and mouth widened into a grin. Maybe his luck was turning around.

The last thing the royal guardsman saw, as his life and the heads-up display in his hood faded away was the soft, leather shoes soundlessly running away.

1

Years later, 262 looked out the window as the bureaucrats argued and discussed and planned. It was raining outside, hard, and it showed no sign of letting up. 262's eyes swept the room, looking at each person as they listened and debated and ate. Her eyes fell on the young Queen Octavia who, despite being only a child, did a pretty good job listening, in 262's opinion.

At least, she did a good job looking like she was listening. It was hard to tell the difference. Sometimes the young queen seemed wise beyond her years and sometimes she acted like any other kid. Satisfied with her visual sweep, 262 looked out the window again. 262's armored hood's face screen and eye augmentations gave her some extra peripheral vision, and, although she was facing the table, she could mostly see out the window. Still raining, and the streets were starting to flood.

As the queen took another spoonful of soup, the elevator made a *ding*. Everyone turned to look, as no one was missing from the role call, and no one should be allowed on the floor during the meeting. The boardroom was completely insulated, cut off from the rest of the giant building-city. 262 walked closer to the queen, now standing directly behind her, ready.

The anticipation was broken when the doors slid open and no one came out of the elevator, instead a massive rush of water flooded the room. 262 had just enough time to grab the queen before the two were swept under. 262, as all royal bodyguards were, was extremely fit. And in the areas in which she was not particularly strong, her armored clothes and augmentations more than made up for any weakness.

Clutching the queen and kicking around a large bureaucrat, 262 swam for the top of the room, hoping the queen had taken a breath before the water hit. Then she felt a small tugging on her leg and her stomach dropped. Somehow, the elevator had moved downward, creating a vacuum that was sucking the occupants into the shaft.

262 fought it as much as she could, and when she finally entered the shaft, she grabbed at a ledge. Holding on with inhuman strength, she let the water run past her and the queen that she held in her other arm.

Eventually, the water stopped and the two sputtered and breathed deeply.

"What-what is happening, Two-Six-Two?" asked the young queen, teeth chattering.

"I don't know, my queen. Let's focus on getting out of here first." She pushed the girl upwards, onto the ledge.

"Oh!" said the queen. "There's an air vent. I can fit in!"

262 shifted her arm and was able to pull herself halfway up the ledge but had to stop before she could climb in all the way.

"It's much too small for you, 262," said the queen matter-of-factly.

"You're right." 262 scanned the shaft, looking for some kind of inspiration for an idea. Then she looked down. The elevator sat a few floors below her and immobile, for now. "Here's what we're going to do, your majesty," 262 said, coming up with a plan. "Go through the vent. If no one is there, see if you can kick out the grill. Then wait a few minutes, count to a hundred, and call the elevator to the floor you're on. Make sure you use this shaft, okay?"

"Which one is it?" the queen's eyes were wide and her brow wrinkled.

"Three. Remember, wait a few minutes before you call it, and if you see anyone, hide right away. You can do it. Now breathe, and crawl."

"Okay, 262." The queen breathed deeply a few times, turned and crawled through the vent.

262 breathed a few calming breaths of her own, then started to climb down towards the top of the elevator, towards the hatch in the roof.

~~~

It had been a normal day starting out for 262, but it seemed that the ridiculous always happened on normal days. She woke up, ate breakfast, showered, got dressed, same routine that she did so often it was automatic, like clockwork. She checked her assignment on her communicator and was happy to see she was guarding the queen. She had looked at her micro-fridge, covered in papers, and wondered where she would fit the next drawing and wondering if it would be odd to start sticking them to the cabinets. She decided against that. She didn't want her apartment to look like a crazy person lived in it.

She got to the Capitol City Building at the same time she did every day, checked in with security just as some pick pocket or thug got caught trying to sneak in, and she went straight up to the royal floors, her right hand and left eye scanned to verify her identity. Just like every normal day. Now she had to try to figure out how someone could flood a room eighty stories up in a massive building with an elevator. And why? Obviously, this wasn't some kind of prank, the suction would have probably killed at least one bureaucrat. An assassination attempt maybe? If so, it was an innovative way of doing it, if also ineffective.

262 stood in the elevator, waiting to see if it would work. She was cautiously relieved when she felt it shift, and overjoyed when the doors slid open to find the waiting queen alone.

"Did anyone see you?" she asked.

The little girl shook her head, slowly drying curls bouncing back and forth. "What do we do now?"

262 pondered. "We should probably find the steward and get you to your safe room. What floor are we on?"

The queen shrugged, "What about my brother?"

Now 262 shook her head, "his bodyguard should be taking good care of him. He was in a different room, so he probably didn't even get a little wet."

"Can you warn his bodyguard?"

262 shook her head again, "I have to remove my comms before going into that room. No communication in or out during those meetings." Then she rolled her eyes behind her face screen and muttered to herself, "the room is supposed to be secure."

"Let's not use the elevator, then, 262."

262 smiled under her face screen and said, "No way. Let's take the stairs."
~~~

2

The Capitol City Building was massive, the largest on the continent. It had to be; it was the entire city. Its colossal atrium was elegant, with seating areas throughout. A coffee shop was the first stop for most visitors, and the gift shop was usually the last. Only the most important people (and their staff) lived on the top floors in the building, but it was filled with rooms, apartments, shopping districts, schools, and even its own jail.

It was in this jail on the ground floor that the thief found himself. He had been caught sneaking in, which was odd, as he had never been caught at that point before. He knew the lower floors of the building like the back of his hands. He looked at his hands as he thought about this, thinking how sad and empty they looked without his lock pick kit. His long, skilled fingers were only long and skilled now. Normally, they were magical, opening any lock or door of any kind.

If he had his tools in his hands, he would have been out of this jail cell within seconds, maybe even microseconds. Instead, he was stuck here, next door to some guy all in black and some woman who sat, meditating, in the middle of her cell.

It wasn't his first time in this jail, but it was the first time the city police had thought to search him for his kit. So here he was, actually stuck. He felt so powerless, so...

"Will you shut up?" the man in the cell next to him said, interrupting the thief's train of thought.

"What?" the thief blinked and turned to look at his neighbor. He didn't realize he had been voicing his thoughts.

"With her humming and you muttering I have a massive headache. Just shut up please." The man sat on the cell's cot, looking sourly at the ground.

The thief crossed his arms and went back to musing. At least, he tried to, but he noticed something was off. His feet, in his clever, silent shoes, were cold and wet. Looking down, he saw water running into the room.

"Um," he said.

"I thought I asked you to shut up," said the man in black, now lying on the cot and rubbing his eyes.

The thief looked down at the ground, finding it was quite wet now. "Listen, guy, I don't know who you are, but there's water everywhere. Or do you not care? I'll just shut up about it." and he glared.

The man in black sat up and looked at the ground. A solid inch of water covered the floor.

"What the..."

"I don't know about you, but I'm getting out of here. Oops, forgot to shut up," and the thief decided to rely on his long, skilled fingers to work at the lock. It wasn't as good as his kit, but…

"You can pick locks?"

The thief didn't answer.

"Listen, if you can pick locks..." began the man in black.

"I'm shutting up here, thank you very much."

The thief could practically hear the eye roll and he allowed a small smile.

"Fine. Listen, I want to get out too. But unless you can turn your fingers into lock picks, you are going to need my help. We need to work together."

The thief stopped and looked at him. "You have a lock pick hidden on you?"

"Something," said the man in black and handing him a long, thin knife.

"How did they not find this on you?" the thief asked, then he quickly shook his head and said, "never mind, don't tell me, yuck." He pulled up on his sleeve to hold the knife handle.

"I didn't hide it there," said the man in black, crossing his arms defensively.

"Sure, sure," said the thief as he unsheathed the knife and started working at the lock again. This time he was successful and, opening the door, he went to a nearby desk and started tearing through the drawers. The water was up to his ankles at this point, almost reaching the bottoms of his pants, which were a size too small and ended a good inch from the tops of his shoes. This was no sewer main back up or water pipe leak. The jail wasn't sealed and the large ground floor of the building too huge to fill up this fast. Or so he thought.

"Hey! Don't forget me. If you try to leave without me, I..." The man in black was standing up against the door, holding the bars in an angry grip.

"I'm not ditching you, I'm looking for my kit," the thief interrupted. He skimmed through a few more drawers on a second desk and, with an "aha!" found his kit: a leather satchel filled with shining, silvery lock picking tools.

"Aw, did you miss me?" he said to his tools, grinning widely, then sloshed over to the man in black's cell. It was open almost immediately.

"Should we help her?" asked the thief, gesturing towards the woman in the other cell.

"Do what you want. I don't care; I'm getting my stuff and getting out of here," grumbled the man in black as he picked his way through the water towards the door.

The thief sloshed to her cell. The woman sat, legs crossed in lotus pose and eyes closed, unfazed by the strange happenings. He banged on the bars, saying, "Hey! Miss! You okay in there?"

Nothing.

"Well, I'm leaving," he turned to go then looked back.

No answer.

"Alright, good luck," he said as he walked out of the room.

The man in black stopped him immediately, a finger to his lips.

The thief chewed his bottom lip and peeked out the doorway. People were rushing in the hallway, the water now halfway up their calves. Looking as casual as possible, the two walked into the crowd, blending in and heading towards the exit. They needn't have tried looking so uncaring. The large atrium was filled with panicking people. They stopped before reaching it, though. The exit doors were closed fast, and for good reason.

The entire street was flooded, the water reaching all the way up the doors and beyond. The doors were dark, the gray clouds obscuring the only light that could make it through the wall of water that cut the building off from the rest of the world. Some people banged on them, screaming for help. Others ran up stopped escalators and stairs, rushing away from the water and looking for emergency exits that may not have been flooded yet.

The man in black cursed quietly to himself, "stuck," he grumbled.

"There're other ways out," the thief muttered, then repeated louder as the crowd around them was growing more panicked and unruly.

"You're familiar with the building?"

"The first fifty floors, yes. After that, not so much."

The man in black nodded. After a moment of pondering he said, "How about we keep helping each other. Help me find another exit, and I'll help you if I can."

It did not take long for the thief to think it through, "Sure." He put out his hand to shake, "Name's Zeke." The man in black shook, "Cutter. Lead on, Zeke."

The two walked with backs against the wall, fighting the press of people rushing through the atrium, once so grand and opulent and now flooded, like a movie Cutter had seen once. He couldn't remember the name. The water was up to their knees and rising faster. They struggled towards a stairwell and started to head up.

* * *

Besides being a kindergarten teacher and writer, **Hayley Nations** is the new mother of twins! She is working on her first full-length novel when she has a waking moment to spare.

Young Adult (Ages 13-17) - 3rd Place **Rose Marie Kern**

Definition of a Lady

You ARE a Lady! You are…every kind of a lady! You have exquisite taste, you manage the staff with tact, kindness and efficiency, and you are BEAUTIFUL!

Kelvin paced the floor of the parlor, exasperated by the stifled sobs of his younger sister. "Ronnie, you cannot let those little snits get to you this way."

Ronetta Josephina de Castellano, youngest daughter of LeRoy de Castellano, Chancellor of Luxainia, blew her nose and looked up at her sibling.

"That is the whole problem," she sniffed. "They are LITTLE snits…delicate, petite, fragile…."

"So what!" Kelvin shot back. "None of them is half the woman you are."

At his sister's glare he amended, "I mean, their accomplishments cannot compare to yours. There is no reason at all to feel inferior to those twits."

Ronetta straightened up and spoke righteously, "Kelvin, I am not crying because they make me feel inferior, I am crying because they make me angry. I cry because if I do not let it out somehow, I am afraid I will hurt one of them."

Kelvin watched his sister flow into her full height and raise hands that span over an octave on the pianoforte. Her long tapering fingers could grasp the halter of a spirited mount, or coax lovely melodies from the harp in the great hall with equal ease.

"If I were to hit one of them in anger, I could kill them. That is why I cry."

Kelvin sighed and placed his hands on Ronetta's shoulders. He smiled into eyes just a trace higher than his own.

"Ronnie, they are young, stupid and full of themselves, next to you they are fireflys whose pale glow wanes beside the fire."

Ronetta snorted, then chuckled. Her big brother had always been able to chivy her out of a frump. "I guess I should be used to it by now, but lately they have been getting those snotty little lordlings that pander up to them to join in the jeering."

"Ah…them." Kelvin grinned. "You know, I would love to see you whomp one of them upside the head…probably be good for them."

"Father would be dismayed."

"Look, Ronnie, you were chosen to be the Lady of Autumn and they are jealous. With every man gazing at you, no one will even look at those twittering magpies."

* * *

Carsten Zetwilligar sniffed and held his lace trimmed kerchief to his nose as he rode past Chancellor Castellano's residence. He was appalled, simply appalled that the Chancellor's outsized beast of a daughter had been chosen to portray the Goddess of the Harvest at Luxainia's Fall festival. His lovely sister, Lillibett, was far more appropriate a choice.

More appalling, the Lord of the Hunt this year would be Prince Marlin Andreyv of Swofford. By centuries old custom, Luxainia and Swofford each sent one member of their higher nobility and his entourage to participate in the major festivals of Spring and Autumn encouraging the younger nobles of both countries to make friends and keep the alliance strong.

This fall Swofford was sending their Crown Prince, and every one of Luxainia's noble houses was maneuvering to bring its marriageable daughters under his eye.

Not that Zetwilligar felt the Chancellor's over-sized daughter would even draw a glance from the visiting dignitary, especially since it was rumored that the prince was a trifle...well...short.

Zetwillegar was ambitious, and having his sister become a queen offered many possibilities.

* * *

Glorious red and gold leaves softly fell to the forest floor as Prince Marlin's party was just emerging into the glow of late afternoon a mile from the city. A deadly and inspired fighter and tactician, Marlin Andreyv, heir to the kingdom of Swofford, was a head or more shorter than most of his nobles. Nonetheless, he had won the respect and love of his people with his shrewd mind and high good humor.

As they approached the city gates, Marlin's trained eye spotted a welcoming party that looked as though they had waited several hours out in the afternoon sun. Quite a few young ladies were fanning themselves. He had known his visit would generate an avalanche of daughters to populate every social event, but he had not thought he would be beset before he even got through the gates!

Chancellor Castellano stepped forward and said "Your Highness" and prepared to utter some formal speech of welcome, but the Prince cut him off.

"Come, my good Chancellor, it has been a long and weary ride. Pray, conduct me to where we can engage in long boring speeches after a bit of refreshment and rest."

The Chancellor was momentarily taken aback, but the Prince's tired smile won a similar one from his own lips as he mounted.

To cut through any embarrassment the Chancellor might have suffered in front of the other nobles, the Prince rode by his side all the way to the palace, which also effectively protected him from unwanted introductions.

That evening the welcoming feast was as delightful and filling as he could wish, and King Gervase's wine cellar provided a pleasant haze through which he could politely smile and nod at the ranks of nobly born young ladies who found excuses to pass by the high table.

A late arrival making her way to the Chancellor's table caused him to perk up. "Incredible", he thought as he sighted the statuesque beauty who gracefully assumed the seat to the Chancellor's left. Marlin had always admired tall women.

The young lady leaned to where her Father could whisper in her ear, then glanced up at the high table, at him. He smiled as her eyes widened, then with a blush, looked away.

Ronetta barely noticed her meal. The brief moment her eyes had locked with the Prince's her heart had skipped. His face was not classically handsome but his eyes were warm and discerning.

When her father had mentioned that her partner, the Lord of the Hunt would be shorter than her it had not meant much, after all, most people were. Later she saw the Prince rise to bid the King good night, and she realized that he might be just over elbow height to her!

She was struck with the realization of how the Prince would be embarrassed as she towered over him during the ceremony.

By morning at least twelve young lords had quietly pointed out to the delighted Prince that the stunning creature he had seen enter the hall would be his Lady Autumn. All of them had hinted that if he found his partner objectionable in any way, all he would need to do was mention it to the King, and by the way had the Prince met his sister?

The formal meeting between Prince Marlin and Castellana Ronetta took place the next morning. Unfortunately, from Prince Marlin's point of view, there were far too many people there to speak with Ronetta privately, though his glance lingered on her lovely face whenever the ceremony allowed, and he would try to smile disarmingly.

Ronetta did not know what to think, other than she was glad he didn't run screaming away as soon as he saw her. He bowed low at their introduction and smiled as befitted a prince, but she had no illusions that the smiles were anything more than royal politeness.

The height variation would not be obvious as both parties led their followers through a slow ritualized line that wove in opposite concentric circles from the outside of the room. They would spiral inwards and eventually meet in the center climbing a stair to their festival thrones. Ronetta decided that by hanging back a tad, the Prince would arrive at the stair first which would minimize the height differential.

When she did that the Prince looked up at her with a conspiratorial grin and taking the next step up he turned and stretched out his hand, and seated her with a flourish first.

The next day the equinox dawned bright and cool. Prince Marlin escaped the cacophony of preparation for a few moments to walk in a quiet corner of the gardens. He noticed a flock of young ladies and lords entering from the patio, and moved into an arbor for privacy.

A movement caught his eye as Ronetta entered through the courtyard arch on her way to the Palace. Her graceful stride put to shame the simpering steps of the other girls. "She moves like a queen." Marlin thought.

Ronetta stopped as Carsten Zetwillegar and his cliché of muffin-brained followers blocked her way.

"Behold! It is a flagpole I see? Or possibly one of the stilt walkers from the Carnivale?" Zetwillegar had every intention of shaking Ronetta's confidence, perhaps he could make her see the idiocy of her partnering the prince.

His companion, Lady Evelyn laughed. "Ah no, it is a tree in skirts!"

Ronetta stared at them a moment, her hands clenched and white. With a level gaze and calm voice she said. "Move out of my way".

"Ahhh," said Zetwilligar, "the Lady of Autumn speaks and we must obey." He moved to the side. "She must hurry along; she has to practice dancing so as not to stifle the Prince as they glide along the dance floor."

The Prince almost burst from hiding at this remark, but Ronetta had had enough. With one hand she grasped Zetwillegar by the throat and lifted him – pushing his back up against a tree.

Holding him there, she said clearly. "You may mock me but do not mock the Prince or the blessed parts we are to play this holy day."

Then still with one hand she lowered the choking Zetwillegar to the ground. He staggered back into his fluttering group of obsequious sycophants. "Did you see that! She tried to kill me!" He turned to face her. "My father and the House of Lords will hear about this…this brazen attempt to…"

Zetwillegar's diatribe cut off as Prince Marlin stepped onto the stone path. "Brazen attempt to…what? It's Lord Zetwillegar, I believe?"

The consortium of noble nitwits immediately bowed and curtseyed with Zetwillegar groveling lowest of all.

The Prince turned to Ronetta, his eyes glowing as he extended his arm. "Come, my magnificent Lady of Autumn, let us ready for the ceremony."

Ronetta smiled at his twinkling eyes and laid her hand atop his. As they walked toward the palace, the Prince asked, "Tell me, my Lady, have you given thought to perhaps visiting Swafford castle during the Spring Festival?"

Rose Marie Kern loves to experiment across the genres. Her most recent book is a humorous look at one of her favorite pastimes – gardening. *The Competently Quirky Parables of an Eccentric Master Gardener* is available on Amazon and local bookstores.

Section Five:

Free Verse Poetry

Loquacious Cascade by Barbara Garvey

Free Verse Poetry - 1st Place   Kathleen Holmes

Notes from Jerome, Arizona

"I want to be water!" yells a toddler
running alongside Bitter Creek.

"It goes fast!'

Her arm jets out to mimic the flow of
water as she wipes out on the ground.

The child's father brushes dirt off
her clothes and stuffs the runaway
arm inside a small coat sleeve.

Whitewater pounds against red rock.
I copy her to become water—
loud,
narrow
tumbling,
almost vertical,
like a waterfall.

* * *

Kathleen Holmes is a resident of Aztec, New Mexico. She has received seven awards in SWW anthologies for short stories and poetry published in *Ramblings and Reflections*—2021, *A Diversity of Expression*—2022, and *Woven Pathways*—2023.

Free Verse Poetry - 2nd Place **Sarah Kotchian**

A Cure for Procrastination

Plunge organic beets in cool water,
trim the rosy globes

of their dirt rich roots;
set to boil.

Sauté greens in olive oil,
remove to a flowered plate.

Simmer golden peppers,
mushrooms, tomatoes, heirloom.

Fluff lemony eggs,
watch them enfold the tender vegetables.

Turn the omelet, note its half-moon shape,
perfect, if you do say so yourself.

Slice beets in lovely quarters,
sip wine with lingering citrus notes.

Slide the omelet onto your best china,
add sides, deep red, gold and green.

Was there another purpose for this hour?

Red stained fingers hold the pen;
the ink that flows is fuchsia.

Sarah Kotchian poetry collection, *Light of Wings*, was published by the University of New Mexico Press in 2024. Her book *Camino* received the New Mexico/Arizona Book Award and Seven Sisters Book Award. A contributor at the Bread Loaf Writers' Conference and Pushcart nominee, her work has appeared in numerous journals. skotchian@comcast.net

Free Verse Poetry - 3rd Place Kathleen Holmes

Desert Rain

Because it's spring,

I open my door to
a solo rain on
the purple mesa.

Wearing a dress
made of water,
lit by the sun and
stitched from a storm,

she wings her way

over lilies
growing wild in
the ancient ruins

searching

for the Spanish man who
carved his name into
pink sandstone in 1762.

* * *

Kathleen Holmes is a resident of Aztec, New Mexico. She has received seven awards in SWW anthologies for short stories and poetry published in *Ramblings and Reflections—2021, A Diversity of Expression—2022, and Woven Pathways—2023.*

Free Verse Poetry - Honorable Mention Jefferson Carter

Driving North

Hands at ten & two,
late Miles on Bluetooth,

I'm driving north, stopping
again & again

to bury roadkill,
a coyote, jackrabbits,

three diamondbacks, even a
young red-tailed hawk.

I'm driving north, where
I once rode my old gelding

around the reservation,
visiting the hogans

of my friends. We'd
drink coffee & laugh

at my little orange horse,
his cow hocks, his blaze face

& nasty disposition.
Listening to Miles play

"Yesternow," I'm driving north,
yes, where it once rained.

* * *

Jefferson Carter's work appears in journals like *Barrow Street* and *Rattle*. Chax Press published his ninth collection. *Get Serious: New and Selected Poems*, a Southwest Best Book of 2013. *Yesternow* is available through his website: jeffersoncarterverse.com. Carter lives in Tucson, Arizona. He taught composition and poetry writing at Pima Community College.

Free VersePoetry - Honorable Mention - Kathleen Holmes

Notes From the Gila River

Bolts of lightning strike
near our feet as we run
from the hot spring.

Safe inside the car, we vanish
with the mountain while you
drive home to Silver City in
the darkness and the rain. Now,

smooth wet stones lead me
back to the hot spring where
Geronimo was born.

Ashes rise as I hang
a tarp above my sleeping
bag next to the Gila River.

Sounds of water on stone
stretch across Picasso shaped
edges of the canyon.

Lines in the palm of my hand
map the Gila merging with the
Colorado before it enters the Grand.

I climb the mountain to watch
my memory of you crossing the
state line—into Arizona.

I'll see you home to California
and leave you there.

Free Verse Poetry - Honorable Mention **Kathleen Holmes**

Notes from Hawaii

A rare monk seal is giving birth on
the black sand beach—lava
lava everywhere.

The moon pulls the sea
—the way it pulls a woman.
The moon turns lava into sand.

Monk seals walked back into the sea
over a hundred million years ago.

I wonder how things might be today
if primates had walked back into the sea.

The mother dives for food in a
corral reef before nursing
her pup on shore.

I shop for T-shirts at the Kings and
Queens before driving back to the condo.

Kathleen Holmes is a resident of Aztec, New Mexico. She has received seven awards in SWW anthologies for short stories and poetry published *in Ramblings and Reflections—2021, A Diversity of Expression—2022, and Woven Pathways—2023.*

Section Six: Nonfiction

Article/Essay

Bad to the Bone by Carol Rawie

Non-Fiction Article/Essay - 1st Place **Paula Nixon**

Alaskan Migrations

Run. Pause. Peck.

He is alone on a large lawn, about half the size of a football field, bordered by sidewalks and flanked by two six-story hotel buildings. It's early April and he spends every day, all day, on the grass. I watch him from the balcony of my hotel room from my first cup of coffee until the sun goes down over the nearby Pacific Ocean.

When I am away a twelve-foot-tall, laughing Buddha at the far end of the lawn keeps an eye on him.

The bird is about ten inches tall with dark eyes and a black face, belly, and breast, which are outlined with a row of white feathers that run low across his brow and down both sides of his chest like a fancy stole. His back is cloaked in a speckled pattern of gold and black feathers. This showy spring look will help him attract a female in the coming weeks.

Pacific golden plovers (*Pluvialis fulva*) live for more than eight months each year, including the fall and winter, in the Hawaiian Islands. Mid-spring, they migrate to the Alaskan tundra to nest, mate, and raise their chicks.

Known as kōlea in Hawai'i, they are not from the islands but found their way here from the north thousands of years ago. Their Hawaiian name means *one who takes and leaves.* With habitats ranging from backyards on Kauai to cemeteries on Oahu to golf courses on the Big Island, the personable birds are well-known by island residents and visitors. Schoolchildren eagerly await their return each fall and try to predict when the first kōlea will arrive.

~~~

As a child, I was told stories about another April before I was born: a young man's journey three thousand miles northwest from Kansas to a vast land of mountains and ice—the territory of Alaska. It was 1957 and although he had some familiarity with the place this experience would be new. Dressed in a uniform he reported for duty on a military base in Anchorage.

He arrived alone and prepared his quarters, a small apartment, for the arrival of his wife.
~~~

* * *

The kōlea on the lawn is nearing the end of his yearly stay on the Big Island of Hawai'i. He continues to hunt and eat—roaches, spiders, earthworms—preparing for a long flight. The boundaries of his territory are invisible to me. Still, this expanse of hotel landscaping is large enough that he isn't threatened by another bird, a female with a similar golden color but muted white and black feather accents. She has claimed the far north end of the lawn. I never see the two of them interact.

Shortly after sundown each evening both disappear, probably to roost on a nearby flat roof where they are safe from roaming feral cats but still must be alert for the occasional passing owl, hunting in the dark.

~~~

Back in Kansas, the young woman was excited but edgy, making preparations for her upcoming trip to Alaska. Except for a brief time after her wedding, she had never been more than a few hundred miles from home. She studied for her university finals and finished sewing the dress she planned to wear under her black robe. On the day she walked across the stage her parents were in the audience but her husband was not.

After graduation, she received a letter from Major Baumgartner with her travel orders. The Army would not provide her transportation but would furnish an allowance for her to ship 350 pounds of household and personal items.

* * *

On Thursday our routine is upended. The hotel yard crew arrives. Not just a riding mower but the whir and grind of weed wackers and hedge clippers. Mowing, pruning, edging—it goes on for hours. I don't see him take flight but the kōlea disappears.

When I return in the evening, he is back. The trimmings have been carted off and the kōlea appears unfazed, probably well-used to the yard routine.

I study the kōlea with a small pair of binoculars but don't see a band on his leg so his history is unknown. It is almost certain that he returns to this same patch of ground each autumn and fights for it if another tries to move in. I wonder how long he has been coming here, three or four years, maybe more? His life expectancy is six or seven years but could extend well beyond that.

~~~

The day finally arrived for the young woman's flight: Kansas City to Anchorage. But her travel plans were fouled up. She discovered she didn't have a reservation for her flight to Alaska when she landed in Seattle. Her husband made more than one trip to the Anchorage airport to look for her. Eventually, she arrived and they were reunited. She could scarcely hear, her ears so clogged from the changing air pressure during the flight. And tired, bone tired. All she wanted was to sleep.

* * *

On my final night in Hawai'i a full moon lights up the lawn. The kōlea is not there but the marble Buddha shines.

The next morning, I rise with the sun but the kōlea has gotten an even earlier start. I pack for my return flight to New Mexico and pull my suitcase down the sidewalk. The kōlea doesn't look up. Not wanting to startle him I bid him farewell under my breath and wish him safe travels.

In three weeks, at the end of April, he will fly to the north end of the Big Island to congregate with other kōlea, all preparing for their flights to Alaska.

I wonder if anyone at the hotel will notice that he is gone.

What happens when the birds gather? How do they sort themselves into flocks? What spurs them on to take flight—something in the wind or the angle of the sun? So many unanswered and maybe even unknowable questions. But they know. The kōlea and his flock take off.

Up. Up. Up.

For three days he flies over the Pacific Ocean. Not a speck of land in the dark water below him. Three thousand miles to the western side of Alaska. He travels at forty miles an hour—sometimes more, sometimes less. It depends on the winds and will test how well he has prepared for the journey.

If adverse winds throw him off course, he'll have to adjust, but there will be no place to stop and rest. His absolute certainty about his destination spurs him onward.

When he lands it will be somewhere in the Alaskan Peninsula or the Yukon-Kuskokwim Delta where he is known not as a kōlea but as a plover.

By the time he arrives on the treeless tundra most of the snow should have melted although the mosquitos and insects will not yet have returned. He will make do with last season's freeze-dried berries still hanging on the low-growing shrubs. It's a remote place with few humans except the occasional researcher or intrepid birder.

Pee-chew-ee! Pee-chew-ee!

The plover stakes out his territory. Compared to his lawn in Hawai'i, it's huge, acres and acres of open tundra. If he cannot reclaim his nesting site from the prior year, he scouts for a new spot on the ground. He scrapes out an indentation with his feet, rubs it with his breast, and lines it with leaves and moss. He works to keep it concealed in the low-growing grasses where it will be safe from the gulls and falcons always on the prowl for eggs and chicks.

He begins to advertise for a mate and makes big, looping flights. He calls and loops until a female appears. She has also recently arrived from Hawai'i.

~~~

Within a few weeks of the young woman's arrival, it was the summer solstice. Recovered from her hectic springtime preparations and arduous trip, she basked in the long, almost endless days. No more textbooks or training manuals for the couple. When their boxes and crates arrived from the Lower Forty-Eight, he was thrilled to find a new fishing pole sent by her father. They celebrated their first wedding anniversary in July.

He told her about the summers he spent working on the Alaska Highway out east near the Canadian border—stories about clear-running rivers and magnificent wildlife. She grew to appreciate his love of the tall, snow-capped mountains.

* * *

The female plover lays four cream-colored eggs with dark brown speckles. Both adults take turns incubating the eggs. He sits on the nest during the day while she roams widely, eating and preening. Late in the day, they trade places.

In less than a month the eggs begin to hatch, four gold and brown speckled fluff balls, well-camouflaged for their first few weeks on the tundra. The adults carry the white-lined eggshells, which might attract predators, to a distant site.

The chicks have long legs and tiny wings.

The family leaves the nest and the chicks soon learn to hunt for bugs and browse for berries. The parents are vigilant, watchful for roaming foxes and lumbering caribou, trying to protect their young from being eaten or trampled. When the air grows cold, they gather the youngsters under their wings.

The days are long and the plover chicks mature quickly. Within a week they begin to grow their flight feathers. Not all of them will survive.

~~~

The couple took a weekend trip to the Matanuska Valley northeast of Anchorage. Fresh fruit and vegetables were a luxury most of the year in Alaska but in this fertile valley, produce was abundant during the short growing season—with twenty hours of sunlight each day it was a place where farmers grew 1000-pound pumpkins. The young woman marveled at the size of the tomatoes and green beans.

* * *

By the end of their first month, the chicks are adept hunters and have started to fly. The adults' breeding feathers are fading. They have finished raising the chicks. The female leaves first, the male a few days later. Each goes off to prepare alone for its solo flight back to Hawai'i.

The remaining chicks stay put and continue to eat. Without the adults to protect them they must be alert to the threat of predators, ready to disappear into the tundra or to take flight.

~~~

By late summer the couple was expecting a baby. The nights grew longer, and the air had a chilly edge to it. She bought a second-hand sewing machine. He checked the power outlet at the pole in the driveway to ensure it would keep their car battery charged during the coming sub-zero nights.

* * *

In early September, the male plover sets off on his return trip to Hawai'i. With less favorable winds on the way south, it will take him four days.

The steadfast Buddha is waiting when the exhausted and thin kōlea lands.

Back on the tundra only a couple of the chicks have survived. They now look like the adults in their winter feathers, buff color all over with a speckled golden back. The males and females are indistinguishable from one another. They sense the coming change—the days grow shorter and the breeze colder—as they continue to forage.

In early October one of the remaining plover chicks takes flight. Like millions of her ancestors before her, some combination of a map and a compass written into her DNA pushes her south. Perhaps she stops on the Alaskan coast for a few days and continues to hunt and eat. But soon with only her instinct to guide her, she will lift off and fly ninety-six hours nonstop to a destination she has never seen. The journey will take all of her strength and perseverance.

If she succeeds on her maiden flight and lands on one of the islands, her next challenge will be to find a patch of unclaimed grass. It won't be easy. The adults, already arrived and settled, won't take kindly to her infringing on their long-established territories.

~~~

April finally returned after a long dark winter. In a snapshot, the smiling couple stands outside their quarters, a blanket-wrapped bundle in her arms.

Years later they will tell me that it snowed on the day I was born.

* * *

Not many kōlea survive their first year. But some do. I often think about one that might have and try to imagine her life.

I hope she found a quiet, unclaimed yard bordered by blooming hibiscus shrubs, the scent of plumeria in the air with coconut palms swaying overhead. A peaceful place where she spent the winter, foraging and gaining weight.

It's April now and she has grown her breeding feathers and is recognizable as a female. She still has a few weeks to prepare for her first flight to Alaska. This trip should be easier. She will gather with a flock of kōlea on the coast before she takes flight, bound for a place not completely unfamiliar to her.

Today she continues to run and peck, pausing to swallow a wriggling worm.

Paula Nixon holds a business degree from the University of Kansas. She has published work with *Earth Island Journal, Sun Magazine, Santa Fe Reporter, Albuquerque Journal, and the SouthWest Sage*, among others. She lives and works in Santa Fe, New Mexico.

Non-Fiction Article/Essay - 2nd Place **Kathleen Hessler**

My Furry Feline Family

I had never been a cat lover. In fact, I had a strong dislike for the independent, haughty creatures most of my life. My husband, Jim, knew how I felt about cats when he brought the orange tabby girl kitten home for the night in October 2010. So, he wasn't surprised when he witnessed the objectionable expression on my face when I came home from work and found this small ball of fur prancing around our kitchen. Before I could say anything, Jim told me he was planning to take the kitten to the Animal Humane the next day.

His daughter Wendy had rescued the cat on the doorstep of her workplace that day. Someone had abandoned the vulnerable kitten there, leaving half a bag of dry cat food. The rest of the food had been spilled over the entry way leading to her office door. Wendy called her dad to ask him to come get the cat because she said it would be too difficult emotionally for her to take the kitten to Animal Humane. She was already a pet parent with two cats and two dogs and couldn't add another to the mix.

Since I had never been attached to these autonomous companions, I didn't understand Wendy's rationale that it would be too hard for her to drop the kitten off at an animal shelter.

That evening, I stole glances at this young, beautiful kitty. I watched Jim as he loved on her. She looked soft and adorable sitting in his lap. I reached over and timidly stroked her back. Jim showed me where and how cats like to be rubbed. He scratched under and over this baby's ears and under her throat—and then on her butt.

When I left for work early the next morning, I suggested that we keep the kitten another night. One more night led to another, and then a week had passed.

We officially adopted her in late October. The veterinarian estimated her age at seven to ten months. In keeping with autumn tradition— and her standout orange coloring—we named her Pumpkin. Pumpkin's color was brighter than other tabbies, and her shiny orange patches were interspersed with large snow-white spots. She was beautiful, gentle and lovable. She became particularly fond of Jim and would sit in his lap whenever he watched TV.

Thirteen months later, we adopted another kitten—a sandy blonde bundle— from an "Adopt a Pet Room" at a local arts fair. We named her Bunker because her coloring is like the sand in the bunkers on the golf course where we live. We took care in introducing Bunker to Pumpkin, similar to bringing a new baby into the house when you have another young child at home.

I researched the proper way to familiarize cats to each other. We followed all the rules. We separated them for several days, keeping Bunker in the spare bedroom with separate food, water, toys and litter box. We introduced them each to the other's smell, rubbing a washcloth over their fur and then stroking the other one with the same washcloth. We traded out their toys, so they each played and chewed on the other's play things.

All these introductory efforts seemed to work since I don't recall much hissing between Pumpkin and Bunker, just playful banter. Perhaps Bunker knew her place as the second child and took it in stride, looking up to her older sister. As adopted siblings, they got along well.

Each had their own special personality. Bunker was more rambunctious from day one and could play for long periods, chasing around the end of the colorful toy fishing poles I dangled in front of her. She still finds these hidden toys and pulls them into the living room, sits next to them, and cries out for me to play with her.

As I learned more about the lives, personalities, and habits of cats, I became fascinated by the apparent similarities between cat siblings and human siblings—for that matter, between feline and human behavior. The wholly individual personalities, body types, and distinct interests are just as apparent in cats as in humans. I realized that cats demonstrate emotions, such as jealousy, longing, excitement, anger, and hunger.

On many occasions, I observed Bunker staring at Pumpkin, then demurely walking away while Jim stroked the orange and snow-white cat. And just as my siblings rushed to grab the favorite TV chair if I got up and didn't announce "saved," Bunker would immediately jump into Jim's lap if Pumpkin got up to get a drink.

Another thirteen months passed. And like a growing family settling into the routines of new additions—and loving the changes the new ones brought to our lives—we were faced with the potential to adopt another girl kitty.

I was shopping at PetSmart one day. And as parents often do, I was keeping an eye out for any cute toys that I thought our girls would like. At the back of the store, I noticed several wire crates occupied by kittens. A shiny, thick, black furred cat with startling green eyes stared at me through the wire mesh of a small crate. I put my finger through the cage and she licked it. I pulled it out as she stared at me. She sat calm and serene with regal like behavior, demonstrating good poise and posture.

The adoption agency asked me if I wanted to hold her. Against my better judgement, I agreed. I walked around with her and felt an instant attachment. I returned her to the attendant and left quickly, before temptation to adopt her took over my resolve to leave.

It was a Saturday. Jim was finished with golf when I arrived home. I told him about my encounter with the black cat. He said, "Let's go get her." Surprised and not sure he was serious, I responded, "We already have two cats. We can't manage three."

"Why?"

He had me thinking, *why not*? "Well, I suppose we could consider it," I said. "Why don't we wait until after golf tomorrow. We'll go up to PetSmart. If she is still there, we can talk about it."

My hope was that she would be adopted. I didn't want to be labeled a "crazy cat lady." I erroneously believed that only lonely, old women had multiple cats.

Jim pointed out that Pumpkin, although still so young, might not be around much longer. She had been showing signs of illness, but the veterinarians could not put a diagnosis to her symptoms. She went blind in one eye and was unable to jump up to the couch. On the other hand, I was thinking that we might have a sick cat that will take more time and attention.

Late Sunday afternoon, as we approached the back of the store at PetSmart, the lady who handed the cat to me the day before expressed her excitement at seeing me.

"Oh, you came back! She's still here," she paused, then added with emphasis, "and no one else has asked to hold her since you left yesterday."

This information pulled at my heartstrings. Sure enough, the black beauty seemed to recognize me too. She watched me with her big green eyes while sitting still and silent. The lady opened the cage, picked her up, and gave her to me.

As I held her, the lady told us how difficult it is to adopt out black cats. "Not many people want them," she said. "Some people are superstitious and think black cats are bad luck. And we never adopt them out around Halloween because some adopters use them in sacrificial or satanic ceremonies," she concluded.

"How could anyone do that?" I exclaimed. My protective instinct kicked in as I looked down at the vulnerable creature nestled in my arms, now purring loudly. Jim gently took her from me and walked around holding her close.

Within thirty minutes, I had signed all the adoption paperwork, including agreeing not to remove the claws on this precious one.

Like a new child to a family, sometimes it takes time to decide on a name that suits the new addition. After a couple weeks, we settled on the name Shadow. Wherever we went in the house, she was several paces behind us. She still follows us into a room and waits until we sit before situating herself within a few feet. She has never been as affectionate as Pumpkin or Bunker and doesn't climb into our laps as readily, but she wants to be near us. She is the quiet child who cries only when she is hungry or wants a treat.

When we arrived home with Shadow for the first time, we initiated the same routine that we did with Bunker. We separated her from Pumpkin and Bunker for nearly a week. However, Bunker never did warm to our new addition. She was a jealous sister, turning to stare and hiss at Shadow whenever they came within a few feet of each other.

Within weeks of adopting Shadow in December of 2012, Pumpkin's downward spiral became undeniable. We sought care at vet specialists to no avail. Jim was distraught and we were both so sad when we were told there was no hope of recovery. We cried at the veterinarian's office.

Three-year-old Pumpkin was laid to rest several months after we adopted Shadow. We decided to cremate her and pay for the services from French Mortuary to have her ashes spread in the mountains east of Albuquerque. She had a yearning for the outdoors. I think of her as free and out exploring the wild.

After Pumpkin's death, I carefully observed Bunker and Shadow for signs of sadness or changes in behavior, such as we might experience after the death of a family member. I didn't notice any overt behavior issues, except that Bunker promptly took over Pumpkin's time in Jim's lap.

We set-up a catio—a screened in sunporch with cat furniture and toys. We also took to placing harnesses and leashes on our precious cats when the weather allows, letting them roam outside on the patio while we relax. If they start wandering too far, we pick them up and bring them back to where we are sitting. The dangling leash seems to be a deterrent for running off.

Bunker has always been the crafty one. I trained her to walk around the perimeter of the house with me on her leash, lightly tugging at it to lead her, like I would a horse's harness. If Shadow starts walking behind us, Bunker turns and lets out several long hisses, seeming to say, "I want to have some time alone with my mommy."

They both like to sit at the kitchen window and chatter at the birds in the birdbath, or the lizards that slither up and down the outside stucco walls. A gecko, sitting outside on the window sill seems to taunt them. The cats put their noses to the window letting out whimpers and nervous chatter as the gecko rests in a death-like posture.

Now, as I walk into the kitchen to prepare their morning food, I look at the little blonde at my feet vying for my attention with her high-pitched voice that only a mother could love. I bend down and whisper, "You are a mean sister."

She looks at me with her big, light green eyes, and lovingly cries for a rub.

I stoop down further and rub her behind the ears and under her throat, and then firmly on her little butt. Bunker, our furry blonde darling, continues to be a bully to her younger, but bigger sister Shadow—our black, full-figured, furry girl.

Even after twelve years together, Bunker continues to maintain her distance from her sister and vehemently hisses at Shadow when Shadow silently approaches to sit on the same colorful blanket or bedspread. Despite the fact that Shadow is bigger—at nearly thirteen pounds to Bunker's eight—and has claws while Bunker has none, Shadow quietly turns away and finds another place to sit.

However, on occasion, like a younger sibling, Shadow will stand her ground, as if saying to Bunker, "Go ahead, come after me." Bunker will get up, stretch, and spit out more hateful hisses and then leave.

While they have never physically hurt each other, it is clear Bunker only tolerates Shadow. Although I envy my friends who have cat siblings who like each other, play with one another, and nestle up to nap together, we love and accept our furry girls. We recognize their strengths and weaknesses and treat them equally with love and attention.

We are entertained by our curious cats. We love watching them trying to fit into little boxes or grocery bags. They seem to find the most unusual hiding places. I have been known to wander around the house looking in all the nooks and crannies for them.

I have come a long way in my love for my furry family. Even my siblings are amazed when they meet my cats, or hear me affectionately tell stories about their antics.

"But you never liked cats," my sister says with surprise.

"I never did, but now they are my pride and joy," I say with confidence.

I reflect back on the years of being a pet parent to my darling feline girls, and how, once I opened my mind to these adorable creatures, my heart cracked wide open with love, affection and pride. Like every parent who hopes their children will show love to each other and be friends, I have not given up on Bunker. I continue to have faith that she will learn to be a nicer sister and start showing affection to her younger sibling.

Now that I know people can change when they open their minds and hearts, I say to Jim, "I still have hope that one of these days Bunker and Shadow will learn to play with each other—and cuddle together on the couch."

Jim may be more realistic. "Dream on," he says. "They are cats."

* * *

Kathleen A. Hessler is an attorney and a registered nurse. She is actively working at being retired from her work in healthcare law by writing, golfing, hiking and traveling. She has won awards from SouthWest Writers, New Mexico Press Women and the National Federation of Press Women for her writing.

Non-Fiction Article/Essay - 3rd Place **Neill McKee**

The Dogs in My Life

When I was five and my brother Glen was six, almost every day we had to carry a blue and yellow honey pail full of table scraps to a pack of hungry hunting hounds kept in a pen beside our dad's farm equipment manufacturing shop in our small town of Elmira, Ontario. We would hum songs together as we walked to the dogs' jail, holding the pail between us. I think the humming built our courage.

These poor dogs only got to go hunting four or five times a year. Otherwise, no one paid much attention to them, besides us. When we approached the hole in the wire mesh, they'd gnash their teeth and growl at each other to gain greater shares of the scraps. We took turns guardedly pouring it in, afraid they'd chomp our fingers too. For this task, we each received an allowance of ten cents a week, which rose to 15 cents after a couple of years. Dad said he'd started at 15 cents an hour as an assistant in a machine shop, so how could we complain?

When I was seven, Dad brought a small female dog home from a business trip—a black and brown Manchester Terrier. I named her "Peggy" and I also gave her a longer name, "Peggy-Peggra-Peg, Elizabeth-Lizzy-Liz, Gala-Poochie-Pup," or just "Peg" for short. I learned to call her using her full name.

For some reason, the dog gravitated to me, and everyone in our family said she was my dog. I watched the feats of Rin Tin Tin on TV, a German Shepherd that helped a boy named Rusty, who had been orphaned in an Indian raid. I imagined Peggy in the same role and took her on hikes in the countryside.

Some of those trips involved following the course of the Canagagigue Creek downstream from Elmira's chemical factory. Starting in the late 1940s, it produced an insecticide called DDT and two "miracle" herbicides—2,4-D, and the stronger 2,4,5-T. With less regulation in those days, some of these substances escaped into the creek. During the summers, my brother and I, with Peggy, explored and fished in the creek. We wore rubber boots but Peggy had to brave the water. We came upon acidic festering pools and creepy things, such as frogs with two heads and fish with only one eye. We didn't try very hard to catch those fish, but if we happened to hook one, we'd throw it back in. They looked too spooky, almost ghost-like, and Mom never liked fish, anyway.

In my early teenage years, I must admit I began to ignore Peggy. I was more interested in fixing up old cars and meeting girls, so Mom had to look after my dog. One time when I returned from a trip with a friend, Dad and Mom asked me to come to the kitchen table for a talk.

I asked, "What's it about? Did I do something wrong?"

Mom said, "No, we just want to tell you that Peggy is dead."

This news shocked me. My little dog had grown old and fat, and I knew she wasn't particularly healthy. No one walked her, and she only was taken to the veterinarian for obligatory shots.

I asked, "How'd she die?"

Dad replied, "Very quickly and with no pain. I took her behind the shop and shot her. She never knew what happened."

I felt like crying but somehow held it in. I thought, *How could Dad do this without asking me first?*

Mom said, "The dog was dying anyway. Your dad just ended Peggy's misery."

This explanation didn't help much. Dad had buried Peggy on the spot, like a piece of trash, whereas I would have liked to bury her in our garden and put a memorial stone above her. For a while, I became fixated on the image of the bullet entering Peggy's skull and her brain exploding—blood shooting all around.

But as I grew older, I forgave my father for the murder and started to wonder if it was the chemicals in the Canagagigue that had made Peggy so sickly. After all, for a small dog, she lived a very short life. Many years later, I found out that in the 1960s Elmira's chemical factory was one of seven North American facilities busily making Agent Orange for America's war in Vietnam. Agent Orange was composed of those two herbicides, 2,4-D and 2,4,5-T, which Elmira's factory had much practice in manufacturing. The US Armed Forces wanted to destroy the enemy's crops and the jungle foliage that concealed troop movements and supply lines. They dropped about 80,000,000 liters of this chemical concoction on Indochina. The formula, which was produced at many times the potency needed to kill vegetation, eventually caused thousands of people to get sick, many dying of cancer and other diseases. Did my dog Peggy suffer from the same fate?

* * *

I had nothing to do with dogs during my late teenage and university years. I earned a B.A. in psychology but didn't know what I wanted to do with my life. So, in 1968, I applied to Canadian University Service Overseas (CUSO) and I ended up teaching high school in a small town called Kota Belud, in Sabah, Malaysia, on the Island of Borneo. It's about 800 miles from Vietnam, across the South China Sea, where the Americans were still dropping Agent Orange on the land and people.

On my first Saturday in Kota Belud, I found myself walking around town with Mr. Yeoh and Mr. Chan, two fellow teachers. My new Chinese-Malaysian friends and I settled in a restaurant. They wanted to treat me to a drink, so I ordered an Anchor beer while they went for the local version of fresh lemonade, *ayer limau* in

Malay, the lingua franca. Chan explained, "Alcohol drinks make me turn all red and dizzy. Many of us Chinese have this problem."

As we chatted, I gazed through the open front of the shop at the town square. I watched customers at the open-air market and noticed many dogs acting as trash collectors, eating anything that could fill their stomachs. I saw some with sparse patches of fur and ulcerated skin clashing over scraps of bone and vegetable waste from the market. My friends told me the Bajau people in the area, like most Muslims, considered dogs and pigs to be at the same low level of existence—unclean animals.

I soon learned to go to bed early in Kota Belud to ensure I fell deeply asleep before the yelps of dogs began, as they fornicated under the streetlight on the road below my government-issued bungalow. If they did wake me, I would hear barking, growling, and yelping as males fought over bitches, the successful ones working themselves into a frenzy and getting stuck.

One morning at exactly 6:00 a.m., I woke to the tremendous blasts of shotguns and wondered if a revolution had begun. I soon learned that on a designated day every year the police devoted about eight hours to shooting these miserable beasts. On "dog day," the Chinese quickly pulled their pets inside their gates and chained or caged them. But strays had no such cover and the firing continued until mid-afternoon, or whenever the executioners considered the excess population sufficiently culled. Meanwhile, canine corpses piled up on roadsides around town until sanitation workers, with handkerchiefs tied around their noses, arrived to hoist the fly-ridden carcasses onto a truck.

For a few nights, I noticed fewer dogs gathered to procreate under the streetlight below my house. But then the surviving dogs returned. I came to understand that "dog day" was a game of survival of the fittest and the most fecund. The smarter creatures would clear out of town with the first blasts, returning when the gunfire ceased and it was safe to continue the search for sustenance in human garbage by day, and breed by night.

But I don't want to paint a completely negative picture of Kota Belud in those days. I loved my ethnically and religiously diverse town and my students—Bajau and Kadazan natives, and more recent arrivals from China. I became a pretty good teacher, focusing on English and Geography. It was also the place where I found my future career. My American housemate was making a movie for Peace Corps in Washington and I asked him if I could borrow his 16mm camera to make a film for CUSO. He agreed and I wrote to Ottawa, surprisingly receiving a positive answer. That led me to travel throughout northern Borneo documenting the lives of Canadian volunteers.

* * *

In August 1970, on finishing my two years in Borneo, I bought Peter's camera and flew to Japan to have a soundtrack put on my first film. I sent a copy to Ottawa, as proof that I was capable of making more films for CUSO on my way home through Asia and Africa. I also met Beth Diemer in Tokyo, an American woman from Iowa who had just arrived to teach English in a Lutheran school. We fell in love and married in 1972, in Lusaka, Zambia, while I was making more films for CUSO. Eventually, we settled in Ottawa for 12 years, while I traveled the world shooting films for Canada's International Development Research Centre. Our two children, Derek and Ruth, were born and grew up in Ottawa, but unlike me, they never could have a dog because Beth was allergic to canine fur and dander.

It wasn't until 1990, when I joined UNICEF as Chief of Communication in Dhaka, Bangladesh that our children experienced the joy of having a pet dog. Ruth wasn't very happy with leaving her Ottawa friends but cheered up when we agreed she could have a dog. She chose a small black-and-white terrier an American family had found in a Philippines slum. They were moving again and wanted to give it away. His name was Tuxedo, or "Tux" for short, because he had white markings on his chest, which looked like he was always ready for formal dinners.

So, what about Beth's allergies? Well, in Bangladesh we could afford full-time domestic help. We didn't have modern conveniences, such as a dishwasher, and Beth wanted to concentrate on her artwork. Every day Mitro swept and washed the terrazzo stone floors of our rented house, while Shuntu cleaned up after Tux in our yard.

At the end of 1993, Derek completed high school and entered university in the US, whereas Beth, Ruth, Tux, and I moved to Nairobi, Kenya, where I became the Regional Communication Officer for UNICEF. We rented a newly completed house with a good-sized yard for Tux and we adopted a young female mongrel that grew to be three times larger than Tux. We asked Ruth what she wanted to call this new addition and she came up with "Doorknob." The name seemed to fit well with the state of our roughly finished house.

Ruth left for university in 1995, but returned for emotional reunions with her two dogs (as well as her brother and parents). Our dogs enjoyed wonderful years in the spacious yard, frolicking together in the mild Nairobi air and later on the grounds of our home in Kampala, Uganda, when I was transferred there. But in December 2000, I resigned from UNICEF to start a job at Johns Hopkins University (JHU), in Baltimore, Maryland. We left Tux and Doorknob with a friendly Dutch woman who promised to care for them as long as they lived.

* * *

In Maryland, we bought a two-story house, located on a hill overlooking the Magothy River, which flows into Chesapeake Bay. It was about 15 miles south of Baltimore and relatively isolated. I had to travel overseas frequently, while Beth was busy making new friends and creating art. She had the same problem with allergies to dogs and no full-time help, so didn't want canine company.

Then in 2004, we moved to Moscow, Russia where I directed a group of Russians in a JHU health communication project. We rented an apartment next to the Moscow River, which meandered through the old city. When I was in a hurry to get to my office near Red Square, I'd walk to Kievskaya train station, where I could take the Moscow Metro most of the way. I found the metro to be almost always on time, like a fine-tuned clock. I also loved the artistry and ornateness of Moscow's metro stations, each one different. This compensated for the gloomy faces I would encounter in the old-fashioned utilitarian metro cars—everyone staring straight ahead, without making eye contact. Such indifference was sometimes broken by a few well-behaved feral dogs that would go down the steep escalators and enter open metro cars, then exit at exactly the station of their intended destination—possibly for an expected treat from a street vendor. Was it because each station had a particular smell we humans couldn't detect? The sight of these canine friends would make some passengers smile.

After three years my mission in Russia was accomplished and we returned to our Magothy River home. In 2008, I joined another development organization in Washington, D.C. Unlike in Moscow, I battled an inefficient commuter train system, which, together with the metro, took up to two hours each way. I decided to buy an apartment near my office and only return home for weekends. That left Beth alone with her art projects most of the time.

By then, our daughter Ruth was married with children, living in Los Angeles, and Beth would frequently travel there to help out or babysit. When she returned home to our lonely place on the Magothy River, she always felt depressed. She claimed it was from a withdrawal of the hormone oxytocin, which is known to induce warm and fuzzy feelings in adults when they care for children. Beth searched online and concluded that adopting a dog could help with this problem. But she knew it had to be a hypoallergenic dog that was unlikely to induce an allergic reaction in her.

Beth found a black male Shi-Poo, a Shih Tzu Poodle mix, and she applied to adopt the little guy. It wasn't automatic. Background checks were in order. The other problem was that this dog was located in Louisville, Kentucky, over 600 miles to the west. That never stopped Beth and she was soon off to retrieve this dog named Samson from a state prison. His temporary caretaker was a criminal, the head trainer of a team of 12 prisoners who trained dogs to American Kennel Club standards, while the dogs taught the prisoners social responsibility and empathy. Beth met this prisoner-trainer, who teared up when she took Samson away, a sign the program was working. She also learned that Samson had spent his first months in a family with several small children, where the parents had no time to house-train a dog, and he continued to pee on their rugs and furniture. So, he was sent to a Humane Society kennel for adoption, and from there went to prison for his crimes against humanity.

Beth renamed him "Samwise," for he was a quiet and friendly companion, and just like J.R.R. Tolkien's Hobbit of the same name, he loved second breakfasts and a regular schedule. Samwise settled down in his riverside home in Maryland. He was most attracted to the herons, gulls, osprey diving for fish, and flocks of Canada geese noisily splashing down and taking off. Beth claimed the oxytocin therapy worked when she returned from Los Angeles.

Samwise was fascinated by water, but only went swimming once when he fell off our floating dock. I had to rescue him by jumping into the brackish mix, my legs sinking into the muddy bottom. But he enjoyed rides, fishing trips, and dinners on our pontoon party boat. What a privileged life he lived after getting out of jail!

If he thought this earthly paradise would be his home forever, he had joined the wrong human family, for in 2015, after I retired, Beth and I sold our riverside house and drove Samwise across the country to Albuquerque, New Mexico, where Beth found a community of artists and I found an excellent writing teacher. I studied creative nonfiction and started to write about my life-long adventures. Samwise had to adjust to a more confined city lifestyle but he loves walking, sniffing, and peeing, leaving messages for other canine friends. He's less partial to dog parks, where he tries to stop excessive romping by unruly dogs. It is good to have a pet who has also lived an adventuresome life. He's gradually growing blind and hard of hearing and we are aging together.

During my life, I have felt the joy of companionship with dogs and have witnessed a wide range of interactions between humans and canines in many parts of the world. In New Mexico, I have also had time to read and explore more on the matter. Humans arrived here from Siberia some 13,000 to 20,000 years ago. They devised special spear points to hunt mammoths, dire wolves, saber-toothed tigers, giant bears, and bison. But they could not have done it without their canine friends, domesticated wolves, who alerted them to the dangers of these fierce predators and helped them hunt for the protein reward of big game, which some scientists believe was responsible for expanding the size of human brains over millions of years. If only all humans could use their enhanced frontal cortexes to learn this simple fact, for some continue to treat dogs cruelly, while others treat dogs better than they treat humans.

* * *

Neill McKee is a creative nonfiction writer who spent 45 years as a teacher, filmmaker and multimedia producer for international development organizations, traveling to or based overseas. In 2015, he settled in Albuquerque, where he has written and published four memoirs, which have won many awards and finalist recognitions.

Non-Fiction Humor - 1st Place Rosie Kern

The Easter Goat

In St. Jude Catholic Church during the 1960's, Easter Mass included a processional wherein a child in the eighth grade would carry a white lamb to the alter. This was to represent Christ as the innocent Lamb of God. The Priest would bless it, sprinkle it with holy water and say a few words to the congregation. Then the child would take the lamb out of the church so Mass could continue.

Since St. Jude was located in a suburban residential area, the lamb usually came from a flock somewhere outside the Indianapolis city limits. The host family would bring it home, clean it up, and place a ribbon around its neck.

One year Easter arrived very early and the farm did not have a male lamb old enough to take away from its dam. What they did have was a female baby goat.

This was the year that my family was chosen to bring the lamb to church – and I was the lucky kid who would carry it in the processional.

Now, we were suburban city folks, so having a goat around was definitely a novelty. Our family had a nice two-story split-level house with a quarter acre yard -- necessary when you have six kids – so we figured it would be easy to tie her up outside with enough grass to munch on.

Dad picked up the goat on a bright, clear warm Saturday morning. He tied her with a rope to a tree at the edge of the back yard. Fascinated by this temporary pet, we fussed over her for a while, bringing handfuls of clover and a water dish. Then Dad went in the house and the rest of us started tossing a football around the back yard with some of the neighbor kids.

The baby goat was evidentially teething, and the closest thing to chew was her rope.

My sister, Bunny, suddenly yelled "The goat's loose!" So naturally all of us ran straight for the goat. With this wall of young humanity all scrambling for her, the goat basically said "I am out of here!" and took off like a shot. She darted around the back for a bit, then ran northeast with all of us strung out behind her, oldest to youngest.

There are no fences between most yards in southern Indianapolis. It's the kind of place where you may mow a couple feet of the neighbor's yard one week, and he does the same for you the next. The goat could pretty much choose any direction and not meet many significant obstructions.

Fortunately, on Saturdays, half the men in the neighborhood were out mowing lawns, but a gang of kids chasing a goat through the suburbs stopped all normal activity. The goat only made it about four houses down the street when several of the neighbors joined the hunt.

Jumping back and forth like a bunch of monkeys, five men owning various amounts of gray hair finally surrounded the baby goat. Old Mr. Gommel was able to grab her when she tried to break out of the circle.

Bunny and I took over just as Dad huffed up – he'd heard squeals that sounded somewhat different from the usual cacophony of kids at play and jogged in pursuit. He grimaced at the rope, figuring, correctly, that the goat had eaten right through it.

Guess goats deserve their omnivorous reputation.

We'd only lived in the neighborhood for about five months, so Dad introduced himself and apologized, though the other men seemed to be very amused at the unusual break in their weekend activities.

Bunny named the goat Rocket. Dad found an old dog collar and chain to hook the goat up to the tree again. After the excitement we all tromped indoors for our peanut butter and jelly sandwich lunch.

After our weekend chores were done, we bounced out into the back yard again to enjoy the sunshine. Other kids in the area were drawn to our house, both because there was a large group of kids in residence and because we had the only back yard big enough and bare of trees enough for a decent size football field.

About a dozen of us between the ages of seven and thirteen were playing when Rocket managed to slip out of her collar.

There we go again! The goat bolted straight for the street this time with the whole gang in pursuit, half of us yelling "DAD! DAD! THE GOAT'S LOOSE! as we pelted down the front hill.

Rocket raced across Lawrence Avenue and up the hill on the other side to the next set of houses. She zigged west between the back yards until she was turned by a short wall, then north again to Radcliffe Lane. I was starting to get a bit winded, but I was the oldest, and I KNEW I'd be the one to get in trouble if she got away.

A large group of children running after a goat naturally attracts attention. We crossed through streets and yards full of other kids playing on swing sets or splashing around wading pools, who all figured chasing a goat was a lot more fun.

The goat turned back east with a horde of us in pursuit and managed to cross at least eight more yards. Suddenly she saw a place to hide – an open garage door. Bee-lining right for it, she reached the garage just as someone opened the door into the house. Rocket leapt up the steps into the house, startling a teenage boy.

I didn't even hesitate but charged right in behind her with my siblings and the whole crowd of neighbor kids behind me. A middle-aged lady with short curly gray hair dropped a stack of plates and yelped, "What was that!" To which my brother Casey stopped and replied, "A goat," in a factual tone of voice.

We gave chase through the living room where a man in a recliner was watching football and drinking beer. His head snapped back and forth as each body flew past and then he looked at the bottle in his hand.

The goat was finally trapped on a twin bed in a small room with purple shag carpeting. The kids, goat and human, all collapsed for a moment to catch our breath, then I picked her up and we proceeded to make our way to the front yard.

The excitement and noise brought out a crowd of neighbors on that normally quiet street. The lady who dropped the plates was telling everyone, "I thought I was seeing things!" The guy from the recliner told a friend he didn't think he was *that* drunk.

After resting a few minutes, I took a deep breath, reset my hold on the goat – who no longer wore a collar, and yelled for the Kern Kids to start on home. I was not about to in any way let her hooves touch earth until we were inside the house. The goat was too tired to struggle, so we got there with no further incident.

Dad wasn't there when we got back. (Later we found out he'd jumped in the car to try and find us – but when he saw the crowd outside a house three streets away and me hauling the goat away...he just kept driving.) Mom had me put the goat in the small bathroom next to my parent's bedroom, where it stayed until Mass the next morning.

After dinner, Dad gave the goat a bath and painted its hoofs with pink nail polish. Things settled down for the night.

The next morning with all of us dressed in our Easter best, we headed to church. Rocket must have been tired out by all the activity, so she didn't even struggle as I carried her down the center aisle to the alter and the priest sprinkled her with holy water.

Immediately after Mass, Dad drove Rocket back to the farm. Rocket had the last laugh though when Dad went into the bathroom to put on his slippers that evening…and they squished.

* * *

Rosie Kern (shown at age 8) writes across multiple genres and is currently organizing Kern Kids stories like this one.

Her recent book is a humorous look at one of her favorite pastimes – gardening. *The Competently Quirky Parables of an Eccentric Master Gardener* is available on Amazon and local bookstores.

Non-Fiction Humor - 2 Place Jasmine Tritten

Only Champagne

How about drinking some water, Mom," I hinted to my mother on her 100th birthday in Copenhagen after she toasted champagne with the mayor. With a smile, she looked up at me, blinked her eyes, and replied, "No thank you, I only want champagne."

On her memorable day, she deserved everything. This included champagne and admiration for having raised three children and lived a long life with good health, a clear mind, a cheerful outlook, and a terrific sense of humor. The local mayor brought her a bouquet of heavenly white roses amidst tiny purple flowers with a divine scent.

Mother thrived at being the center of everything. She bathed in flattery and had a mind of her own. For this occasion, being the oldest sibling, my duty remained to keep an eye on her, making sure she behaved herself. My two younger brothers passed away during the last ten years and so did three of her close friends. But for Mom life continued.

The overwhelming attention she got made her appear fifteen years younger than when I first arrived from New Mexico only two days ago. She received a letter from the Danish Queen Margrethe, congratulating Mom on her landmark, and it cheered her up even more. Close friends and twenty-five family members arrived from various parts of Denmark and the world for this significant event. Everybody loved and admired my mother for her great personality.

A month earlier, my oldest son Chris and his family bought airline tickets from Houston to Copenhagen for the occasion. My son Brendon, his wife and two children planned to drive from Stockholm to attend. I also purchased tickets from Albuquerque to Denmark for the celebration.

In one of my daily long-distance phone conversations with my mother I reminded her before the event,

"Okay, Mom, since we all bought our tickets and are planning to celebrate your big day with you, it is your job to stay alive through your 100th birthday. You can depart this earth plane any time after the party even the following day if you so desire."

After we giggled, she answered, "I think I can manage that." Both of us broke into unstoppable laughter.

Not only did she manage to stay alive, but she surprised us throughout the birthday celebration with her vigor and humorous quality. Every hour I asked if she needed to take a rest.

"No, I am not tired. I do not want to miss anything," she said.

For four hours, she socialized, drank champagne, consumed delicious food, and nibbled on the three-tiered chocolate cake my niece brought. None of us had any clue where she got her strength from and were unable to keep her down. At last, she pulled herself up from her chair at the table. In a soft voice, my mother thanked every one of us for having traveled a long distance to be present for her significant birthday. At the end of her long speech in English, she finally announced,

"I thank you for coming here today from afar, and now I thank you for leaving. I am tired." Everyone applauded.

Immediately, two of my strong, handsome nephews rushed over to each side of her chair, lifted it high and carried her towards her apartment. For one moment she sat still, then flapped her arms in different directions and demanded,

"Please let me down. I am not so old you need to carry me. I want to walk back to my own apartment."

Flabbergasted, my nephews lowered the chair and let her out. Laughter filled the air in the whole restaurant because of my mother's independence and determination at her ripe age. After steadying herself on her feet, she grabbed her cane, and we all followed to her lovely apartment with flowers in assorted colors of the rainbow and a multitude of presents. Finally, she crashed into her bed after an unforgettable day. Did the champagne keep her going, we wondered?

Another year went by before my mother passed away peacefully in Denmark, surrounded by love from family members and me, her daughter. The day before she died, we waited for her doctor of twenty-two years to arrive in the afternoon,

"When is the doctor coming," she asked me in an anxious tone.

"Doctor Williamsen will be here soon, Mom," I reassured her, after which she slowly lifted her right arm. With shaky fingertips, she touched upon her lips and whimpered,

"But I don't have on my lipstick or my eyebrows."

"Mom, your doctor doesn't care if you have lipstick on or not, I guarantee," I responded and broke into a grin. The attending nurse chuckled. Even on her deathbed, my mother remained vain and attempted to look her best. I loved her for that.

When Mom stopped breathing, I stood by her side with my son Brendon, two of my grandchildren, my niece, and two nephews. Each one kissed her goodbye, and we held hands around her in a circle. After my niece recited a Danish prayer, we continued to stare at her for about one hour, mesmerized. Luminous energy radiated from her face, and a faint smile of peace from her lips. It must have been the champagne still lingering.

* * *

Jasmine Tritten is an award-winning author, artist, and photographer. She has written numerous short stories that have been published in various anthologies. *The Journey of an Adventuresome Dane* was published in 2015. *Kato's Grand Adventure* was published in 2018. *On the Nile with a Dancing Dane* in 2019.

Non-Fiction - Humor 3rd Place Annette Thies

Why I Didn't Write

Writing was at the top of my to-do list today like this !!!WRITE TODAY!!! It held the top spot of what I wanted to accomplish by the end of the day. Yet it's 9:00 p.m. and I haven't written a thing. Here's why.

I sat down with my cup of coffee and opened a new Word document when the phone rang, and the caller ID showed it was a dear friend. She was my best friend in grade school when we used to turn cartwheels to each other's houses rather than walk the three blocks. With thousands of miles between us there are no cartwheels in our future and probably wouldn't be anyway, given our age. When we ended our conversation an hour later, I had to pee, so I ran to the bathroom. In the bathroom, I became absorbed in the article written about fraud in the latest *AARP Bulletin*.

Back in my office, I sat down at the computer to do a quick email check before I started writing. An email from AARP caught my attention. They're looking for people interested in participating in research about the brain. I clicked on the "Learn More" tab. But I couldn't learn more without logging into my account. Easy enough, right? After four attempts I realized I'd forgotten my password and needed to create a new one. I pride myself on creating very intricate passwords, even for the AARP website. You never know when someone might use my password to find out what six foods you shouldn't eat after sixty, or the supermarkets that give old folks a discount.

My special sequence for fraud-proof passwords usually consists of my initials, my favorite letter, a plus sign and the year. Since I needed to create a new password, I decided to change my sequence (at least for AARP). It was my measurements when I was thirty (yes, I can remember them), my favorite day of the week and then I added sh**! At the end to signify my frustration that was building. I wouldn't forget this password again. Armed with my new password I logged in. Then AARP requested two-factor authentication. This signifies to me that AARP also thinks that people are going to want to hack their website, so I'm not the only one who is crazy. I elected to have the special code for two factor authentication sent to my phone, but when I reached for my phone, it wasn't on my desk. I grew frustrated after two trips up and down the stairs to find my phone. My heart rate peaked at 115 when I finally found it in the bathroom beside the *AARP Bulletin* I'd been reading earlier.

Once on the site I read that the research would be AARP members taking tests and playing brain games on the AARP website, which sounds interesting, but I decided not to participate because you had to sign-up with a new password specific to this research. What if part of their research was keeping track of how many passwords I created just to take the test?

I was ready to close the screen when I noticed an email from Spotify with the subject line "Monthly Charge." Why would I have a monthly charge from Spotify? I thought I paid for a full year. Had someone hacked into my Spotify account? I decided to check the account to make sure someone wasn't using it. I tried to log in and couldn't get in. I tried again with no luck. Whoever said, "if at first you don't succeed, try, try again," didn't know a thing about getting into websites. Again, I needed to create a new password.

I discovered I'm billed monthly, and it costs a lot more than I remembered. So, I did a quick check to see what other streaming services cost. Then I created a spreadsheet to make it easy to compare the costs. As I was perusing the spreadsheet I felt hungry and noticed it was time for dinner. Just as I finished dinner the phone rang. Another friend, this one needing advice. I'm always up for giving advice.

An hour later I decided to treat myself to ice cream since I'd had a frustrating day. I opened the freezer and no ice cream. No problem, the grocery store was less than five minutes away. It did take awhile to find my favorite ice cream on the shelf. There was one pint left, and it was mine!

I'm happy to report that my mood improved two-fold after I finished that pint. The perfect end to the day. Writing, well, I always have tomorrow if I don't do anything that requires a password.

* * *

Annette Thies previously wrote profiles and book reviews for national coaching magazines. After moving from New Mexico to Pennsylvania to be near family, Annete turned her focus to fiction, specifically stories for her granddaughter. When she isn't writing she is babysitting or swimming.

Non-Fiction - Humor - Honorable Mention **Michelle Smith**

Bullfrog Bungle

One spring morning with nary a cloud in the powder-blue sky, I was anxious to implement new swing changes I'd learned in a golf lesson. After spending extra time on the practice range, I headed to the first tee with three girlfriends and launched the most magnificent drive. This remarkable demonstration of enhanced distance with pristine trajectories continued throughout the first three holes such that I contemplated qualifying for the LPGA Tour. Even my companions were playing well; but as any regular golfer knows, it only takes a blunder or two to set off a treacherous cascade of errors that ruins what appeared to be the start of an exceptional round. Any regular golfer also knows there's nothing worse than the inability to self-correct a downward spiral in a timely fashion.

Golf is a capricious game wherein players are sometimes seduced into thinking they're better than they actually are. Perhaps this is the reason some unleash the most unflattering behavior when an otherwise pleasant outing suddenly turns into the golf round from hell. I've witnessed countless meltdowns where golf clubs are chucked or f-bombs are dropped from the mouths of some of the most unassuming folks. Theoretically, hurling expletives should stave off one's descent into a full-blown rage. But sometimes, such outbursts merely hint at what's to come.

In my case, I try to keep epithets to myself. But after fumbling on the par-3 fourth hole, I directed my frustration at the wrong entity. The greenskeeper must have been in a foul mood that morning because he'd placed the target flag only a few yards beyond a bunker strategically located between the green and a small tranquil lake in front of the tee box, necessitating a well-struck tee shot.

The true test of honing new swing changes is implementing them during a golf round. Given my exceptional prowess thus far, and as the lowest handicap player in my foursome, I felt up to the challenge of pin-seeking. Mother Nature had something else in mind for me. With its requisite showers and blossoming flowers, spring is mating season for bullfrogs. Basking atop lily pads, those annoying amphibians were especially rowdy with their full-throttled, guttural bellows. As I teed off amid the raucous cacophony of mating calls, I struggled to maintain my focus and ended up hitting a skanky tee shot that barely cleared the lake. While I was pleased my ball reached the bunker, I was disappointed to be the only player who missed the green. In hindsight, I should have done the same as my savvy companions who chose to play it safe by aiming for an open part of the green. But, no—I allowed my ego to commandeer my better judgment.

I turned toward the lake and cursed the bullfrogs, imagining they might retaliate by leaping out of the water and latching onto my bare legs. Then I proceeded to the green, determined to get up-and-down for a sandy-par. After a couple of practice swings, I stepped into the bunker and took the proper wide-leg stance I'd also learned in a golf lesson. Leaning a little left, I bent my knees and lowered my derriere into a hover at the very moment a bullfrog in hiding let out the loudest "croak" I'd ever heard.

Sinisterly reminiscent of a particular bodily function, the piercing, resounding din led me to momentarily question from whence it emanated. Confident I was not the culprit, my immediate objective was to discern whether my playing companions suspected I'd just let one slip. Standing eye level to their knees like a gnome in the headlights, I sheepishly glanced at their faces. I'm not sure whether it was the croak itself or the dubious manner in which I searched my fellow players' eyes with seeming culpability that prompted all three ladies to belt out disconcerting chuckles. Even though I declared that the blast was not of my essence, their cackling, which went on far too long, indicated they weren't buying my version of what just happened.

My forehead as tight as my golf grip, I still faced the thorny task of extracting my ball from the bunker. Tuning out the chortle fest as best I could, I returned my focus to the little dimpled dickens staring up at me from its sandy repose. In furtherance of my mortification, my first effort at extrication failed. Despite a notable ratchet up in body heat, I maintained my composure. The last thing I needed was to intensify my humiliation by futilely hacking away in the sand trap. Fortunately, I executed a decent bunker shot with the second attempt. This time, I cursed myself in silence.

Loathed to glance back at the group behind us whose members had been waiting to hit their tee shots, I quickly raked the bunker back into shape. Glimpsing the now peaceful lake, I observed a stately white egret wading amid a floating field of pink and white water lilies. The bullfrogs were curiously silent after apparently getting the last laugh.

* * *

Michelle Smith is an award-winning writer and poet. A top-10 finalist in the 2019 She Writes Press and SparkPress Toward Equality in Publishing competition, and a First Place winner in the 2021 SouthWest Writers annual writing competition, she placed 19th in the *Writer's Digest* 2023 international poetry competition.

Non-Fiction - Memoir - 1st Place **Katy Hammel**

Village

Dear Passengers :

I'm writing about a flight we shared. You've probably forgotten it. At least I hope you have. But I think of this particular trip often. I'm thinking about it today, for reasons you'll soon understand.

I'm back at the airport, which should make this letter easier to deliver. That's a silly idea, because I won't be posting this letter. For one thing, I haven't the slightest idea who the passengers were on that plane. It's not like I have the manifest from a flight we took twenty years ago. But I want to tell you the steps I took up to that day, to show you my sincerity in writing this letter.

I was going to be traveling with my two children. My older son, Ben, would soon be turning six. He was a confident child, always curious about how things worked. Ben was always keen to explore and touch and learn.

Henry was four. He was different: precious and foreign. Henry was as pretty as any child in a Tonka truck commercial, an enchanting tow-headed boy with olive skin. He, too, had a quick mind, but it came with a series of significant stressors.

All I can tell you is that Henry landed on planet bewildered and upset. After his birth, I wondered where he was from. Perhaps he had previously abided in a two-dimensional realm. Perhaps he had not been carbon-based. He was clearly from somewhere less fathomable.

He screamed while I made the introductions as gently as possible. "These are your legs," I would say as I lifted and bent them alternately during diaper changes. "Bicycle racing, bicycle racing, downhill!"

"These are your lungs. Breathe in. Breathe out. Blow."

"Latch. Suck. Try."

Henry would scream into my breast.

When I say "scream," you're probably thinking something like "colicky." But I'm using the word euphemistically, like when a doctor says you'll feel a "pinch" or "some discomfort."

Arched back, body stiff as a board, Henry's shrieking was so persistent and penetrating my best friends, my husband, and I would take turns taking the baby outside in fifteen-minute shifts just to give the rest of us some auditory relief.

This wasn't gas; this was existential panic.

"It's the cranky ones who grow up to change the world," my doctor declared. And that was encouraging, though suspiciously aphoristic.

Henry grew into an exquisitely beautiful boy, bound by strict rules. There was only one babysitter who could row this boat. Just one barber who could wield the "bumblebee" and cut his locks without a tantrum so distressing it would drive the other customers away.

George Bernard Shaw famously said, "A family is a tyranny ruled over by its weakest member." Henry was our weakest member but we did not falter; instead, we developed expertise.

Really, it came down to managing two things: transitions and novelty. Here's what I mean. Bath time was fine but getting out of the tub was not. Grocery shopping was acceptable but the shift from rolling through the aisles to standing still in the checkout line was unbearable.

Learning how to parent this child made me shameless. I composed a song, sung lightly but audibly in the supermarket, that signaled we were about to stop putting items in the shopping cart and take a place in the check-out line. Another song was specifically for the purpose of easing the boys out of the bathtub and into their pajamas.

Errors on my part had consequences, so I read this child like an organic chemistry textbook, reading ahead to the next chapter to make sense of the previous. I became his channel of explanations about the world. I spoke flexibility into his being. I programmed him, benevolently, if you take my meaning.

Over time, Henry added to his repertoire of experiences. Ice cream melted predictably when hot fudge was added. The lights would come down in the planetarium when the show was starting and come up again when the show was over. Henry developed a mental map of reference points and comparators.

And that brings us to this first flight to his grandmother's house in Pennsylvania.

My pre-flight steps started with the White Pages, where I located a direct phone number to the Southwest Airlines' ticket counter.

"Hello, Southwest? I have a four-year-old with special needs. He'll be flying for the first time and it will be challenging for him."

I eyed the ceiling; "challenging" was an understatement bordering on an outright lie. "It would help if he could practice first. Is that something we can arrange? Like a field trip?"

"Sure!" the cheery voice said. "Mid-afternoon is the slowest time. Around three."

"Three o'clock today?"

"Yes, that will work."

"Wonderful. Who should I ask for when I get to the airport?"

"Any of us, but I'll still be here. Ask for Antonia."

"Thank you, Antonia. I'll have my sons Ben and Henry with me. We'll see you then!"

This was a blessing.

We had already completed our research at home, which consisted of checking out from the library all the picture books about airplanes and the airport experience. Ben was fascinated by them. Henry wandered off to watch *Blue's Clues*.

That afternoon, confident the excursion would be well worth the cost of airport parking, I loaded both boys into their car seats. Henry clung to "Swagon," his stuffed dragon.

We found Antonia without difficulty, and she had a surprise in store. "Would you like to see where the luggage goes?"

Of course, we would. We watched the suitcases trundle along the conveyor belt and disappear through the rubber curtain. We didn't crawl through the curtain. Instead, we took a side door and entered the secret world passengers never get to see, the grand cavern where luggage embarks on its parallel journey through screeners and sorters.

Antonia had secured two other miracles. One was permission to take us through airport security, which was remarkable to me in the post-9/11 era. The other was that she had identified a plane whose turnover on the ground would be longer than most. We could actually board an aircraft.

Would Henry be willing to relinquish his shoes and pad through the screener? He would. Could he stand in boarding line A, B, or C? Could he step from the jetway onto the plane? Could he take a seat and have a seat belt secured snug around his middle? He could and he did.

The cockpit door was open and the pilots came out to say hello. I recalled the days when Pan Am pilots would present first-time fliers with a Junior Clipper pin and children's activity kit. It appeared Henry would earn his.

Ben was invited into the cockpit and up into the pilot's seat. What a grand adventure. The outing was a success all around.

On the day of the trip, we followed the exact same sequence. Toys and snacks in Henry's *Blue's Clues* backpack. Swagon in the car seat. Shoes off through airport security. Line up on our spot. From the jetway onto the plane. Ben in the window seat, Henry in the middle, and me at the aisle. Seatbelts. Click.

That's when Henry crumbled.

And began to scream.

We had made it so far. We had come so close.

At that point, there were no further preparation to be done. There was no talisman, no remedy. There was no way out but through. Just this one first flight and thereafter flying would take its place securely in Henry's reservoir of life experience.

All of you took your seats, and the flight attendant approached me: "Does he need a cup of water?"

I lied to her. Immediately. Without shame or hesitation. "Oh yes, thank you. That would help."

She brought water. I thanked her and she backed away. Of course, we were only a minute into the screams. No sip of water would dent this trauma. I knew better than to hand him a cup that he would fling away.

A moment later, the flight attendant was back, boldly. "How about milk?"

"Oh, of course. Why didn't I think of that? Milk would really help." That was lie number two. And she backed away.

I felt compassion for her. She had her job. But I had mine.

Please take off, I summoned the wheels. As soon as the plane lifted off, as soon as wheels were up, we would cross the wavery divide.

Of course, I felt compassion for you, too, my fellow travelers. Of course, I was sorry. But I knew something you didn't know, which was that Henry only had to do this once. I ruthlessly and without consent deputized you all as his village.

The flight attendant returned. She said, "If he doesn't stop crying, you will have to get off the plane."

And I assured her, "Oh, he's going to stop crying in just a minute." That was lie number three.

She backed away. As I waited for the *coup d'é-tat*, I felt the plane pull and roll forward. We began to taxi. Victory was mine.

It wasn't long after takeoff that Henry, exhausted, fell asleep.

Then something truly stunning happened.

There was a tiny woman, an elderly African-American lady, sitting catty-corner from me in the seat across the aisle. Her hair was pulled into a white and gray bun pinned neatly at the nape of her neck. Her feet barely reached the floor. She was eighty if she was a day and likely weighed no more than that in pounds.

She twisted back toward me and gently placed her hand on my knee. "They're all angels, aren't they?"

And I agreed, yes, they all are.

Likely, hers was the only voice of compassion we would hear that day. I nearly wept.

What I'm saying is that this letter isn't an apology. It is a thank you. There can be little doubt that woman is no longer on planet. She can't know I never forgot her words. She can't know I wear her words emblazoned on my heart. She's my slogan, my siren, my trumpet call.

You see over there? That's Henry heading through Security. I still watch my boys while they go through the TSA screen-o-matic. They wave to me from the other side. Then I walk back to the parking garage alone.

Henry has graduated from college. He's headed to Dublin for graduate school. This is his first solo trans-Atlantic flight.

That is where we were then. This is where we are now. The in-between wasn't easy, mark my words. It took a village.

But I had a village. And you were in it.

* * *

Katy Hammel is the award-winning author of *Meg Goes to America*, which won the Douglas Preston Award for Published Fiction; *Meg and the Rocks*, which won a WILLA; the recently published novel *The Kitten: A Kerrie Rasmussen Attorney at Law Yarn*; and over twenty published short stories.

Non-Fiction - Memoir - 2nd Place **Lynne Sebastian**

An Unsolicited Testimonial

Because I drew the short straw, *again*, I'm sitting in the *Wash 'n' Go* laundromat in Richfield, Utah, on a hot July afternoon with Calvin as my laundry buddy. The laundromat is an archetype of its species – sickly green paint on the cinderblock walls, the floors covered in dull brown asphalt tiles spattered with flecks of blue, yellow, and orange. Large windows on either side of the front door are plastered halfway up with fliers advertising trucks and hay and various used appliances for sale, a fundraising dinner and dance benefiting a family whose little girl has cancer, posters for lost dogs, and an offer from someone wanting to trade a lawnmower for a chainsaw.

A double row of washers, back-to-back, runs down the center of the floor; the far wall is lined with industrial-sized drum clothes dryers. Along the wall where I sit, there is a row of hard plastic chairs, a vending machine for tiny boxes of detergent and fabric softener, and a change dispenser that turns $1 and $5 bills into quarters. The year is 1978. The air is permeated with the smells of overheated fabric and *Clorox*.

There is no one in the place except the old lady who runs the laundromat, my archaeology field school classmate, Calvin Ross, and me. The old lady, like her business enterprise, is a classic of her type. Short and dumpy, with gray, frizzy, badly permed hair, she is wearing a dingy white sleeveless blouse, a baggy, dun-colored skirt, cotton anklets, and scuffed tan oxfords. A brassiere strap hangs down one of her pale flabby upper arms, and a cigarette occupies the corner of her mouth. She moves slowly down the row of washers, wiping them off with a damp, ragged piece of an old towel.

Calvin, too, is something of a classic. Tall and skinny, with an unfashionable crewcut, straight-legged jeans, white t-shirt, and horn-rimmed glasses, he looks a bit like Buddy Holly, but not in a good way. He has an uncanny ability to say things that annoy people. We all view him as having been badly socialized. A later, kinder, more knowledgeable generation will probably classify him as being on the high-functioning end of the autism spectrum.

Our field school director, who is both a prude and a martinet, will not allow the nine of us students to go into town as a group to do our laundry. Apparently, he believes that if we were all together, we would be seduced by the fleshpots of this small Mormon ranching community and engage in wild debauchery. Neither are we allowed to go into town alone, even though all of us are over 21 and three of us are over 30. Therefore, we all make the 15-mile trek from field camp to the laundromat in town each week in groups of two or three at a time.

I should note an exception to the statement that "we all go" to town to do our laundry. Sometimes one or more of us is not allowed to go do our laundry that week because we are being punished for some infraction of the field director's rules. In those cases, one of the other students hauls the miscreant's laundry to town and washes and dries that person's things in addition to his or her own. The good news this week? No one is being punished. The bad news this week? When we drew lots for "laundry buddies," I got Calvin.

I'm reading a day-old copy of the *Salt Lake Tribune.* Calvin is reading McGregor's *Southwestern Archaeology*, which is widely recognized as the most soporific textbook ever published in our field. The door opens and five men walk in. They are big men, heavily muscled, bearded, tattooed, and swarthy from long hours on the road in the desert wind and sun. They are all wearing do-rags, leather vests, shirts with the sleeves cut off, jeans, and heavy, thick-soled boots with silver studs and outsized buckles. As they swagger through the door, they fan out in a ragged line and stand silently surveying the room and those of us in it through dark sunglasses. I freeze, scarcely daring to breathe; the old lady backs slowly toward the rear of the shop. A few months ago, in another small central Utah town, a motorcycle gang beat and stomped a young man to death. The people of Zion are still very wary of their kind.

The men open two of the washers and take out wet clothing, carelessly tossing the items into one of the big dryer drums. I sit absolutely still, pretending to read my newspaper. In fact, I am watching desperately out of the corner of my eye for any indication that Calvin is planning to say or do something. So far, he still appears to be engrossed in McGregor, but given his personality, we are skating on thin ice.

The biggest of the bikers stalks over to the change dispenser, which is bolted to the wall not four feet from where Calvin is sitting. The man pulls from his pocket a wallet that is connected to his belt by a long shiny chain and extracts a bill. Suddenly, Calvin shifts his body, trying to fold his boney frame into a more comfortable position on the hard plastic chair. The huge, grizzled biker, whose biceps appear to be as big around as my thighs, turns slowly and stares down at Calvin, his eyes invisible behind dark, wrap-around sunglasses. I am silently pleading, *please don't say anything, please don't say anything, please don't say anything.*

Just then, the washers holding Calvin's and my laundry both finish their cycles and fall silent. I stop breathing. Calvin continues reading. The biker continues to loom over him. It seems to me that there is no sound left in the world except a faint sizzling noise from a failing fluorescent tube in the ceiling fixture above me. Just as I start to feel faint from hypoxia, the man turns back to the dispenser, inserts the bill, and collects his handful of quarters.

He returns to the dryer, inserts some of the quarters in the slide tray of the machine, and rams the slide home. The machine begins ponderously tumbling the clothes. The slap of wet denim and the clatter of metal rivets and zippers against the metal drum fill the ominous silence. With one last glare around the room, the men turn and walk out. A motto is visible on the backs of their vests: "BORN TO DIE" with a death's head forming the O in TO.

The old lady and I make eye contact. She shakes her head slightly, lights a new cigarette from the stub of her old one, and picks up her cleaning rag. I sit still, not yet trusting my shaking knees to carry me to my washer and then on to a dryer. Suddenly the door opens again, and the huge biker who operated the change machine stands alone, silhouetted against the light like the villain in a B movie.

By now, I'm experiencing an adrenalin crash, so my main response to his reappearance is weary resignation about my impending untimely death. He looks toward the old lady, raises one huge fist holding a small white cardboard box with bold orange print on it, and says, "I forgot to put in the *Bounce*." He marches over to the dryer, yanks open the door, tears off a fabric softener sheet from the roll in the box, throws it in, slams the door, mashes the "restart" button, and walks out.

For a long moment, the rumbling of the dryer is the only sound. Then I look at the old lady, and she is looking at me, and we instantly become hysterical. I laugh so hard that tears begin to run down my face. She leans on one of the washers, alternately laughing and coughing a deep smoker's cough. Calvin emerges from his McGregor-induced coma, looks blankly back and forth between the old lady and me, and says, "What's the matter? Did something happen?"

* * *

Lynne Sebastian is a retired Southwestern archaeologist who has discovered the joy of telling good stories. She recently published her first novel, *One Last Cowboy Song*. Her second book will be a memoir volume about an unforgettable archaeological field project in which she and her husband participated in 1981.

Non-Fiction - Memoir - 3rd Place **Charles Garcia**

Garlic

Our family loved to gather in the backyard under the dense and welcoming shade of our ever-giving elm tree. The meetings in this comfortable place were never scheduled on the calendar or announced ahead of time. Mother would occasionally take a break from her daily chores and find a peaceful spot in the shadow of our great elm tree. Mother did not have to pound a gavel to assemble her children and call a meeting to order. Mother's simple appearance under the deep-green elm leaves summoned her children to her side.

One by one all of her children would find a perfect spot near Mother. With well-used toys, favorite books, and worn-down crayons in hand, we would come together and create a quorum that fully represented our family. Below thousands of quivering green leaves our hushed meeting began. The usual sole item on our agenda was to just be together. In this lovely assemblage of family our voices were calm. We listened carefully to anyone who wanted to share. We especially loved the stories Mother retold about the days when she first met Father. We all had a difficult time believing there was a time when Mother and Father had no children.

Sitting on our concrete patio during a summer afternoon was not at all uncomfortable. The hard surface was refreshingly cool to the touch. There was plenty of room to stretch out upon a carpet that was woven from uncountable soft threads of shade. Busy ants constantly scurried and drifted nearby while on mysterious errands, not at all interested in our discussions. The only audience paying attention to our gathering was made up of a few curious starlings that impolitely clicked and squawked at us from their lofty perches.

The most rewarding time beneath the rustling canopy was when we waited for Father to return home from his day-shift at the steel mill. We all knew, along with the entire city of Pueblo, when hundreds of workers were heading for home after difficult hours of laboring in the sweltering factory.

The steel mill would announce the departure and arrival of its workers by sounding a blast of a loud horn. The signal from the familiar horn, or whistle as some of us liked to call it, carried across the entire city. The wailing call traveled at the speed of sound, entering the ears of every living thing in the vicinity. The unmistakable blare painted everything around me in a coat of happy anticipation. For others the blast may have been a nuisance, disturbing naps or calling a new collection of weary workers into the steel mill.

There came a particular day when the sound of the steel mill whistle brushed across my family in a masterful stroke. We gladly became an open canvas that anticipated the colorful arrival of our father. The portrait we sat for would soon be completed with Father's presence. The landscape that created the background of our family and home would be cleverly captured and framed, forever belonging to us.

Two chairs from the kitchen table set were placed squarely in the thickest shade beneath the elm. Mother sat in one, and the other was reserved exclusively for Father. The rest of us relaxed on the backdoor steps or found a nice place on the hard-but-cool concrete. We chatted, but intently listened for the sound of Father's car pulling into the driveway.

Our patience was always rewarded. The harmonized noises of rolling tires and a humming motor filled our ears. The unmistakable sound of a car door opening and slamming shut signaled us, just like the steel mill whistle, that Father was finally home. My siblings and I would rush to the backyard gate to greet Father. His face would brighten when he met us. We cheered, jumped, and hugged him in welcome. Father would gently pat each of us on the head and make his way to his comfortable chair. He would plop down and look rather regal, strong, and gratified. We all knew he was tired and hot. He was adorned with a coating of thick dust and dingy grime from the steel mill. We were grateful he was now home in his shady retreat.

A satisfying air of completeness saturated our gathered circle of ten. Father was home, now we can get back to the important things that must be completed before this bright day is over. Some drifted back into the house to continue reading their favorite books or to find more toys to play with. A couple returned to the unorganized pile of mechanical parts waiting to be reassembled into a much improved bicycle. A few of us lingered and sat quietly, listening politely to Mother and Father's conversation.

I remained, hovering near Father like a curious hawkmoth studying a phlox garden. I felt safe and strong in his presence. A light-red dust covered his boots. His jeans were stained with rust-colored streaks. His work shirt was terribly wrinkled. The wrinkles of the shirt poured onto Father's skin and spread, rippling like a gentle creek across his face, settling as crow's feet near the corners of his eyes.

While I sat studying Father's appearance he opened his dented and black lunch box and reached in. He took out a brown paper bag. Now his eyes turned to me. Father was tired, but his eyes sparkled with liveliness.

"I brought something for you," Father announced while looking down at me.

My heart skipped, wondering what could possibly be in the paper bag. I reached out and took the mystery from Father's hand. I had no idea what this could be. Could it be a tasty treat like candy? Maybe a small pet, like a lizard.

While snatching the bag I heard a slight rustle or rattle. I was certain the bag contained a small animal. I unrolled the top of the bag and cautiously peeked in. If there was a living thing inside of the bag I did not want to frighten it. I didn't want the small creature to hop out or quickly fly away.

To my great surprise the bag did not carry a small animal. The bottom of the bag was filled with tiny objects that resembled polished stones. They were uniform in size and shape, something like a teardrop. A somewhat pungent odor escaped from the bag and caused my eyes to widen and my brows to rise. My confused face looked at Father. I wondered if this was some kind of joke.

"What are these?" I managed to ask.

Father smiled. He knew I was confused or maybe disappointed. "Garlic seeds."

"Garlic seeds?"

"Yep. Someone at work gave them to me. You can plant them in the garden."

My confused fog was gradually lifting. "Okay, where should I plant them?"

"Plant them along the fence line. It is good place, nice and sunny."

I smiled and nodded at Father. I rolled up the top of the bag just like when I carried my lunch to school. I stood and headed for the garden. I think Mother and Father were quite surprised that I went right to work.

I was still a bit muddled thinking about Father's surprise. My hope was to receive a gift meant strictly for me. Instead, I was given a task to plant something my entire family could share in. Father did not grow his garden for himself. He planted and tended his garden for all of us. I understood that someday, the offering Father gave to me today, will be shared at our kitchen table.

The late afternoon heat did not bother me. I had explored the muddy banks of the nearby ditch in much hotter weather. I never complained about the temperature when I played baseball on a day like today. The best time to explore the neighboring prairies was when the sun was brightly shining.

I grabbed Father's hoe that was leaning on the garden shed. I stepped upon the soft and fertile soil of Father's garden. I tiptoed cautiously around the bushy vegetable plants that were happily thriving. I made my way to the chain-link fence that separated our yard from the neighbor. With one hand clinging to the fence and my other hand grasping the hoe I surveyed the narrow area where the garlic seeds were to be planted.

I decided that I could easily scrape out two rows about a foot apart along the fence line. I held the hoe in both hands, just like Father, and began scratching out a furrow. The soil easily gave way to the sharp blade of the hoe. The dirt was dark and rich. I disturbed the quiet and private lives of many earthworms. The soil's distinctive odor rose up to greet me. The fragrance of the ground was always a pleasure to smell.

Within minutes I completed the first furrow. I was proud that the row was somewhat straight in its alignment. I was fairly certain that the narrow channel was about two inches deep.

I leaned the hoe against the fence and reached for the nearby bag of garlic seeds. I opened the bag and the sharp smell of garlic rushed out and mingled with the aroma of the soil. I reached in the bag and grabbed a handful of seeds. They were purple in color and had a glassy-smooth texture. I could easily make out a pointed top and a rounded bottom.

I knelt down next to the dug-up soil. I placed a seed in the bottom of the furrow. I placed another seed about six inches away from the other. I continued moving on my knees and dropping seeds into the ground. When the last seed in my hand was planted I began to gently cover them with soil. My hands pushed the cool soil, covering the seeds in a promising blanket of dirt. I firmly patted my hands on the soil, trying to lock each seed into place.

I continued planting the seeds until they were all in the ground waiting to come to life in Father's garden. My hands reeked of the sharp smell of garlic. The odor was almost overpowering, bringing tears to my eyes.

I took the garden hose and gently sprayed my two rows of garlic seeds. The soil greedily soaked in the water, delivering a life-giving drink to the dormant seeds. The place where I once dug in the garden now looked undisturbed. There was no trace of my work. The small garlic seeds were hidden in a perfect place. Now I must patiently wait for the soil, the water, and the sun to unlock the seeds.

I stood in Father's late spring garden hoping the garlic seeds would magically sprout in front of my eyes. I wasn't sure why Father asked me to plant the garlic seeds. I wondered if Father possibly *chose* me out of all of his children. Nevertheless I was happy to plant the seeds. I was honored that Father entrusted me with a small piece of his beloved garden. Father always stood tall in his garden. This little spot of land could very well be Father's most favorite place on Earth.

Maybe Father saw me as a seed he could plant in his garden. I felt my shoulders rise and reach for the sun while I gazed at my small plot. My confidence swelled, germinating like a seed, ready to take root in a most respected area. My feet felt truly welcomed in the delicious soil Father worked so hard to maintain. While lost in this musing a simple feeling of happiness blossomed inside of me.

Mother and Father have nourished us with warmth and comfort. We have all sat together at the kitchen table and enjoyed the gorgeous flavors, textures, and colors of Father's garden. Our entire family greatly respects the place where Father toils with the earth.

I watch as more of Mother *and* Father's garden run around the yard with the sounds of laughter pollinating a field of contentment. My parents have skillfully cultivated a splendid variety of life that thrives under their careful and tireless watch. I take the old hoe back to the garden shed. I lean it against a wall, so that Father will easily find it. I rush to join the swirling and surging of joy that the chain-link fence of our yard struggles mightily to contain.

Days later I am rewarded with the view of bright green slivers spouting through the dark soil. The tiny emerald blades are in two rows, aligned like valiant soldiers on parade. I am delighted. I run and ask Father to come and see the wonderful sight.

We stand at the edge of his garden. We are surrounded by a happy silence. I am very proud. I actually planted seeds, and they grew.

"When will the garlic be ready?" I had to know.

Father gave a knowing reply, "We will have to wait until next spring or summer. They take a long time to grow. Maybe we could dig up a few plants late in the fall. We just have to wait."

"Okay!"

Father walked over to the garden shed. He reached out and grabbed hold of his trusty hoe. He took a quick glance into the sky. His eyes then focused on his garden. He stepped smoothly into his lush realm and blended into all that grew around him. Father himself continued to grow gracefully in his garden.

I ran into the house to tell Mother the good news.

* * *

Charles J. Garcia lives in Erie, Colorado. He was an elementary educator for forty years. He is the author of several journal articles focusing on literacy instruction in the elementary classroom. Charles has self-published books for children and adults. He loves to write about his childhood days in Pueblo, Colorado.

Non-Fiction - Memoir - Honorable Mention **Mark Fleisher**

Tale of a Working Man

If I may paraphrase an iconic line from the Oscar-winning 1955 movie "Marty."

"What do you wanna do today?"

On more than one occasion I would ask this question of my best friend Marty Stein as we grew up together in the Brooklyn of the 1940s and 50s. Marty and I lived in similar houses – two-story brick homes each with four apartments. In real estate jargon the homes along East 94th Street were semi-detached. Two buildings separated from two identical buildings by a narrow alley.

"I dunno," Marty might reply. "Maybe play catch in the alley."

We would emulate our favorite baseball pitchers. My guy was Dodger righthander Carl Erskine, "Oisk" in Brooklynese. Marty liked Elwin Roe, nicknamed "Preacher," a crafty southpaw often accused of throwing an illegal spitball. I'd hide the pink rubber ball known as a Spaldeen in my Bobby Veach model glove and throw as hard as I could. There were no radar guns in those days so the speed of my fastball was never calculated.

Our seemingly innocent activity was sometimes interrupted by the shouts of Mrs. Narinsky who lived on the second floor of Marty's building.

Her script never varied.

"Stop making such noise, you no goodniks. If you don't I'll pour hot water on you."

No wonder Mr. Narinsky had disembarked from this shrew some years ago, or so went the story.

Rather than risk being scalded by a lucky pour, Marty and I retreated down the block. Around the corner from Solo Dry Cleaning an inviting brick wall seemed the perfect venue for an abridged version of handball.

One summer afternoon Mr. Solomon, the proprietor of Solo's, came around the corner as Marty and I were engaged in a stirring match. Thinking Mr. Solomon did not appreciate turning his brick wall into a handball court, Marty stammered our apology and promised we'd play elsewhere.

Mr. Solomon simultaneously shook his head and said "No, no. I know you two are good kids. I wonder if you'd like a job."

Job was a word alien to our young ears. A job meant working and that activity was reserved for grownups like our parents.

We gingerly inquired of Mr. Solomon the nature of the work he held out for us.

"Okay. You know the cardboard strips on the wire clothes hangers? Well, the hangers don't come that way. I'd need you to attach the strips. I'll pay you a penny a hanger."

Today that trifling wage would be considered slave labor. Perhaps we should have lobbied for free dry cleaning for our families. But we weren't exactly skilled at labor negotiations. So Marty and I jumped at the opportunity, figuring we each could handle at least a hundred hangers a day. That would net us a buck apiece and by the end of a week we would be rolling in dough. Maybe we would not be so enthusiastic if we knew of carpal tunnel syndrome.

One August day the boss called me into his cubbyhole of an office. Uh-oh, I thought. Here comes the pink slip, the axe. The gravy train would screech to a stop.

"You know where Kings Highway is?" Mr. Solomon asked.

"Sure. Cross Clarkson Avenue, stay on 94th past Lenox Road and you come to Kings Highway."

Mr. Solomon walked to the back of the dry cleaning area and returned with a stack of clothing on hangers tied together with wire and sheathed in protective plastic. He handed me a slip of paper with a King Highway address written in bold script.

"Is this a little too heavy for you? I don't want you getting hurt and then have your mom and dad sue me."

"Nah," I confidently answered. "Take me 15 minutes to walk up there."

I marched out the store, crossed Clarkson and strode past Public School 219 where I'd soon enter Mrs. Paulsen's fourth grade class. Before reaching Lenox Road I could feel the hangers biting into my palm and I quickly shifted the clothes to my left hand.

Turning right onto Kings Highway I quickly found the address Mr. Solomon had given me. Wow, I thought, this is some house. Whoever lives here must be rich. Later in life I would know enough to recognize the Tudor-style architecture. A massive wooden front door stared me in the face as I rang the bell.

After a few seconds, a man about age 50 opened the door and I announced I was delivering his dry cleaning.

"Oh, good," he said as I handed him his clothes. "Wait just a second, please."

He disappeared into a room off the hallway. Upon his return he stretched out a hand that I could plainly see held an image of Andrew Jackson.

"This is for you, young man."

I'm sorry. I don't have any change."

"No, it's yours. Just promise me you'll spend it wisely."

"Thank you and I promise."

As I walked home I thought of what 20 bucks could buy. Any number of Topps baseball card packs...a few model airplane kits...movie tickets...comic books...hamburgers and Cokes at Berman's Luncheonette on Clarkson.

I've had some interesting jobs before my Air Force years and subsequent newspaper and government careers. I inspected basements for use as possible fallout shelters; erected metal book cases; sold women's shoes (one day); messenger for a company delivering court papers for attorneys; and researcher for a major Wall Street law firm.

But none left a lasting impression like my time stringing hangers and my very lucrative dry cleaning delivery experience.

* * *

Mark Fleisher's fifth book – *Knowing When* – was a finalist for the New Mexico-Arizona Book Co-Op and Military Writers Society of America awards. He is an Ohio University journalism graduate, a former newspaper and magazine writer and editor, and decorated Air Force veteran serving in Vietnam as a combat news reporter.

Non-Fiction - Memoir - Honorable Mention **Terence Cady**

Blossom Ladies

The northeast Texas town of Paris entered the cultural lexicon in 1984 with the award-winning film "Paris, Texas" by German filmmaker Wim Wenders. The film's story is not about the town. The town was merely a fixture in the imaginative life of the protagonist, Travis, who purchased a vacant lot there while passing through.

1984 was when the seventy-seven-year-old widow, Ruby Pearl, left California to return to her native Texas. When she arrived, she didn't pitch a tent on Travis' vacant lot but settled into a brick cottage in Blossom, a small rural hamlet ten miles to the east, where she soon became "Miss Ruby."

1992, eight years later, I'm coming to Blossom.

Mom's friend who can still drive picks me up at the country airport. We approach town as twilight droops into darkness. I observe details of the passing landscape: collapsing barns capped with rusted tin roofs, houses stitched with weeds up to the rafters, loose shingles and peeling paint, sagging front porches and shell back metal chairs set in talking circles in front yards shaded by umbrellas of ancient trees, and porch swings suspended by rusty chains fixed to the ceilings of wrap-around galleries, some screened against bugs.

Miss Ruby has finished fixing a homecoming supper for her prodigal son. She scurries about the kitchen. After reminding me that my last visit was eight years ago, she becomes the serving lady, moving into the dining room in her sleeveless worn and faded flower print house dress. Her frame is sparer now due to a strict diet to control her diabetes. Large folds of skin hang from her arms like atrophied bat wings. Supper is roast chicken, "light" salad (made entirely of ice-berg lettuce), toasted homemade bread, sweet tea, and lemon meringue pie, all served with smiles and happy energy.

"Try my Chow-Chow," Miss Ruby commands, and plops a heaping tablespoon onto my plate. The blob consists of finely diced bits of cabbage, onions, green tomatoes, red and green peppers in a vinegar marinade. With a teaspoon, I tip some onto my tongue. It's bitter-sweet. "Yum."

"Tell me about Chris (her grandson). He hasn't come back to see me since he was sixteen."

"I don't think there's much attraction for Chris in Blossom, grandma – other than you," I amend.

"Guess not," she says. "I think Chris was shocked by his first time in a little town."

"Indeed, it is a little town," I reply. "That sign out on the highway still says, 'population 1,400.' That number hasn't changed since I first saw it eight years ago. Can't be right. The town has withered and shrunk since then."

"Maybe they just don't subtract the old folks who pass on, son. The number didn't go down when Millie's husband Frank died, and it didn't go up when Aunt Polly came back here."

Millie and Polly are Miss Ruby's younger sisters. She had other sisters before she herself was born in 1907, but she never knew them; they died soon after birth.

Millie was the first sister to return to Blossom after Frank's knees gave out and he could no longer work. Polly, the baby sister, had worked in Tucson at a Christian bookstore for a *very friendly* pastor who hired her after her older husband died. When the friendly pastor went to his reward, Polly moved back to Blossom.

"Polly moved into Neil Hardy's old crumbling-down house,"

"Remind me who Neil Hardy was."

"He was my stepmother's brother. He's been long gone now, buried with all the Moores out at Knights of Honor Cemetery. Nobody had lived in it for years – the *house*, not the cemetery. Polly moved in and folks said it's getting even more run down. She's got the housekeeping sense of a hippie. Have some more Chow-Chow," Mom orders. "It'll grow on you."

"If I keep eating this, I'm sure something will grow on me." I inhale my pie to kill the astringent aftertaste of the Chow-Chow. "I'm sorry I didn't get back sooner, to see Uncle Frank before he died."

"You wouldn't have known him. He went downhill fast the last few years."

"Like the town." Miss Ruby ignores my sarcasm.

"He couldn't read any more, his eyesight was going. He loved to read. Winter, he'd sit by the fireplace; good weather he was reading out on the porch. Mildred tried to get him out of the house, encouraged him to talk to the old-timers over breakfast at the KKK – that's the Kountry Kitchen Kafe. Frank said 'Hell, I get to talking to those old guys and my whole day is shot. They go on forever.' He didn't fit in here. He was Irish-Catholic. He called folks here chicken eatin' Baptists and common-as-gnats holy rollers who shunned papists like him; said his books were more interesting. By the end, he was sitting on the porch watching cars and trucks, passing on the frontage road. Frank just faded away and died – from boredom most say."

I slurp the last of my sweet tea and tell Miss Ruby how much I appreciate her home-cooking, and how it evokes fond memories of the good parts of my childhood. Mom understands what that means. Silently, she turns away from me and starts clearing up the supper dishes.

I step outside to avoid kitchen clean up. Before the door closes behind me, I'm enveloped in a cloud of thick hot air and gasp for breath. I relax, exhale, and slowly begin to breathe again.

I sit on the porch, eager to savor a fine cigar. Moist air and cigar smoke coalesce to bathe me in a convalescent analgesic.

The porch steps descend to lawn bounded at the street by crepe myrtle trees.

I sit in shadow-less slumber immersed in twilight's blue balm. The night is heavy and liquid. Womb-warmth and sticky darkness envelop me in a milky placental cocoon. Cigar vapors encapsulate my face. My sinews loosen and unravel. My mind slips, unhinged. Fireflies! The air is filled with flickering incandescence as fireflies float from the grass. Crickets chirp in the shrubbery. Frogs belch from the drainage ditch. Cicadas emit a chorus of steady, rhythmic buzzing. Honeysuckle and Confederate jasmine climb entwined, conspiring to embrace the leaning wood tool shed, their cloying fragrance seeks and finds my senses–nearly nauseating. Dogs bark down the road.

I'm suspended in foliage, heavy at its verdant August zenith. Trees in varying sizes and shapes spread garden-like over a carpet of lush grass: live oaks, sweet gum, crepe myrtle, dogwood, red bud, billowing weeping willows.

The edges of things – of trees, houses, fences, are softened by embracing vines and bathed in a luminous, soft gray light, soon gone. Eyes adjusted to the thickening darkness; I'm startled by an electric light snapping on across the way. It's out of place here, in this moment, in this feeling. Into my fractured reverie steps Bubba! The neighbor across the road emerges through a screened door and walks his potbelly, protruding bare from a worn and dirty "wife-beater" undershirt to the half-cut oil drum rib smoker where he bastes and turns pork ribs by porch light. Moths circle. Smoke – venting from the rib smoker – disperses, crosses the gravel and heat bubbled tar of the road to where I sit. Sweet barbeque fragrance embraces me, complementing the soft nutty, woody buzz of the cigar that lingers on my tongue. The night is tantalizing, intoxicating, a soft hallucinogenic, inducing a feverish, languid repose.

Breakfast is on the table when I wake. Bacon, eggs, and hot biscuits, strong coffee, home-made jam, Miss Ruby's way of telling me to get up early so she can spend as much time with me as possible. I come to the table in my bathrobe. The ceiling fans are spinning.

"The day is fixin' to be a scorcher," Miss Ruby announces. She scurries about making sure I have everything I want for breakfast. At eighty-five, Miss Ruby remains spry, lively, curious, and voluble – more voluble than me, so soon after rising and before breakfast and lots of coffee.

Miss Ruby has a cat. Actually, four cats that depend on her, fittingly, for sustenance and survival. Miss Ruby claims only one of these cats as kin: Samantha, a sleek Siamese, friendly yet characteristically independent.

"I feed all the others, too," she says, "because I went hungry so often as a child, I can't stand to see anyone or anything go hungry. These old hard country people here would just take these little extras out and kill 'em, like they would a snake or a mosquito, because they're not useful."

"How do you like my 'permanent'?" Mom asks, pointing to her hair. Her tone tells me she's hurt that I haven't noticed or volunteered a compliment without having to be prompted. Her thinning hair has been professionally brushed and set to give it greater body. She had the good sense to talk the beautician out of coloring it, but had it rinsed with a "highlighter" to achieve a light, mousy brown.

"Looks real nice, Mom." Miss Ruby smiles.

"Can't wait to show it off at the yard sale."

"What yard sale?"

"Pauline Whittle is having one of her big yard sales. We're goin'."

I groan.

"Don't be giving me any of that, now. We're goin'. That's all there is to do here – yard sales and funerals. Letha will be here in a minute, so hurry up with your breakfast. I want to be there when it starts. I get bargains that way."

There's a quick rapping at the front door and it opens directly. Letha pokes only her face and silver curls through the small opening in the door. "Ruby?!" She is announcing her arrival more than she's asking if it's okay to come in, because she enters immediately afterward. "I'm hee-er. Y'all ready to go? Whew-eee, already a scorcher. I put out a wash this mornin' before it got hot. Little yellow butterflies dancing all around me. Think I pinned a couple on the line. Oh, Polly told me about the big snake." Miss Ruby shivers at mention of the snake, but that doesn't stop Letha.

"Polly told me it was at your back door, Ruby."

"Thank God I didn't see it. Polly saw it when she was coming to visit and warned me off. She knows how I feel about snakes ever since that Jasper boy in Hope, Arkansas put one down inside of my shirt when I was a girl."

"Polly told me," Letha continues, oblivious to Miss Ruby's discomfort, "that Butch came runnin' right over and killed the critter."

Miss Ruby signals with her hands that she wants the snake talk to stop. Letha veers off in a new direction.

"Ruby, did you hear about the little Meyers girl? Kaylynn." Without waiting for Ruby to say 'yes,' she had heard about Kaylynn already from her neighbors, Elbie, Euna, Irene, and from both Paulines.

Letha pushes on. "Dead from a spider bite. Only nine years old, poor thing. Only child, too. And they can't have no more children. Poor things. I've cried and prayed ever since I heard."

Now that her news delivery is spent, Letha begins to fidget, signaling her eagerness to get on over to the yard sale.

"Come on, now, let's make like the wind and blow."

Letha sees me staring vacantly at her over my eyeglasses. Without missing a step, she moves up real close to me and declares loudly, "Okay, then, mister city slicker, let's make like a cow patty and hit the road!"

I'm speechless. Letha senses my lack of appreciation for her self-parody, and yells in her broadest country accent, "Betcha ya' don't hear talkin' like that back in Berkeley."

"No ma'am."

The yard sale sits on a treeless lot fronting the highway. Used clothing hangs from discarded department store racks that totter precariously on the grass. Rusted tools cover rough-hewn benches. Worn out saddles and tack gear hang from sawhorses.

As they emerge from the car, Mom and Letha become twenty years younger. The place energizes them. Letha entwines her arm in mine. "Now you stick real close to me, like a cicada to a pecan tree."

It's clear that yard sales here are not merely shopping opportunities but social events for ladies, much as some old men go to bars. Pauline Whittle walks over and tells me to pay for all of Miss Ruby's bargains.

While escorting me around the sale site, Letha explains, "As a proper Christian lady, I must act discreetly and take pains to avoid any suspicion about my character and propriety."

After making polite introductions to almost everyone she and I encounter, Letha approaches a particularly dour and sour faced cluster of older ladies who've been watching our cozy promenade, and announces loudly, "Oh, ladies, we're not lovers, just sweethearts." She turns and walks away, holding me even tighter and closer. Miss Letha is in her seventies. I am twenty-five years her junior.

Suddenly, we are surrounded by "church ladies," middle to late-aged women who don't waste any time inviting me to their respective assemblies. Letha tells me straight away what denomination she is, which is her way of telling me *who* she is. "I'm Baptist," adding, "That's First Baptist. Burgie Thompson's the pastor."

The Methodists and the Baptists, compulsive proselytizers, are competing for my attention and a possible visit to a devotional service Sunday morning or Wednesday evening. The lady recruiting for the Methodists is named "Pug." Her husband's name is Buck. Pug warns me off the Baptists, saying, "You don't want to be goin' to the Baptists. The things that go on there. Terrible!" (I learn later that Pug is alluding to a scandal about a preacher and a parishioner. Not Reverend Thompson). Seizing the opportunity to seed an unfavorable impression, I declare to the assembled church ladies, "That sounds like the place for me!"

Side-stepping my remark, Pug says, "Oh, it's so nice of you to be visiting your mother. Bless your heart."

Another lady asks, "How long you going to be staying with Ruby? You're going to be here for a while, aren't you?"

I know where this is leading. I feel wanted and needed in a way I neither want nor need. Next I'll be invited to a devotional for aging singles. I feel the urge to inoculate myself from further importuning, so I announce, "Years ago I took a solemn vow to stay out of churches." My blasphemy falls on the ladies like a smothering quilt and brings up belly laughs from the good old boys standing nearby.

Letha quickly changes the subject. "Nathan, Pug and I have a dark secret that we need to share with you. I have to confess that we were responsible for the deaths of two famous singers; country-western singer Marty Robbins, and – Elvis!" Pug and Letha pause and wait for the desired effect.

"Really?!" I exclaim, playing along.

"Oh, yes," Letha continues. "You see, Pug and I were at those boys' last concerts – the very last ones just before they died. And the way we know we were responsible, and that it wasn't just by chance they died after we were there, was that singer Tom Jones didn't die. You see, we had tickets to Tom Jones' concert, but we gave our tickets to someone else. We didn't go. And he didn't die."

Mom is scowling. "I'm disgusted. I can't find a thing here worth buying. I've a mind to have my own yard sale. Let's go."

We pile back into Letha's car and drive to her house. She escorts me into her modest white wood country home. She gestures broadly to the abundant clutter strewn and piled throughout the house and declares, "Honey, I just look rich, but I'm really not!"

The following day, Miss Ruby and Aunt Polly sit at the kitchen table, working-up a large box of sun-spotted apples. By day's end they have put up several jars of apple sauce and apple butter, the latter for winter biscuits. Aunt Polly is the "hippie" in the family. Unkempt frizzy hair and, most of the time, weather permitting, barefoot – indoors and out.

Mom points with the peeler in her hand to the mounting pile of skin shavings and corings, "The hogs would sure love to have this."

"Yessir," Aunt Polly replies, "We got everything out of these apples but the squeal."

"Where is Aunt Millie?" I ask.

"*Mildred* is not talking to us," Polly says. "She prefers "Mildred".

"She thinks she's too good for us," Mom says.

"Snooty is what she is," adds Polly. "We're just too small town for her."

Mom says, "Mildred hasn't come calling since she came over one day –and saw the changes I was making to the house. She let me know that she didn't approve. Too 'country' for her. You'da thought I was living in The Ozarks. She got me so upset I had to take a relaxin' pill."

Aunt Polly screws up her face in mock pretentiousness. "Ruby, if you want to put tin cans on your chandelier, you can do it!"

Bird sounds come in from beyond the window, loud, clear, distinct, emphatic.

"I can hear those birds speaking," asserts Aunt Polly. "Jee-um, Jee-um." "Sweee-ut. Sweee-ut."

"What?" I ask. Aunt Polly is making no sense.

"'Jee-um,' like your brother. 'Sweee-ut,' like tea."

Next day is shopping day. Letha and I cross the Wal-Mart tarmac through withering heat and take refuge in the air-conditioned store. Letha discovers a display of decorative rub on transfers. Letha tosses a handful back on the pile, sniffing, "I wouldn't buy something I couldn't do more with than just rub on."

Over the store's public address system, Willie Nelson's whisky baritone speaks of "Angels flying too close to the ground." The mood is shattered by a woman's high-pitched, reedy twang announcing, "Little girls to lay away; little girls to lay away." I am not making this up.

* * *

Recovering trial lawyer, nationally certified Child Welfare Law Specialist, **Terence Cady** is a graduate of the University of California, Berkeley. "I have lived and worked in Santa Fe, New Mexico since 1993. Most of my work features the darker sides of socially and economically marginalized people."

Non-Fiction - Travel - 1st Place **Cornelia Gamlem**

La Posta

What did he just say? I was listening halfheartedly to a newly hired employee who was in my office chatting away. For some reason they loved to hang out in their recruiter's office, and you learned to humor them and listen—at least for a while.

He was talking about his wife's family who owned a Mexican restaurant in Rancho Cordova, California, and it served New Mexican style food. Suddenly, he had my attention.

Her family is from New Mexico, he explained, and the local establishment had its origins in a restaurant in Mesilla called La Posta. The family owned another restaurant, El Pinto, in Albuquerque. I responded that I knew El Pinto well since I once lived in Albuquerque while I was scrambling to get information about the Rancho Cordova restaurant.

No surprise that during our California years, La Posta de Rancho Cordova became our go-to place when we needed a New Mexican food fix, and it never disappointed. But I vowed that someday I'd visit the original.

It took a few years—well decades to be honest—but the journey to Mesilla, New Mexico, finally happened. And the original La Posta de Mesilla did not disappoint either.

Arriving in neighboring Las Cruces, New Mexico, we were advised at the hotel that the parking around the Plaza in Old Mesilla could be a challenge, but La Posta did have a dedicated parking lot. It was early afternoon, so we took a short drive to acquaint ourselves with the Plaza and the local landscape.

Like so many old New Mexico towns, there is a plaza in the center surrounded with businesses. These plazas were the focal point for community and commerce during the days when their respective settlements and towns were emerging. Mesilla was no different. The buildings housing the current businesses are rich with history, even if the shops today are typical tourist traps. We intended to explore Mesilla's history the following day.

La Posta de Mesilla was located just south of the Plaza—it's parking lot just a short block away. On a Thursday evening, it was enjoying a brisk business. Having had the foresight to make reservations, we were promptly seated at a table painted with bright flowers with a note greeting us. It was March and St. Patrick's Day decorations adorned the fireplace—an interesting but festive contrast to the Mexican tiles that framed it.

Yet, it was food and drink we came in search of, having been advised that the drinks there were the best around. The selection of Margaritas (What else do you drink with Mexican food?) was extensive, if not overwhelming. My husband opted for a Blood Orange Silver Coin, while I finally chose the La Patrona—a bit more traditional for my tastes. Both, however, are highly recommended.

Time to decide on the main event—dinner. We were of like minds, choosing something familiar and similar to what we likely ate in La Posta de Rancho Cordova. I ordered the Sour Cream Enchiladas—Green Enchiladas with chicken topped with sour cream and smothered in green chile. My husband indulged in his favorite, Chile Rellenos. Both came with refritos (refried beans) rice and something new—Mexican Slaw, a tangy, welcomed alternative to the usual shredded lettuce with chopped onions and tomato.

The food menu was as extensive as the drink menu. Beyond the traditional New Mexican fare were selections from the CharBroiler—entrees we didn't recall from Rancho Cordova. This left us contemplating a return visit on Friday night, perhaps to enjoy their patio dining.

Unfortunately, our adventure to Mesilla got literally blown away. It was March in New Mexico and the wind blew, spoiling our plan for any outside exploring, like taking the La Morena Walking tour around the Plaza. Thus, the Mesilla bucket list grew, rather than shrunk. On Friday, we had to settle on wandering around the Plaza, ducking into stores and making small discoveries like a tea shop, Old Barrell Tea Company, with an interesting assortment of loose-leaf tea.

Another discovery was the NM Vintage Wine, Beers and Cigars just half a block south of the Plaza, offering wine and beer tasting, a cigar nook, and live music on certain nights. It was a little too early in the day to indulge, but it is a planned stop on our next visit. During the pandemic, the shop began offering take out from La Posta, which is right across the street, that can be eaten in their courtyard. They have continued this service because of its popularity.

Our browsing took us into Mesilla Book Center—housed in an historic mercantile building on the Plaza—numerous gift, curio and craft shops including the Billy the Kid Gift Shop located in a building that was once the courthouse in which he was sentenced to hang, and the usual clothing and apparel boutiques.

We ultimately stumbled into Double Eagle Restaurant on the Plaza. Say Double Eagle to me and I immediately think of Ben Abruzzo, Maxie Anderson and Larry Newman crossing the Atlantic in August 1978 in their hot air balloon. After all, New Mexico is the Hot Air Balloon Capital of the world, right? But Robert O. Anderson, Roswell native and longtime CEO of Atlantic Richfield Company (ARCO), and for whom University of New Mexico's School of Business is named, bought the building and turned it into a restaurant in 1970. He chose the name of the twenty-dollar gold piece of the 1880s—The Double Eagle—for the restaurant's name.

After entering, we sat down at the Imperial Bar for an afternoon (adult) beverage to wash the dust and sand away, and I became mesmerized by the French Baccarat crystal chandeliers. This led the *barkeep*—well it is the Old West after all—to suggest dinner in the Maximilian Room. We were convinced. An encore at La Posta de Mesilla would have to wait until next time. This trip was evolving into a food adventure.

The Maximilian Room, named for Maximilian the Emperor of Mexico, features three Baccarat crystal chandeliers, an 18 and 20 carat gold pressed metal ceiling, a music balcony with an 18 carat, gold leafed brass railing, and a stained-glass panel above double doors leading to a patio. I felt terribly underdressed surrounded by this elegance. But it is New Mexico and relaxed dress codes are acceptable.

Amazingly, the first thing I noticed on the table when we were seated was a tasteful St. Patrick's Day decoration. *It's surprising that this holiday is so widely celebrated in the Southwest,* thought this New York girl who once cut high school to go see the St. Patrick's Day Parade on Fifth Avenue in Manhattan.

After repeating the afternoon cocktails along with appetizers of crab stuffed mushrooms and Italian calamari (the Bison sausage was tempting), it was time, once more, for the main event—the entrees. Contemplating everything from fish—Pacific Salmon or Blackened Mahi Mahi—to fowl—Pan Seared Duck Breast or Roast Pheasant Under Glass—I settled on Chicken Mesilla.

Being a green chile enthusiast, I couldn't pass up a Bone-In Chicken Breast with sautéed onions and green chile and Monterrey Jack cheese served with chile con queso mashed potatoes. The green chile and jack cheese were both subtle, but definitely present to the palate. The chile con queso surrounded by a moat of mashed potatoes—delicious!

My husband, a die-hard carnivore in his younger years, passed on the House Aged Beef and Steaks, short ribs and pork chops, and delighted his palate with the Sea Bass served with a lemon caper and white wine sauce, seasonal vegetables—including broccoli, his favorite—and mille-feuille (crispy, layered) potatoes. The fish, he said, melted in his mouth.

For dessert we shared Mile High Cheesecake—almost, but not quite, equal to Juniors in New York—and Vanilla Bean ice cream with raspberry sauce. Both were excellent choices.

We discovered that the Double Eagle, like everything else in Mesilla, had quite a unique history. Next visit we'll plan more time wandering through the remaining rooms—The Billy the Kid Patio, the Lew Wallace Salon, the Gadsden Room and the Charlotte Salon or ghost room, where legend has it that a teenage servant girl and a teenage son of the family fell into forbidden love and subsequently met their untimely demise. Sitting in one of the two upholstered arm chairs in the room today is said to provoke a strong reaction.

Our short trip was not complete until we had breakfast the next morning at Rincon de Mesilla, a half block south of the Plaza next to the wine shop. This delightful coffee shop and artisan market also serves breakfast and lunch making a perfect ending. It didn't disappoint.

Breakfast consisted of an order of Huevos Rancheros—two eggs served with their special green chile salsa, beans, green salad and a corn or flour tortilla. If La Posta de Rancho Cordova in California was a taste of New Mexico, Rincon de Mesilla was a taste of Old Mexico just like its owners intended. The portion of food was a perfect size—enough to satiate but not overindulge. Their green chile sauce was flavorful, yet not overwhelming. It was a perfect complement to the eggs.

On the way out, we purchased muffins baked on the premises and took the opportunity to talk with Juan Albert, who owns the establishment with his wife, Claudia Gonzalez, who had been our server. Turns out that Juan spent many years, as did we, living in Northern Virginia, right outside Washington, DC, and his son lives in New York City.

The connections we discover over travel, food and drink are priceless. And this story started because so many years ago I happened to hire a gentleman in Sacramento, California, who had familial connections to Mesilla, New Mexico.

Until next time…

* * *

Management consultant and speaker, **Cornelia Gamlem** took her expertise and shared it through her award-winning books. She coauthored three editions of her first book plus four more. Three have been translated into other languages. Two were recognized by internationally acclaimed Next Generation Indie Book Awards. www.bigbookofhr.com

Non-Fiction - Travel - 2nd Place **Theresa Nichols**

How to See an Elephant

"We go to the jungle. See elephants." My Sri Lankan friend drew out the word "jungle," saying it with a lilt. I don't think he meant to be mysterious, but that's how it sounded.

I was interested. Lal had mentioned taking me to the jungle several times, hoping to make a few rupees by serving as my adventure guide. The lanky lad, some ten years younger than me, was tourist savvy, eager to please, and spoke passable English. Surely, he'd escorted other travelers into the jungle to see these magnificent animals.

It was a perfect activity to include on my nine-month journey in Asia. Five months earlier, at age twenty-nine, I'd quit my job and set off from New Mexico with a backpack, a few thousand dollars, and a yearning to experience the world. I met Lal at a humble guest house in the ancient Sri Lankan kingdom of Anuradhapura. Back in 1984, tourists there were sparse. I could pedal a bicycle along quiet paths to the ruins of monasteries, Buddhist stupas, shrines, and irrigation features. Occasionally, I'd meet a bullock cart, people on foot and pedaling bicycles, or a motorized vehicle.

Lal wasn't pushy like other touts I'd encountered on my travels. In his shy and soft-spoken way, he earned a small commission by steering tourists to guest houses. He was new to the game, forced into making money however he could. Uncertain of what to do with his life and where he belonged, he spoke of shifting between his parents' and brother's houses and dealing with rankled family relationships. His sense of humor made up for his frequent moodiness and impatience.

Attempting to conquer his own boredom, he joined me on bicycle rides to fourth century water reservoirs, or to clusters of stone columns marking an old palace. I examined architecture while he tossed rocks and drove away roving bands of monkeys intent on snatching my bag. Sometimes I gave Lal money to buy biscuits or candy that we would share. I enjoyed his company.

One day we settled in a grove of broad-leaved trees where birds hid among the branches and called softly. That's where he showed me the secret of the Edna chocolate bar, made from Sri Lankan-grown cacao. It was wrapped in thin white paper, ideal for rolling a ganja joint. Naturally, he carried a supply of the herb and showed his skills. Those snaky tree branches were positively mesmerizing and the milk chocolate divine as we enjoyed his hand-rolled reefer. The cartoon character sticker included in the packaging of every bar was a delightful bonus.

I entrusted the jungle journey arrangements to Lal. Setting out on a rickety bus, I carried water and a bag with a few snacks. Lal carried nothing. After a couple hours of traveling bumpy rural roads, we got down at a lonely tea stall where we sat on a wooden plank and drank tea. A male pig snorted and stomped in a pen behind the building. Everything about the animal was massive. Rounded and massive. Someday, his bulk would become a fine feast.

Lal chatted in Sinhala with the shop owner. The previous evening, elephants had trampled through a nearby village, destroying a dwelling or two. At least the animals were in the area. I shivered with excitement. We might actually get to see one.

Across the road, the brushy thicket sprinkled with a few tall trees didn't look like a real jungle. It wasn't dark or mysterious or dripping with vines and echoing with jungle sounds. I saw no path, which didn't bode well for my attire of a long skirt and sandals. But Lal also wore sandals, like everyone in Sri Lanka. If I could make it to the elephant viewing area, I didn't need to worry about my poor jungle-hiking clothes.

Refreshed by the tea, we crossed the road and plunged into the tangled vegetation, picking our way around sticky bushes and pushing through branches. A short walk brought us to a narrow stream running at the bottom of an open, sloped hillside. Tree branches hung low over a shallow pool. It was a perfect play spot for elephants to wade and squirt water at each other with their trunks. Alas, there were no elephants. Not even a single pile of elephant dung to suggest they used the area.

"Where are they?" I asked. Lal had led me on a useless, uncomfortable trip, where the most interesting thing I'd seen was a pig. The jungle wasn't even that intriguing. It was way too close to the road and people to attract any wildlife.

"There." He nodded toward the pool, empty of elephants.

Right. We'd come all that way and would have to turn around without seeing an elephant.

Lal gathered dead wood in the fading light and dragged it to a spot on the bedrock slope. "We sleep here."

Sleep in the jungle? I hadn't exactly planned for an overnight experience. But I was young and adventurous. Maybe a little foolhardy. If I had to sleep outdoors on a rock overlooking their swimming pool to see an elephant, then that's what I'd do.

The wood pile grew. I stretched out on one side of our campfire and Lal on the other. Our feet pointed downhill toward the stream and pool about seventy-five yards beyond. The fire bathed me in smoke as the unpredictable breeze shifted. Night settled in, and I resigned myself to sleeping on a rock mattress. I lay down and dozed.

A blood-curdling blast shook me awake. I sat up, peering into the darkness, straining to see something, hear something that would tell me what made that noise. All I heard was my thumping heart, my panicked breath. Total blackness. Clouds obscured the stars. The campfire had burned to a glowing mound of coals. I needed to pee in the worst way. My guide and protector snoozed away.

"Lal! Lal!" I whisper-yelled. "Wake up! Wake up!" He sat up, rubbing his eyes. I could barely see him in the faint light.

Another screeching bellow. Wailing, angry, loud, like a lion's roar. But lions didn't live in Sri Lanka.

My insides tumbled. I was sure I'd lose all that pee, right through my clothes and on to the rock. I didn't move.

"Mmm." Lal nodded, his eyes squinting. "Elephant."

No kidding. His monotone baffled me. Not a hint of concern.

Lal piled branches on the fire. It sparked and flared. Shadows danced across his face, contorting his cheeks and chin. I trembled, looking at him for reassurance. None came.

Had he actually done this before—brought a traveler to this very spot, slept on the rock, watched for an elephant? Right then, I didn't want to learn the truth.

Another trumpeting siren echoed across the ravine. I shook. I sweated. I still needed to pee. How close was the animal? How big? How many? Crackling flames billowed light against a black wall just beyond my companion and me. I could see nothing but Lal's pinched face and wide eyes. Trying to quell my terror, I imagined the firelight creating a protective barrier between me and the wild. Me and the enormous body of an Asian elephant.

When the rain came, my body was already saturated with adrenaline—paralyzing adrenaline that rooted me to that unyielding grave. Lal fed more wood to the fire before he pulled the back of his shirt up and over his head for a pathetic umbrella. The downpour soaked my hair and my clothes, ran in rivulets around and under me. No sense trying to stay dry. I was dead anyway. But I'd be clean when the elephant's tusks found me and tossed my body around.

The rain lightened. Our campfire sputtered. We sat on the rock listening to drips and water splashes and insect buzzes. I pinned my bent legs against my belly with crossed arms. My breathing slowed and evened out. *Make it to dawn. Make it to dawn.*

A couple hours later the world turned grey, and I could detect the treetops. I peeked up the slope behind me. No big four-legged animals peered down at us, waving their trunks. Nothing below us, either, splashing around in the pool.

After I worked up the nerve to stretch my crumpled legs, I rolled to my feet and limped to the side to finally relieve myself. The earth was squishy soft from the rain.

As I walked back to Lal, I noticed a depression in the mud. Round, a few inches deep. The size of a large doggie bed, I could have crawled into it and curled up. Several similar spots sank into the soil nearby. A few feet away was a fresh pile of crumbly greenish dung.

An elephant foot had landed within fifteen yards of my sleeping head.

Seeing the elephant track was more than enough adventure for me. We gathered our wits and hurried through wet vegetation toward the road to catch the first bus back to Anuradhapura.

Lal and I spoke little about our jungle adventure. In my remaining days in the area, we continued to explore the ancient city and Sri Lankan culture. He taught me simple phrases in Sinhala, while I helped him with his English. In the mornings, he took me to street food vendors for the local breakfast specialty of rice steamed in coconut milk in bamboo. I counseled him as he struggled with his angsty life. We enjoyed more Edna chocolate bars, the warm days, and the lush vegetation lining the ancient irrigation canals and lakes. One day, he and his buddy stalked an enormous lizard up a tree. They poked it with a long stick and pelted it with rocks. I screamed at them to stop, saving the creature from the fate of becoming lizard curry.

Days later, before I traveled on, Lal presented me with a gift. His eyes gleamed as he gave me an elephant, carved from dark wood, the finish dented and scratched. One of its white eyes was missing. Two gaping holes on both sides of its trunk showed where the bone tusks had fallen out. Lal admitted taking it from his brother's house. He figured his brother wouldn't miss it.

I still treasure Lal's pilfered gift, offered with such gratitude. Gratitude for spending time together. Gratitude for surviving the overnight adventure in the jungle.

Where we did not see an elephant.

* * *

Terry Nichols is a retired National Park Service ranger who spent most of her career in the American Southwest. Her middle grade fantasy, *The Dreaded Cliff*, stars a word-mangling, hopelessly lost packrat. She writes and talks to desert creatures from her home in Aztec, New Mexico.

Non-Fiction - Travel - 3rd Place **Suzanne Stauffer**

The Children of Panamint Springs

We arrived at Panamint Springs Resort on the western edge of Death Valley early in the evening of the fourth day of our honeymoon trip back in December 2006. We'd spent the night before at Stovepipe Wells, more or less in the center of the Park and the night before that at Furnace Creek Ranch.

We started our day by watching the sun rise over the Mesquite Flat Sand Dunes just east of the motel. In the silence of the freezing morning, the silhouette of the dunes was gradually exposed as the horizon lightened by degrees. Soon, the shadow cast by the rising sun slowly crawled up the faces of the slopes until the sun was sitting on the crest of the mounds. The sun then climbed higher to reveal the vast expanse of rolling hills of sand. We stood immersed in wonder until the sound of cars starting at the motel broke the spell.

After breakfast at the Badwater Saloon, we gassed up the car and took Scotty's Castle Road to Scotty's Castle and Rhyolite. Driving a rental sedan, we avoided the "high-clearance vehicle recommended" Titus Canyon Road, despite the National Park Service promising "colorful rock formations… petroglyphs … and spectacular canyon narrows." We drove northeast through the vast ancient lakebed, like the bottom of an immense bowl whose sides were formed by the jagged peaks of the surrounding Amargosa and Panamint Ranges to the east and west, and the Grapevine and Owlshead Mountains to the north and south. We'd long ago run out of adjectives to express our wonder and amazement at the vistas and simply stared in silence.

We made a quick detour to the Ubehebe Crater, attracted as much by the name as by the description. The six-hundred-foot-deep crater, caused not by a meteorite crashing to Earth but by a volcanic explosion, is striated in rusts and ochres, with a wide band of charcoal cinders around the top. Because we were on a schedule, we did not take the time to walk around the rim. Walking down to the bottom and back up was not even contemplated, although someone else was doing it at the time.

Scotty's Castle — more properly, Death Valley Ranch -- is a short drive to the east and up Grapevine Canyon to an elevation of 3,000 feet. I was feeling the cold when we got out of the car, so I bought a sweatshirt at the visitor center gift shop while we waited for our living history tour to begin. The Castle, a California Mission-style mansion, is a testament to the excesses of the 1920s. Built by Chicago insurance magnate Albert Mussy Johnson as a vacation home, it soon became known as "Scotty's Castle" when his friend and partner, cowboy and miner Walter "Death Valley Scotty" Scott claimed to have built it using the proceeds of his secret mines. The interior is as lavish as the exterior suggests, with intricately carved hardwood railings, ceiling beams and doors, tiled fireplaces, and wrought-iron banisters and chandeliers, as well as the almost-obligatory mounted hunting trophies. The tile floors are covered with Oriental rugs on which stands custom-made furniture imported from Spain. We left feeling slightly drunk with all the opulence.

Continuing east, we left the Park and ascended another thousand feet or so to the ghost town of Rhyolite, Nevada. The wind chill was well below freezing, so after a few minutes exploring the Bottle House (yes, a house made from empty bottles) and the intact train station, I returned to the car. I wouldn't have been able to do even that much if not for the sweatshirt I had just purchased. Mike toughed it out a bit longer, then also sought refuge. We drove slowly down the main street of the town and viewed the ruins of the bank, the jail and other identified buildings from the comfort of the heated car, then turned and retraced the road back to Stovepipe Wells, where we stopped for lunch at the Saloon, before returning to the road leading southwest toward Panamint Springs.

Just past the Stovepipe Wells Campground, we turned off the main road and followed the unpaved road to the parking lot at the trailhead to Mosaic Canyon. We walked into the canyon — the bed of an ancient river that fed the prehistoric Lake Manly — and soon reached the polished marble walls rising at least twenty feet above our heads. We could clearly see the eponymous mosaic, formed of small fragments of polished rock of various colors held in a natural cement matrix. Some prehistoric earthquake had shattered the bedrock, and mud and water and time had created this natural collage. When we reached the boulder jam about a mile into the canyon, we did what most people do and turned back rather than attempting to crawl through the narrow passage to one side.

It was dark when we pulled into the dirt and gravel parking lot in front of the Panamint Springs Resort "lodge," a one-story wooden building with a narrow porch running along the front. The painted wooden sign on the porch roof above the door proclaimed "Restaurant Pizza Burgers Salads." Ours was the only car in the lot. A low-watt bulb burned over the door and the windows on either side were dimly illuminated. We could just make out several dark neon signs advertising different brands of beer. The resort had opened around 1940 and the current owners had chosen to maintain its historical character.

"This is a resort?" Mike asked.

I shrugged. "It is in Panamint Springs."

"It looks like a roadhouse that's fallen on hard times. Where's the hotel?" He looked behind us at the empty lot across the road. I knew from my previous visit that it was a campground and RV park, but there weren't any campers there now.

"As far as I remember, the rooms are behind this building. It's an old-fashioned motor court. We check in inside here."

We climbed the four or five steps up to the porch and entered the lobby/bar. We didn't see or hear anyone. The neon signs over the bar facing us had been turned off. The bakery/deli display cases were empty and dark. Fluorescent lights flickered in the ceiling. To the right of the entrance and perpendicular to it was a small counter with a cash register and chrome service call bell. Behind it, a door led across a narrow hall into what was the general store, but the lights were off and its door was closed. To our left, another door led into what we later discovered was the "restaurant."

"This is where we checked in last time," I said and tapped the bell. It sounded loudly in the eerie silence. We waited.

"Did you hear something?" I asked Mike. He shook his head, but my hearing is better than his. I was sure I heard the distant murmur of voices. Now I could hear a sort of shuffling sound, coming from deep down the hallway behind the "registration desk," gradually growing louder. Eventually, a young man shuffled into view. He had neck-length dark hair that hung in his eyes. He was wearing jeans and a hoodie and moccasins on his feet. He peered at us through his hair.

"We have a reservation," I said. "We're here to check in."

He nodded and slouched across to the counter. He opened a registration book that looked like it had been in use since the 1940s. He ran his finger down the page, and said our name.

"That's us," I said.

"Uh-huh. You got room 5."

"With a king-size bed?" I asked.

"Uh-huh." He gave me the room card and I filled in our names and other information. He handed me an old-fashioned door key with a large plastic hotel fob on it, all without a word.

"Where do we park?"

"Uh, you can park in front of the room."

"Yes, but how do we get there?"

"They're behind here." Which did not answer my question, but I decided that it would be less work to just find them on our own. They couldn't be far and there was nothing else out there to confuse us.

"Is the restaurant still open?" If not … we'd have to either backtrack to Stovepipe Wells or continue on out of the Park and hope to hit something on 395.

"Uh-huh. We could do something." He looked resigned.

"Should we eat first?" I asked Mike, who so far hadn't said anything. I learned later that he was wondering if we were going to enact the "two strangers take a wrong turn and end up in a mysterious town" trope of horror films and was working out a defense and an escape.

"Yeah, it's been awhile since lunch," he responded.

We waited.

"Could we get dinner?" I finally asked.

"Uh-huh." He — we never did learn his name, so he'll be He from here on in — wandered over toward the door on our left and we followed Him, hoping He was leading us to the dining room, and that we were not on the menu. This room, too, was dimly lighted. Square tables with fake wood tops ran down the center and along both walls. Four chairs stood at those in the center and two at those on the sides.

"Sit wherever," He said.

We selected a table for two near the door and away from the windows. He handed us menus. Mike ordered a beer. I asked for diet Coke. He slouched away. We perused the menus. We were surprised to see, among the burgers and pizzas, spinach lasagna and spaghetti and meatballs.

When He returned with our drinks, Mike ordered the spaghetti and I ordered the lasagna. We worried that He didn't write down the order, or even repeat it, but hoped for the best. He slumped away.

We sipped our drinks and talked about the sights we had seen that day and where we were going the next day. He re-appeared sooner than expected.

"Uh, yeah, there's a problem." We were more surprised at the length of the sentence than the meaning of the words. He looked at me. "Yours is ready." He turned to Mike. "But, the chef dropped yours on the floor, so he's going to have to make it again." He looked back at me. "Do you want yours now?" I shook my head. "Ok. He said to tell you we can make you some jalapeño poppers while you wait."

Mike looked at me questioningly. I shrugged and nodded. "Yeah, ok," Mike replied. "And another beer."

He nodded and shuffled out. I shook with suppressed giggles as soon as he was out of the room. "Dropped it on the floor?"

Mike shrugged. He was still laying plans for our escape, if necessary.

I had only just got the giggles under control when He returned with Mike's beer and a plate of breaded deep-fried jalapeño peppers. We thanked Him and he wandered off.

I examined the poppers for signs of having spent time on the floor, but seeing none, ate a couple. They were crispy, but not burned, and filled with warm cream cheese, so we knew the chef could operate a deep-fryer. We'd consumed most of them when He showed up with a plate in each hand. The spinach lasagna he placed in front of me was a perfect rectangle, with ruler-straight sides. Two sides of the noodles retained their curly edges. I've heated enough frozen single-serve lasagna in the microwave to recognize it when I see it. Mike's meatballs rested on sauce-coated spaghetti, looking like leftovers reheated for lunch the next day.

We ate our food, which was edible if uninspired, paid the check, got in the car and drove around to our room. The fourteen-room motel was a long one-story building with a wooden shingled roof, similar to the "lodge." There were a couple of cars parked at either end of the building. We parked in front of room 5, opened the door, and walked into a screaming tropical nightmare. The king-sized four-poster bed constructed of faux bamboo nearly filled the room. The bedspread, curtains, and wallpaper all assaulted our senses with palm trees swaying on sandy beaches lapped by turquoise water, glowing red, green, blue, and yellow hibiscus flowers, and raucous parrots flying through the palm trees. Exactly what you'd expect from a Western-themed rustic "resort" run by the children of the damned. Thankfully, the assault was easily quashed by turning off the lights, and the bed was comfortable.

The next morning, as we walked over for breakfast at the "lodge," Mike wondered aloud whether "He comes out during the day." We guessed not, as He was not in evidence when we arrived at the restaurant, but She was. Young, thin, pale, dressed all in black with black hair and multiple piercings, where he had avoided eye-contact, she stared at us with withering indifference. We humbly requested breakfast and meekly followed her to a table in the dining room. We must have ordered and eaten breakfast, although I remember nothing about it. When we were finished, we approached the cashier's desk. It was now staffed by a tall, thin young man with a short hair cut wearing oddly ordinary slacks and polo shirt. He avoided eye contact by staring at some point behind us or to one side or over our heads.

"Everything all right?" He asked as he rang up the amount due for breakfast. I turned to see who he was talking to. There was no one else there. "You wanna check out now, too?" He seemed eager to have us gone.

"It was fine. Yes, let's do that and save time. Room 5."

I handed him our credit card. He processed the charges and gave me the receipt to sign.

"What do we do with the key? We still need to pack and load the car."

"Just leave it in the room." They only wanted to see the back of us.

* * *

We stopped at the turn-off to Darwin Falls, but the sign at the entrance declared the road suitable only for high-clearance vehicles, so we continued on to the Father Crowley Vista Point and its view of the aptly-named Rainbow Canyon. We left the car in the parking lot and walked to the fence at the edge of the overlook. As I gazed around, taking in the view of Panamint Valley, it unleashed one last surprise. I saw a small black speck in the sky to the west. It quickly grew into an Air Force fighter jet, likely from Edwards Air Force Base on the other side of the mountains. The clear air and angle of view made it appear that the jet was headed straight toward us, and I smiled at the thought. Until it became apparent not only that it was headed straight for us but was descending. I stared at it in disbelief. The pilot dipped the plane low enough to make out the make and model of the car, then pulled up and away. I called to Mike, "Did you see that guy buzz us?"

He shook his head. "Are you sure?"

"Well, if you don't believe me, here he comes again." The plane had circled around and was coming toward us again. Once again, it descended, then pulled up just before he was close enough to read the license plate. This time, he continued east.

"Some joker having fun with the senior citizen tourists," Mike shook his head. "He'll be telling his buddies all about giving the two old people a thrill."

"It would be something to tell the grandkids, if we had grandkids."

We got back in the car. The rest of the morning is a hazy memory until we were well out of the Park, leaving Panamint Springs and its denizens far behind. It was as if a veil had lifted. We never did see the chef.

* * *

Suzanne Stauffer is a retired librarian, professor emerita of Library Science, and author living in Baton Rouge, but soon moving to Albuquerque. Her historical mystery, *Fried Chicken Castañeda*, set in Las Vegas, New Mexico in 1929, will be published in Spring 2024 by Artemesia Publishing.

Section Seven: Opening Pages of a Memoir

Mosaic Voices from Beyond by Barbara Garvey

Unpublished Memoir - 2nd place **Brenda Beck**

Changing Woman Speaks

CHAPTER ONE
Between Two Worlds

The Phoenix sky is dark and ominous as I step out of the airport terminal and climb into the front seat of the car beside the Navajo medicine man. Great jagged streaks of searing white lightning tear across the heavens and slash down to the earth in every direction. They are relentless and all around us as we head north out of Phoenix towards Flagstaff and the Rez.

As many times as I've been to Phoenix, nothing seems familiar. The lightning is disorienting, and he's driving on back roads I've never seen before to avoid the rush hour traffic. I'm in his territory now, and this Navajo man who I've known for several years is taking me somewhere way up north tonight to the Navajo Indian Reservation where he's going to sneak me into a private ceremony.

Just an hour ago I was on a plane flying in from New York, having spent a week with the editors of Reader's Digest in our corporate headquarters in Pleasantville, thirty miles north of Manhattan. Three other top advertising sales executives and I had been chosen from our New York, Detroit, Chicago, and West Coast offices to be immersed in the magazine's unique editorial process while honing our own editing skills.

I'd spent this morning working on our final assignment in a private office, sitting at an antique French writing desk and gazing up at a lovely painting of ballerinas hanging on the wall in front of me. Suddenly, I realized it was an original Degas—later to be sold by Sotheby's for over six million dollars—and I was sitting at the desk of Lila Wallace, Reader's Digest's beloved co-founder, art collector, and philanthropist. I immediately felt my spirit lift and my back straighten. The beauty and elegance of this room and Mrs. Wallace's legacy inspired me to do my very best work.

My colleagues and I had been given only one hour to edit a nine-page Newsweek article down to one and a half pages for Reader's Digest. The editor apologized for the time limitation as he hustled us off to private offices, saying, "It's an impossible task in an hour, but please do the best you can."

Exactly one hour later, a senior editor reviewed my work and was thrilled that I'd nearly replicated, word-for-word, his own edit of the same article which was about to be published. News of my achievement quickly circulated the hallowed offices, and I was patted on the back and told they would hire me on the spot if I were applying for an editor's job. It was obvious they hadn't expected this from an advertising salesperson. It had been a good week for me, and I would be remembered for it.

I bid farewell to my colleagues at noon and climbed into the Lincoln Town Car that would take me to John F. Kennedy Airport. I had less than an hour to figure out a wardrobe change from my corporate suit and heels to a Navajo ceremonial outfit, whatever that might look like. On the way to the airport, my driver graciously dropped me off at the White Plains shopping mall and waited while I tore through the racks at The Limited looking for something that would work. Thirty minutes later I emerged wearing a calf-length, tiered denim skirt, a western-style blouse, and a tooled leather belt which paired with the boots I had worn to New York. I told the salesgirl I was headed to Arizona, and she envisioned me at a fancy dude ranch. *That's close enough,* I thought to myself as I hustled out.

In the car, I plaited my long brown hair in a single French braid down my back. I'd read traditional Navajo women don't leave their long hair hanging loose but arrange it in a special bun. I couldn't do that, so the braid was my effort to be respectful, and I hoped I looked appropriate. It was the best I could do in a pinch, and I was amazed I pulled it all together so fast.

Before my plane took off, I left a message for my best friend back in San Francisco telling him where I was going and with whom. He thought I was flying back to the Bay Area tonight and would assume I'd check in when I decompressed from my week in New York. Without this call, no one would ever know I changed my flight to land in Phoenix and would soon be somewhere deep in the native lands of northern Arizona. My voicemail ended with, "If I don't call you by Sunday evening, I want you to know where I was last headed and with whom!"

Five hours later, my plane dropped down through the altitude levels into a different climate, a different culture, and a totally different reality. As we taxied to the gate, I tried to prepare myself for what I'd signed up for. I wasn't scared, but very nervous with a million questions. This wasn't another Navajo workshop but the real deal, a chance to go to the Navajo Reservation with my teacher and friend and attend a real ceremony. I wasn't going to miss it for the world, as I might never have another opportunity to do this.

I met James three years ago in Nine Gates Mystery School, a spiritual retreat program in northern California which focused on the nine energy centers of the body. The teachers included an African shaman from Togo, a Sufi, a Navajo medicine man, and a Tibetan monk who shared their traditional teachings, songs, and ceremonies with our group. When the program ended, many of us continued to study with our favorite teachers, and most of us gravitated to James whenever he could come back to California.

He was introduced to us as a full-blooded Navajo medicine man who was raised in Tuba City, Arizona on the Navajo Indian Reservation. His father was a Navajo

Code Talker in World War II, and his paternal grandfather was a formidable Navajo medicine man himself, and the first Vice Chairman of the Navajo Nation. James' teachings run deep, and he has helped a lot of people through his people's traditional ways.

I was surprised to learn that he's also a college-educated businessman. When I met him, he was working for a large financial services company in Phoenix, with large corporate clients in northern California. Now he lives in Flagstaff, Arizona where he owns a computer consulting business and a Chinese restaurant on the Navajo Reservation. He opened the restaurant over a year ago to provide jobs for his son, his eldest daughter, and her partner, who is a Chinese chef. But now something has gone awry, and evidently this ceremony is the only thing that can uncover what that is.

Peking Gardens was a success from the moment it opened in Tuba City, a small town on the western side of the Reservation not far from the Grand Canyon. The Chinese food was excellent, and the restaurant was the only game in town aside from the Navajo tacos and burger stand across the street from the gas station. They were full every night and James's family was having fun running it, until the business started to implode.

One weekend, the chef flew back to San Francisco's Chinatown to visit his family and was spirited away and not heard from again. Six weeks passed before he was able to secretly relay a message back through a friend that he couldn't return. Evidently, his traditional Chinese parents didn't think too highly of their first-born son being with a Native American woman, and they had no intention of letting him return to Arizona. Never mind that they had a beautiful baby daughter together. That probably made it worse. He was essentially kidnapped, and it was clear he wouldn't be back. Ever.

With the chef gone and the staff devastated, the sous chef stepped in and did a great job replicating the traditional Chinese dishes. The restaurant was always busy, but the business began bleeding money. He's looked at the books, spent time in the restaurant, and talked with the staff, but couldn't figure out the problem. Then bizarre car accidents started happening in rapid succession, first with James, then with different family members in the restaurant's parking lot.

I was in New York when he called to tell me he'd hired a medicine man do a reading. The medicine man had read the crystals and said there was black magic involved and that a protection ceremony was needed as soon as possible. It was scheduled for this weekend, the weekend I was flying home from New York.

I jumped at the chance to be invited. He's my spiritual teacher, but we're also now business confidantes. He's been talking about his restaurant problems for months, so I knew the issues and how precarious things were. Plus, a lot of things were getting weird for me in our California ceremonies, jealousy and mean things being said behind my back, so maybe I can learn something that will help me too.

He explained this would be a private ceremony without his family or the restaurant staff. It would just be him and the medicine man. But I pleaded my case hard, coming from the place of supportive friend and colleague, while trying not to sound too pushy. It would be so easy for me to stop in Phoenix on the way home, so I felt like it was a sign I should be there. Finally, he decided it would be safe to invite me. He said if I could swing it, he'd pick me up at the Phoenix airport and we'd drive up together.

So that's how I got here, fresh off the plane from New York, and heading into the unknown. James is being unusually quiet, and I can't tell if he's nervous about the ceremony, wondering why in the world he invited me, or just concentrating on what needs to be done. He's only a few years older than me but looks so much older. He's my height, five foot six inches, with balding grey hair, and a stocky build. In business settings, he suits up and looks nice, and often wears a diamond ring on his right hand. This evening he's in blue jeans and cowboy boots, with no diamond ring. He's dressed down for the Rez.

We exit the interstate at Flagstaff and head towards Kmart to buy supplies.

"What do you need for the ceremony?" I ask.

"For this one," he says, "we need to provide a rifle and ammunition, along with breakfast food that I've already gotten, and cash, all as the exchange."

"What's the rifle for?" I ask, as nonchalantly as I can.

"I'll explain on the drive to Tuba City. Right now, you can come in with me, but I need you to lay low and let me go to the gun counter by myself. There's going to be Navajos in here, and I don't want to take the chance that someone will figure out what we're doing."

How could anyone possibly guess what we are doing? I wonder. *And why would it matter?* He seems a little anxious now, and that is making me nervous.

We enter the Kmart separately, a grey-haired Navajo man and a white lady in crisp new western clothes. I can see why he doesn't want to walk in with me. I look out of place here, and walking in together would certainly raise eyebrows. I move slowly through the aisles by myself, picking up a few things to snack on while he goes to the gun counter at the back of the store to purchase the rifle and ammunition. I feel like every Indian in the place is watching me.

As I walk by one native couple, the skin crawls on the back of my neck. I sense suspicion in their eyes as they discreetly glance at me. Have they guessed what we're up to? Is it because I'm a white woman? No, there are lots of other Anglos in the store. It's because of what James said when we walked in. He doesn't want to take chances. I still don't know what that means, but the power of suggestion is strong.

Leaving Kmart with supplies in hand, we head east out of Flagstaff along old Route 66, then turn north onto Highway 89 towards Page, Arizona. The landscape begins to change as the pine forests give way to sandy outcroppings and strange windswept formations that I can just make out in the darkness. We pass a wooden sign that reads, "You Are Now Entering the Navajo Reservation," and this escapade starts to get very real.

I ask about the rifle again. "What is it for?"

"The rifle will be placed inside by the door," he says, "in case something happens."

"What do you mean? What kinds of things might happen?" I ask.

"Anything can happen when you do a ceremony like this. Sometimes things come to the door. Just keep your eyes and ears open and stay alert."

That's all he's going to say, so no point in asking anything else. We don't talk much for the last hour of the drive, and I'm grateful for the silence. It's been a long day, and I'm trying to switch my head from the euphoria of being with the Readers Digest editors to suddenly being here, heading towards the unknown.

I've been fascinated with the Navajo teachings since I first met James and have always wanted to visit the Reservation. But this is bigger than that. This is a secret journey so completely different from the corporate world I normally live in. It feels like a powerful force is pulling me into the Navajo world, calling me towards something I still can't see but I know is waiting for me up ahead.

Was I crazy to come? Absolutely. I could be home right now, relaxing from my long week with a glass of wine in my hot tub. But this door opened, and I stepped through it. In fact, I insisted I needed to be here, so no matter what happens, it was my choice.

Maybe the better question I should be asking is, "Am I safe?" I don't know what I'm getting into, and that's scary. But I have a trusted guide, so I shouldn't be worried. Right?

* * *

Brenda Beck is an author, film producer, and practitioner of the Navajo Beauty Way. She's dedicated to helping save the ancient wisdom of indigenous people and believes the integration of this knowledge is vital to navigating the challenges we face in today's modern world.

Unpublished Memoir - 3rd place **Michael Andryc**

X-Rated Trout Fishing

Anyone who has ever pulled a trout in through a second story window will know what I mean.

There is (thank God) an *unwholesome* side to fishing. Luckily, in the annals of the sport, there are bad influences galore – men (and women) who have not killed the wild thing in themselves. Wild men after wild fish in a wild world.

And so, it should be.

And so it is that I have my old man to thank for having originally led me astray.

He was quite a character.

For one thing, he was nuts about trout. To him, there was nothing more beautiful than a native brook trout. Trout-crazed, he would do anything for trout. I sometimes thought he would even kill for trout.

He did things like bribe kids with ice cream so he could fish a favorite hole.

To ward off adults, he'd flash his honorary deputy game warden badge and soon they'd be racing to their cars.

We'd be out fishing at night in our small boat, and he would tell me stories that raised my hair of his life. Trainyards and whorehouses and bums and drinking and falling out of canoes.

Who wanted to go to school when he could fish, listen to stories, have a swig on the jug, a puff on a cigar?

We did not simply go fishing, we went on expeditions, in those New England hills. He prepared for these ventures days in advance. And when, like speeding turtles, we finally lit out in the old Studebaker, he wasn't satisfied to go straight to the fishing hole. Oh no. Not my old man. He had to visit every bar along the way. And as if that weren't bad enough, he had to recite the history of the area we were fishing. The crumbling foundations, the washed-out dams, ancient gristmills, Indians, etc. Over and over and over. Then we had to unload the gear (in a certain order) and load it upon our backs (with yours truly carrying the unpoetic things like frying pan, bacon strips, bait, beer) and then we would hike miles through thick brush – the old man going along like a rusty tractor – and then and only then would we begin to fish. The rest of the tedious details will be left to the reader's imagination. Keep in mind that we almost always caught trout.

Trout, as I said, even came through the second story window.

How?

Well, the old man had a flower shop. Which seems innocent enough. And, in fact, the front of the store looked most respectable: a few decorations (according to season) in the window, a pair of cut-off wagon wheels for handrails, two huge bottles of colored water for ornamentation and the sign. But it was a front, a coverup for what went on in back.

For behind the store was a river. And if the customers could see through the big icebox behind the front counter, they would see a flyrod out the back window. How many flowers wilted in their hands while the old man executed his secret vice?

What hope can anyone have for a normal childhood who has a father that fishes *at work?*

But worse than the old man's unwholesome deeds were those of his cronies. Such actions on their part have permanently warped the mind of the writer.

Of course, he knew characters who had actually killed fish with shotguns or brought them stunned to the surface with dynamite. But these were evil, unsportsmanlike beings. Only a step above them was an artless individual named Alex. This gent slept outdoors on an old rat-chewed mattress, caught fish indiscriminately on a trot line and *sold* them. But in the end, he got his just reward and was compelled to lecture pigeons from park benches for the rest of his life.

Not so evil but equally misleading were Beauregard and Tripp.

Art "Colonel" Beauregard and Frank Tripp were always together, always fishing, always drunk and always seventy (at the time I was always ten) so I thought of them as being one and the same person.

Maybe they were.

The only difference was that the "Colonel" kept a trout down his well (against hard times?) and Tripp it was who showed me the "proper" way to cut brush.

But I never did see these whiskey-drinking tobacco-chewing trout-fishing old timers actually fishing.

Having caught so many real and imaginary trout, the act itself must have been unimportant now, a mere detail. They had merged with the fish – they even looked like trout.

They now spent much of their time discussing the finer points of the sport:

Tripp: "Don't pay no attention to Beauregard, son. Senile old (blank) can't tell a skunk's (blank) from a Royal Coachman."

Beauregard: "Hell, Tripp thinks his (blank's) a trout!"

They died on the same day, lured out of their holes by the Ultimate Trout passing slowly over the horizon. Years later the old man found their initials on a tree near a favorite fishing spot. Needless to say, he added his. But can the reader imagine the effect of all this on an up-and-coming trout fisherman?

Then there was Joe Lambert.

Joe worked engraving patterns on steel rollers in textile factories – but in real life (the life we all live in our hearts) he was a fisherman extraordinaire, a French-Canadian trapper, 'coon hunter and all around wildman.

Ok. Maybe he did smoke crippled cigars and chew Life Savers at the same time, but he tried. We put in our fifteen minutes at church before sneaking into a certain posted reservoir. I mean, the fifteen minutes must have counted for something.

And harrowing minutes they were. Standing in the back of the church and dressed for ice fishing, you might have thought we were wearing fish hides – based on the looks we got.

In our misdoings, however, we were highly invisible.

Joe taught me that even if you have no cover, if you don't move no one is apt to see you. There is nothing quite like being a small boy and hiding behind the trees preparatory to a run across the road into posted land.

In order to increase our invisibility, we only fished on the worst days, in the deepest snow. Then we could be sure that the man who patrolled the reservoir wouldn't be out. What joy and crazy ideas a kid has. Since fishing was forbidden, there must be bass as big as buildings – man-eating bass – ancient and uncatchable. And one cold day while we were imbibing some of Mother Goldstein's finest with a deer poacher, the flag went up and we pulled in a bass that weighed seven pounds.

It is a fact that we dragged branches to cover our tracks. It is a fact that we never left any trash. Soon the woodland returned to its natural state and the bluejays, no wiser, ceased hollering. All of which led to the overwhelmingly demented act of catching a trout with your bare hands, admiring its beauty and *letting it go.*

Far from New England, in the mountains of southeastern Wyoming, there is a creek which no one – including myself – can accurately describe. You could say that the water was clearer than air or colder than ice. Which would be true. You could say it was a heartbreaking creek, and it flowed along like a well-structured sentence. Which would also be true. But, if Libby Creek, in the Snowy Range Mountains, is beyond description – what can you say for a rainbow trout that takes the wrong turn?

I can see the headlines now:

Thrill-Crazed Trout Meets Extraterrestrial Fisherman

For, insane with the woodlands, cursed and blessed with a love of fishing – one fall day when the aspens were going full blast and the sky was so blue it throbbed – I took that same wrong turn.

It was water not meant for fish – so shallow a trout would get a suntan swimming through it. Never mind a gravel autograph on its undersides. What, I still ask, was a fourteen-inch rainbow doing in a place like this?

Beauregard, were you responsible for this?

Tripp, was this the "proper" way for a trout to conduct itself?

The trout fishing sins of the father had surely been visited upon the head of the son. But I was not content to leave it that way.

In true mountain man style, I would show my own son how to catch a trout. Abandoning all thought of flyrods and tackle, not bothering to roll up my pants or take off my boots, I jumped into the tiny runoff. I chased that fish from one end of its rainbow to the other. I could hear Beauregard and Tripp and Lambert and the old man – trout fishing heroes all – laughing in the woods. Finally, the fish ran aground, and I took it in my hands.

Of course, I had learned from Ernest Hemingway (and the old man) to wet my hands first. But I remembered nothing from any of his stories about a "corral" like the one we had built. It was made of stone and the water flowed through it, but the trout could not.

Words fail, fall down upon their knees and beg forgiveness because they cannot cope with what we felt looking at this wayward trout, that certain day in Wyoming autumn. Yes, we must have been totally out of our skulls trying to communicate with this fishy being. But every true fisherman knows that what is caught on a fishing trip is not just the fish. But how many fishermen have gone fishing and gotten caught themselves?

We were in a spell, we were caught. What more beautiful thing was there than this fish that had swum away with all the colors of the fall up a wrong turn in the creek?

Having taken wrong turns all our lives, we knew what it was like. There was only one thing to do.

My son carried the beautiful fish to the best pool in the creek. He did not cry when the trout swam away and neither did I. It was hard to let go, as it is always hard to let go. But as I thought of it, we had let nothing go. We left the place as we had found it but with one difference.

Waiting at the bottom of Libby Creek in the Medicine Bow National Forest is one angry, much-wiser, blood-thirsty trout!

But what I want to know is, what kind of fisherman will a boy turn out to be whose old man lets fish go?

* * *

Michael Andryc is an award-winning writer and artist living and working in Albuquerque, New Mexico. His writing has been published in the *North American Review*, and his artwork has been exhibited at the New Mexico State Fair, Albuquerque Museum's Arts Thrive, and the StepUp Gallery in Los Alamos, New Mexico.

Unpublished Memoir - Honorable Mention **Eva Nevarez St. John**

When Tough Cookies Crumble

Prologue

Missing

My calls to my best friend Janice from early morning to late at night went unanswered, and her weekly letters stopped appearing in my mailbox. When I learned she hadn't been to school or work since early November, I feared the worst.

The two hundred miles I drove from Alexandria to Chesapeake, Virginia that cold November morning in 1981 would prove to be the longest drive of my life. It was Friday the 13th, an ominous sign of the nightmare ahead.

Was there something I could have said or done to protect her?

Janice was like a sister to me. We were roommates in 1978 at the Yongsan Army Base in Seoul, Korea. After we were discharged in the summer of 1979, we moved to the Washington, D.C. area together. Two years later, she moved to southern Virginia. After three months there, she was missing.

Why didn't I take the things she wrote about in her last letters more seriously? She suspected her life might be in danger and she told me who would be responsible if anything happened to her.

Where was Janice?

Chapter One

Kimchi Land

What should we wear?" I asked Janice. We eagerly anticipated a Saturday night out at the Crossroads Club, a Non-commissioned Officers (NCO) Club not far from our barracks.

"Let's wear our gray pinstripe suits with our white silk blouses," Janice answered.

I joined the Army in January 1976, to get away from my abusive alcoholic husband and finish my education. Janice joined in July 1976 after she graduated from high school, to escape bad relationships and be independent of her parents. I followed my boyfriend to Korea in the spring of 1977. Janice arrived in January 1978.

Monday through Friday, we were at the mercy of Uncle Sam, wearing unflattering uniforms and keeping our hair above our collars. The weekends were our chance to literally let our hair down and have fun. When we went out, we transformed ourselves into hot mamas. We painted our nails, put on make-up, curled our hair, and put on a dress or one of our custom-made three-piece pantsuits and a silk blouse. It was a ritual that required extra effort in the barracks. Our rooms only had steel cots with a single mattress, dressers, and steel lockers instead of closets. We had to use a common bathroom down the hall.

Janice was the prettier one. She was tall, with thick dark brown shoulder-length hair, warm brown eyes, a beautiful smile, and skin that tanned easily. I was petite, barely 100 pounds, and more of a plain Jane. My long dark brown hair and almond-shaped eyes hinted at my father's Native American heritage. I got my hazel eye color and fair skin from my German mother.

We were different in other ways, too. Janice grew up in an upper middle-class community in Miami. I was an Army brat who lived all over the United States and in Germany. Janice was a shy girly girl, and I was an assertive tomboy. At twenty-one, I was two years older and had more life experience.

Even though Janice had become a Mormon the year before, after a couple of months in Korea, she picked up my vices of drinking alcohol, smoking cigarettes and marijuana, and was sexually active again. Janice and I were among a small minority of single heterosexual American women in Korea, surrounded by thousands of young American soldiers. We were like kids in a candy store!

During the day, the Crossroads Club was a place to eat when we didn't want mess hall food. At night, it transformed into a disco. When we walked into the club, the lights were low and the disco music immediately put us in the mood to party. The drinks were cheap, so we knew it wouldn't take long for us to get a buzz.

We barely sat down when a guy named Billy came up to our table and asked Janice to dance. When they came back, he invited us to join him and his friend Ronnie at their table. Ronnie was a real fox, with a mustache, glasses, and a big smile. We danced with them until 3:00 am. The next day they took us to see *Saturday Night Fever*. After the movie, we sat around smoking herb and talking for hours.

I was attracted to Ronnie, and I thought he liked me, too. We both had a sarcastic sense of humor and enjoyed "shooting the shit" together. I was surprised when Janice told me later in the week that Ronnie called her, and they went to lunch together. I was disappointed that Ronnie appeared to be more interested in Janice and that Janice didn't ask me how I felt about it before she went out with him. I gave Janice the benefit of the doubt, because she knew I was seeing Wally and probably didn't think I was serious about Ronnie.

Janice and I were always looking for Mr. Right. Unfortunately, the objects of our affection were too often Mr. Wrong. SSG Wally Holmes was my Mr. Wrong. I left Thomas Henry, my partner of two years, for Wally. We ate lunch together almost every day during the week, but he only let me go to his house about twice a month. Although he wanted us to be faithful to each other, expecting me to go without sex for two or three weeks at a time at my age was too much to ask. If Wally couldn't meet my needs, I considered myself free to date other people.

The following Friday night, when Ronnie, Billy, Janice, and I went to the Crossroads Club, Ronnie spent most of the time talking to Janice. After we left the club, Billy walked Janice home and I went with Ronnie.

"You sure spent a lot of time talking to Janice tonight. Do you like her better than you like me?"

"To be honest, yes I do."

"Why didn't you just tell me?"

"I didn't want to hurt your feelings."

"I'm a big girl. I can handle it."

Ronnie was cute and fun to be around, but if Janice liked him and he liked her, more power to them. Ronnie and Janice only dated for a short time, and it wasn't long before she moved on to her next love interest.

* * *

Janice and I considered Korea a Third World country. Outside of the city, people lived in primitive conditions. Even in the city, Koreans often dressed as if they still lived in the country. They had an odd habit of squatting instead of standing and they ate strange food, including dogs. The whole country had an unpleasant odor that seemed to leach from the pores and breath of every Korean, which we called the kimchi smell. Kimchi is fermented cabbage with spicy seasoning.

We were both Administrative Specialists (i.e., clerks). I received the maximum score on my evaluations and was promoted twice, from Private First Class (PFC) to Specialist 4 in July 1977 and to Specialist 5 in May 1978. I was described as "an extremely competent soldier" and my "devotion to duty performance" was "superior to individuals in her grade. She exemplifies the modern professional soldier." I was even recommended for "integration into the Commissioned Officers Corps and promotion ahead of her contemporaries."

Although I was considered a model soldier, women in the military faced sexual harassment and discrimination daily. As part of the Women's Army Corps (WACs), we were a very small minority in the Army, in general, and in Korea, in particular. We wanted to fit in and be treated as equals, but we represented a threat to many men who saw us as part of the women's liberation movement that was redefining what it meant to be a woman beyond the stereotypical roles of wife and mother.

Korean women weren't comfortable with us either. They were raised to be totally subservient to men, and they saw American soldiers as a meal ticket and possible escape from Korea altogether. Almost every GI had a Korean *yobo*, who for a small financial investment served his every need. If they were really lucky, they got married and came to the U.S.

Korean waitresses on post usually didn't serve American women until all the men were served. When we were served, they were often very rude to us and messed up our orders. In a typical incident, a friend and I went to the Hideaway Club for lunch. All the men who came in after us were served.

I told the manager, "My friend and I have been here for almost half an hour. Your waitresses are ignoring us and serving all the men who came in after us."

"You can fill out a complaint form if you don't like it," was the rude and indifferent response I received.

"What I want is to get served," I said firmly. He made no effort to see that we got service, so we stormed out of the club and went back to work hungry.

We were literally card-carrying members of these clubs. We were protecting this Third World country from its communist neighbor North Korea. There had never been an official end to the Korean War and "incidents" between North and South Korea happened relatively often, although they weren't publicized in the U.S.

I filed an official complaint. The response that I received from the Chief of the Equal Opportunity Office was less than satisfactory. He wrote that the treatment we received was "not intentional, but an extension of the customs and values existing in Korea" and "is unconsciously influenced by the Korean socialization process and perceived to be sexist by persons who are not familiar with Korean custom." He went on to say that the "recent influx of USA female soldiers in the ROK and lack of understanding about the cultural differences, is contributed as the cause of the behavior you received." His response pissed me off. It was clear that American men at all levels loved the royal treatment they received from Korean women, and they didn't appreciate us trying to interfere with our ideas of women's liberation and equality.

Another issue we had to deal with was Korean hostesses, a euphemism for prostitutes. They lined up outside the gate waiting for men to escort them on base and turned "our" NCO Club into a brothel. One payday, as Janice and I came into the gate past the throng of hostesses, we saw a Master-at-Arms from the Crossroads Club escort two "hoochie mamas" onto the base and into the club. We went into the club and found the acting manager.

"Your Master-at-Arms is escorting hookers into our club. The letter posted on your bulletin board says: "Under no circumstances will the Master-at-Arms or anyone affiliated with the club system sponsor females on or off the installation."

He gave me a complaint form, but refused to do anything and the women were allowed to remain in the club until it closed.

Janice and I wrote a Letter to the Editor of the military newspaper. "As members of the military service stationed here in Korea, we should be able to enjoy the use of our own club system, of which we are paying members. One of the things that interferes with our enjoyment is the abundance of Korean "hostesses" in the clubs." No action was ever taken as a result of our complaint or our letter.

* * *

In May, I graduated with a Bachelor of Arts in Government from the University of Maryland's Far East Division, the first on both sides of my family to earn a college degree. I had to overcome homelessness and an abusive marriage to complete the first two and a half years. After I joined the Army, I attended night classes at the University of South Carolina. I finished my last year in Korea by taking a full-time load of classes at night.

Now that I had graduated, I had more time to hang out with Janice. Our favorite thing to do off base was to go shopping in Itaewon, the Korean neighborhood next to the base. We bought custom-made pantsuits and athletic suits with our names and designs embroidered on the back, copper kettles, chop sticks, mother-of-pearl vases, bookends, carved wooden figures, and macramé plant hangers. Janice bought a beautiful thick red Korean blanket.

One night, Janice and I decided to go clubbing off base. We went to several clubs in Itaewon, but none of them played our kind of music. We caught a bus to Sam Gotchi to look for a club that played soul music. I saw a Black man and asked him if he knew where the People's Club was. He looked surprised but gave us directions. The music was good, and we danced until we were soaked in sweat.

Like Cinderella, we had to get back to the base before the midnight curfew. No one was allowed on the street in Korea between midnight and 4:00 am. You could be fined or put in jail and soldiers could also get in trouble with the military authorities.

The more time Janice and I spent hanging out, the better we got to know each other, and our friendship grew stronger. On the other hand, my love life was getting chaotic. I started seeing a cute Captain named Benny Leonard. Socializing between officers and enlisted soldiers, officially known as fraternization, was not allowed, and having sexual relations was even worse. But life in Korea was like going to Las Vegas. What happened in Korea stayed in Korea.

The next lover I added to my roster was Marvin Carter, who lived on the first floor of my barracks. One day, our Top Sergeant called a barracks meeting because he said the barracks was a whorehouse. The sexual revolution that started in the 1960s was in high gear in the 1970s. What did they expect in a co-ed barracks of young single soldiers?

The relationship between Wally and I came to an ugly end one night, when I showed up at his apartment around 11:45 pm. Since it was close to curfew, I thought he would have to let me spend the night. Wally's roommate Fred answered the door. After I came in, we both heard moaning coming from Wally's room. When Fred let him know I was there, Wally came out of the room, picked me up, and literally threw me in the hallway.

"I told you never to come over without calling first!" he snapped.

"How can you throw me out? Is she more important than I am?"

"Yes, she is," he yelled. "I love her. I'm going to marry her. She understands when I say yes and when I say no."

Fred drove me home. I tried to sleep, but all I could think of was the sound of Wally screwing that Korean chick.

* * *

Janice had moved off base with a guy she was dating. By the time I had my going away party at their house, they had broken up and were only roommates. Marvin came with his friend Vic, who liked Janice.

Then next time I saw Janice, she told me, "I slept with Vic last night. Candice was right, he was a lousy lover."

Then Janice became irritated. "Why did you tell Marvin that Candice said Vic can't screw?"

"I didn't expect him to tell Vic."

Janice's irritation turned to anger. "Vic said when he told you that he liked me, you told him to tell me because I'm insecure and I need to hear it."

"I'm sorry, but it's true. You don't believe in yourself. You're good-looking and smart. I just thought he should tell you himself."

When I got back to the barracks, the lights were out. Blackouts were a regular thing in Korea. When I saw Marvin, I told him, "I'm pissed at you for telling Vic what I told you in confidence."

"I'm sorry. Vic shouldn't have told Janice what I said."

We went to his room where we talked and made love for hours.

"Would you ever marry me?" he asked.

"I'm too young for that." I didn't tell him I had already been married.

"I love you. I don't want you to leave Korea." I was surprised at his declaration and not sure how to respond. We hadn't even been dating for a month.

A couple of days later, Janice, Vic, and I went to the Crossroads Club. Marvin walked in with one of the new sisters in the barracks. Marvin spoke to Vic, but ignored me. I was shocked and hurt. *Two days ago, he was professing his love for me and talking about marriage. Now he acts like he doesn't know me.*

Later when Marvin was alone, I went by his table.

"Can we talk?"

"We have nothing to talk about."

"You had a lot to say the other night."

"I would only have twelve hours with you. I can have twelve months with her. This is my last opportunity with her. I've turned her down too many times because of you."

I thought he loved me. Now it was my turn to play the fool. I turned around and walked out of the Crossroads Club for the last time

Earlier that day, Captain Benny had invited me over to his place, but I declined because I thought I would be with Marvin. Since I didn't want to spend my last night in Korea crying alone in my room, Benny would once again be a substitute for the man I wanted to be with.

The next morning, I went back to my room to finish packing. I called Janice to say goodbye before I got on the bus to Osan. I was more than ready to fly away from Kimchi Land forever.

* * *

Eva Booker Nevarez St. John has been an Army brat, soldier, lawyer, and nonprofit manager. She continues to be a social activist, writer, genealogist, mother and grandmother. Eva currently lives in southern New Mexico. This is her first memoir.

Unpublished Memoir - Honorable Mention **Claire Wilcox**

The Tipping Point

Mr. Smith was incoherent, writhing and moaning about his belly pain. The stench of stale alcohol and vomit swirled all around me, surging, like waves, into my nostrils. I held my breath as I approached. I placed my hands on his upper arms in an attempt to calm him down.

But my pager kept going off. *Beep beep beep. Beep beep beep.*

This would later come to be a sound that would cause a reflexive, vibratory, almost painful surge in my chest and a slight out-of-body experience for decades to come.

I'd been dashing around between the top floor of an eight-story high-rise built in the 1950s—Denver General Hospital ("D.G."), Intensive Care Unit—and the ER on the first floor, for over an hour. It was the first day of my first rotation as an Internal Medicine intern.

The pager went off again. I wondered how many calls I would be needing to return when I was done with him. My growing to-do list threatened to blow up my brain.

The previous two days – orientation - I had spent sitting in front of PowerPoints, overeating free sandwiches, chips, and cookies. It had given me no sense of what work-work would be like.

Today, I was on call, which meant I wouldn't leave the hospital for thirty-six hours. I still delusionally believed I would get sleep that night and maybe even also find a few minutes for an afternoon snooze.

I hoped so since I had overdone it at the Coyote Club the night before. The cool-looking joint had piqued my interest on my first night in Denver; the second I entered, I intuitively knew it would be my new Cheers. That place would soon become my lifeline. Until it wasn't.

I had thought it was an over-exaggeration—what people had said about intern year. Samuel Shem, the notorious author of *House of God*, had spoken at our medical school graduation. The 1978 book was a cult classic—an uncensored, horrific, portrait of what training to become a doctor is truly like. I didn't believe it would be even close to like that. It wasn't possible that people didn't sleep *at all* on their 36-hour call shifts.

My pager went off, several more times. I looked at its tiny digital screen to see who was calling, 2-3422. Repeated seven times. Someone needed me. Bad. "I'll be right back, Mr. Smith," I said, turning away. He groaned.

I walked to the nurses' station and punched the numbers into the phone, and my resident—the intern's direct superior in the hospital hierarchy—picked up and said, "You have an admission," and without pause continued, "Mrs. Peake is a 45-year-old with a history of coronary artery disease status post cabbage..." (What's cabbage, I wondered, knowing it sounded familiar...oh yeah C.A.B.G. for coronary artery bypass graft) "...complaining of left substernal chest pain and shortness of breath worse with exertion. Her EKG shows—"

I felt around at my hips for my pen, which I couldn't find anywhere in the pockets of my long white coat, its length a sign that I had stepped up in rank from student. How old was the patient again? Did he say 45? Shit, what was her name?

The pager went off again. The resident was still talking to me through the phone receiver. I finally recovered my pen from my back pants pocket—strange location for it—and I looked down to see a new five-digit number on the little digital screen. Another nurse's station, somewhere else.

A loud prolonged beep started somewhere out there in another room. It sounded like an alarm clock, shrill, repeating, reverberating. Next the loud chant, "Internal medicine line one, internal medicine line one" echoed from somewhere above.

The voice of my resident shrilled, "Shit, ER, I hope it's not another train wreck admit." Apparently, the announcement had gone hospital-wide; he had heard it too. He quickly recited a room number to me for the patient with the chest pain, said he'd deal with the overhead page, and hung up.

I felt around in my pockets for the notepad to record the number. My pen was gone. So were the index cards—one per patient, the recommended way to keep track of the people under your care and to pass them off during shift-change. I felt a surge of dizzy panic. I hoped the cards were in Mr. Smith's room.

A nurse gestured to me over the tall podium-like counter. I hung up the phone. She said, "Are you taking Jennifer Solstice? Her B.P. is 70/30 what do you want us to do?" I had no idea who Jennifer Solstice was and picked up another phone to call my resident until I realized his pager number was on the missing index cards. Defeated, I returned the phone to its carriage.

Then a blood-curdling scream came from the direction of Mr. Smith's room. He was bellowing in agony. I felt a hand on my shoulder and hot breath against my neck, as a nurse said, "Dr. Wilcox, what can we give Mr. Smith for pain?"

I thought, maybe if I logged in quick to the medical records system, I could at least look the guy up and find out his allergies and medical history and order some pain medication. At least I could do that one thing. And my pager went off again.

It went that way all night.

* * *

An admission is a time-consuming and important task—perhaps the most important one for an internist. It involves a thorough evaluation of the patient—interview, physical exam, chart review, test ordering, results reviewing, coming up with preliminary potential diagnoses, and developing a treatment plan. This is followed by the composition of a note, documenting observations and thoughts, and then order-writing so that the nurses know the next steps.

This was the year 1999 before the verdict in the Libby Zion case had led to widespread reforms for residency training: Ms. Zion had died in a New York hospital due to a sleep-deprived trainee's error in 1984. Therefore, this was a time before "caps" which required training programs to limit the number of admissions per intern to ten and before 80-hour work week regulations were adopted for all U.S. training institutions by the Accreditation Council for Graduate Medical Education.

That first night, I would admit fifteen patients, maybe sixteen. I'd never really know for sure. In med school, I'd never admitted more than two. I would soon find out that a 100-hour work week was not uncommon.

As a medical student, I'd enjoyed being on call, a little, in a weird self-torturous sort of way. Even with only a couple of patients, I'd stayed up all night with my nose in the books, reading about HIV-associated illnesses or cancer staging procedures, following the typewritten clues to figure out the next most important test to properly diagnose. I looked forward to wowing my attendings with my thoroughness when I presented the case orally the following morning. And I did.

Being a real doctor was an entirely different beast.

At 7 AM the following day—I'd had no rest for over 24 hours—I found myself in rounds. A dozen and a half people, all in scrubs, were either gathered around a large round table or sitting on the floor. The smell of coffee breath and sweat permeated the room.

The duty of "presenting" after a night on-call usually fell to an intern in a teaching hospital. The point of this task was to communicate key pieces of information about each admission, review the treatment recommendations, and get the attending—the highest-ranking person on a team, and the senior physician—to sign off.

We had learned about and practiced presentations in med school. "Mrs. X is a 54-year-old woman with a history of X who presents with X," one would start, followed by a full description of a case. All the data included was to be relevant, lead the listener to a rational conclusion, and justify a plan for the future. The perfect presentation was about five minutes.

New interns, being naturally a little flustered, tended to drag on and report more information than was necessary. Attendings hated the last week of June, which is when all internships started.

I was grateful I had been able to find the coffee machine, but I had only had time to chug one small cardboard cup of it, and my brain was foggy, and it was now my turn to present. The silent crowd stared. I flipped through the cards before me, trying to read my own scribbles. Which patient was this? My thoughts mirrored my own unintelligible scribbles on the index cards—chaotic, agitated, desperate.

I started with Mrs. Peake, the card at the top of the pile, squinting at my writing. I reported her symptoms, her medical history, and her lung and heart sounds.

I said, "She had an S4."

My resident scoffed, "S3 actually."

I said, "Sorry," and tried to find my place in the notes again.

In the brief silence that resulted, the resident barked, "So, Dr. Wilcox, what is this morning's echo going to show, given what you've said about her heart sounds?" (an echo was a cardiac ultrasound, and he was "pimping" me—aka grilling me—to test my knowledge).

I couldn't remember what either an S3 or S4 implied, so I stayed silent, and the attending and resident exchanged unveiled disappointed looks with one another.

I moved on to Mr. Smith. I said that we were still working up the cause of his pain.

My resident breathed out through his teeth and said to the attending, "Nope, we know. Lipase elevated, pancreatitis, NPO, Demerol, all taken care of."

The attending gave the resident an empathetic look that said, "Too bad, you got a dumb one, huh."

I would not go home until after 8 PM that night. I would be at the hospital again at 6 AM the next day.

* * *

In internship, I would soon learn how to make the most of that moment, of leaving. I would learn that there was nothing more freeing than the sensation of pulling out of the hospital after a 36-hour shift, rolling down the car window, blasting Tribe Called Quest, and lighting up a Camel light. It felt like a big old f-you, I'm free. It punctuated the transition. It was transporting.

The Coyote Club became my second home—the perfect combination of collegiality and funk. The jukebox was excellent, and its patrons drank alone, played pool, and gathered in small groups in red booths or at the bar.

Because I didn't know anyone in Denver in the early days, I'd go alone, and would often scribble thoughts on bar napkins as they came to me, sipping microbrew pints and chain-smoking cigarettes. My belly and heart would warm, and the edges of my lips would tug, wanting to make a smile.

I'd imagine and wonder about the patrons. That man with the stubble and thin, narrow, but athletic body: what had he done in his lifetime, what adventures had he been on? Maybe he had climbed Everest. He had long fingers, and the hands were calloused. He was not looking to meet people, keeping his eyes averted. Maybe I'd get lucky and he'd notice me, find me cute even, or be intrigued by my writing and want to know what creative magic was seeping out of my fingers. Being here near him was practically like being on the top of the mountain myself, only easier to get to.

And then reality would shock me awake, after a while. No man had ever tried to pick me up. Who was I kidding? I wasn't going to meet my rescuer in a bar. I was gaining weight—and fast. The bathroom mirror told me I looked exhausted and grey. The notes I wrote weren't poetic, they were unintelligible and infantile. I was living in a dream world.

Sometimes I'd see couples in booths, chattering with each other, sitting on the same side of the table, kissing. I'd wish one of them was me.

Maybe I'll have just one more beer, I'd console myself. Maybe if I have just one more, my mood will improve, the impossible will happen, and I'll find romance or even just stumble into a death-defying adventure of my own, filled with surprise and challenge and joy. Just one more beer.

The next day, after nights like that, back at the hospital, I'd feel hazy with confusion and fatigue. The nausea and headaches would wane by evening, but the exhaustion would linger.

* * *

I wasn't one of those people who wanted to be a doctor from a young age. I never really knew what I wanted to do; I had always loved to read in my room, play and adventure in the outdoors, write stories and thoughts in my journal, explore new landscapes and cultures, and hang out with dogs. None of these passions seemed particularly adaptable to a money-making career.

I had enjoyed science and math in high school—they gave me concrete answers about how things worked—and I had a brain that absorbed what the teachers and books taught me. I got great grades, people were impressed and told me I was smart, and I liked that. I went straight through from high school to college.

As the end of college approached, I waffled between grad school and med school. I could definitely see myself as a scientist, with hair frazzled doing experiments past midnight, determined to find truth and solutions, at any cost. But I didn't love the idea of being limited to living in Illinois or Ohio or some such place: I knew there was more competition for jobs as a PhD than as an MD, and that academia could be limiting geographically when it came to seeking a permanent position.

Medicine would offer me a highly transferrable and flexible skill. I could help people, live anywhere, and still do research, in the end, if I wanted.

Family history inched me towards medicine, too. Many of my relatives were doctors—dermatologists, internists, gynecologists—or worked in the medical field—scientists, hospital administrators. My parents believed strongly in education and hard work and pushed us toward careers with tangible utility. They wanted their children to be financially secure, well-established, and mainstream members of society. Their desires made sense.

Therefore, my decision to choose medical school was a practical, theoretical, and (slightly) altruistic one, rather than one derived from self-knowledge. I wasn't tuned into my own likes and dislikes, passions and repulsions. I was unskilled in attending to myself.

I applied to med school and got in.

* * *

Four years later, there I was, moored in a land of beeps and mechanical sighs surrounded by sterile chemical smell, and putrid body odors, while countless nameless, often faceless, often bitter, nurses and doctors and patients barked at me and called me to attention, incessantly. I had little time to ask myself: how the heck did I get here?

Call rooms were sometimes shared—that hellish room with three bunk beds, a concert hall orchestral with pager sounds. Occasionally, we got our own rooms, which was heavenly. Either way, during the rare periods when things would quiet down—usually between 1 and 4 AM—I'd lie in bed, squeezing my eyes shut tight, begging for sleep. My brain, anxiously anticipating the next piercing alarm from the tiny black box that was my jailkeeper, would not let me, though.

I often hated my patients, especially in the middle of the night. A nurse would call me to address an oozing wound or to deal with a complaint of an achy shoulder. I'd enter the hospital room, rage like a hot white ball in my stomach. It was not fair that they got to be prone, still, watching TV passively, while I had to serve them, always exhausted, often desperately achy in my feet and hips from standing and walking all day in a body that was gaining weight from all the junk food, my bladder aching with un-voided urine. Residency gifted me with back pain, plantar fasciitis, and recurrent urinary tract infections.

I fantasized often about coming down with cancer or heart failure myself. I, too, could be lazy and lie in bed all day, watching sitcoms and old movies, with a remote in my hand. If only I were dying: I could sleep when I wanted, get meals brought to me, pee into a bag, and demand things.

I was jealous, even, of Mr. Jones—deep yellow from alcoholic cirrhosis, smelling of rotting cotton candy. He had been a patient on my service for several weeks. He would ignore me when I came in—his illness gave him a right to relinquish social niceties. His life was luxurious compared to mine.

How good it would feel to throw down my stethoscope, wriggle out of that fucking white coat, and tear up each and every last white index card in my pocket. It was ridiculous: expecting a 3x5 piece of cardboard to stand in for a human being, their survival dependent on how clearly you wrote your checklists on it.

I often wanted nothing more than to get in my car and leave. But I did not. Because beyond the chaos, there was nothing. I'd disappear in a cloud of smoke. I was empty inside. I didn't know what I loved.

Or, more accurately, maybe it was what I loved was no good. I had loved the college boyfriend, but he was bad for me. I loved my cigarettes, but they killed you and smelled of trash. I loved dive bars and mountain tops. But they didn't make you a living.

Plus, I didn't get myself all the way through medical school for nothing, right? It was my duty to progress through to the end, to the certificate, or whatever.

* * *

Claire Wilcox is an addiction psychiatrist and neuroscientist living in New Mexico. She writes fiction, creative non-fiction, news articles, and academic works. While wrapping up a trade book about food addiction, she is pursuing an MFA in fiction at IAIA in Santa Fe. Her writings can be found at www.wilcoxmd.com.

Published Memoir - 1st Place **Wanda Whittlesey-Jerome**

Flying Fancy: A Fly Girl's Memoir

PART ONE

Preparing for Boarding and Takeoff

I was driving across the burning desert
When I spotted six jet planes
Leaving six white vapor trails across the bleak terrain
It was the hexagram of the heavens
It was the strings of my guitar
Amelia it was just a false alarm
~ *Joni Mitchell*

The Interview

Full of excitement, I looked around the marble-floored foyer of the skyscraper. While I stood just inside the front door, I hesitated for a second. Then, I breathed in and imagined my confidence building.

After I scheduled the interview a couple of weeks before, I began to get nervous as the time approached. This interview was so important to goals I held for the rest of my life, and I knew this interview with *Fancy Airlines* would open the door to my dreams. I arrived there early and had time to brush up my looks. Makeup – check. Dress – check. Shoes – check. I walked up to the front-desk receptionist and introduced myself.

"Hello, I'm Ella Volé. I'm here for an interview with *Fancy Airlines* for a stewardess position. Could you please direct me to the interview suite?"

The receptionist looked up and softly whispered, "We don't call them stewardesses any more, honey, we call them *flight attendants*." She sighed and continued speaking.

"Take the elevator to the 40th floor. The doors will be in front of you. Go on in and let them know who you are and they'll take it from there."

Gulping, I said my thanks and scurried off to find the elevators. For what I considered the job of a lifetime, I started a little shakily.

Exiting the elevator at the 40th floor, I found myself surrounded by windows three stories high. A modern metallic sign hung in the open atrium. "Welcome to *Fancy Airlines*" it exclaimed. A beautiful woman in a company uniform sat at a modern metallic desk in the middle of the atrium. I introduced myself.

"Hello. I'm Ella Volé, and I am here for an interview for a flight attendant position."

She smiled, put a checkmark next to my name on her paper schedule, and asked me to sit in the foyer. Everything sparkled. Jazz music softly wafted in the air, and the smell of expensive perfume encircled my body. I knew that I belonged here. I knew it in my bones.

While breathing methodically in and out, I closed my eyes and imagined a perfect interview. Suddenly, I heard my name.

"Ella Volé?" the woman at the desk called, looking at me, "You may enter the conference room now." She pointed to large double doors at one end of the atrium. Shiny metallic handles in the shape of airplanes were set at the center of each door.

"Good luck, Ella" she said with a smile as I walked past her desk. I felt ready for the interview. I opened a door. At the head of the conference table sat a beautiful woman also in a company uniform. She greeted me.

"Hello, Ella, my name is Gretchen and I will be interviewing you today. Please sit down," she said as she pointed to a lush leather swivel chair at the other end of the table.

The interview started. The questions were what I had imagined, until, to my surprise, I learned that most commercial airlines were about to start hiring men. That new title I heard for the first time was meant for *all* of us. We would be called "Flight Attendants" – and men would be joining us in the sky-high world of commercial airline travel. No longer relegated to the cockpit, men were to become part of the cabin crew and provide service alongside women.

The interview felt good. With my hands folded neatly in my lap, I sat with my legs together at an angle under the table. The lady interviewing me smiled a lot. Very pretty for her age, she had probably flown as a flight attendant before getting promoted to Employee Services.

My answers to her last two questions cinched it for me. She asked why I wanted to work for this particular company.

"I love *Fancy Airlines'* glamour and reputation," I said, with sparkling eyes. Then, she asked me why I wanted to be a flight attendant.

"Because I love people," I replied, with a genuine, heart-felt smile. She nodded in the affirmative, stood up, walked to where I sat, reached out and shook my hand.

"Congratulations, Ella – you are going to be a flight attendant," she said. Then she added,

"It was because of that last thing you said. You have to love people to do this job and do it well."

I remember her words to this day. I got the job. To enroll in Training School in a couple of months, I had to get my life in order right away. All of the sudden it hit me. To be ready to start flying that fall, I had to tell my boyfriend that I would be in training soon to become a flight attendant. Pursuing a career at 35,000 feet, I didn't know how he would take the news, but it didn't matter. A woman on a mission to accomplish her dreams is a formidable force.

This *Fancy Airlines* interview opened doors to every job I've had since, for I know that flight attendants get some of the best training for dealing with people from all walks of life and in all kinds of circumstances. They see the best and worst, experience the highs and lows, and taste the bitter and the sweet all wrapped up in a beautifully diverse package called *humanity*. Recognizing there are, and continue to be, people who sincerely love people and love to serve people and care for people, my heart is thankful that many of them are, or will become, flight attendants.

The Initiation

For *Fancy Airlines* to have their own physician seemed natural. All the major airlines of the day had medical doctors on their payroll. During the initial interviews, young men and women clamoring to become flight attendants needed to pass a physical with the company doctor before getting hired and starting Flight Attendant Training School.

Prospective flight attendants for *Fancy Airlines* had to schedule physicals with Dr. Chadwick, one of several highly esteemed female medical doctors practicing in the Big Apple. Dr. Chadwick, who preferred to be called *Dr. C*, conducted the initial physicals and provided some aftercare for *Fancy Airlines* employees who chose to stay with her as their personal doctor.

Not knowing exactly what to expect, I sat down in the crowded waiting room. Fancy metal chairs held men and women waiting to be seen. Nurses behind the plexiglass wall moved constantly – shuffling files from one place to another and answering phones. The Muzak offered relaxing *elevator music* in the background. A couple of seats away, I overheard a quiet conversation between two women who had just walked into the waiting room together. I imagined they were friends since they sat down next to each other.

One picked up a copy of the latest *Fancy Airlines* magazine and started filtering through it with her fingers. She hummed a little tune along with the Muzak. Then, she said,

"I just want to get this *done*, Anna. Get the job and start flying," she whispered to her friend, who gave a not-so-sure kind of nod back. I could see remnants of an uncomfortable little frown on her face and she shook her head.

"Beth, I gotta tell you," Anna replied, "Dr. C has a reputation for being a little quirky… if you know what I mean." I listened intently, my ears straining to hear more.

"What do you mean, Anna?" Beth replied, turning to her with curiosity in her voice.

"I mean," whispered Anna, "that I know of others who will tell you Dr. C asked them to do *some* things during their physical, that's all," and then she went back to reading the *Fancy Airlines* magazine.

It suddenly became very quiet in the waiting room, and it seemed that others may have overheard the conversation between Anna and Beth – as had I. After a certain amount of squirming in our metal chairs, I heard a nurse call my name.

"Ella – Ella Volé – please follow me," she instructed as she turned, extending her arm and pointing in the general direction of an open examination room. Slowly I walked down the hallway, perusing many framed certificates and diplomas hanging on the walls. One indicated that Dr. Chadwick graduated top of her class. I could see more framed certifications and degrees lining the walls of some of the examination rooms, including the room I entered.

The nurse closed the door behind me and asked me to disrobe, except for my panties, put on an exam gown, leave it open in the back, and have a seat on the exam table. Then, she left, and I waited. I played the conversation between Anna and Beth over and over in my head. I wondered, *What did 'being a little quirky' mean? What 'some things' did she ask others to do?* I wished I had been brave enough to ask them to clarify what they meant when we were all sitting together in the waiting room, but now it was too late.

Sitting on the exam table, I imagined my getaway. Getting my clothes on fast, I would run out the door and out of the building as fast as my legs would carry me. Jumping into my car, I'd drive somewhere – anywhere. But my imagination soon came to a halt. I would never become a flight attendant for *Fancy Airlines* if I ran away. I would do anything to become one.

Sitting at the point of no return, I had to tough it out. Taking a deep breath, I closed my eyes and thought of my safe place – where I could lounge under a willow tree by a nearby lake and whittle pieces of driftwood into *objects d'art*. I always went there in my mind when I needed an escape.

Just then, Dr. Chadwick arrived. Opening the door, she seemed pleasant enough. Short of stature and old enough to be my mother, she didn't seem weird or strange. I felt comfortable even if it was just the two of us in that exam room. She introduced herself.

"Hello, Ella. I'm Dr. Chadwick. But everyone calls me Dr. C. I am *Fancy Airlines'* physician, as I'm *sure* you know. So, you want to be a flight attendant," she asked, with what sounded like a British lilt in her voice.

"Yes, Dr. Chadwick – ah, er… Dr. C," I replied, smiling as I nodded. Then I noticed that the two of us were alone in a really cold room.

"It will be just you and me," she replied. "My nurses are very busy this afternoon. But that is okay with me. Is it okay with you, Ella," she asked, sounding sincere.

"Sure," I said, catching myself wriggling a little as I sat on the exam table. A feeling of discomfort began enveloping my body. I began to worry that she could tell.

"Good. Well…" she replied, looking at me up and down. Silence. I gulped. After a long pause, she added, "In order to fly, you must pass my examination, you know," she said, sporting a faint smile.

"Yes, Dr. C, I know," I replied, nodding, rubbing my tight neck muscles with my hands. Suddenly, out of my mouth came the words, "I'm sure you are a wonderful doctor – I've heard nothing but great things about you." Choking, I immediately became aware of my mistake.

"I mean, I heard some women talking about you in the waiting room, and they were very, very positive," I said, mentally grasping at straws. I coughed several times, as if clearing my throat.

"You did, Ella? How nice. What did they say?" Dr. Chadwick asked, setting her stethoscope down on the nearby Formica counter top. She turned toward me, her eyes catching mine. I panicked.

"They said you were very… thorough," I stuttered, summoning a weak smile, averting my eyes only to find a wall chart of the female reproductive system glaring back at me.

Dr. Chadwick smiled and picked up her stethoscope. She listened to my heartbeat through my gown and then asked me to cough. At the time, I smoked about a half a pack of cigarettes a day. Back in the '70s, smoking cigarettes was considered normal and nothing to worry about. She then took my temperature (from my mouth) and my blood pressure.

"Hmmm. 120 over 80. Good," she spoke out loud, as if only to herself. Then, she took out a flashlight, shined it into both of my eyes. Afterwards, she looked into my right ear, and said,

"It's amazing you can hear with this ear, Ella, it's really blocked. Does it bother you," she asked, inquisitively.

"No, not really, Dr. C," I answered, nodding. Seconds seemed to drag. I could hear myself breathing rapidly.

"You should clear the earwax out, Ella," she suggested, before moving to the other ear. Sitting on the exam table, I became acutely aware of my surroundings. I think I shook – maybe due to the frigid air – or possibly due to other worrisome thoughts ruminating in my brain.

"Very well, Ella," she replied, and continued the physical by tapping each of my knees with a rubberized hammer to test my reflexes.

"Good," she said, after tapping each one. Then, presuming the physical would be winding down, as there wasn't much else for her to examine, I began to gather the edges of my gown and readied myself to jump down from the exam table.

"Ella, I need you to do one last thing for me," Dr. Chadwick asked, firmly.

"Yes, Dr. C," I answered, noting that my gown now physically shook in my hands.

"Jump down, and stand here," she said, as she pointed to an "x" made out of black tape in the middle of the examination room's floor. "Then, I want you to bend over and touch your toes. If you can, press your hands flat on the floor in front of your feet. I need to see how flexible you are."

I extended my arms far out in front of me to get the most flexibility out of my spine. My gown parted on either side and fell forward. As I bent over, Dr. Chadwick walked around me in a circle, her eyes on my flat hands. At the time, I thought, *Whew, it's a good thing I practice this every morning when I do my stretching exercises.* Still, I became increasingly uncomfortable as I stood there, stretched and bent over, holding my position, palms flat on the floor in front of my toes. God help me if I tried to do that today!

"Good – you pass," she said, without any emotion in her voice. "Please see the nurse at the front desk for your Letter of Approval. Take it to *Fancy Airlines*' headquarters and they will clear you to begin Flight Attendant Training School." Then, she turned, opened the door, and with a quick look back at me – I was still standing in the middle of the exam room with my gown hanging limp at my sides, she added,

"Congratulations Ella. I know you'll be great." And, with that, she smiled and exited the exam room leaving the door partially open. Hurriedly, I dressed, then stopped by the front desk.

"Hello, I'm Ella Volé. Dr. C said I passed the exam and I am to pick up my letter here," I whispered to the nurse at the front window.

"Congratulations, Ella. We hope you enjoy Training School," the nurse replied, smiling as she handed me a piece of paper from a stack of papers on her desk. Safe in my hands, the letter sported Dr. Chadwick's signature and a checkmark in a box indicating I was fit and ready for Training School. I hurriedly left the building, clutching my Letter.

On the way back to my apartment, I had a hard time driving. I couldn't see the road for tears of relief mixed with tears of joy and vindication fogging my eyes and dribbling down my chin. But – and this was a big but, I had passed *The Initiation*. My heart skipped a beat. For the first time in a long time, I finally felt free to pursue my newly chosen career! After all, I wanted this job more than anything in the world, and if every other flight attendant for *Fancy Airlines* went through the same initiation, I could do it too. And I did.

Late at night, after training school wrapped up for the day, fellow flight attendants-to-be often gathered in conversation tucked into the four corners of the school's foyer. These comfy nooks were designed for casual social gatherings. Soft, overstuffed chairs and ottomans provided a pleasant escape from the classrooms' chairs and desks. I spent many an evening scrunched together with a few colleagues, sharing our experiences, our stories, and most especially – any and all gossip. During those whisper-filled, afterhours sharing sessions, I would hear stories confirming what I'd hope to be true – that Dr. C made everyone do the *stretch, bend over, and hold* exercise. It was all really quite normal.

During Training School, we shared many a good laugh about a number of challenges we confronted and surmounted on our way to becoming official *Fancy Airlines* flight attendants. But our shared experience with *The Initiation* meant that we were finally – *officially* – on our way to airborne adventures.

* * *

Wanda Whittlesey-Jerome (aka Wanda W. Jerome, or Ella Volé) is a New Mexico award-winning author. Her books include; *Flying Fancy: A Fly Girl's Memoir*, *Magical Morning Moments: Awakening to Love and Light* and *Crow Wisdom: A Seasonal Journey.* She is crafting a poetic trilogy *Journey Beyond the Veil: Awakening the Heart to Love.*

Published Memoir - 2nd Place **Edith Tarbescu**

Beyond Brooklyn

FOREWORD

My partner Dick Dumas was an anomaly. He cried during sad movies, Italian operas and when I called to tell him my dog suddenly died, hardly the type you would think would own a handgun. I never knew about the pistol, never got a glimpse of it even after he used it to "check out," as he called it. A policeman removed the gun from the scene as evidence. In a state of shock I asked the cop, "Am I a suspect?" He shook his head.

Later, I asked one of the Emergency Medical Technicians, "If Dick died of cancer, why was there blood?" He said softly, "I guess you didn't notice the gun on his lap." "There was no gun," I shouted. "There was never a gun in this house." I was shaking uncontrollably as he reached for my hand and led me outside where we sat on a bench in the freezing cold and talked. It was December 26th, the day after Christmas. Bad timing? Suicide doesn't come with a timetable.

After Dick's death I found a box of bullets in the back of his closet. I was guilt-ridden at not surmising what was happening and preventing his suicide. But I couldn't have. Nobody could have. I realized that after I found an article in his file cabinet from *The New York Times* detailing which pills to swallow and how many in case of terminal illness. The newspaper article was yellowed with age. But I was still angry at him for abandoning me and leaving a mess to clean up. I didn't clean it up. I hired a special cleaning service. There were also two bullet holes in the tile above the tub. According to one of the policemen on the scene, practice shots are often taken to get psychologically ready for the "big one" and to make sure the gun works.

After being treated for two years for a rare form of blood cancer known as Myelodysplastic Syndrome, Dick's oncologist told us one afternoon that he only had a couple of months to live. Based on that *New York Times* article and a few things he told me he had decided long ago that he would not go gently into that good night. The day before he died he told me, "I'm going to ask my doctor for enough pills so I won't have to suffer any more." I looked at his thin, drawn face across the dining room table and whispered, "You can't do that. It's illegal." He nodded in agreement. "Will you move to Oregon with me?" he asked, an obvious reference to assisted suicide. I shook my head. "There must be something the doctor can still do." Dick didn't respond. He obviously realized that I was in denial, hoping for a last minute reprieve, a miracle.

I met Dick Dumas, my significant other and the last man in my life, on match.com. As a writer it struck me as ironic that I met somebody whose last name was the same as a famous writer. He jokingly referred to Alexander Dumas, author of "The Three Musketeers," as a distant relative. It was possible. Dick's paternal ancestors emigrated to America from France, his maternal ancestors from Ireland. He was fair skinned with blue eyes, more Irish looking than French.

There were several other ironies, including the fact that we met at all. I had been divorced a year when a friend suggested I join match.com. It was late January: cold, dark, snowy, and even though New Mexico where I now live has shorter winters than back East where I used to live, I felt the need for a companion. After coffee or lunch with three men that I had little in common with, including an avid golfer, an avid hockey fan, and someone I can't even remember, I spotted a picture on match of a good looking man in biking shorts. Underneath the photo the caption read: "I spend most of my time outdoors: biking, hiking, skiing." I didn't relate to that but I related to his next comment, "Just returned from Chicago where I saw *Wicked,* a great show." I sent him a note saying, "I love the theatre, I'm a playwright." He answered and told me more about the musical. His next e-mail said, "Since we're both Librans we should at least meet for coffee." An interesting response, but I wasn't immune to the fact that many of my friends share the same sign as me. Scientific? Probably not. Coincidence? Probably. But I agreed to meet him for coffee. It was early February and he asked if I would be wearing a tutu so he would recognize me. I loved his sense of humor.

Every time I met a match man for the first time I left my dog, Sugar Bear, in my car for a quick escape. If I felt my eyes starting to glaze over, I would say, "My poor dog must be cold by now. I'd better go." I waited longer than usual to tell Dick about Sugar Bear because I was enjoying our conversation. As he walked me to my car he stopped under a bright light in the parking lot and said, "You look just like your picture," then added pointedly, "My subscription to match.com is expiring in two days. I'm not planning to renew so hope we can continue writing to each other using our private e-mail addresses." As soon as we reached my car I opened the door to let Sugar Bear out, then asked him to hold the leash while I reached in my purse for a business card.

After tucking the card in his jacket pocket he bent down to pet my dog, whose tongue was hanging out by then from all the attention. I laughed, said good-bye and opened the car door to let my dog back in. Dick was not immune to Sugar Bear's looks either. She was a gorgeous blonde, part Golden Retriever and part Labrador.

On our first date we went to an art museum. We shared a lot of information about ourselves while we viewed the paintings, which prompted him to tell me later,

"We talked a lot, that's good." Next date was a museum and dinner. A few weeks later on Valentine's Day Dick handed me a heart-shaped box filled with chocolates. Was it fate that I wrote to him two days before he was about to unsubscribe from match.com? Never a big believer in fate, that experience nearly changed my mind.

We were together seven years and I lived in his house for over four years. During that time we were companions, moviegoers, museum goers, theater goers, hikers, travelers. I introduced him to New York City where I was born and bred. He was born in Chicago, later lived in San Francisco and Houston so he loved big cities. We ended up visiting New York eight times during our seven years together. We attended plays, concerts, operas, ballets, and museums including the Frick, the Metropolitan Museum of Art, the Whitney, the Guggenheim, MoMA, (the Museum of Modern Art.) On my birthday one year, we walked across the Brooklyn bridge on a day that was warm and sunny especially for mid-October.

After reaching Brooklyn from downtown Manhattan we continued until we were in an area filled with lofts, art galleries, and restaurants called Dumbo, Down Under the Manhattan Bridge, where we stopped for lunch. Later, we walked to Brooklyn Bridge Park, abutting the East River, where I rode the antique carousel while Dick took pictures of me.

One of our favorites places in New York was the Neue Museum on the Upper East Side which focuses on German and Austrian artists such as Gustav Klimt. Once a private mansion, the Neue hasn't lost any of its luster. I loved strolling through the museum; I also loved climbing the intricately curved staircase from the lobby. We usually visited on a Monday when most museums in New York are closed. On our first visit we wandered into the elegant cafe on the main floor, ordered apfel strudel mit shlag, apple strudel with whipped cream, and drooled over the taste as well as the aroma. After that, it became a tradition to visit the Neue during every trip to New York. We shared the apple strudel the first time. After that we ordered our own portion of warm apples nestled in a flaky crust, topped with real whipped cream. Sweets were Dick's obsession: cakes, pies, cookies, chocolate bars. Having gone through AA and successfully given up alcohol, he developed a sugar addiction. I have never seen anybody eat as many sweets as he but he wasn't overweight. He worked out at a gym, hiked in the mountains around Albuquerque, and skied in Colorado, Utah, or in nearby Santa Fe.

In addition to strolling all over Manhattan we rode the subway one day to Brooklyn so I could show him the Brooklyn Botanic Garden near Park Slope, where I had lived for many years. Having spent time in Tokyo while he was stationed in the Navy, he fell in love with the Japanese garden, its flowering trees and shrubs and a pond filled with koi.

Whether we were traveling or at home we always talked, laughed, ate, but only I drank. He never joined me in a glass of wine at dinner. As a recovering alcoholic, he hadn't had a drink or even a sip of alcohol in twenty years. After I would come home with a bottle of wine, he would often sniff it and deem it good, bad, or indifferent. He even bought me a split of champagne every New Year's Eve but never tasted the French bubbly he splurged on.

I introduced him to my friends and family in New York. They all loved him. He was funny, smart, a good conversationalist, and a Liberal, despite having lived and worked in Texas for many years. After he finished college, where he had been a chemistry major he joined the Navy,. then ended up in Houston selling building material to architects and contractors. He also had an artistic side to his nature: he played the piano, dabbled in watercolors and shared my love of classical music and Italian opera.

The few arguments we had usually ended with him raising his voice a notch as he told me, "Do you always have to get WHAT you want WHEN you want it?" I would nod and try to be more compromising.

In addition to New York we enjoyed cities here in New Mexico such as Santa Fe, only an hour from Albuquerque. We had a favorite restaurant there with an outdoor patio. One of the best times to eat outside was during June when the orange poppies were in bloom. After lunch, we'd stroll a few short blocks to the Georgia O'Keefe Museum.

I loved Dick and learned a lot from him including the art of gratefulness, a trait I never possessed. I also adopted one of his favorite expressions: "Don't waste a worry." I had always been a worrisome child filled with fears, anxieties, apprehension.

"Regrets, I have a few but then again too few to mention." sang Frank Sinatra. I have a few regrets, I'll get to them later. Loving Dick is not one of them.

* * *

Edith Tarbescu is the author of four books for children, as well as a produced playwright. She studied playwriting at the Yale School of Drama. She's also the author of two books for adults: a mystery titled *One Will: Three Wives* and a memoir titled *Beyond Brooklyn.* www.edithtarbescu.com

Section Eight:

Limerick

Limericks by William Stotts

1st Place

The Belle from Aurora

There once was a belle from Aurora
Who obsessed about fauna and flora.
She bathed with her mice
And named each of her lice
That itchy young belle from Aurora.

* * *

3rd Place

The Sage Named Olanthee

There once was a sage named Olanthee
Who grew bright orange pyrocanthae.
She grew rather large
and left home on a barge.
That peripatetic Olanthee!

Limericks by William Stotts

Honorable Mention

The Hack from Ohio

There once was a hack from Ohio
Who lied frequently in his own bio.
He said he spoke Dutch,
ate acorn, and such!
That fallacious old hack from Ohio.

Honorable Mention

The Man from Racine

There once was a man from Racine
Who lived very near a latrine.
One day he fell in,
smelling like sin.
That odiferous man from Racine!

* * *

Will Stotts, Jr. is a retired teacher of Creative Writing, Theatre, and English. He studied Criticism at UT-Austin. His play, *Tales of Lavender Yo*uth, was performed in Milwaukee by Different Drummer. His poetry is published in *Espresso Poetry*. He is currently completing a YA fantasy series in Albuquerque, New Mexico.

Limericks - 2nd Place **Rose Marie Kern**

Haiku?

I wanted to write a Haiku
About seasons and fruit trees and you
But the rules are confusing
My brain cells are bruising
Not poetry, but nonsense I spew

Rose Marie Kern loves writing limericks, but will admit that is about the length and breadth of her poetry skills. Her most recent book is a humorous look at one of her favorite pastimes – gardening. *The Competently Quirky Parables of an Eccentric Master Gardener* is available on Amazon and local bookstores.

Limericks - Honorable Mention **Rolf Jansen**

Love Hurts

There once was a man named Fred
He jumped off a cliff, now he's dead
His love unrequited
He even felt slighted
Because of another named, Ted

Rolf Hilding Janson is a career locksmith by day and sometimes by night in Albuquerque, New Mexico. In his forty-five years helping thousands of people secure their lives and property, he has had many story-worthy encounters and manages to unlock hearts and minds with his writing in various genres.

Sign Language submitted by Barbara Garvey

Behind the Scenes

The Leaders, Reviewers and Coordinators of the

2024 SWW Writing Contest

Contest Committee and Entry Review Teams

Judy Castleberry, Chair spans the writing world including grant writing, numerous articles on senior care and business, *The Caregiver Zone A Guide to Senior Care,* award winning stage plays, short stories, and creative nonfiction. She has worked in entrepreneurship support and healthcare administration assisting baby businesses and senior adults.

Chris Allen's work has appeared in a number of anthologies, and her latest book co-authored with Pat Walkow, a romance mystery called *Alchemy's Reach*, was published in the fall of 2023. She has won numerous awards as both a writer and an editor.

For **Brenda Cole,** devouring the written word has always been a passion. Writing them began in earnest at age 13, winning her first contest with a science fiction short story. Brenda is an award-winning author and editor in life sciences, poetry and non-fiction. She has served as a Judge for the last four SWW writing contests.

Rose Marie Kern is President of SouthWest Writers. She's authored over a thousand articles published in regional and national magazines, seven books, three stage plays and two industry training film scripts. Rose owns RMK Publications, assisting authors on their literary journey. She designed the cover art for this book. www.rmkpublications.com

KL Wagoner loves creating worlds of fantasy and science fiction. She's currently working on *The Last Bonekeeper* fantasy trilogy and short stories in the same universe. A member of SouthWest Writers since 2006, Kat has worked as the organization's secretary, newsletter editor, website manager, and author interview coordinator. Kat is also a veteran, a martial art student, and a grandmother. Visit her at klwagoner.com.

D. E. Williams is the award-winning author of *Child of Chaos*, The Chesan Legacy Series Book One and *Chaos Unleashed*, The Chesan Legacy Series Book Two. An avid reader and writing mentor, she lives in Albuquerque with a collection of books, movies, and manga, works full-time with a national software company, and travels to visit family when she can.

Joe Badal is an Amazon #1 bestselling author, with 18 award-winning suspense novels. He has been recognized as "One of The 50 Best Writers You Should Be Reading." Named Writer of the Year by the Military Writers Society of America (MWSA) in 2021, he's won the Tony Hillerman Prize for Best Fiction Book of the Year, the MWSA Gold Medal Winner, and is a four-time Finalist in the International Book Awards competition.

New York Times bestselling author **Parris Afton Bonds** has published nearly 50 novels in several languages. She co-founded both Romance Writers of America and SouthWest Writers. SWW's most prestigious award, the Parris Award, honors a published SWW member who has given outstanding time and talent to other writers. Past recipients include Tony Hillerman and Pulitzer nominee Norman Zollinger.

Cornelia Gamlem is a management consultant and speaker, who has taken her expertise and shared it through her award-winning books. She coauthored three editions of her first book plus four more. Three have been translated into other languages. Two were recognized by internationally acclaimed Next Generation Indie Book Awards. www.bigbookofhr.com

Mike Hays is an old, out of shape, recovering alcoholic gay guy who's retired five times now (he gets bored easily.) By training, he's a clinical social worker and health policy analyst. He writes short stories, screenplays, speculative fiction, and memoir, and lives in Albuquerque next door to his best friend.

Allen Herring is a local, award-winning writer and artist. He is a former newspaper features writer and has written for television. He enjoys writing sci-fi, fantasy, and magical realism. He has a master's degree in Cultural Studies. He lives in Albuquerque with his cat, Nadia.

Kirt Hickman wrote award-winning science-fiction thrillers *Worlds Asunder* and *Venus Rain* as well as several other sci-fi and fantasy novels. His writer's guide, *Revising Fiction—Making Sense of the Madness* won a New Mexico Book award for Best How-To and was a finalist in the international IBPA Benjamin Franklin Awards.

Jacqueline Murray Loring has yet to find a genre she prefers to write in. Poetry, screenwriting, nonfiction all demand her attention but working with other writers, especially as a contest judge, energizes her own creativity.

Carol Holland March publishes fantasy novels, short stories, and essays. *When Spirit Whispers* was a 2022 New Mexico-Arizona Book Award Winner. Her latest nonfiction book is *Open the Door to Your Creative Life.* Carol teaches creativity, storytelling, and memoir at UNM Continuing Education and works as a book coach and editor.

Lisa McCoy loves helping authors turn their writing dreams into reality! As a freelance developmental and line editor of fiction and non-fiction, she seeks to connect with each writer's voice and purpose. Her shared goal is to give readers a story they'll want to read to the last page.

RJ Mirabal enjoys writing, music, volunteering, and adventure. RJ and his wife spend a lot of time with Trixie—their famous rescue dog—family, and friends. He has written/published six fantasy and two dog books.

Elaine Carson Montague cherishes friends and open spaces. Her book *Victory from the Shadows* won eight national and international literary awards. Her poetry is in *Open-Hearted Horizons*, published by the City of Albuquerque, and in *Holes in Our Hearts* by SWW. She is working toward passage of The Essential Caregivers Act. (www.elainemontague.com)

Evelyn Neil's award-winning short stories appear regularly in anthologies and journals. Her memoir, *Dancing to the End of Our Rainbow*, took first-place in the Arizona /New Mexico contest and third place in the New Mexico Press Women contest. It is available on Amazon. Learn more on rmkpublications/authorspages/evelynneil.com

Donna Pedace is Executive Director Emeritus of the Eugene O'Neill Theater and Museum, and the Spanish Colonial Arts Society and Museum. She previously wrote and published *The Traditional Spanish Market of Santa Fe, History and Artists* and *Scandalous Women of the Old West – Women Who Dared to be Different.*

Lynne Sebastian is a retired archaeologist and historic preservation consultant from Corrales, New Mexico. In retirement she took up creative writing, recently publishing her first novel, *One Last Cowboy Song*. She is currently at work on a memoir about an archaeological field project with her husband which occurred in 1981.

Dan Wetmore has judged in numerous writing contests in New Mexico and Colorado. His poetry and prose grace several anthologies. He's the author of two poetry collections—*My Mother's Gentle Unbecoming* and *Phoboudenopanophobia*, exploring the effects of Alzheimer's on the leaving and the left behind—currently working on a third.

* * *

Welcome to the New Mexico State Poetry Society!

The New Mexico State Poetry Society (NMSPS) is a diverse and inclusive community of poetry aficionados whose collective purpose is literary and educational, with a good dose of fun thrown in. As of 2024, they have chapters in Albuquerque, Santa Fe, Silver City, and Valencia County, and a number of At Large members across the state and out of state. They would like to establish more regional chapters (especially in southern NM) or chapters devoted to particular genres, such as slam or multimedia.

NMSPS often collaborates with other nonprofits, municipalities, and cultural groups to bring nonpartisan education and entertainment to various venues. Examples are their long-running Poets in the Classroom Project at which SouthWest Writers once helped send about 50 poets into various Albuquerque elementary and middle schools for a day of inspiration and poetry writing by the students. Another is the increasingly popular Poets' Picnic held each May at the Albuquerque Open Space Center. The event draws together poets, musicians, calligraphers, bookbinders, artists, and the general public for a day of fellowship and fun in a lovely outdoor setting.

Visit their website at www.nmpoetry.org to learn more about their 55 years of promoting poetry in the Land of Enchantment and beyond. Then, come create and share your poetry with them. They thrive on mutual support and mentoring.

www.nmpoetry.com

Our thanks to the **New Mexico State Poetry Society** for their assistance as judges for the three poetry categories: Haiku, Free Verse, and Limerick. For more information on how you can join NMSPS go to: nmpoetry.com

Shirley Blackwell has served on the boards of NMSPS (president, 2009-11) and its parent federation, the NFSPS, since 2008. She is cofounder of the NFSPS Black Berry Peach (BBP) Prize for performance poetry and its offshoot, the BBP National Slam Competition. She has poems and essays in over two dozen publications, plus two collections of her own.

A member of the Texas Institute of Letters, Albuquerque poet **Scott Wiggerman** is the author of three books of poetry and the editor of several volumes, including the craft books *Wingbeats I & II: Exercises & Practice in Poetry*. In recent years, haiku and art have become more central to his work as an artist of both the page and canvas.

John Roche lives in Placitas, New Mexico, helping run Jules' Poetry Playhouse and edit Poetry Playhouse Publications. Along with editing the five-volume *Poets Speak* series, his poetry books include *On Conesus*, *Topicalities*, *Road Ghosts*, *The Joe Poems*, *Joe Rides Again: Further Adventures of Joe the Poet,* and the latest, *Tubbables*.

The Society of Children's Book Writers and Illustrators: New Mexico & West Texas Chapter

The Society of Children's Book Writers and Illustrators provides resources, professional networking, and community-building opportunities that support writers, illustrators, and translators throughout their careers. Their mission is to support the creation of an abundance of quality children's books, so that young people everywhere have the books they need and deserve, working to establish a more imaginative and inclusive world through the power of children's literature.

They value not only creativity and professionalism but also community connection—essential for supporting one another in lasting and meaningful careers. Stop by one of their free virtual events to meet their community and see what it's all about!

First Wednesday of the month:
Virtual Coffee House Chat 4 p.m.-5p.m. MST
Second Tuesday of the month:
Shop Talk 7 p.m.-8:30 p.m. MST
Third Wednesday of the month:
Virtual Coffee House Chat 7 p.m.-8 p.m. MST

Website: www.scbwi.org/regions/newmexico

Regional Advisor Susan Metallo is also available to answer questions via email at newmexico@scbwi.org. Drop her a line; she'd be thrilled to meet you!

More kudos and thanks to the New Mexico chapter of the **Society of Children's Book Writers and Illustrators** for their assistance in judging the Children's and Young Adult categories of the contest. Founded in 1971, SCBWI is an international organization with over 200K members. More information is available at www.scbwi.org.

Chris Eboch has over 100 children's books published, including *The Eyes of Pharaoh*, a mystery in ancient Egypt, and *The Well of Sacrifice*, a Mayan drama. Her writing craft books are *Advanced Plotting* and *You Can Write for Children*. She is a popular workshop leader and developmental editor. Visit chriseboch.com.

Susan Mctallo is an author, youth librarian, and *Publishers Weekly* contributor. Her debut novel, *Reasons to Hate Me* (Candlewick 2025), won the 2022 SCBWI YA Work-in-Progress Award, and her short fiction has appeared in *Ladybug, Cricket*, and *The Seven Hills Review*. She lives in New Mexico with her family.

Photo and Art Submissions

Mosaic Voices from Beyond (P.343), *Sign Language* (P.387) *and Loquacious Cascades* (P.269) photos by Barbara Garvey

Barbara Garvey is a small business owner in the field of advertising and promotions. A retired high school English and journalism teacher in Albuquerque, she advised fifteen consecutive student newspaper staffs, supported new teachers in the district, and worked in administration. She strives to capture decisive moments via feature photography.

Mosaic Voices (Prologue & Forward Page artwork) by Allen Herring

Allen Herring is a local, award-winning writer and artist. He is a former newspaper features writer and has written for television. He enjoys writing sci-fi, fantasy, and magical realism. He has a master's degree in Cultural Studies. He lives in Albuquerque with his cat, Nadia.

Mosaic Voices (Cover Art) and *Painting the Chama* (P.95) by **Rose Marie Kern.**
A self-styled "Jill of all trades, mistress of none," writer, photographer, and artist, Rose explains her panorama of interests "I have a very low boredom threshold."

Bad to the Bone (P.277) and *Crow Sees All* photos by **Carol Rawie**

In 1983, Carol began a sci-fi novel. Forty years later, the future has become the past and her novel morphed into historic climate fiction set in 1988. Carol traded arroyos for beaches when she and her husband left New Mexico to live in Huntington Beach, California.

Busted (P.233) art by Deborah Ranniger

Deborah Ranniger is a writer, visual artist and pet portrait painter, urban chicken farmer and foster shelter animal mom. A lover of learning, she has degrees in Art, Landscape Architecture, and Speech Communication, all of which she uses to help make the world a better place.

We, The Dream (P. 7) artwork by Raymund Tembreull

R.M. Tembreull is a husband and father, a 26-year USAF combat veteran, and a career law enforcement and security professional. Humankind's extremes and the beauty of the natural world experienced in his travels and endeavors fuel his "Blighted Earth" writings. His passions are eco-themed literature and art.

SouthWest Writers Information

SouthWest Writers is a non-profit organization devoted to helping both published and unpublished writers improve their craft and further their careers. With over 400 members, SWW serves authors worldwide in every fiction and non-fiction genre through both in-person and virtual meetings, classes, workshops and by providing writing opportunities.

SWW has a database of professionals who offer services to potential authors including editing, web design, mentoring, formatting, illustrations, cover art, blogging, and information about self-publishing. For more information go to: www.southwestwriters.com

Books by SouthWest Writers

*NOTE: Every book written by the SWW membership has received one or more national and/or regional awards.

Available on Amazon and at local Albuquerque bookstores

Pictured above are:

Holes in Our Hearts
A collection of stories and poetry by New Mexico military veterans, their families and caregivers.

Annual Writing Contest Anthologies

2023 – Woven Pathways
2022 – A Diversity of Expression
2021 – Ramblings and Reflections
2020 – Seeing the World in 20/20

2019 – The ***SouthWest Sage Anthology 2019***, a collection of short stories, poetry and articles about writing by writers, first published in the *SouthWest Sage* newsletter.

More books by SWW

KiMo Theatre: Fact & Folklore
The Storytellers Anthology

www.southwestwriters.com/sww-publications

Made in the USA
Middletown, DE
30 October 2024